The
becom

FIRE
FORCE

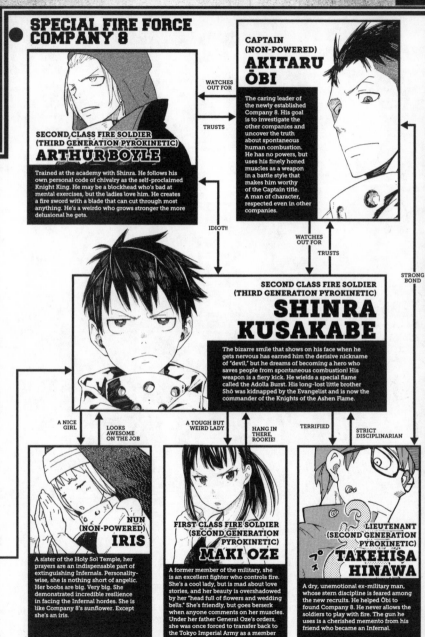

SPECIAL FIRE FORCE COMPANY 8

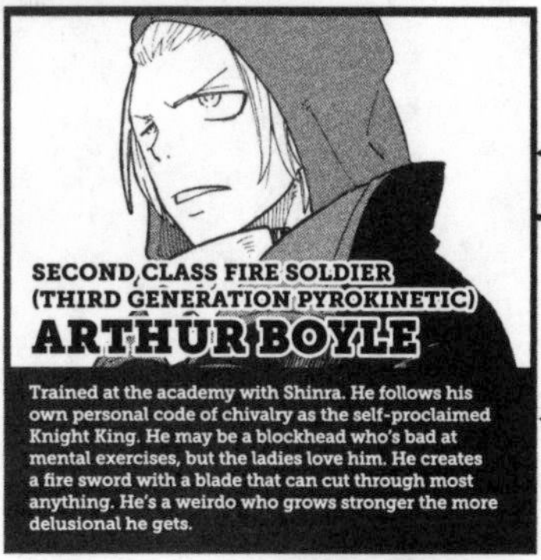

SECOND CLASS FIRE SOLDIER (THIRD GENERATION PYROKINETIC)

ARTHUR BOYLE

Trained at the academy with Shinra. He follows his own personal code of chivalry as the self-proclaimed Knight King. He may be a blockhead who's bad at mental exercises, but the ladies love him. He creates a fire sword with a blade that can cut through most anything. He's a weirdo who grows stronger the more delusional he gets.

WATCHES OUT FOR

TRUSTS

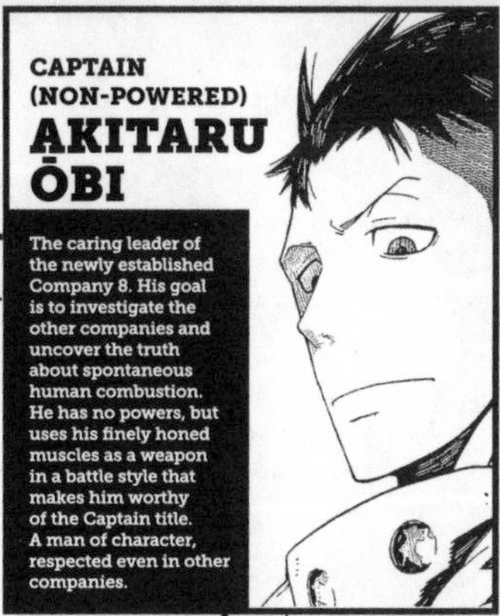

CAPTAIN (NON-POWERED)

AKITARU ŌBI

The caring leader of the newly established Company 8. His goal is to investigate the other companies and uncover the truth about spontaneous human combustion. He has no powers, but uses his finely honed muscles as a weapon in a battle style that makes him worthy of the Captain title. A man of character, respected even in other companies.

IDIOT!!

WATCHES OUT FOR

TRUSTS

STRONG BOND

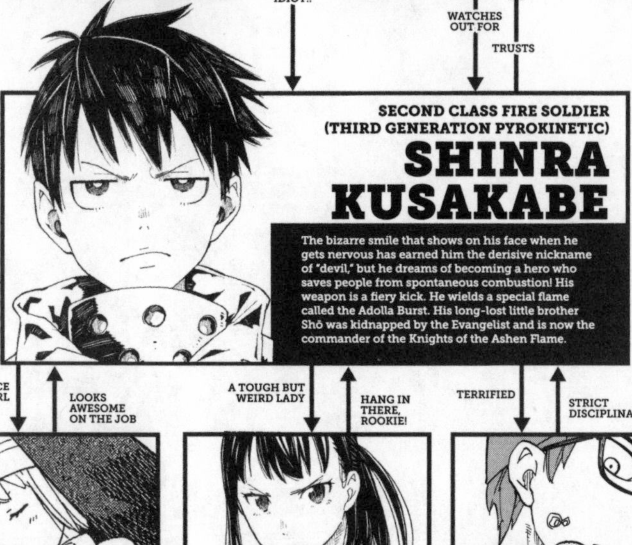

SECOND CLASS FIRE SOLDIER (THIRD GENERATION PYROKINETIC)

SHINRA KUSAKABE

The bizarre smile that shows on his face when he gets nervous has earned him the derisive nickname of "devil," but he dreams of becoming a hero who saves people from spontaneous combustion! His weapon is a fiery kick. He wields a special flame called the Adolla Burst. His long-lost little brother Shō was kidnapped by the Evangelist and is now the commander of the Knights of the Ashen Flame.

A NICE GIRL

LOOKS AWESOME ON THE JOB

A TOUGH BUT WEIRD LADY

HANG IN THERE, ROOKIE!

TERRIFIED

STRICT DISCIPLINARIAN

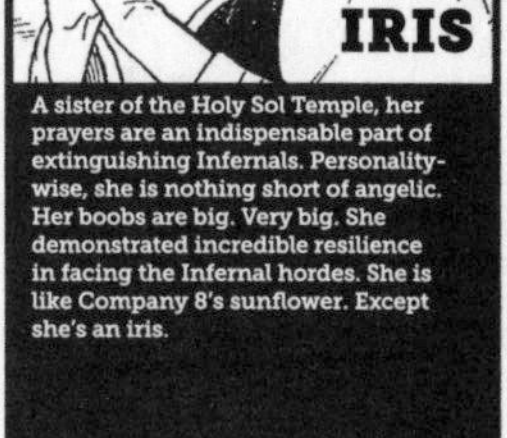

NUN (NON-POWERED)

IRIS

A sister of the Holy Sol Temple, her prayers are an indispensable part of extinguishing Infernals. Personality-wise, she is nothing short of angelic. Her boobs are big. Very big. She demonstrated incredible resilience in facing the Infernal hordes. She is like Company 8's sunflower. Except she's an iris.

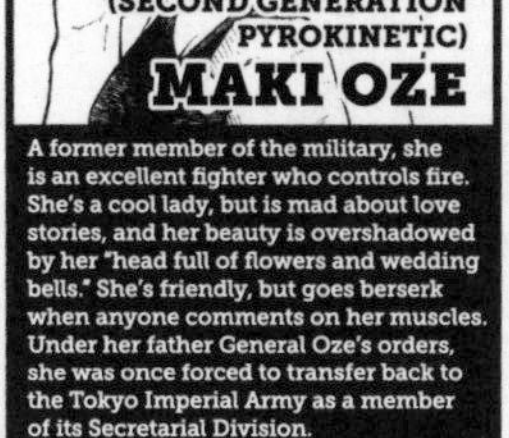

FIRST CLASS FIRE SOLDIER (SECOND GENERATION PYROKINETIC)

MAKI OZE

A former member of the military, she is an excellent fighter who controls fire. She's a cool lady, but is mad about love stories, and her beauty is overshadowed by her "head full of flowers and wedding bells." She's friendly, but goes berserk when anyone comments on her muscles. Under her father General Oze's orders, she was once forced to transfer back to the Tokyo Imperial Army as a member of its Secretarial Division.

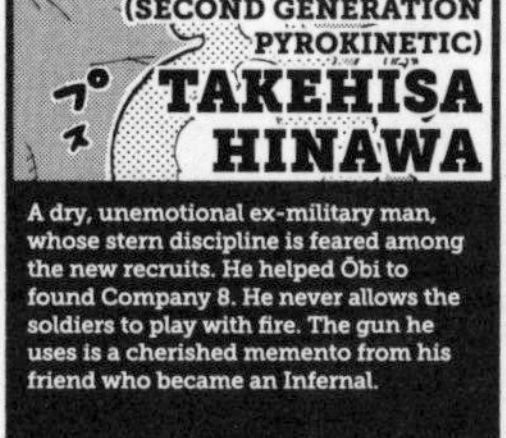

LIEUTENANT (SECOND GENERATION PYROKINETIC)

TAKEHISA HINAWA

A dry, unemotional ex-military man, whose stern discipline is feared among the new recruits. He helped Ōbi to found Company 8. He never allows the soldiers to play with fire. The gun he uses is a cherished memento from his friend who became an Infernal.

THE GIRLS' CLUB

RESPECTS

SPECIAL FIRE FORCE COMPANY 7

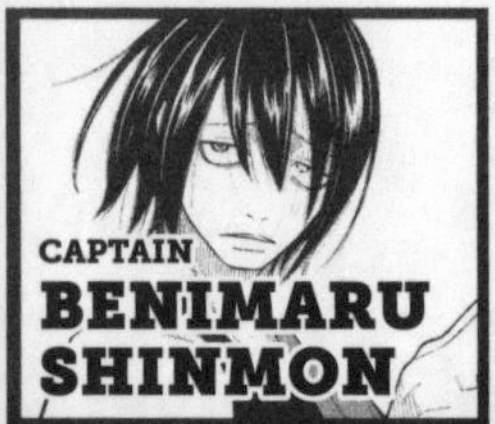

CAPTAIN
BENIMARU SHINMON

A composite fire soldier, with the powers of a second gen and a third gen pyrokinetic. Rumor has it he is the toughest soldier on the force.

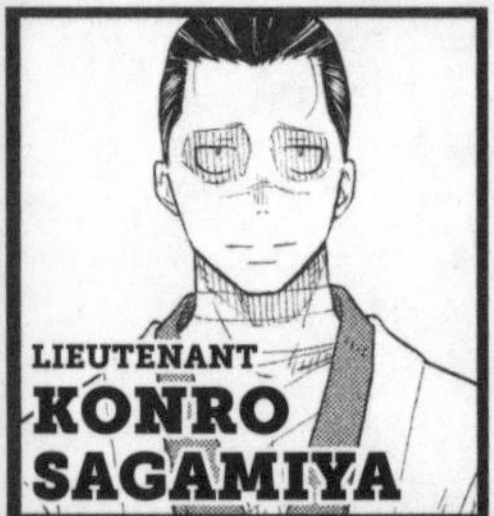

LIEUTENANT
KONRO SAGAMIYA

Has the "holy scar" of one who has experienced an Adolla Link. Refers to Benimaru as Waka.

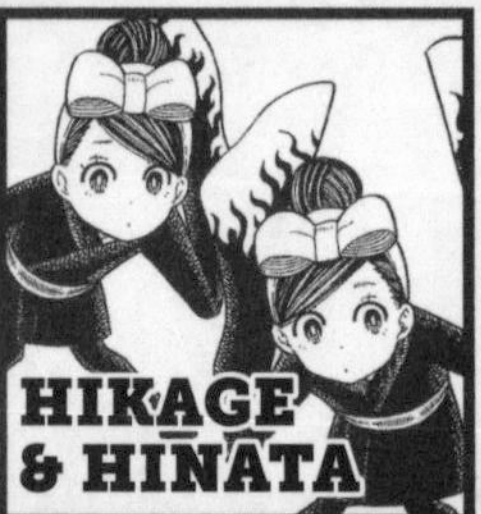

HIKAGE & HINATA

Twin sisters who talk rough and are tough as nails.

FOLLOWERS OF THE EVANGELIST

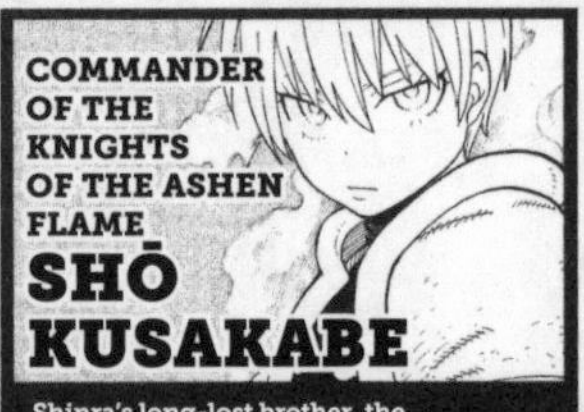

COMMANDER OF THE KNIGHTS OF THE ASHEN FLAME
SHŌ KUSAKABE

Shinra's long-lost brother, the commander of an order of knights that works for the Evangelist. He can use his powers to stop time for all but himself.

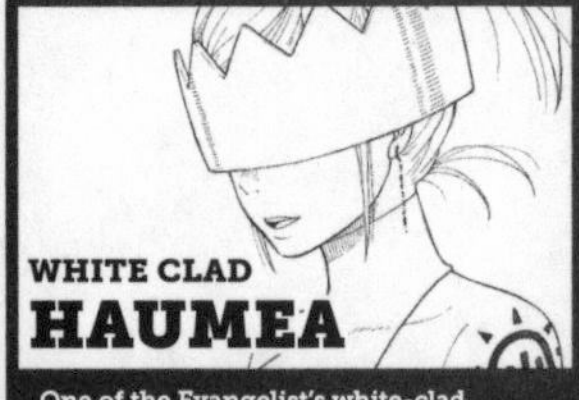

WHITE CLAD
HAUMEA

One of the Evangelist's white-clad combatants. She is a troublesome opponent who can control others with her mind-jacking powers.

OTHER SPECIAL FIRE FORCE COMPANIES

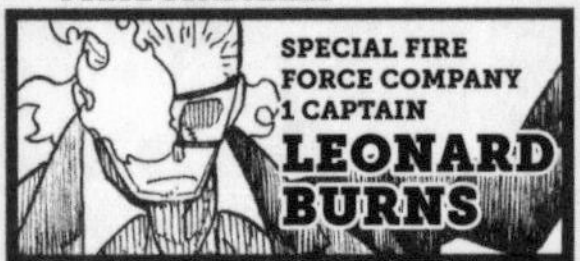

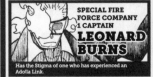

SPECIAL FIRE FORCE COMPANY 1 CAPTAIN
LEONARD BURNS

Has the Stigma of one who has experienced an Adolla Link.

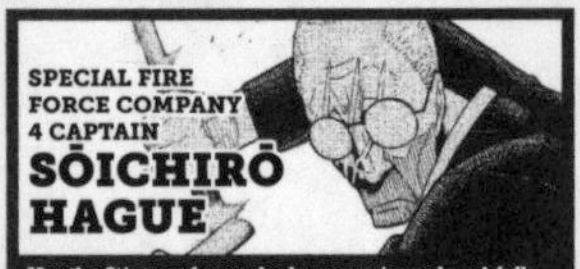

SPECIAL FIRE FORCE COMPANY 4 CAPTAIN
SŌICHIRŌ HAGUE

Has the Stigma of one who has experienced an Adolla Link. Extremely masochistic.

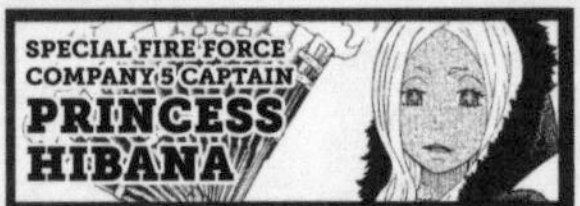

SPECIAL FIRE FORCE COMPANY 5 CAPTAIN
PRINCESS HIBANA

Joined the Fire Force to find the truth about spontaneous human combustion. She's an innocent, pure-hearted queen bee who has a crush on Shinra.

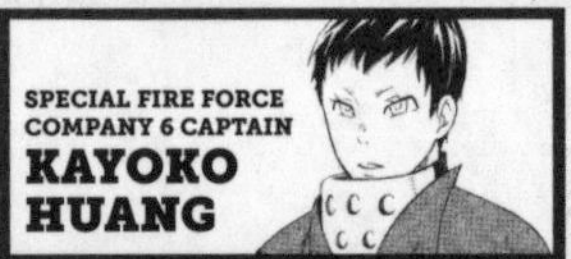

SPECIAL FIRE FORCE COMPANY 6 CAPTAIN
KAYOKO HUANG

Has the healing power called Rod of Asclepius.

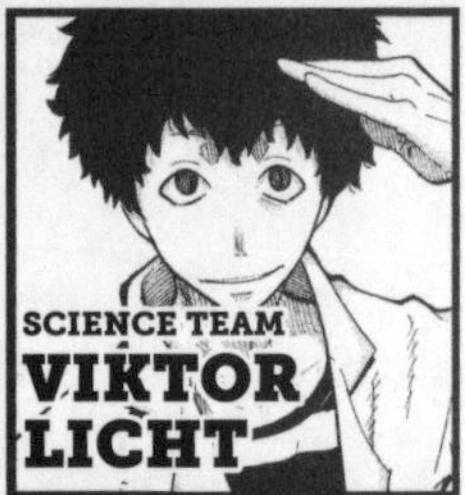

SCIENCE TEAM
VIKTOR LICHT

A suspicious genius deployed from Haijima Industries to fill the vacancy in Company 8's science department. Has confessed to being a Haijima spy.

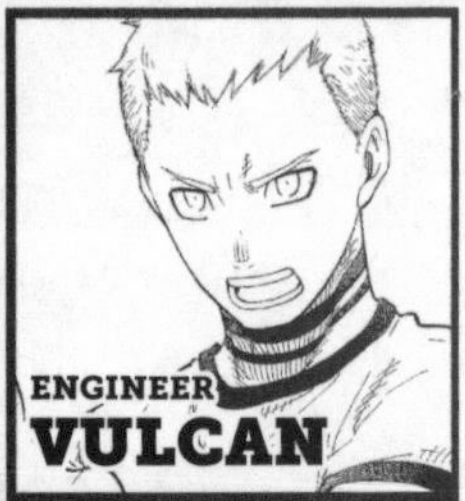

ENGINEER
VULCAN

The greatest engineer of the day, renowned as the God of Fire and the Forge. The weapons he created have increased Company 8's powers immensely.

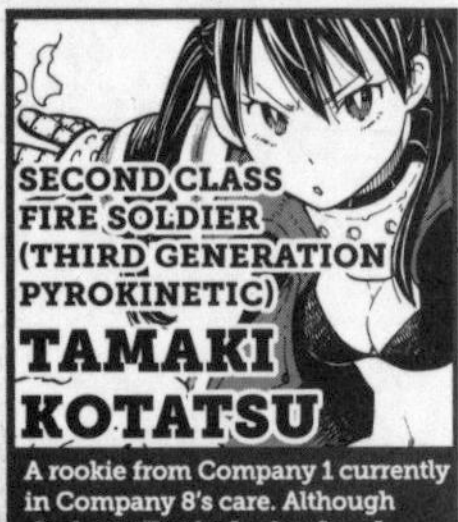

SECOND CLASS FIRE SOLDIER (THIRD GENERATION PYROKINETIC)
TAMAKI KOTATSU

A rookie from Company 1 currently in Company 8's care. Although she has a "Lucky Lecher Lure" condition, she nevertheless has a pure heart. She is now training with Company 7 to get stronger.

HAS EACH OTHER ON THEIR MIND

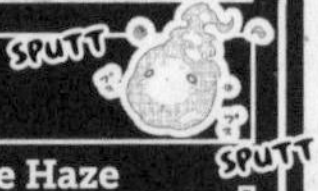
SPUTT
SPUTT

SUMMARY

With attacks from Infernal hordes and Purple Haze knights, the battle in the Nether is the fiercest one yet. Shinra is confronted by Dr. Giovanni, who has turned himself into a monster. He tells Shinra of the Evangelist's plan of destruction before Arthur fights him off with his sword. Then, when Maki risks her life to return to Company 8, she makes sure the White Clad zealots' scheme to wipe out the Tokyo Empire using Infernals as a massive bomb ends in failure.... With the White Clad enemies growing stronger, Shinra and the other rookies return to Asakusa to undergo more training in order to master the secret arts...

FIRE FORCE 20 CONTENTS

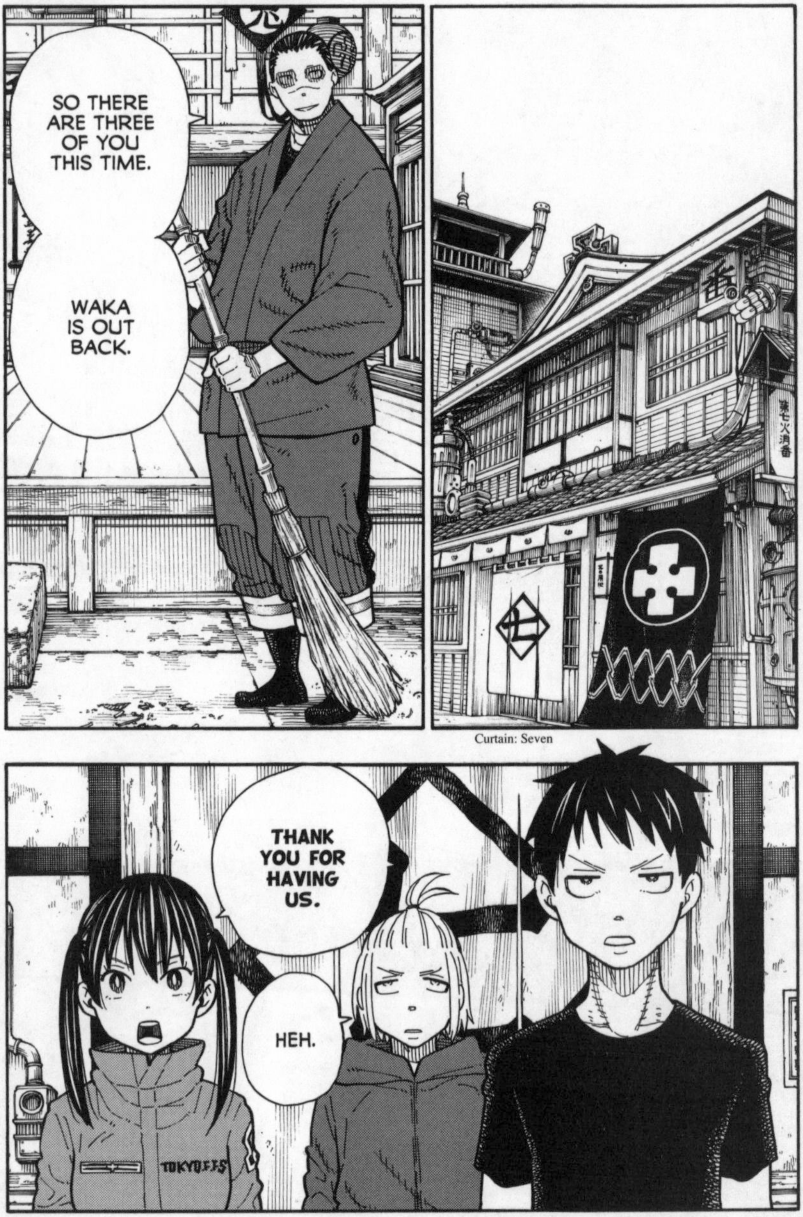
SO THERE ARE THREE OF YOU THIS TIME.
WAKA IS OUT BACK.
THANK YOU FOR HAVING US.
HEH.

Curtain: Seven

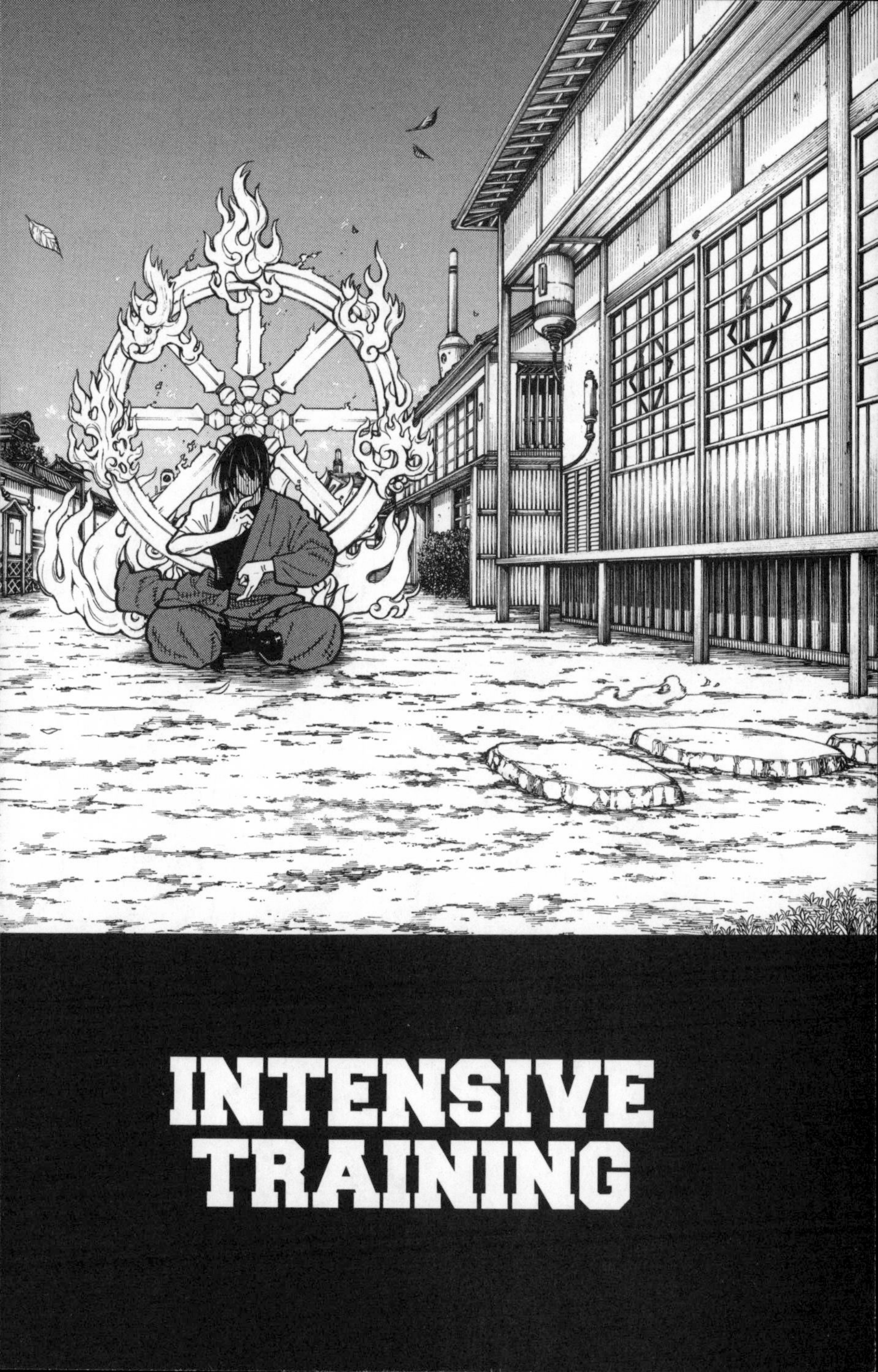

INTENSIVE TRAINING

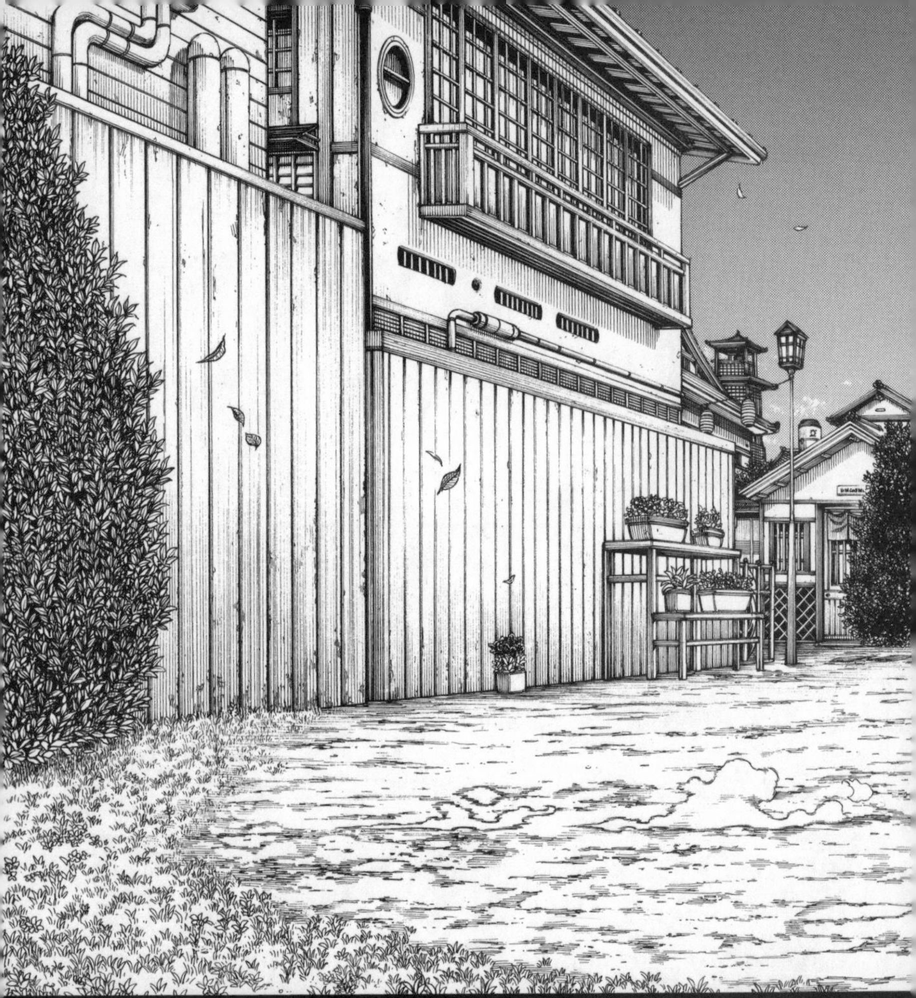

CHAPTER CLXIX:

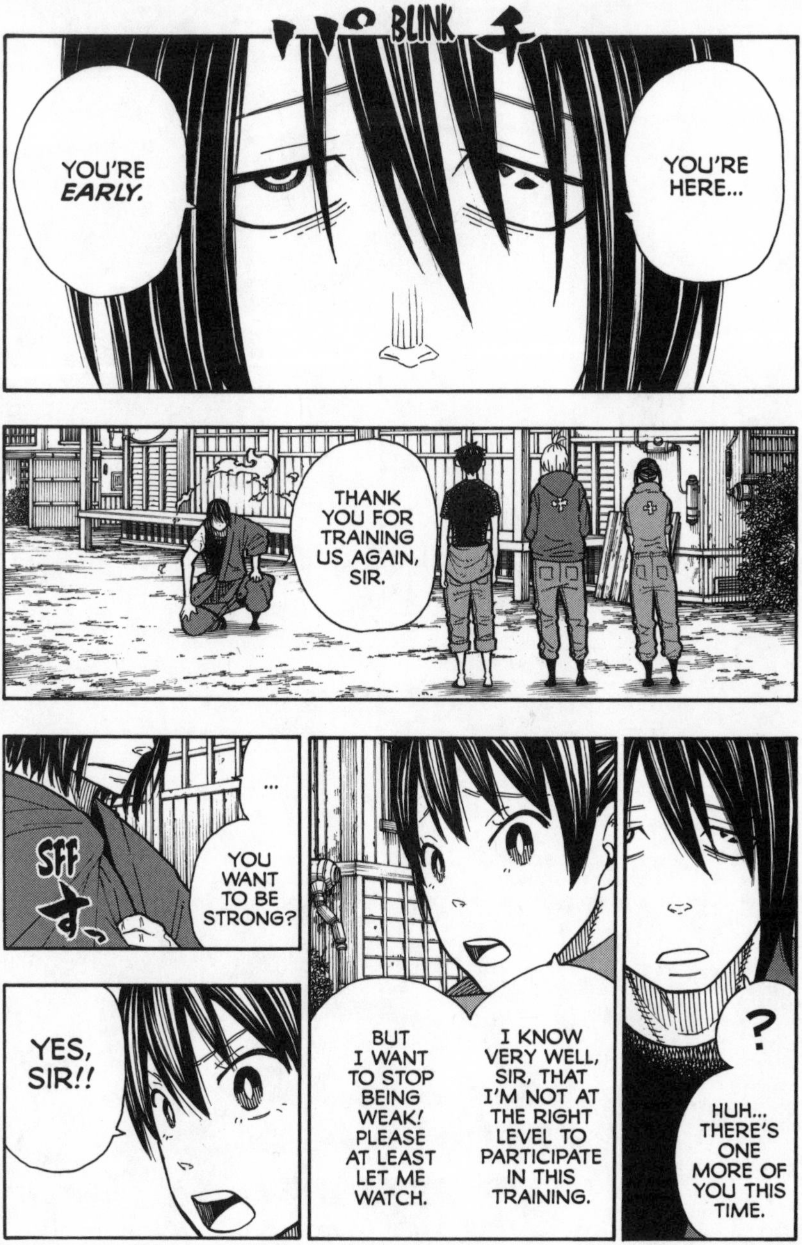
BLINK
YOU'RE HERE...
YOU'RE EARLY.
THANK YOU FOR TRAINING US AGAIN, SIR.
?
HUH... THERE'S ONE MORE OF YOU THIS TIME.
I KNOW VERY WELL, SIR, THAT I'M NOT AT THE RIGHT LEVEL TO PARTICIPATE IN THIS TRAINING.
BUT I WANT TO STOP BEING WEAK! PLEASE AT LEAST LET ME WATCH.
...
YOU WANT TO BE STRONG?
SFF
す
YES, SIR!!

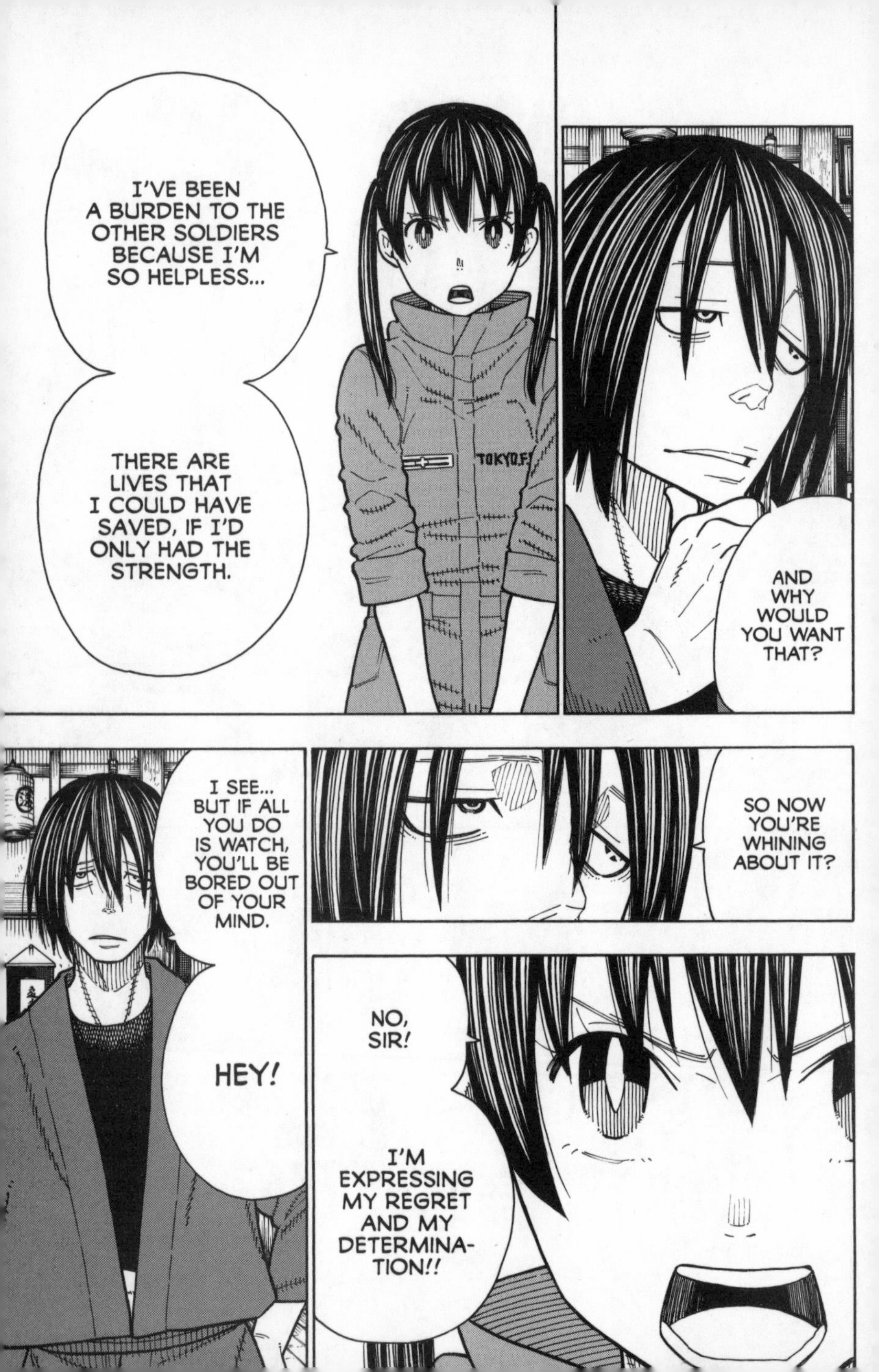

TOKYO F.
AND WHY WOULD YOU WANT THAT?
I'VE BEEN A BURDEN TO THE OTHER SOLDIERS BECAUSE I'M SO HELPLESS...
THERE ARE LIVES THAT I COULD HAVE SAVED, IF I'D ONLY HAD THE STRENGTH.
SO NOW YOU'RE WHINING ABOUT IT?
NO, SIR!
I'M EXPRESSING MY REGRET AND MY DETERMINA-TION!!
I SEE... BUT IF ALL YOU DO IS WATCH, YOU'LL BE BORED OUT OF YOUR MIND.
HEY!

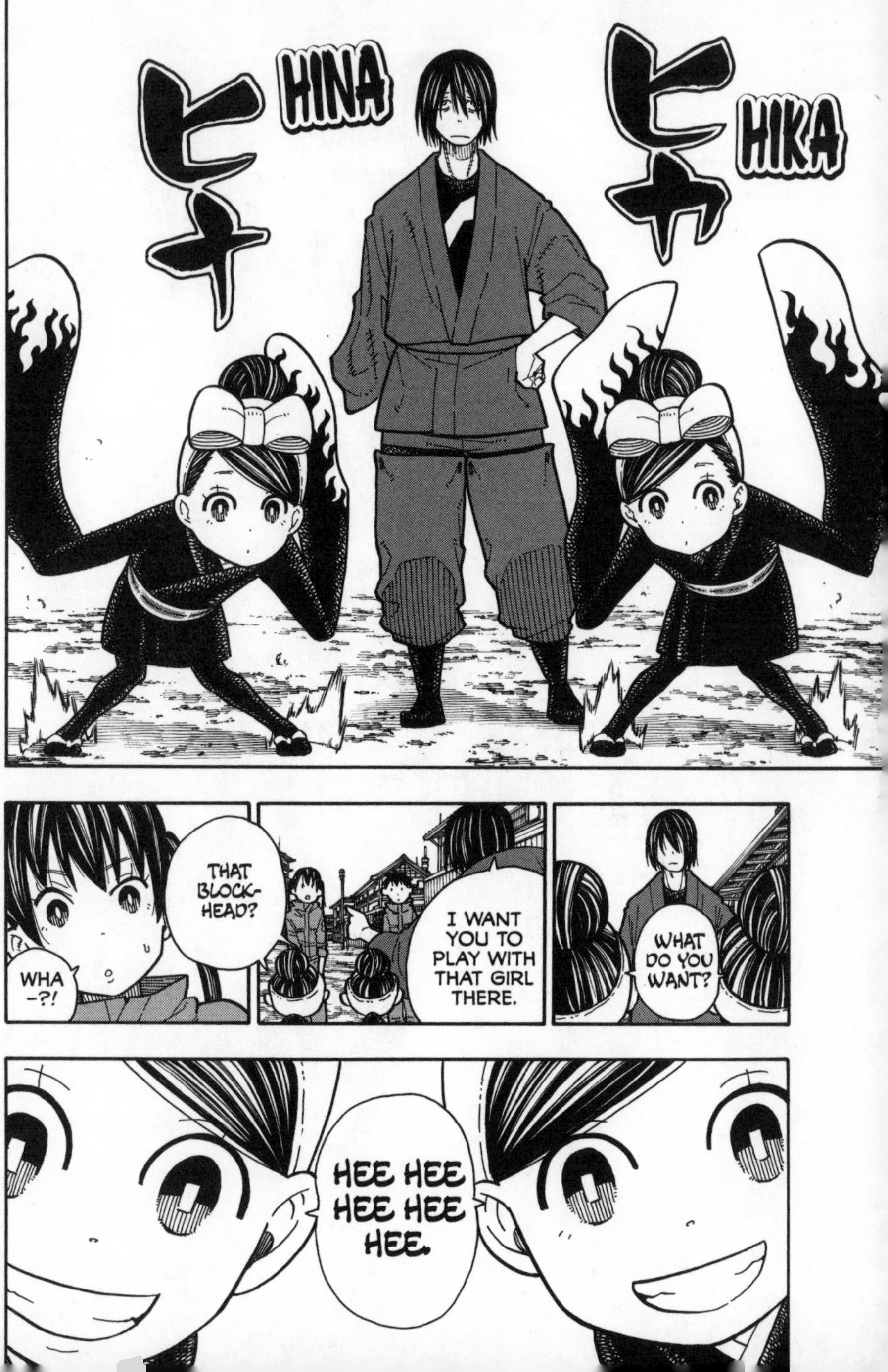
ヒカ
HIKA
ヒナ
HINA
WHAT DO YOU WANT?
I WANT YOU TO PLAY WITH THAT GIRL THERE.
THAT BLOCK-HEAD?
WHA-?!
HEE HEE HEE HEE HEE.

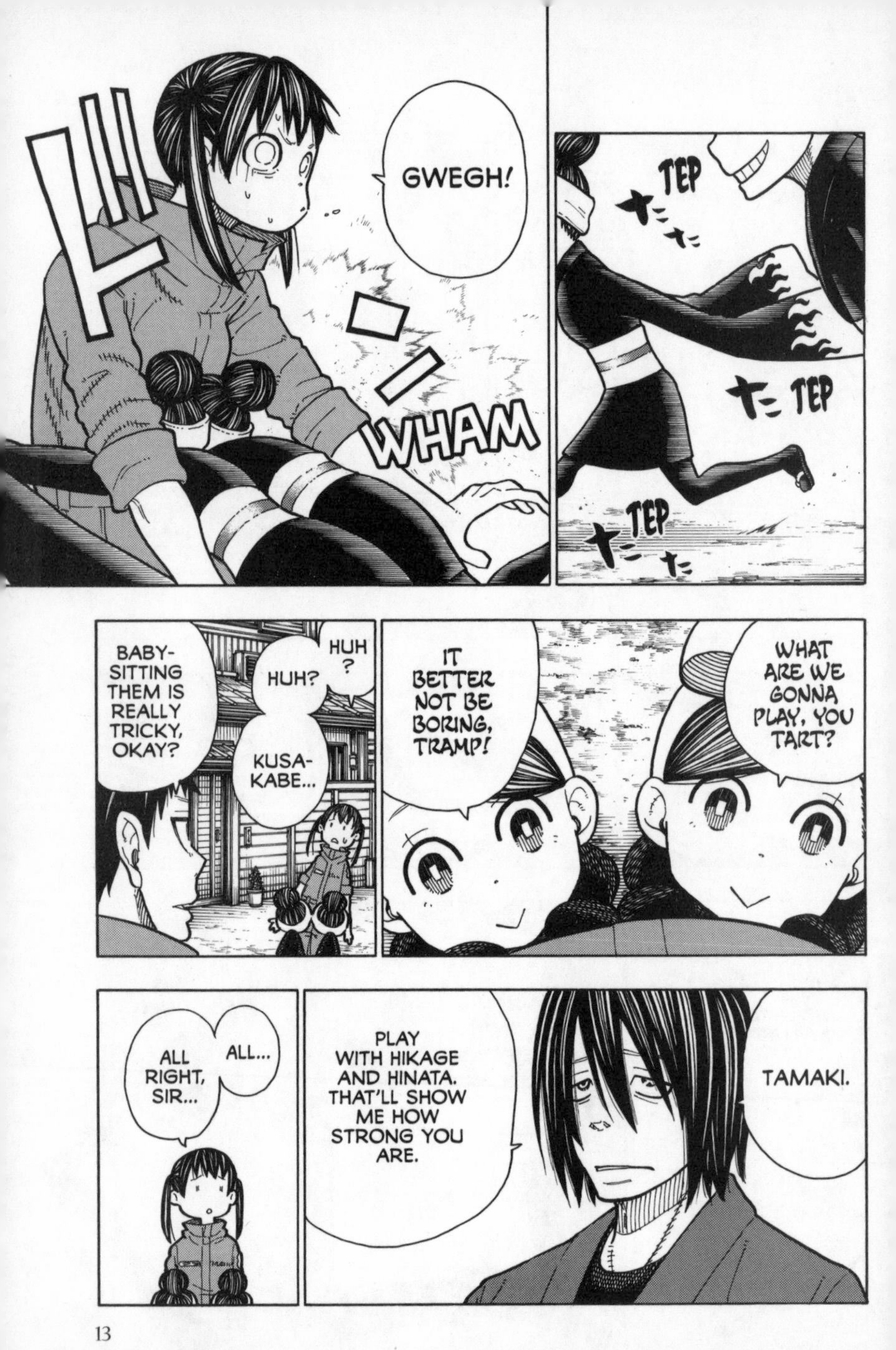
TEP
TEP
TEP
GWEGH!
WHAM
WHAT ARE WE GONNA PLAY, YOU TART?
IT BETTER NOT BE BORING, TRAMP!
HUH?
HUH?
BABY-SITTING THEM IS REALLY TRICKY, OKAY?
KUSA-KABE...
TAMAKI.
PLAY WITH HIKAGE AND HINATA. THAT'LL SHOW ME HOW STRONG YOU ARE.
ALL...
ALL RIGHT, SIR...

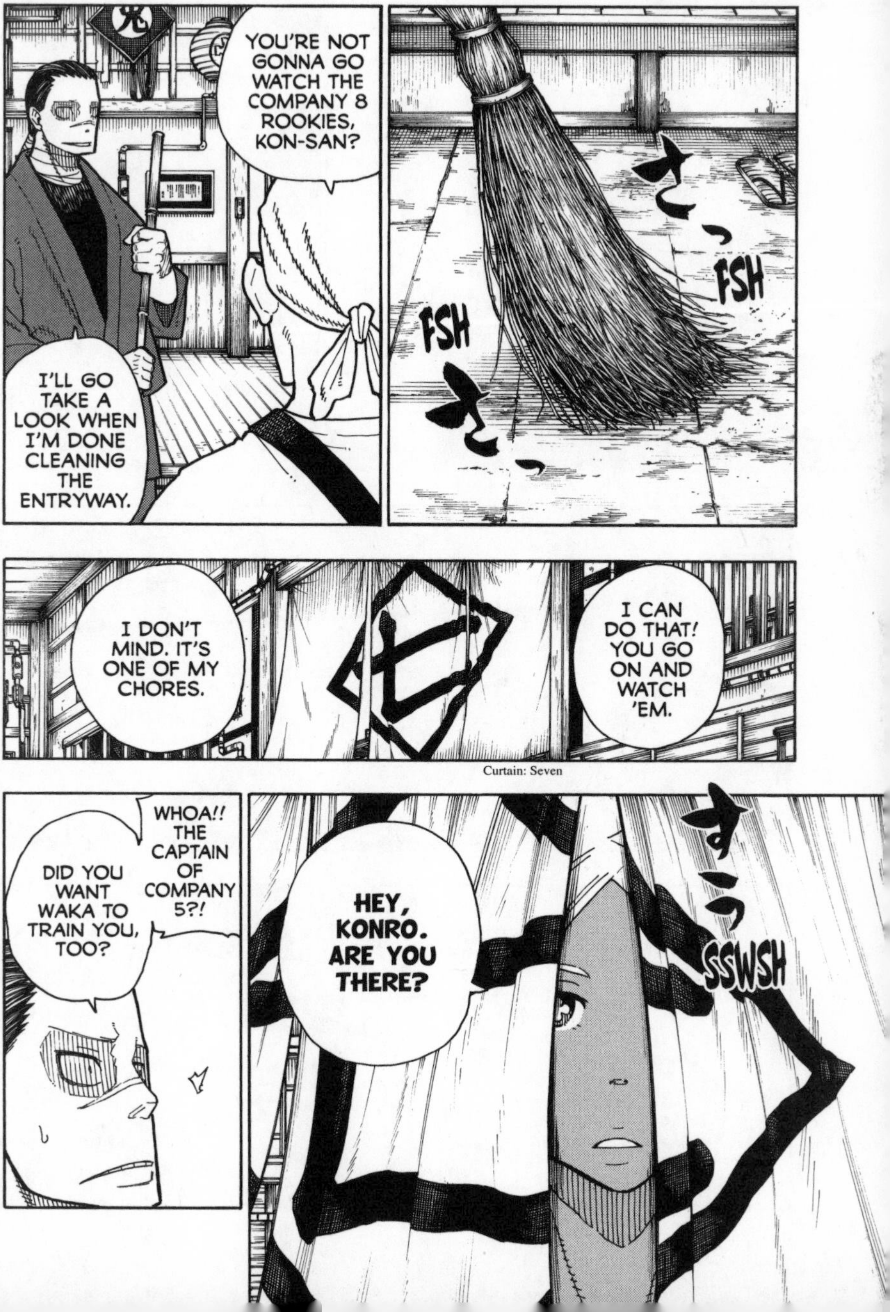
FSH
FSH
YOU'RE NOT GONNA GO WATCH THE COMPANY 8 ROOKIES, KON-SAN?
I'LL GO TAKE A LOOK WHEN I'M DONE CLEANING THE ENTRYWAY.
I CAN DO THAT! YOU GO ON AND WATCH 'EM.
I DON'T MIND. IT'S ONE OF MY CHORES.
Curtain: Seven
SSWSH
HEY, KONRO. ARE YOU THERE?
WHOA!! THE CAPTAIN OF COMPANY 5?!
DID YOU WANT WAKA TO TRAIN YOU, TOO?

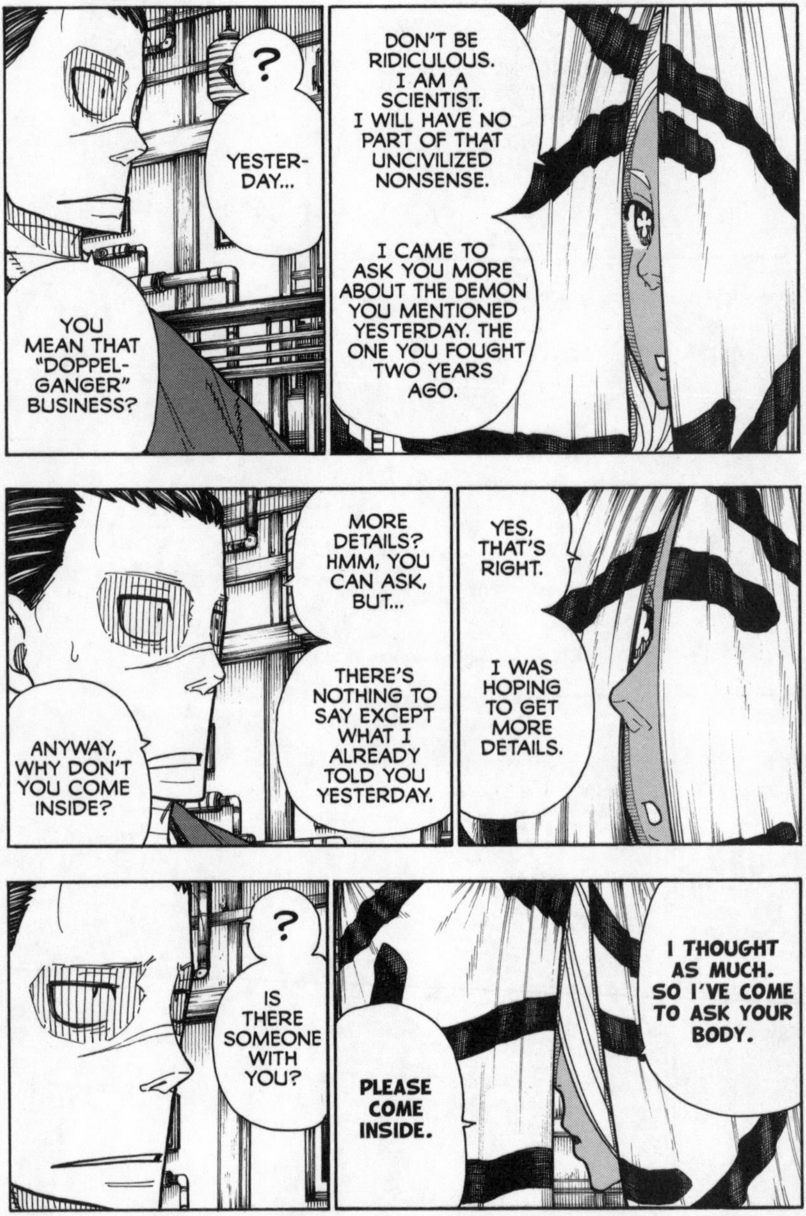
DON'T BE RIDICULOUS. I AM A SCIENTIST. I WILL HAVE NO PART OF THAT UNCIVILIZED NONSENSE.
I CAME TO ASK YOU MORE ABOUT THE DEMON YOU MENTIONED YESTERDAY. THE ONE YOU FOUGHT TWO YEARS AGO.
?
YESTER-DAY...
YOU MEAN THAT "DOPPEL-GANGER" BUSINESS?
YES, THAT'S RIGHT.
I WAS HOPING TO GET MORE DETAILS.
MORE DETAILS? HMM, YOU CAN ASK, BUT...
THERE'S NOTHING TO SAY EXCEPT WHAT I ALREADY TOLD YOU YESTERDAY.
ANYWAY, WHY DON'T YOU COME INSIDE?
I THOUGHT AS MUCH. SO I'VE COME TO ASK YOUR BODY.
PLEASE COME INSIDE.
?
IS THERE SOMEONE WITH YOU?

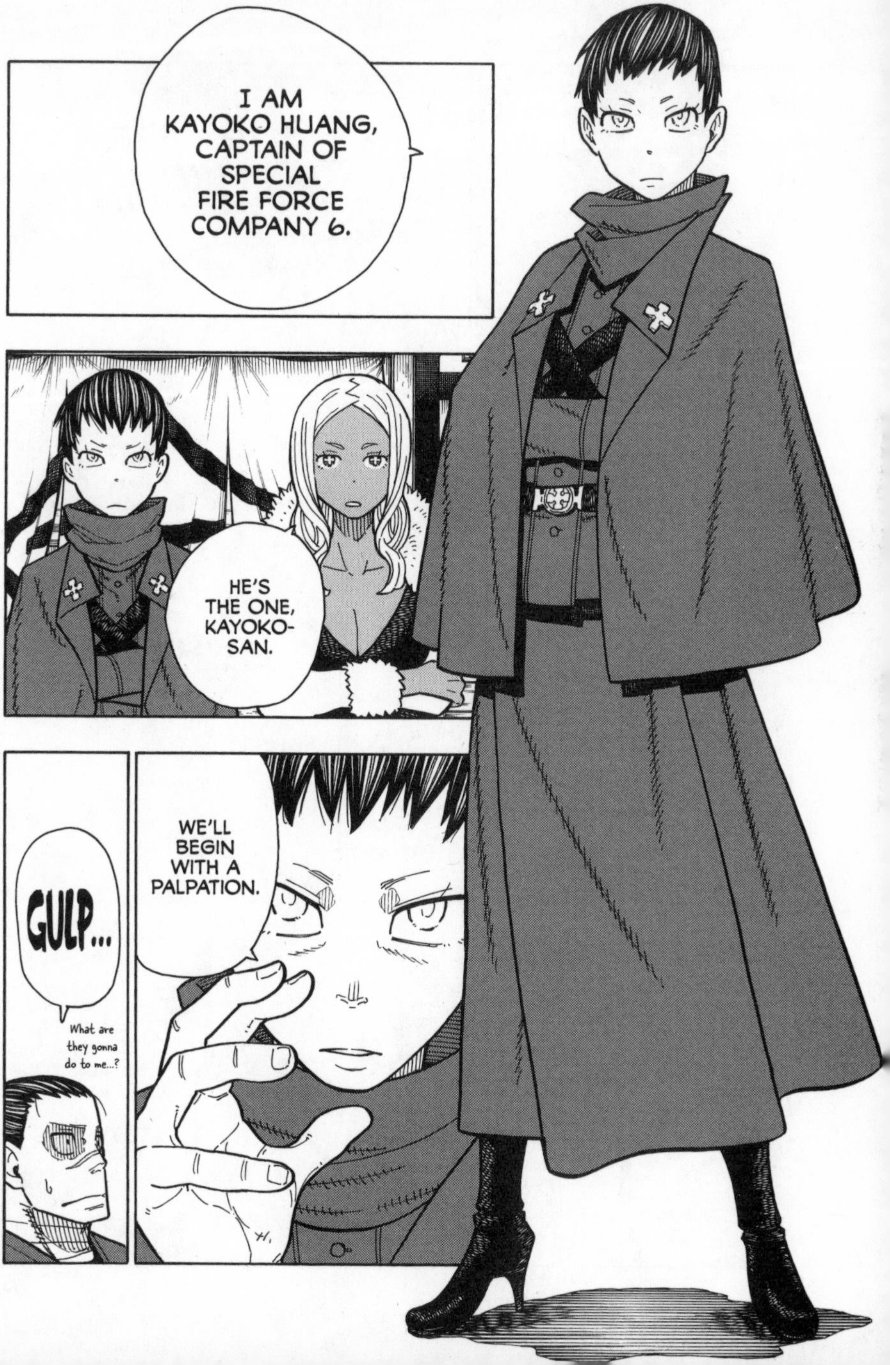
I AM KAYOKO HUANG, CAPTAIN OF SPECIAL FIRE FORCE COMPANY 6.
HE'S THE ONE, KAYOKO-SAN.
WE'LL BEGIN WITH A PALPATION.
GULP...
What are they gonna do to me...?

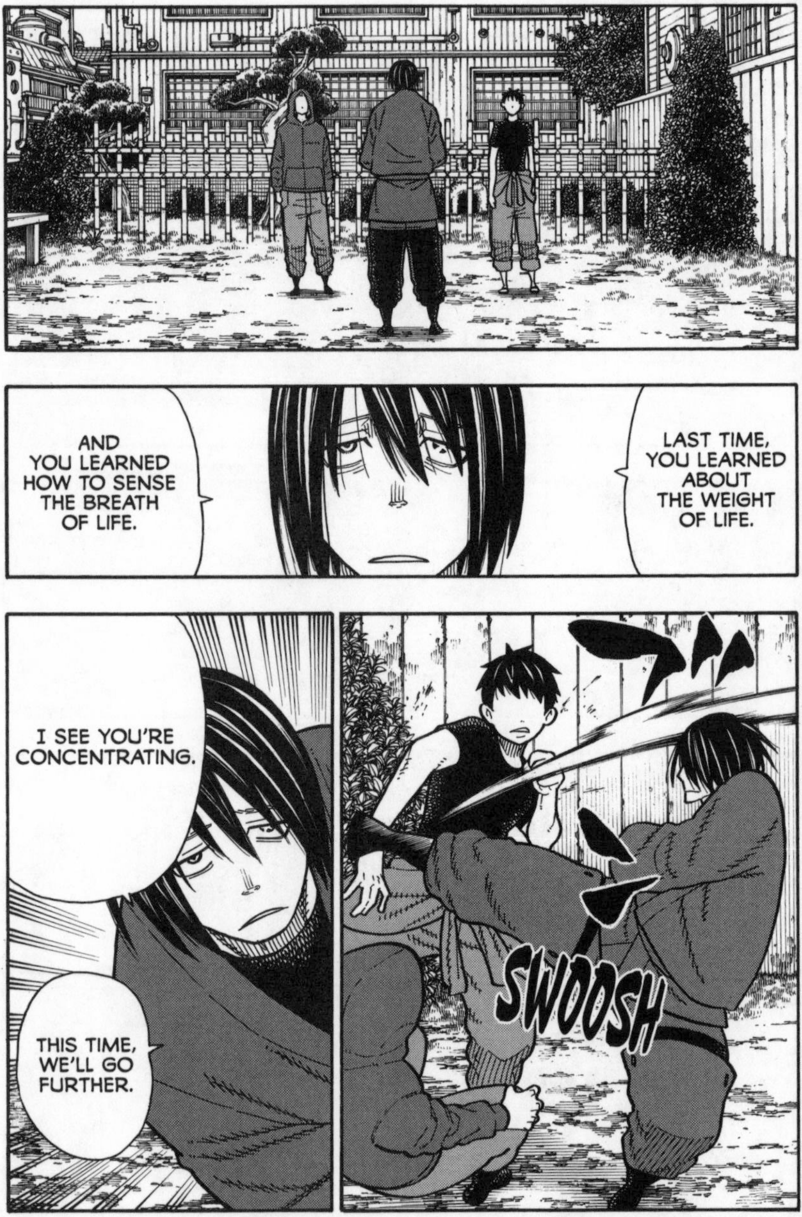
LAST TIME, YOU LEARNED ABOUT THE WEIGHT OF LIFE.
AND YOU LEARNED HOW TO SENSE THE BREATH OF LIFE.
SWOOSH
I SEE YOU'RE CONCENTRATING.
THIS TIME, WE'LL GO FURTHER.

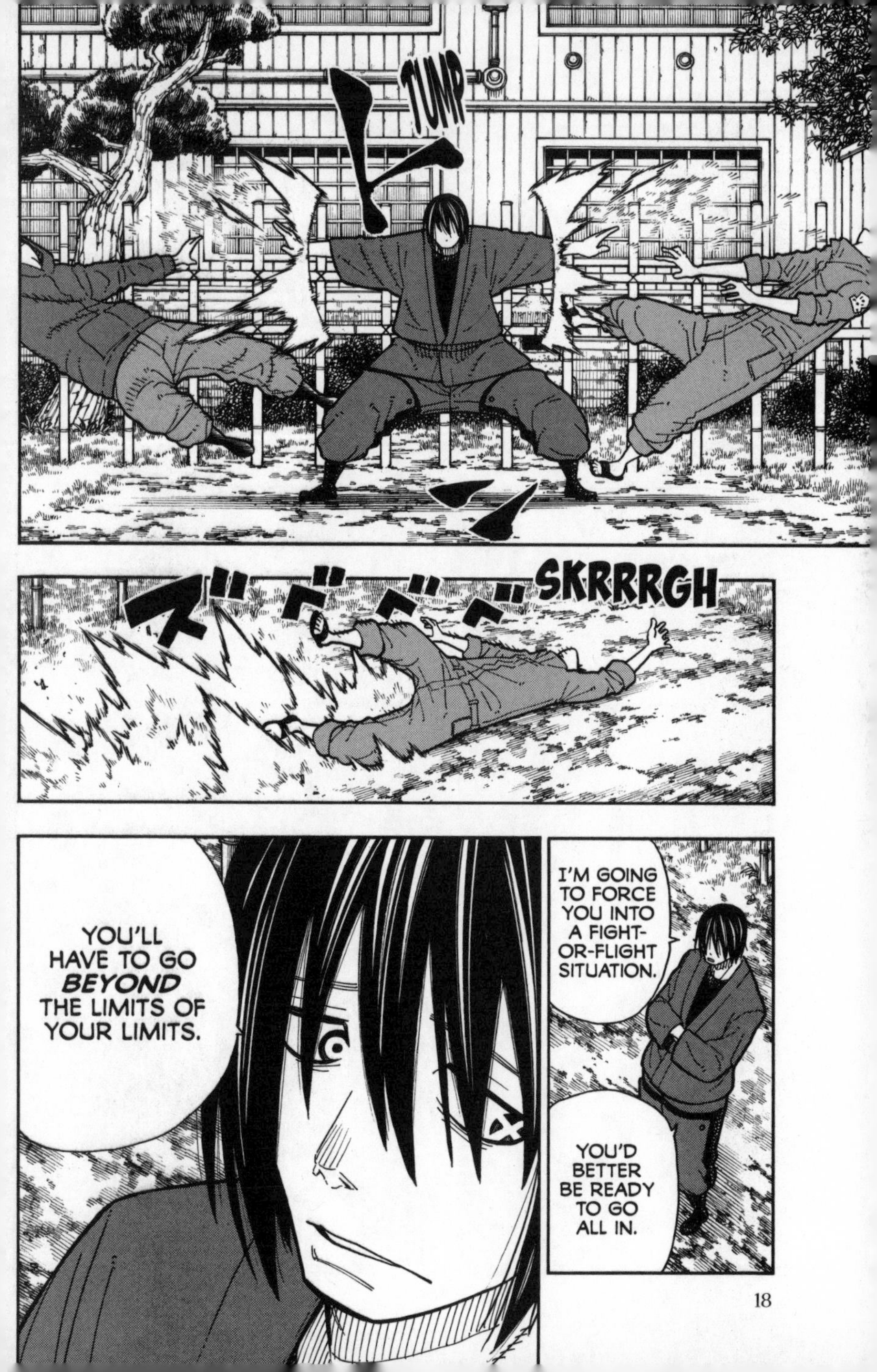
TUMP
ズドドド
SKRRRGH
I'M GOING TO FORCE YOU INTO A FIGHT-OR-FLIGHT SITUATION.
YOU'D BETTER BE READY TO GO ALL IN.
YOU'LL HAVE TO GO *BEYOND* THE LIMITS OF YOUR LIMITS.

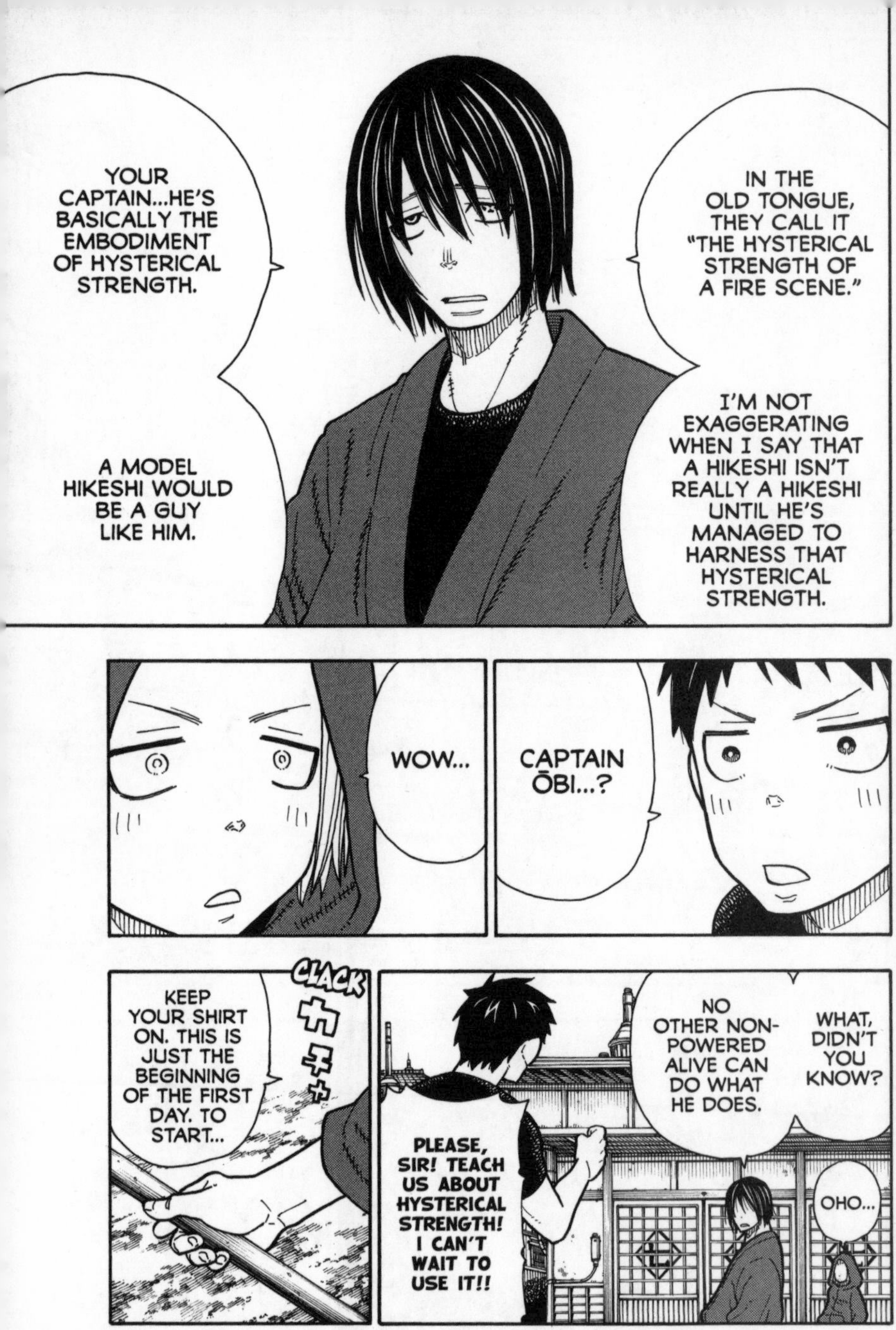
IN THE OLD TONGUE, THEY CALL IT "THE HYSTERICAL STRENGTH OF A FIRE SCENE."
I'M NOT EXAGGERATING WHEN I SAY THAT A HIKESHI ISN'T REALLY A HIKESHI UNTIL HE'S MANAGED TO HARNESS THAT HYSTERICAL STRENGTH.
YOUR CAPTAIN...HE'S BASICALLY THE EMBODIMENT OF HYSTERICAL STRENGTH.
A MODEL HIKESHI WOULD BE A GUY LIKE HIM.
CAPTAIN ŌBI...?
WOW...
WHAT, DIDN'T YOU KNOW?
NO OTHER NON-POWERED ALIVE CAN DO WHAT HE DOES.
OHO...
PLEASE, SIR! TEACH US ABOUT HYSTERICAL STRENGTH! I CAN'T WAIT TO USE IT!!
CLACK
KEEP YOUR SHIRT ON. THIS IS JUST THE BEGINNING OF THE FIRST DAY. TO START...

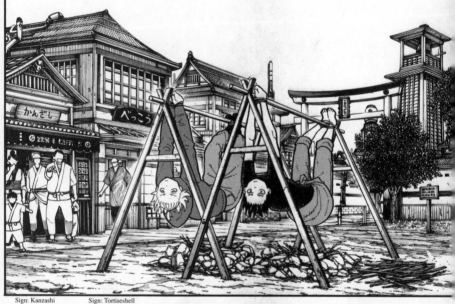

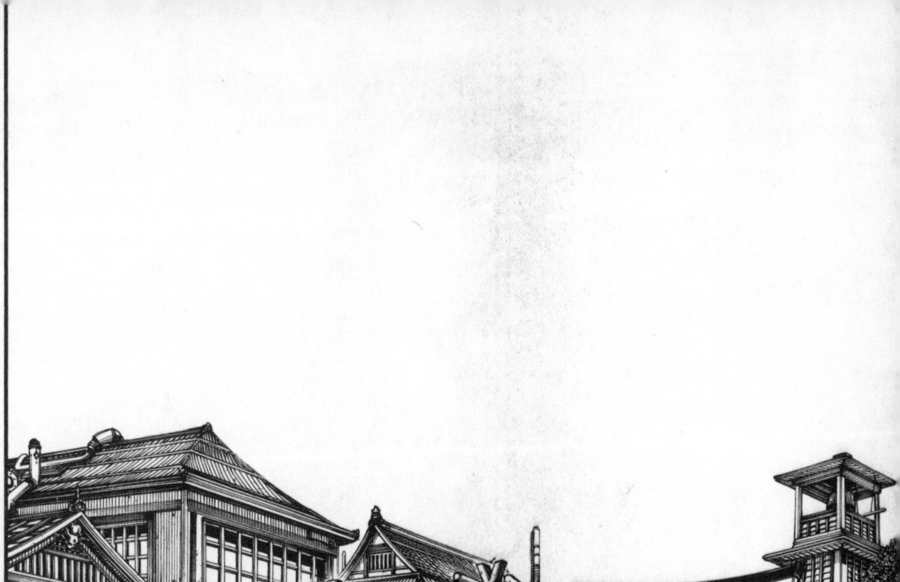
かんざし
べっこう
Sign: Kanzashi Sign: Tortiseshell

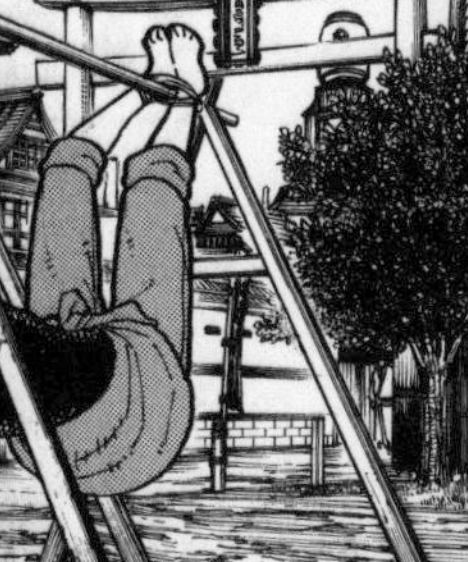
MAN, I HAVEN'T SEEN THIS IN AGES.
NOT SINCE BENI-CHAN.

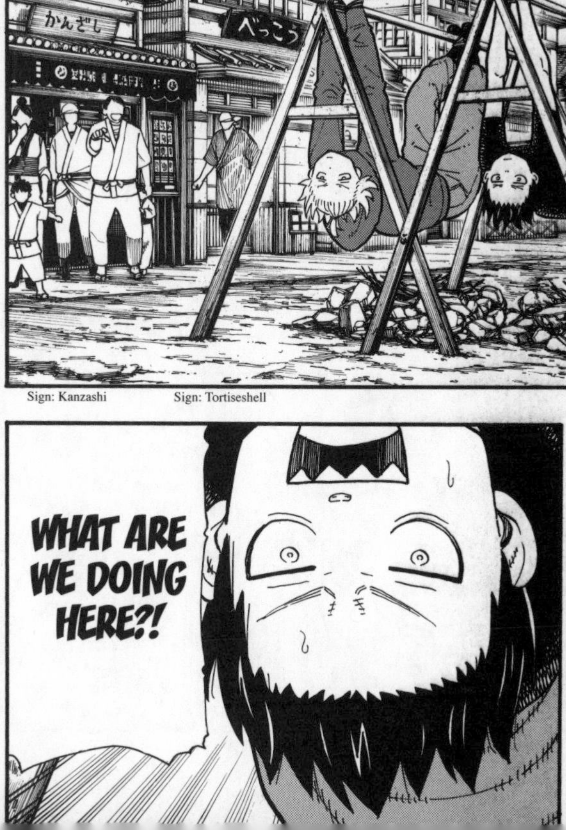
WHAT ARE WE DOING HERE?!

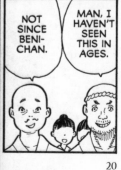

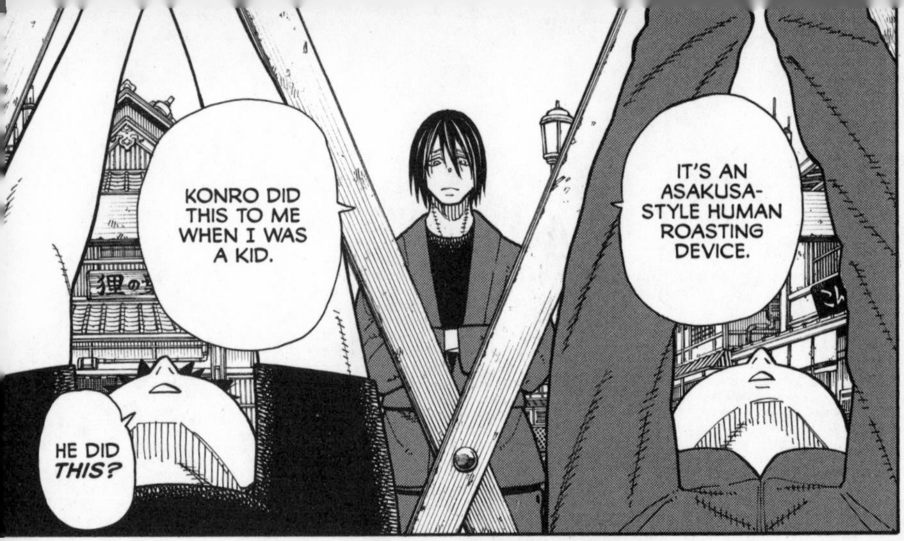
IT'S AN ASAKUSA-STYLE HUMAN ROASTING DEVICE.
KONRO DID THIS TO ME WHEN I WAS A KID.
HE DID *THIS?*

Sign: Tanuki Leaf

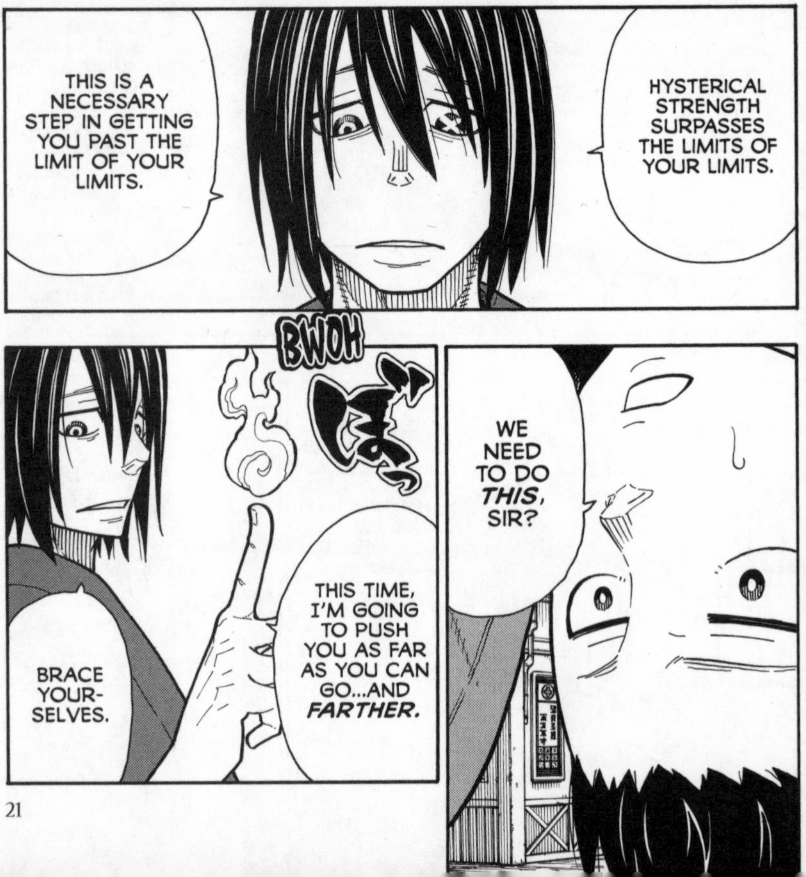
HYSTERICAL STRENGTH SURPASSES THE LIMITS OF YOUR LIMITS.
THIS IS A NECESSARY STEP IN GETTING YOU PAST THE LIMIT OF YOUR LIMITS.
WE NEED TO DO *THIS*, SIR?
BWOH
THIS TIME, I'M GOING TO PUSH YOU AS FAR AS YOU CAN GO...AND *FARTHER.*
BRACE YOUR-SELVES.

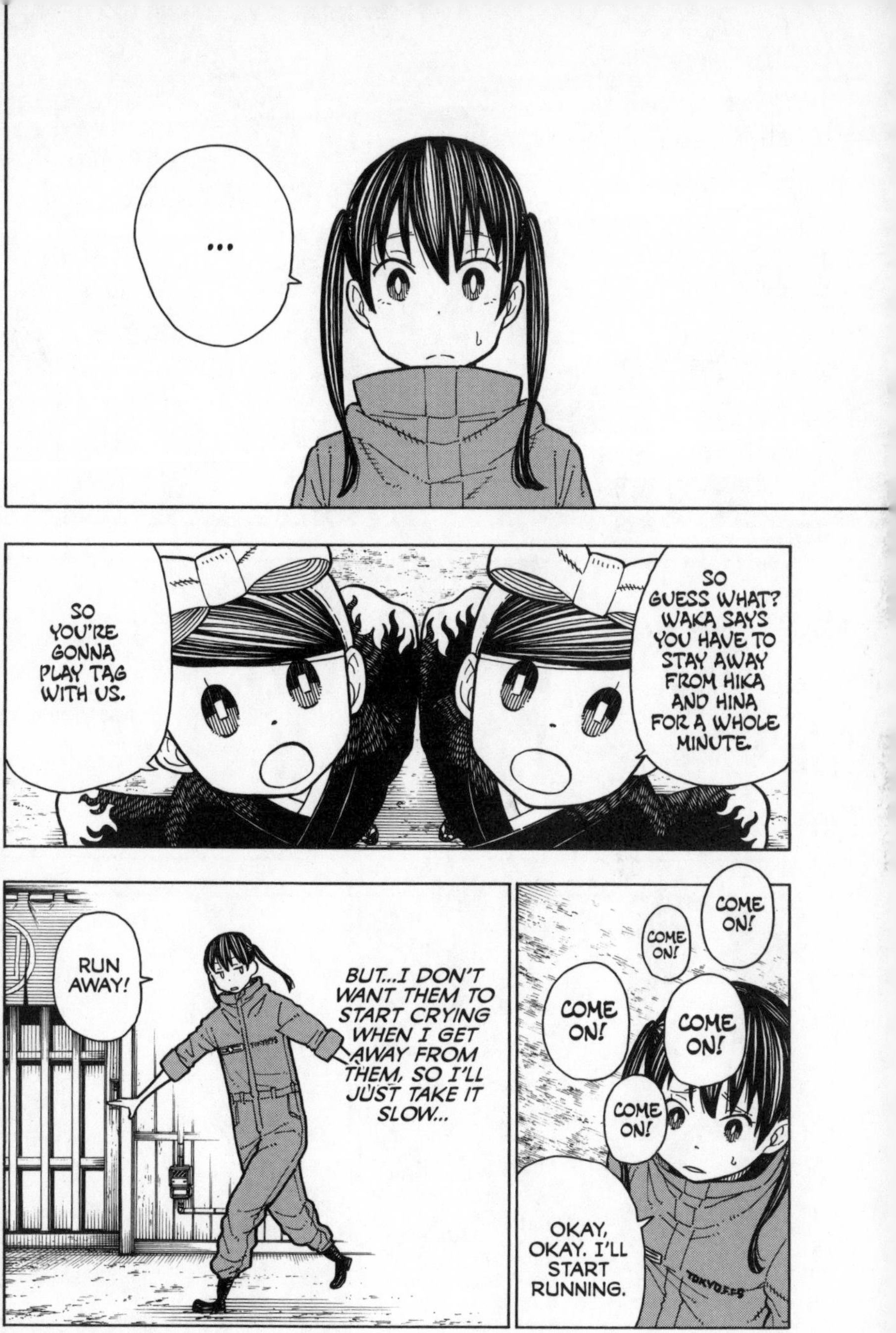
...
SO GUESS WHAT? WAKA SAYS YOU HAVE TO STAY AWAY FROM HIKA AND HINA FOR A WHOLE MINUTE.
SO YOU'RE GONNA PLAY TAG WITH US.
COME ON!
COME ON!
COME ON!
COME ON!
COME ON!
OKAY, OKAY. I'LL START RUNNING.
RUN AWAY!
BUT...I DON'T WANT THEM TO START CRYING WHEN I GET AWAY FROM THEM, SO I'LL JUST TAKE IT SLOW...

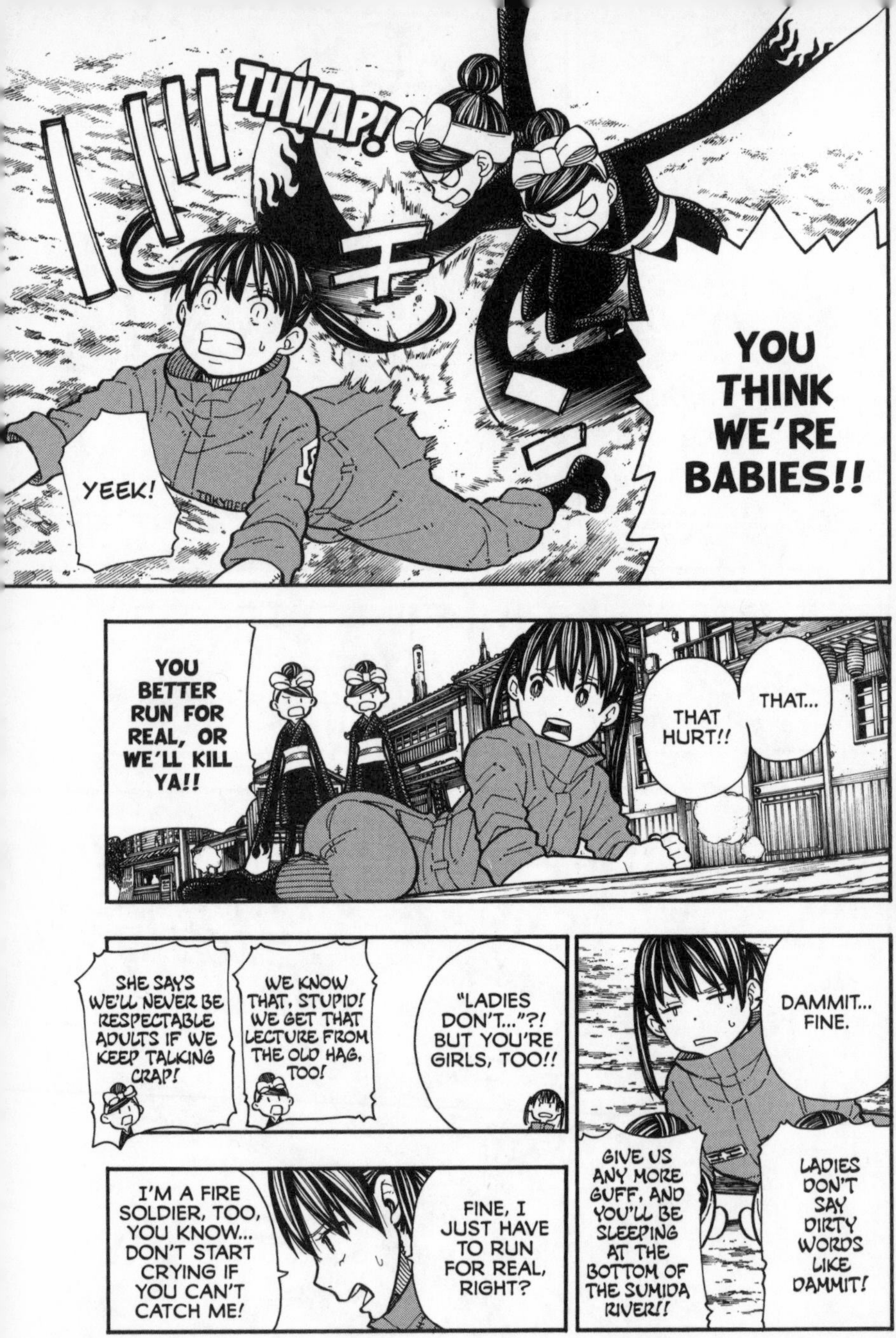
THWAP!
YOU THINK WE'RE BABIES!!
YEEK!
THAT...
THAT HURT!!
YOU BETTER RUN FOR REAL, OR WE'LL KILL YA!!
DAMMIT... FINE.
LADIES DON'T SAY DIRTY WORDS LIKE DAMMIT!
GIVE US ANY MORE GUFF, AND YOU'LL BE SLEEPING AT THE BOTTOM OF THE SUMIDA RIVER!!
"LADIES DON'T..."?! BUT YOU'RE GIRLS, TOO!!
WE KNOW THAT, STUPID! WE GET THAT LECTURE FROM THE OLD HAG, TOO!
SHE SAYS WE'LL NEVER BE RESPECTABLE ADULTS IF WE KEEP TALKING CRAP!
FINE, I JUST HAVE TO RUN FOR REAL, RIGHT?
I'M A FIRE SOLDIER, TOO, YOU KNOW... DON'T START CRYING IF YOU CAN'T CATCH ME!

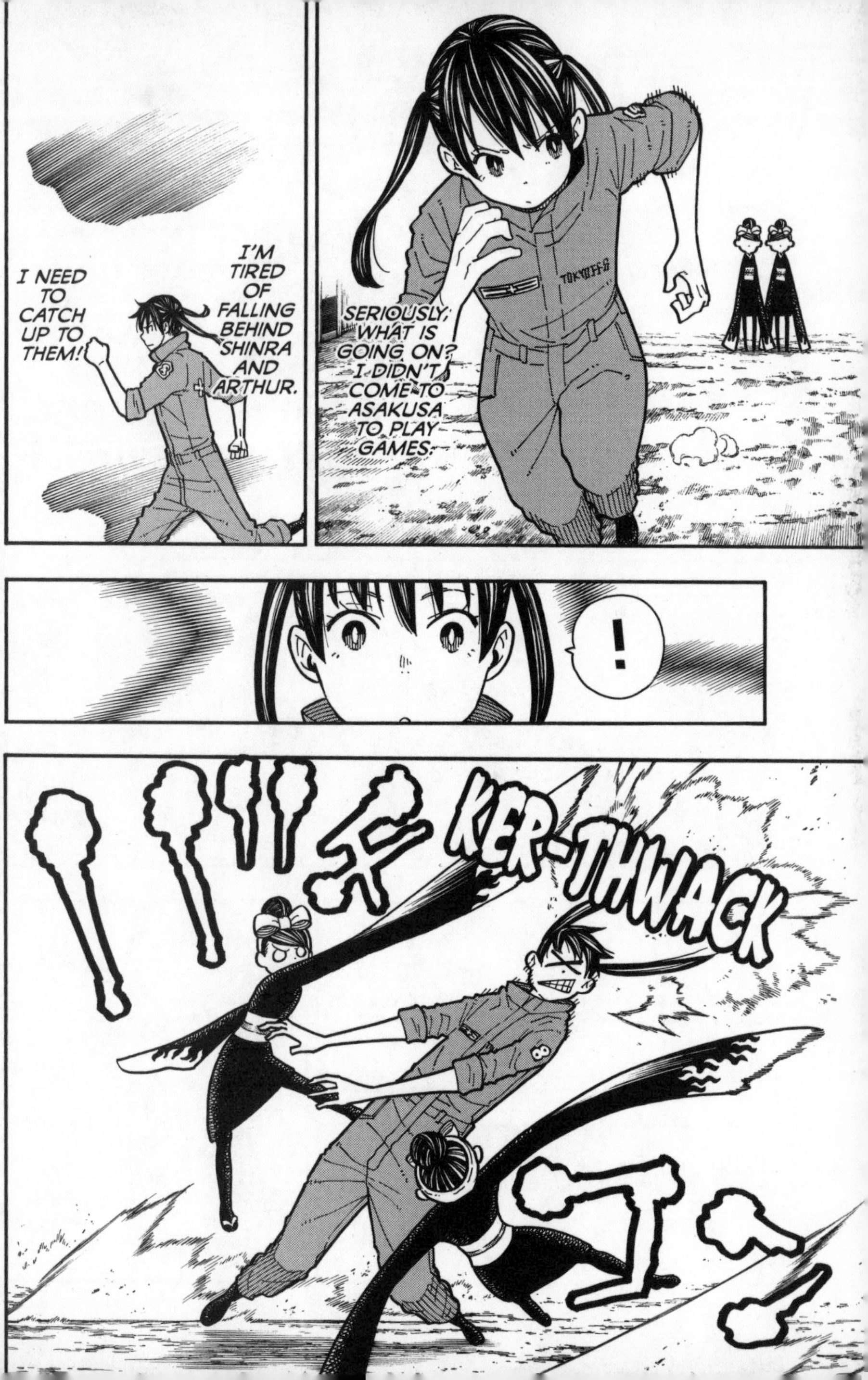
SERIOUSLY, WHAT IS GOING ON? I DIDN'T COME TO ASAKUSA TO PLAY GAMES.
I'M TIRED OF FALLING BEHIND SHINRA AND ARTHUR.
I NEED TO CATCH UP TO THEM!
!
KER-THWACK

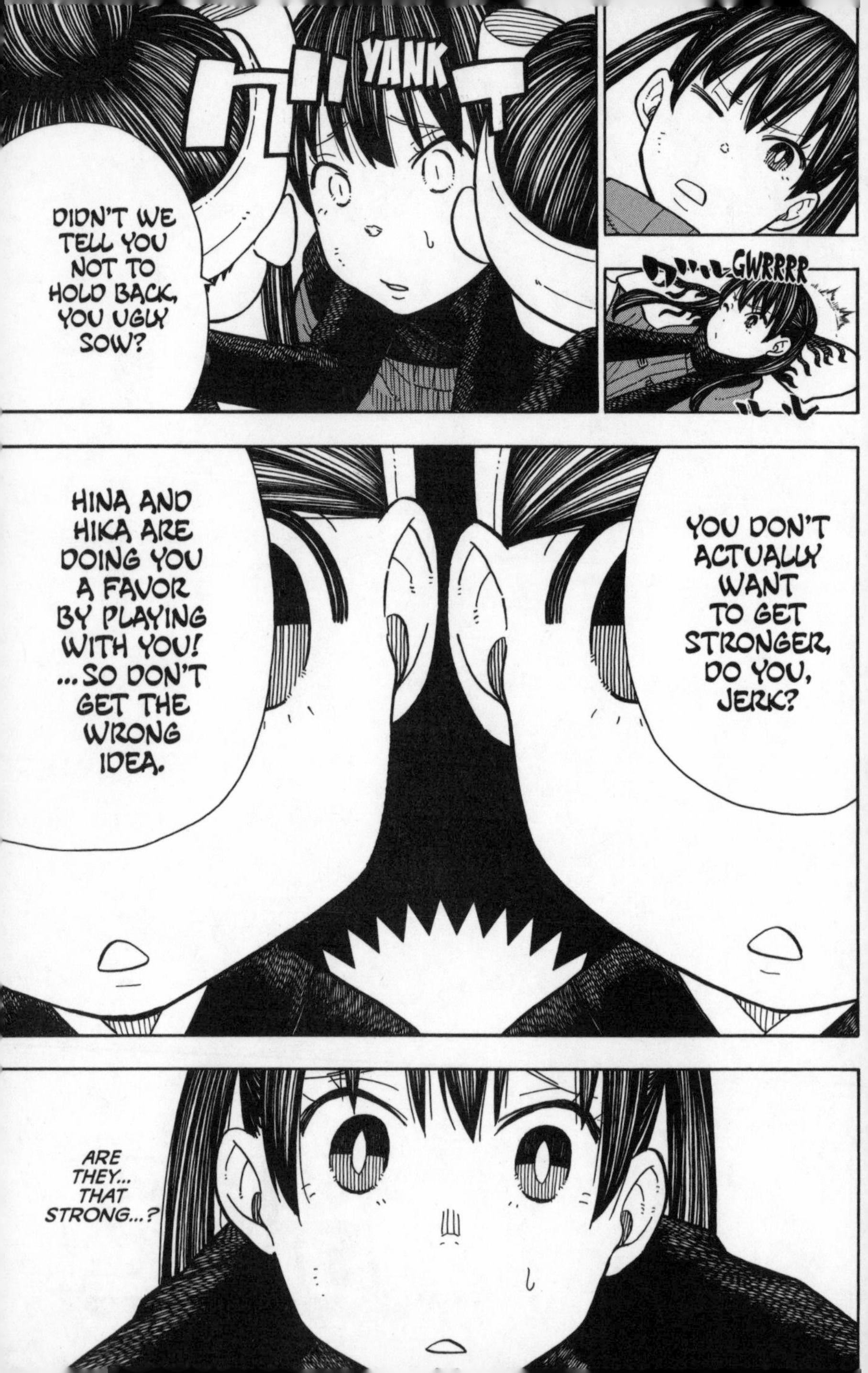
GWRRRR
YANK
DIDN'T WE TELL YOU NOT TO HOLD BACK, YOU UGLY SOW?
YOU DON'T ACTUALLY WANT TO GET STRONGER, DO YOU, JERK?
HINA AND HIKA ARE DOING YOU A FAVOR BY PLAYING WITH YOU! ...SO DON'T GET THE WRONG IDEA.
ARE THEY... THAT STRONG...?

FIRE FORCE

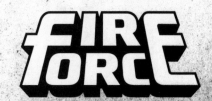

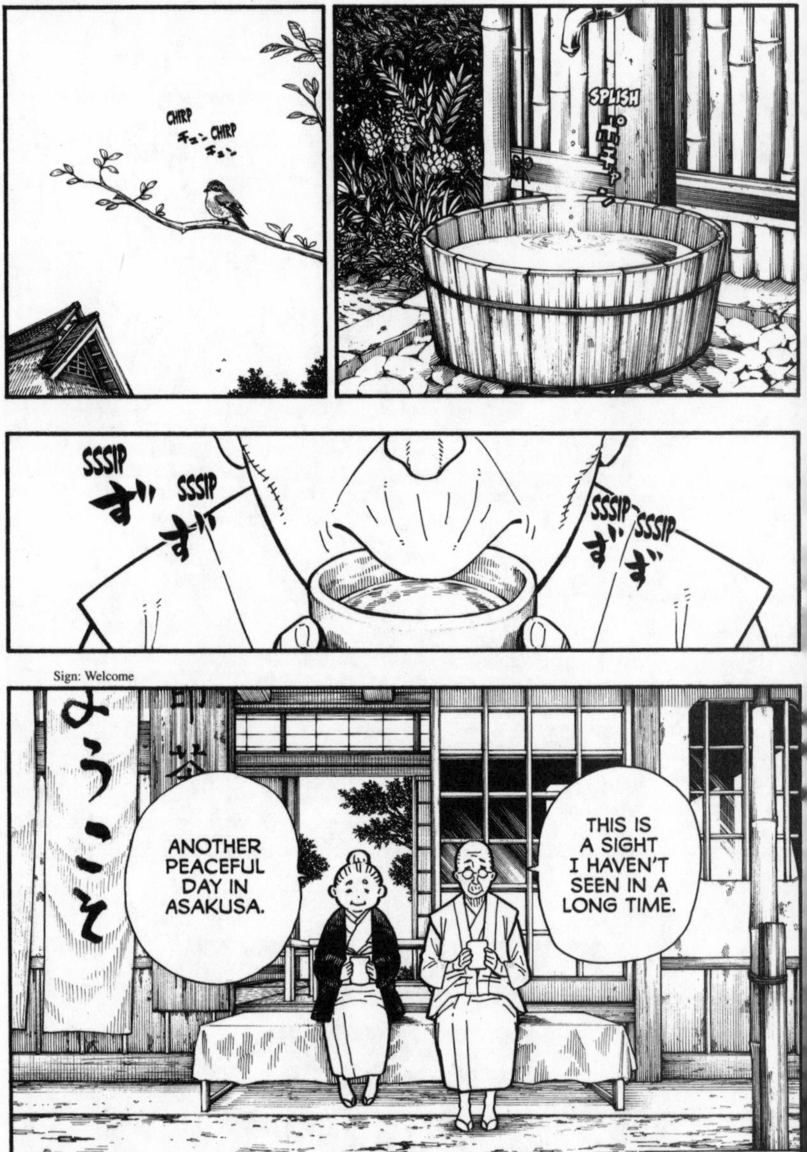
SPLISH
CHIRP
チュン
CHIRP
チュン
SSSIP
SSSIP
SSSIP
SSSIP
ようこそ
THIS IS A SIGHT I HAVEN'T SEEN IN A LONG TIME.
ANOTHER PEACEFUL DAY IN ASAKUSA.

Sign: Welcome

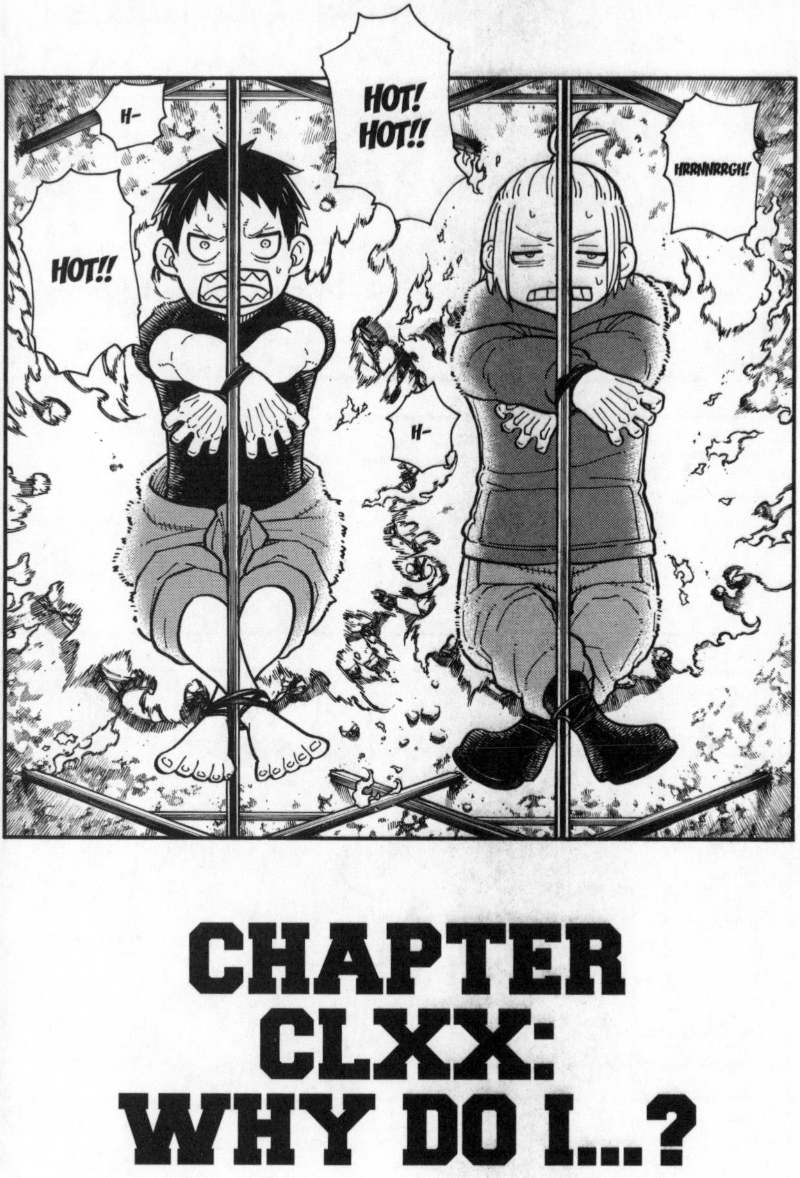
HRRNNRRGH!
HOT! HOT!!
H-
HOT!!
H-

CHAPTER CLXX: WHY DO I...?

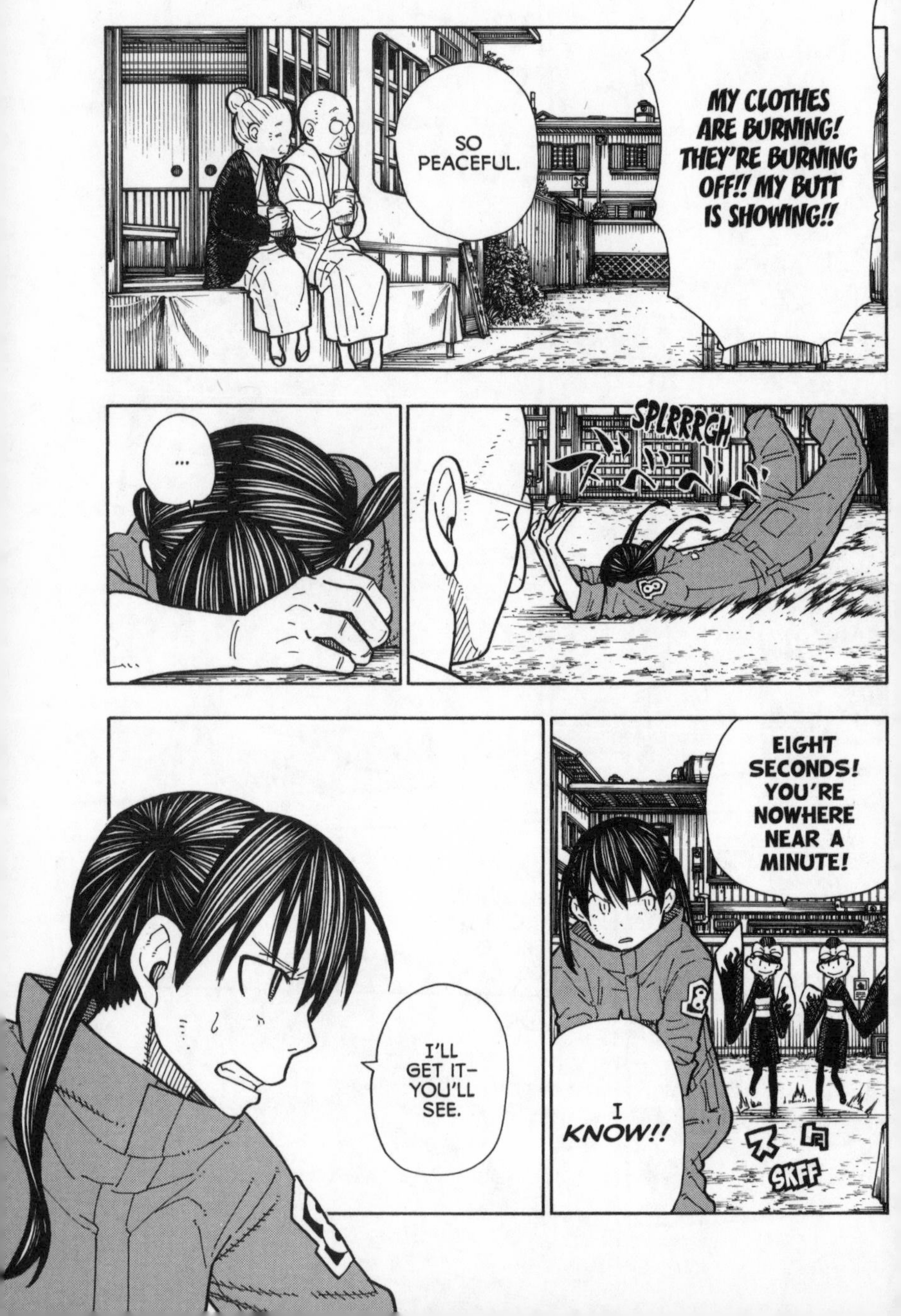
MY CLOTHES ARE BURNING! THEY'RE BURNING OFF!! MY BUTT IS SHOWING!!
SO PEACEFUL.
SPLRRRGH
...
EIGHT SECONDS! YOU'RE NOWHERE NEAR A MINUTE!
I KNOW!!
SKFF
I'LL GET IT—YOU'LL SEE.

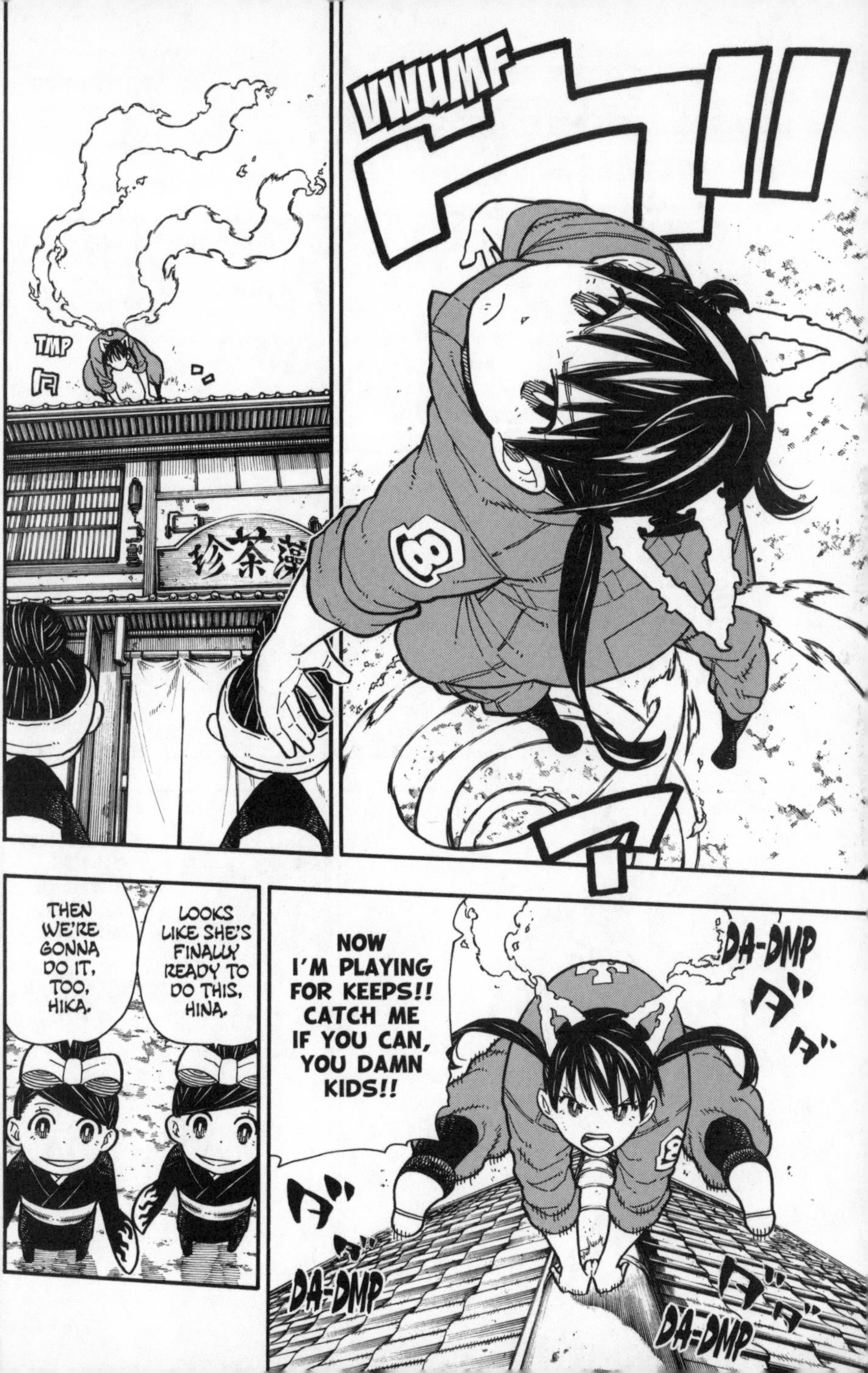
VWUMF
TMP
DA-DMP
NOW I'M PLAYING FOR KEEPS!! CATCH ME IF YOU CAN, YOU DAMN KIDS!!
DA-DMP
DA-DMP
LOOKS LIKE SHE'S FINALLY READY TO DO THIS, HINA.
THEN WE'RE GONNA DO IT, TOO, HIKA.

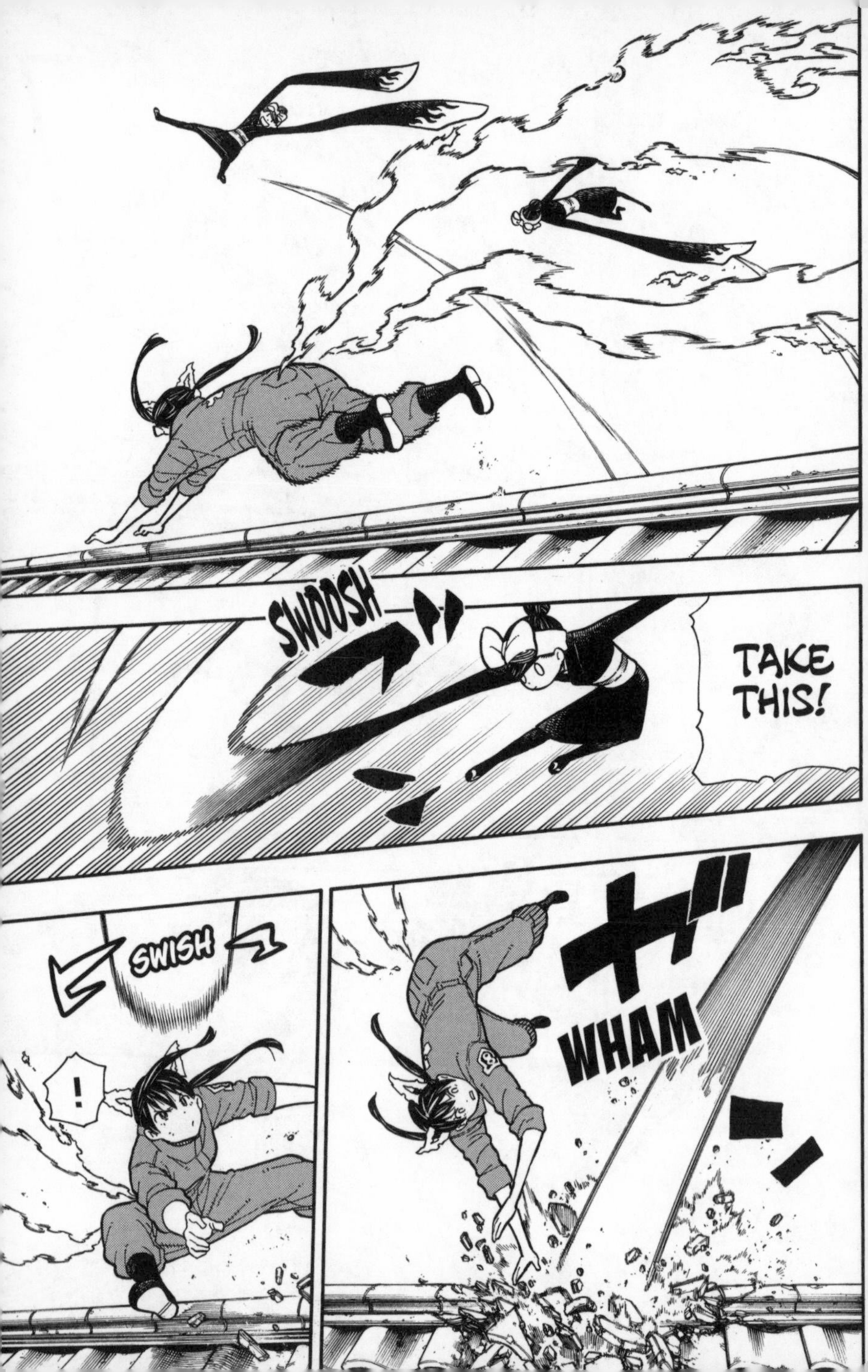
TAKE THIS!
SWOOSH
WHAM
SWISH
!

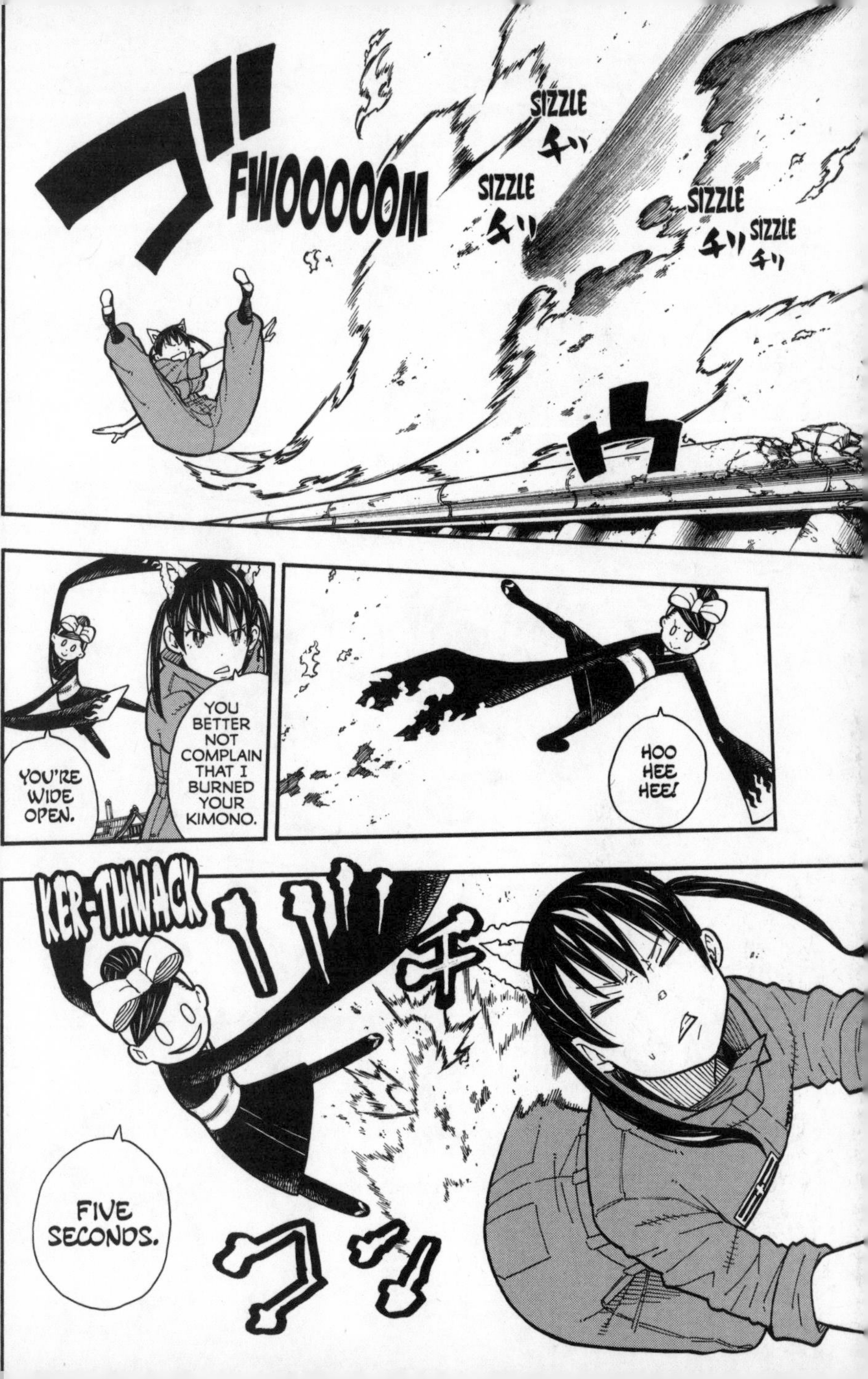
SIZZLE
SIZZLE
SIZZLE
SIZZLE
FWOOOOOM
HOO HEE HEE!
YOU BETTER NOT COMPLAIN THAT I BURNED YOUR KIMONO.
YOU'RE WIDE OPEN.
KER-THWACK
FIVE SECONDS.

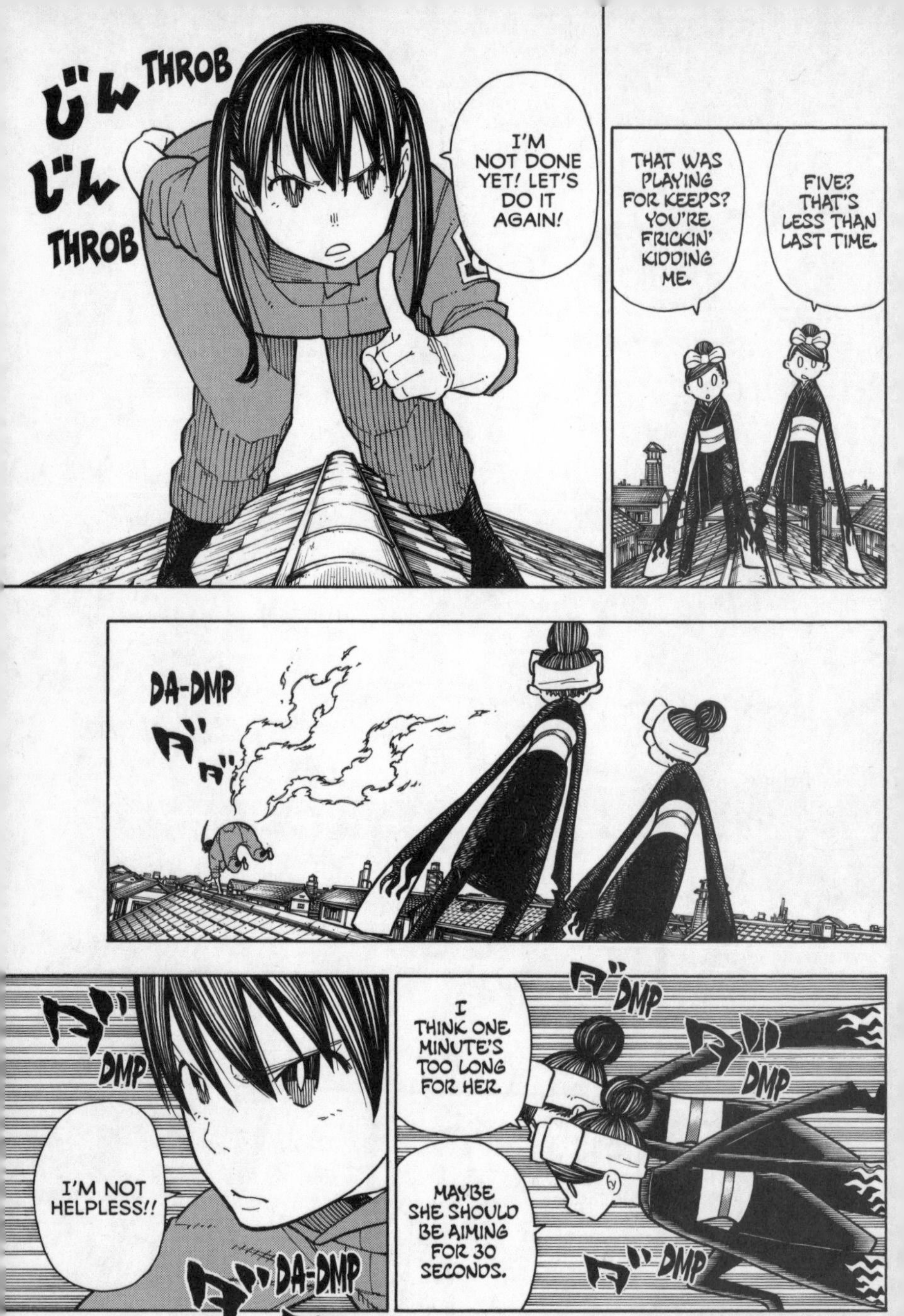
FIVE? THAT'S LESS THAN LAST TIME.
THAT WAS PLAYING FOR KEEPS? YOU'RE FRICKIN' KIDDING ME.
じん THROB
じん THROB
I'M NOT DONE YET! LET'S DO IT AGAIN!
DA-DMP
DMP
I THINK ONE MINUTE'S TOO LONG FOR HER.
DMP
MAYBE SHE SHOULD BE AIMING FOR 30 SECONDS.
DMP
DMP
I'M NOT HELPLESS!!
DA-DMP

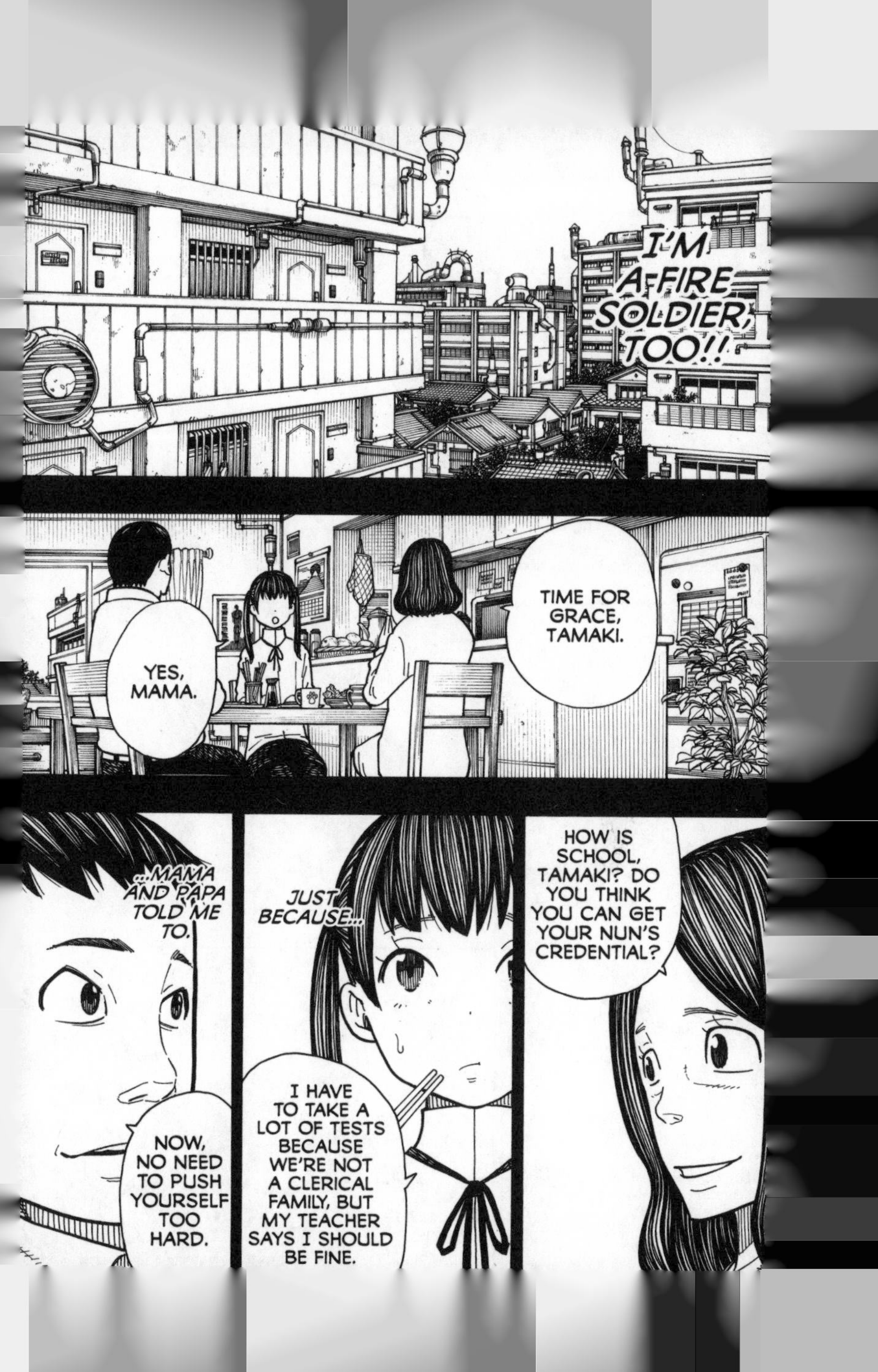
I'M A FIRE SOLDIER, TOO!!
TIME FOR GRACE, TAMAKI.
YES, MAMA.
HOW IS SCHOOL, TAMAKI? DO YOU THINK YOU CAN GET YOUR NUN'S CREDENTIAL?
JUST BECAUSE...
I HAVE TO TAKE A LOT OF TESTS BECAUSE WE'RE NOT A CLERICAL FAMILY, BUT MY TEACHER SAYS I SHOULD BE FINE.
...MAMA AND PAPA TOLD ME TO.
NOW, NO NEED TO PUSH YOURSELF TOO HARD.

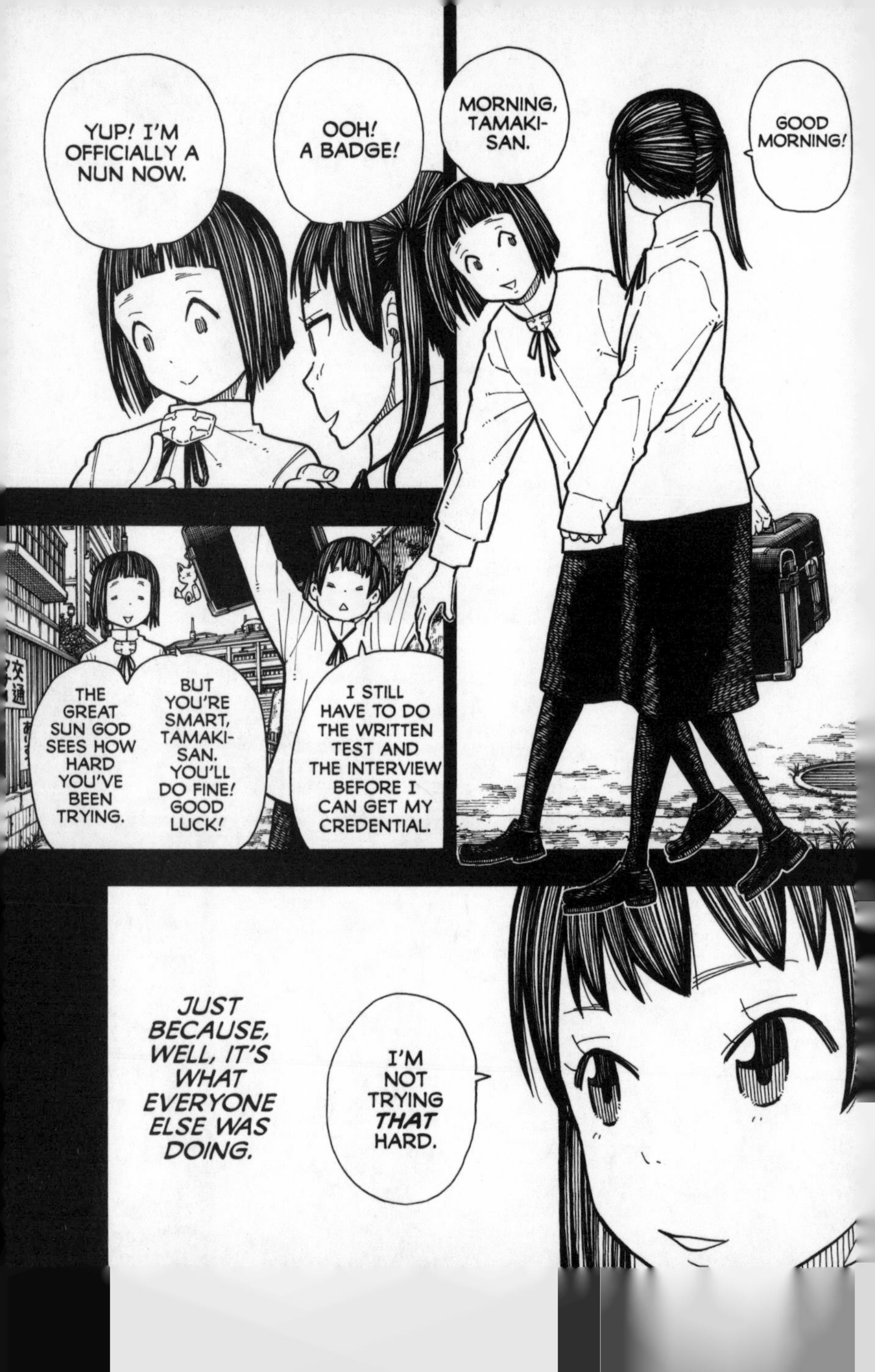
GOOD MORNING!
MORNING, TAMAKI-SAN.
OOH! A BADGE!
YUP! I'M OFFICIALLY A NUN NOW.
I STILL HAVE TO DO THE WRITTEN TEST AND THE INTERVIEW BEFORE I CAN GET MY CREDENTIAL.
BUT YOU'RE SMART, TAMAKI-SAN. YOU'LL DO FINE! GOOD LUCK!
THE GREAT SUN GOD SEES HOW HARD YOU'VE BEEN TRYING.
I'M NOT TRYING *THAT* HARD.
JUST BECAUSE, WELL, IT'S WHAT EVERYONE ELSE WAS DOING.

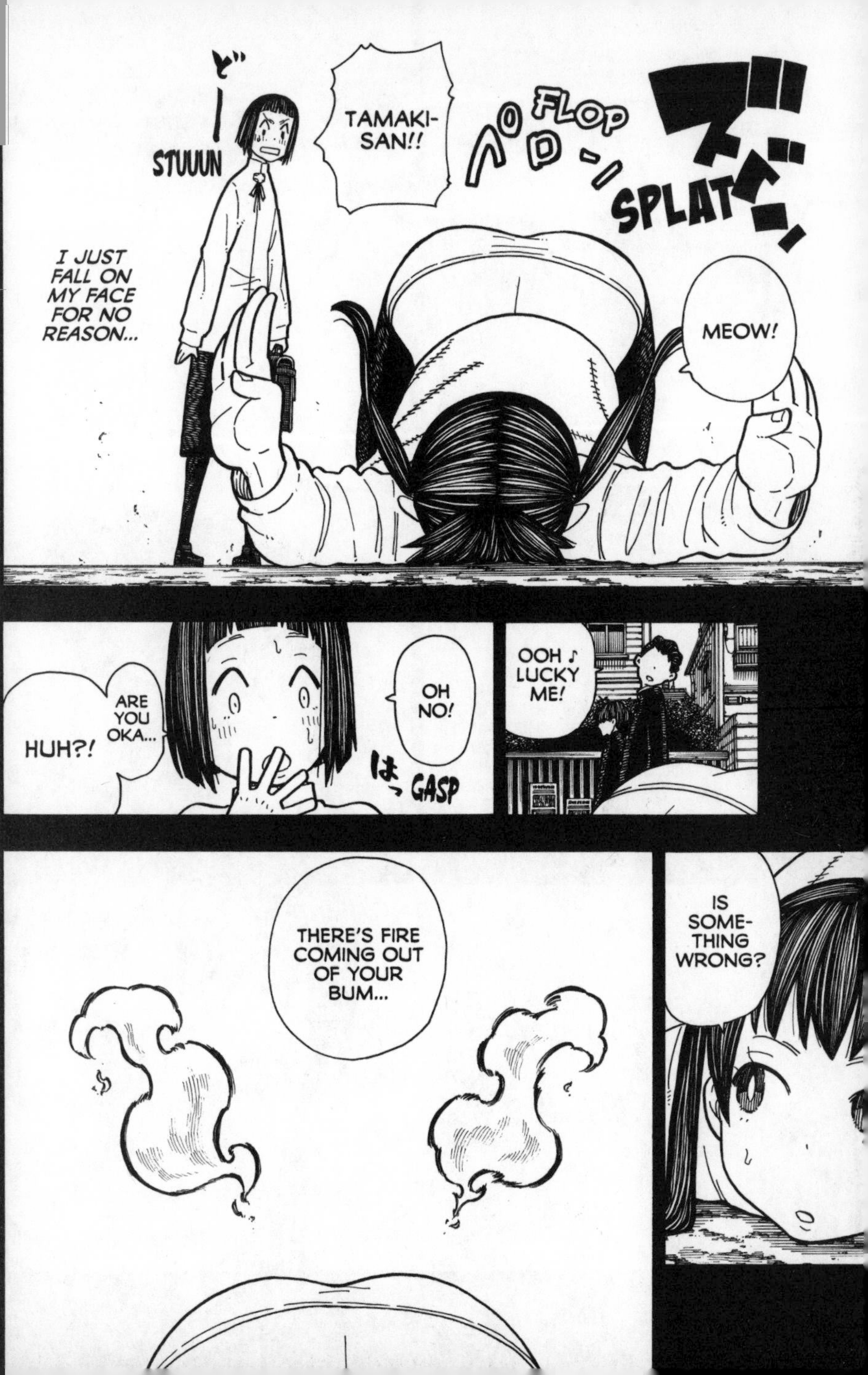
SPLAT
FLOP
MEOW!
TAMAKI-SAN!!
STUUUN
I JUST FALL ON MY FACE FOR NO REASON...
OOH ♪ LUCKY ME!
OH NO!
ARE YOU OKA...
HUH?!
GASP
IS SOME-THING WRONG?
THERE'S FIRE COMING OUT OF YOUR BUM...

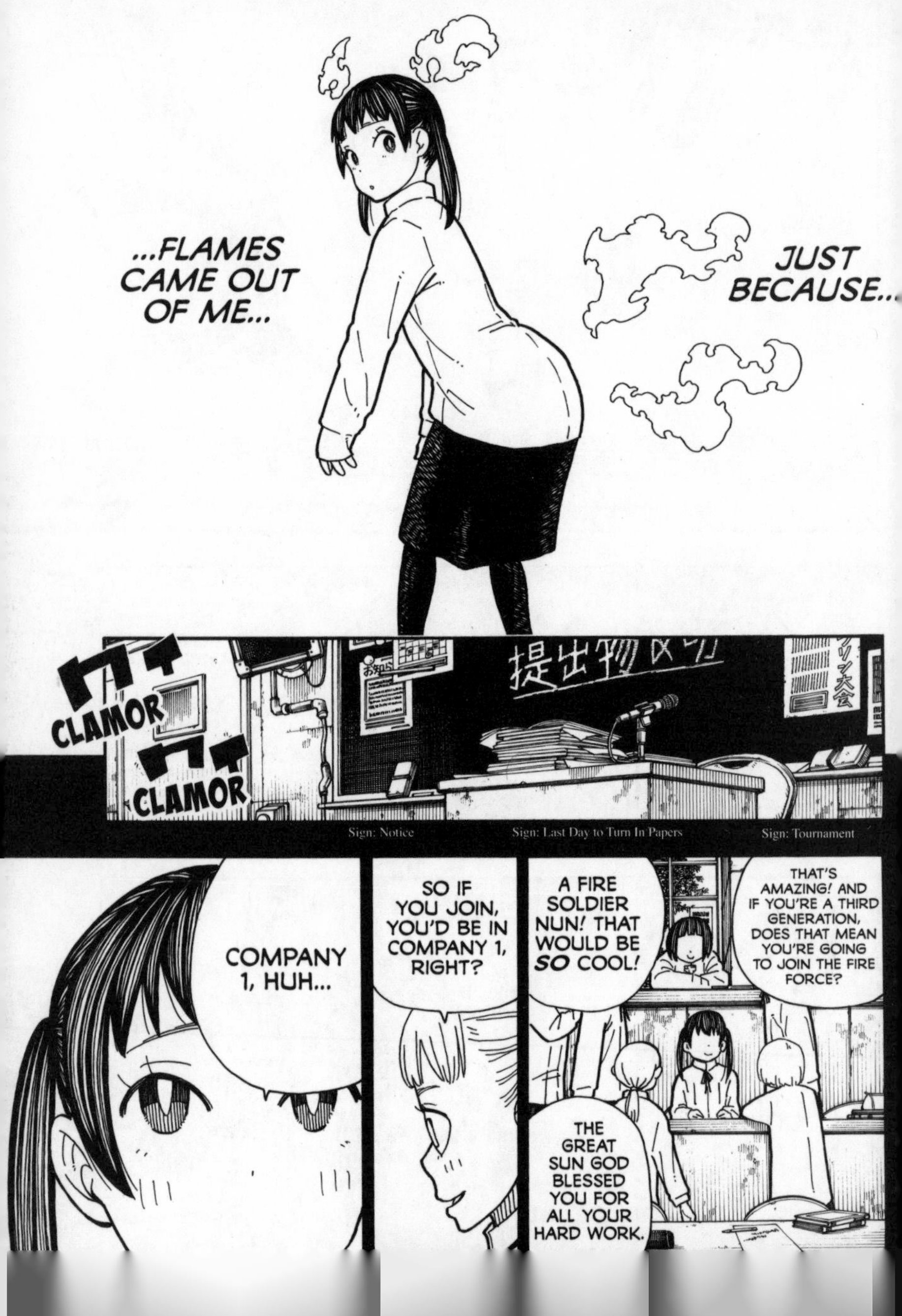
JUST BECAUSE...
...FLAMES CAME OUT OF ME...
CLAMOR
CLAMOR
Sign: Tournament
Sign: Last Day to Turn In Papers
Sign: Notice
THAT'S AMAZING! AND IF YOU'RE A THIRD GENERATION, DOES THAT MEAN YOU'RE GOING TO JOIN THE FIRE FORCE?
A FIRE SOLDIER NUN! THAT WOULD BE SO COOL!
THE GREAT SUN GOD BLESSED YOU FOR ALL YOUR HARD WORK.
SO IF YOU JOIN, YOU'D BE IN COMPANY 1, RIGHT?
COMPANY 1, HUH...

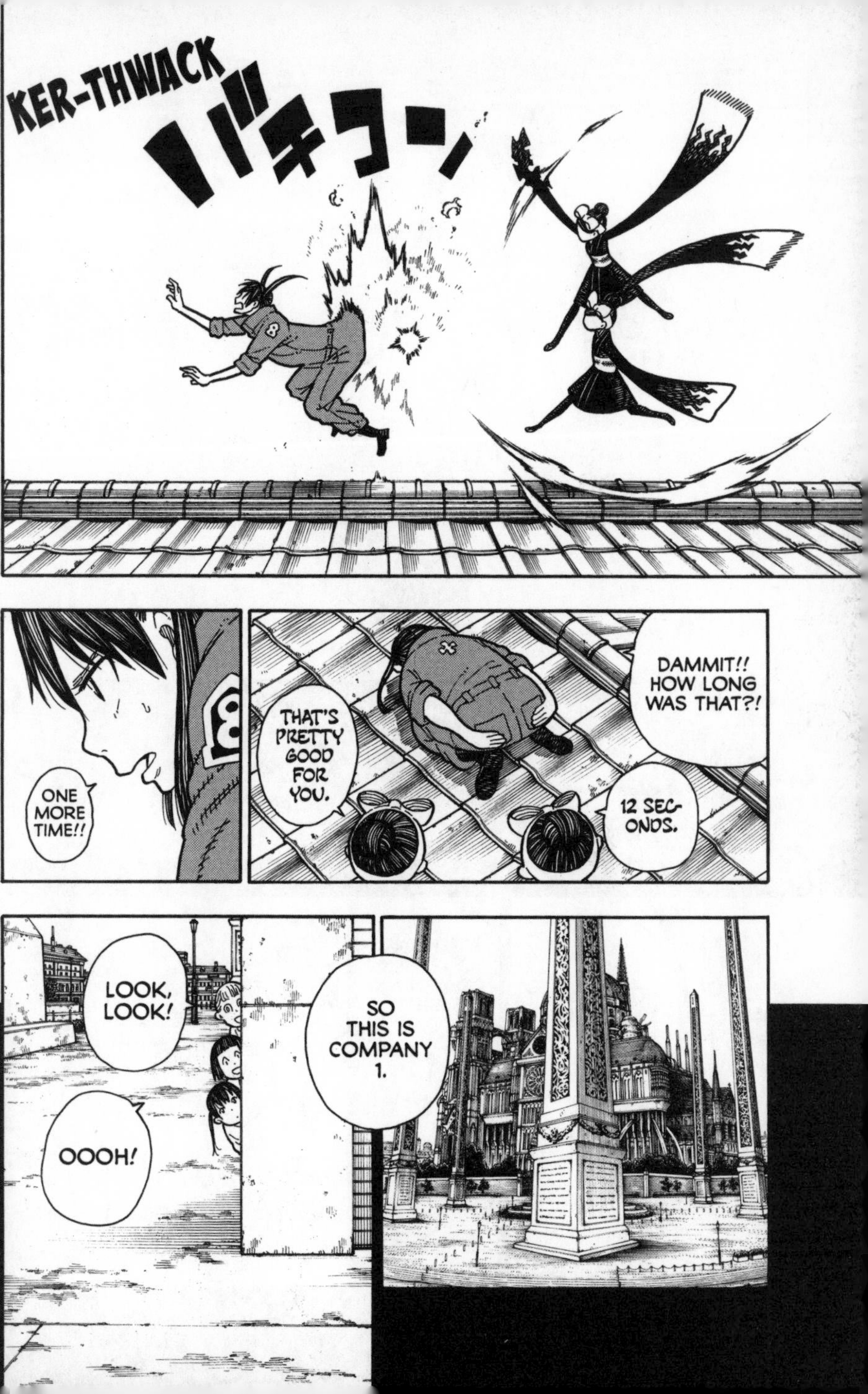
KER-THWACK
バチコーン
DAMMIT!! HOW LONG WAS THAT?!
12 SECONDS.
THAT'S PRETTY GOOD FOR YOU.
ONE MORE TIME!!
SO THIS IS COMPANY 1.
LOOK, LOOK!
OOOH!

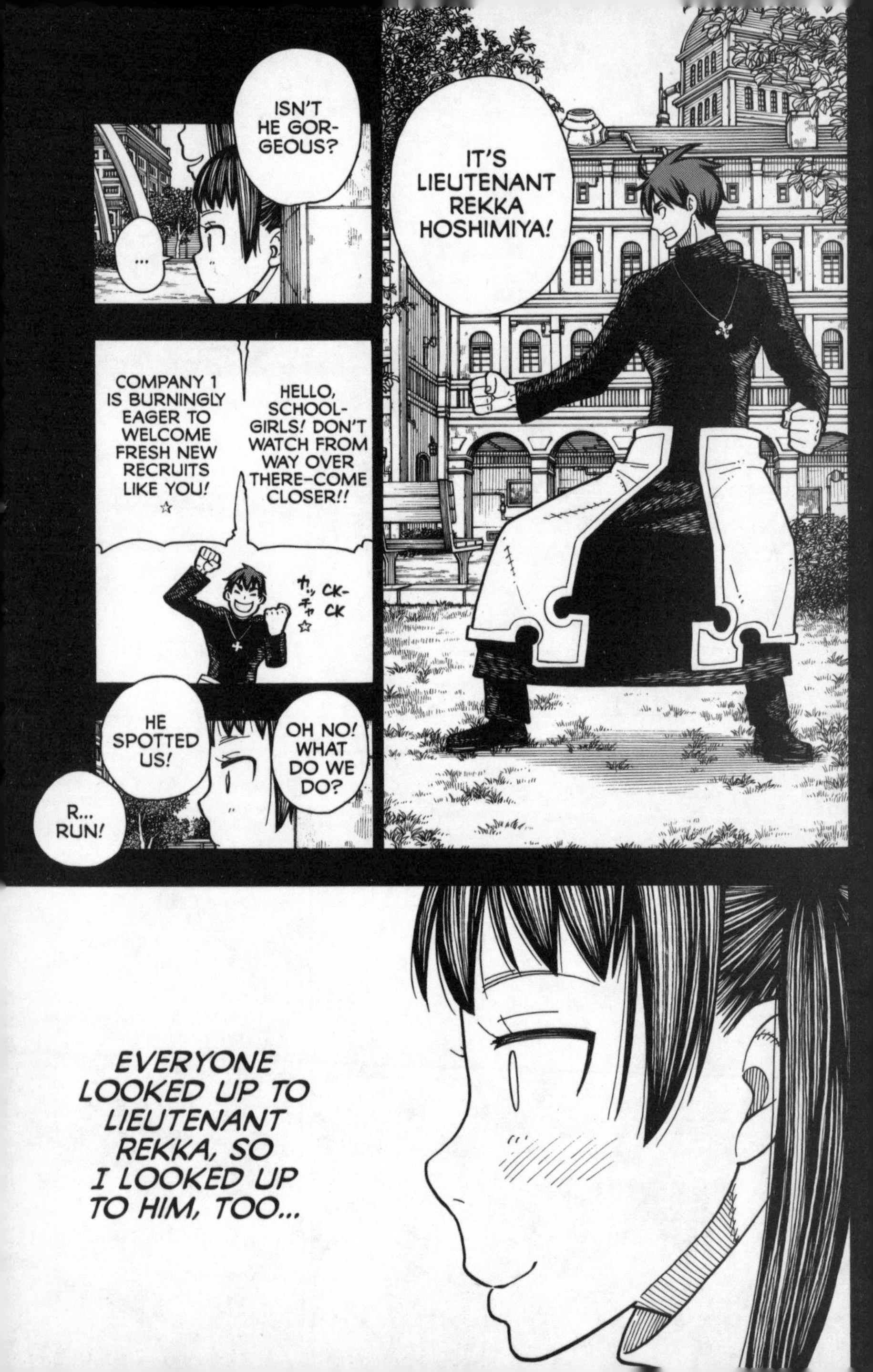
IT'S LIEUTENANT REKKA HOSHIMIYA!
ISN'T HE GOR-GEOUS?
...
HELLO, SCHOOL-GIRLS! DON'T WATCH FROM WAY OVER THERE–COME CLOSER!!
COMPANY 1 IS BURNINGLY EAGER TO WELCOME FRESH NEW RECRUITS LIKE YOU! ☆
CK-CK ☆
OH NO! WHAT DO WE DO?
HE SPOTTED US!
R... RUN!
EVERYONE LOOKED UP TO LIEUTENANT REKKA, SO I LOOKED UP TO HIM, TOO...

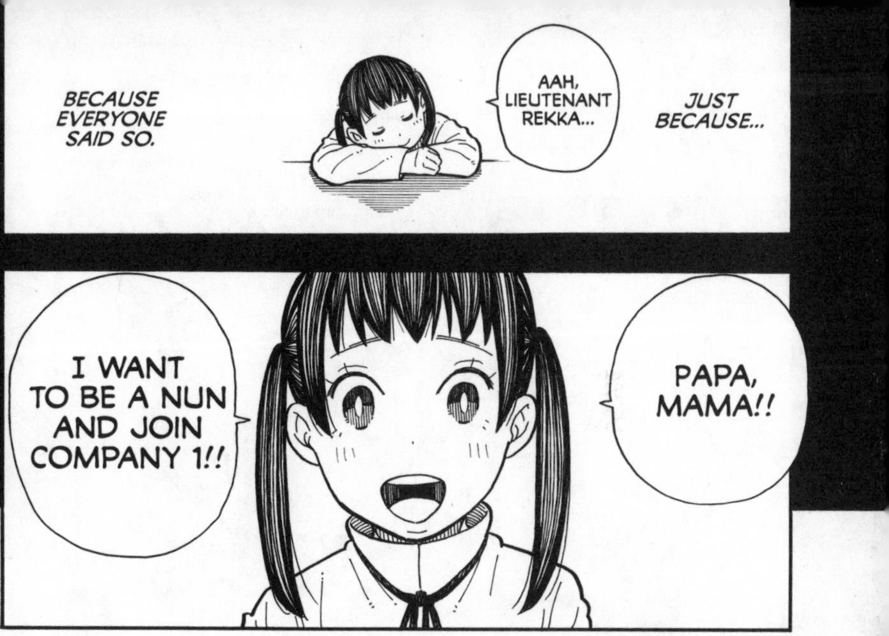
JUST BECAUSE...
AAH, LIEUTENANT REKKA...
BECAUSE EVERYONE SAID SO.
PAPA, MAMA!!
I WANT TO BE A NUN AND JOIN COMPANY 1!!

Signs: Shiromitsukan

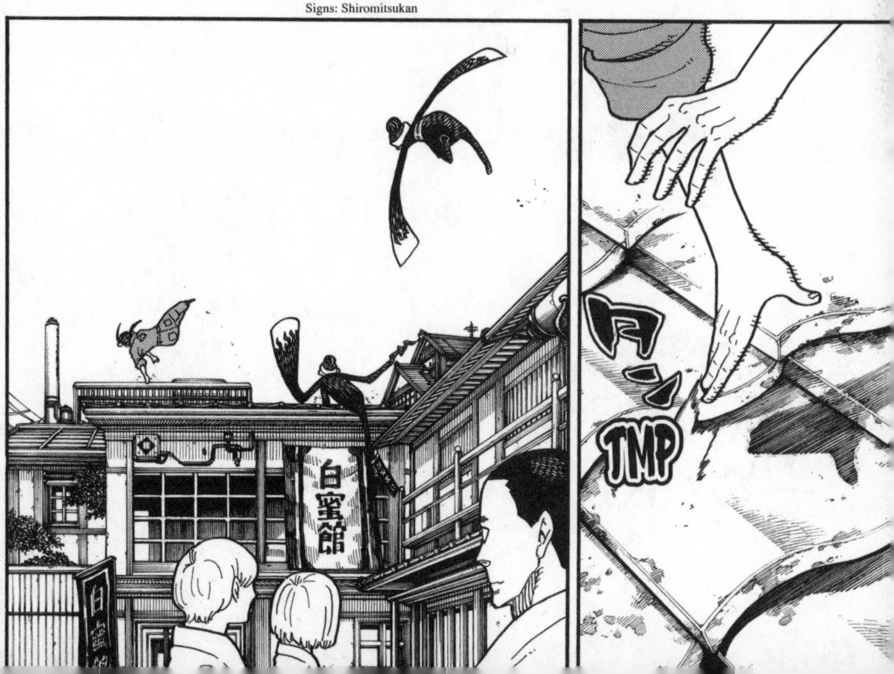
TMP

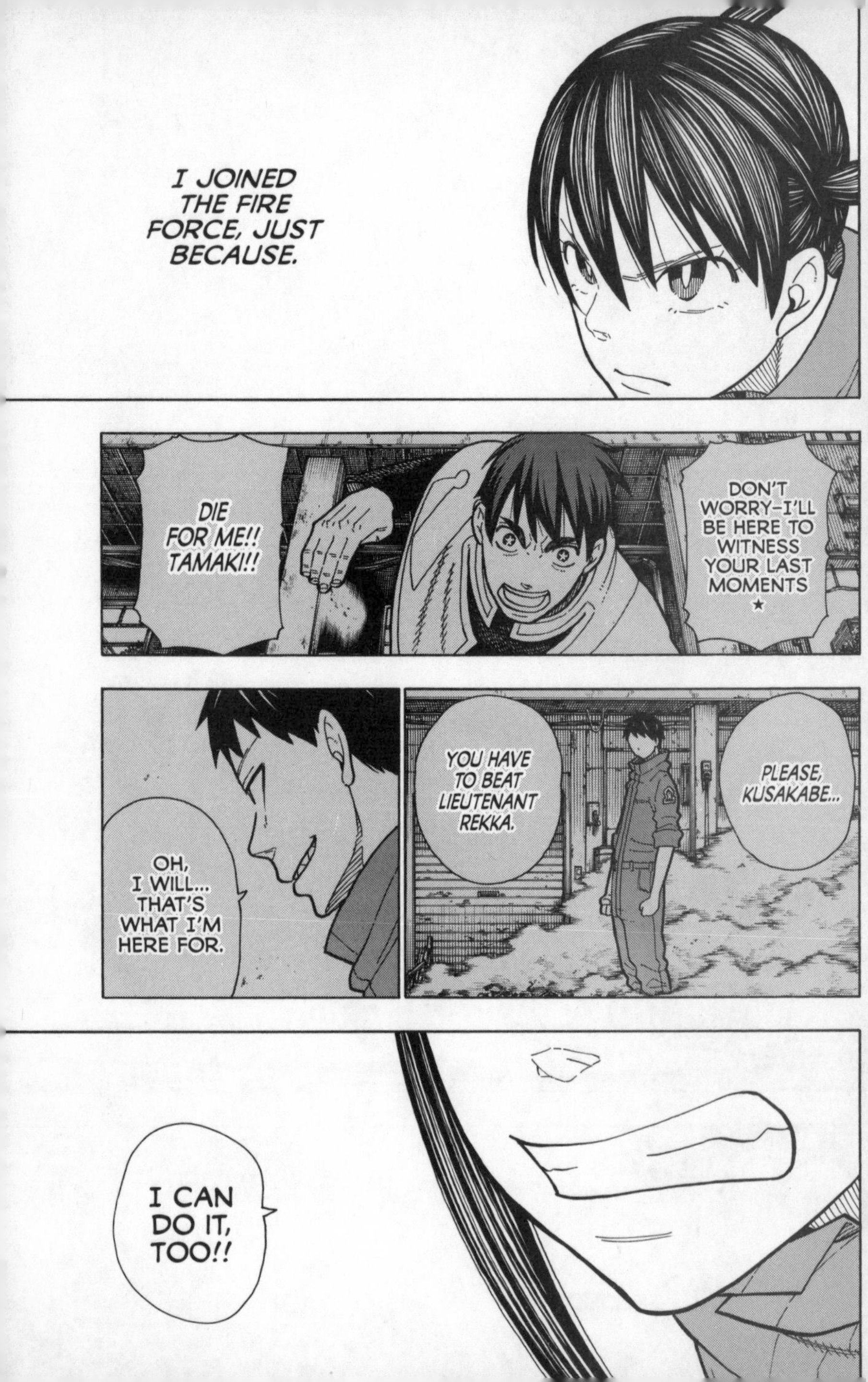
I JOINED THE FIRE FORCE, JUST BECAUSE.
DON'T WORRY–I'LL BE HERE TO WITNESS YOUR LAST MOMENTS ★
DIE FOR ME!! TAMAKI!!
PLEASE, KUSAKABE...
YOU HAVE TO BEAT LIEUTENANT REKKA.
OH, I WILL... THAT'S WHAT I'M HERE FOR.
I CAN DO IT, TOO!!

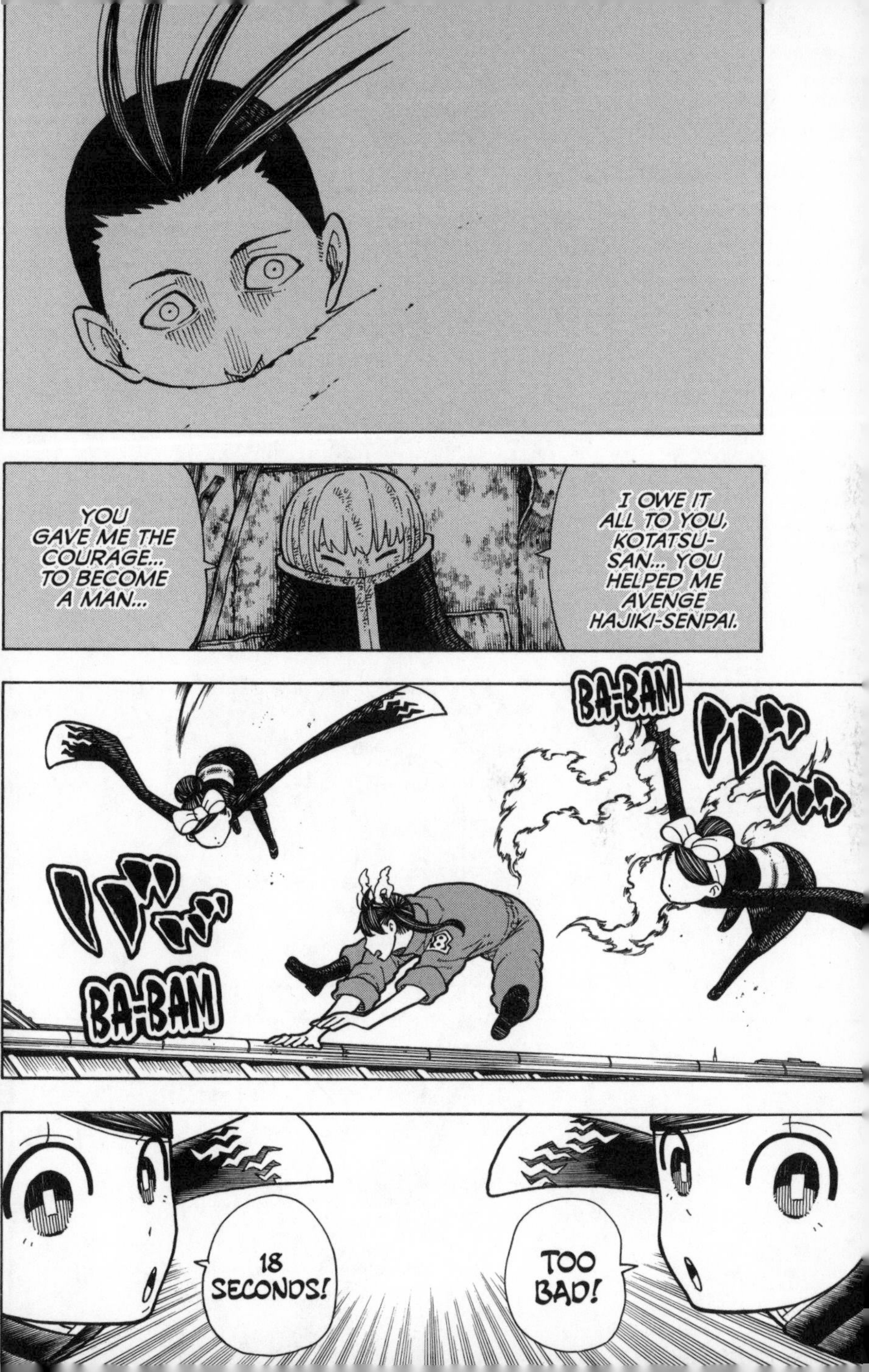
I OWE IT ALL TO YOU, KOTATSU-SAN... YOU HELPED ME AVENGE HAJIKI-SENPAI.
YOU GAVE ME THE COURAGE... TO BECOME A MAN...
BA-BAM
BA-BAM
TOO BAD!
18 SECONDS!

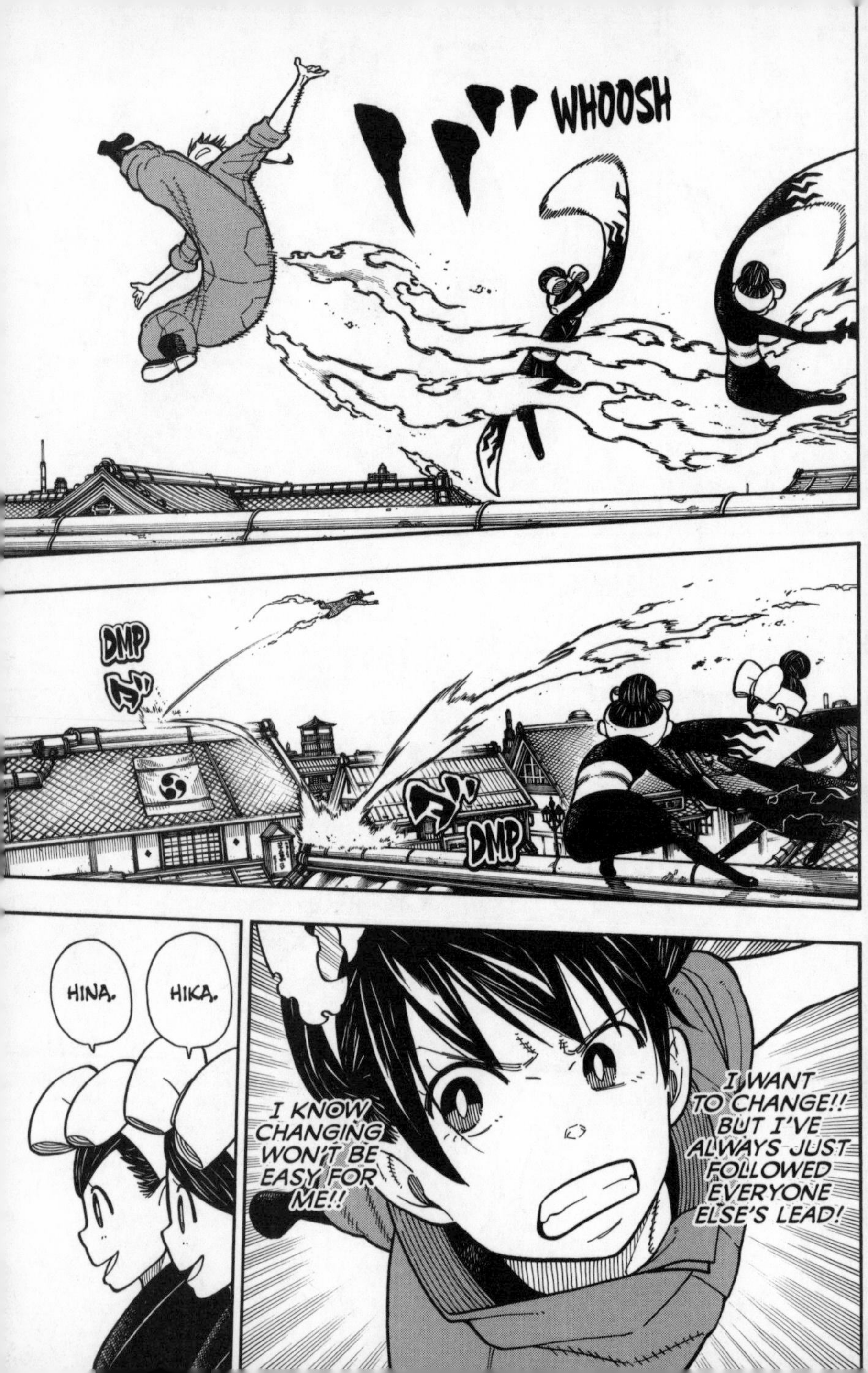
WHOOSH
DMP
DMP
I WANT TO CHANGE!! BUT I'VE ALWAYS JUST FOLLOWED EVERYONE ELSE'S LEAD!
I KNOW CHANGING WON'T BE EASY FOR ME!!
HIKA.
HINA.

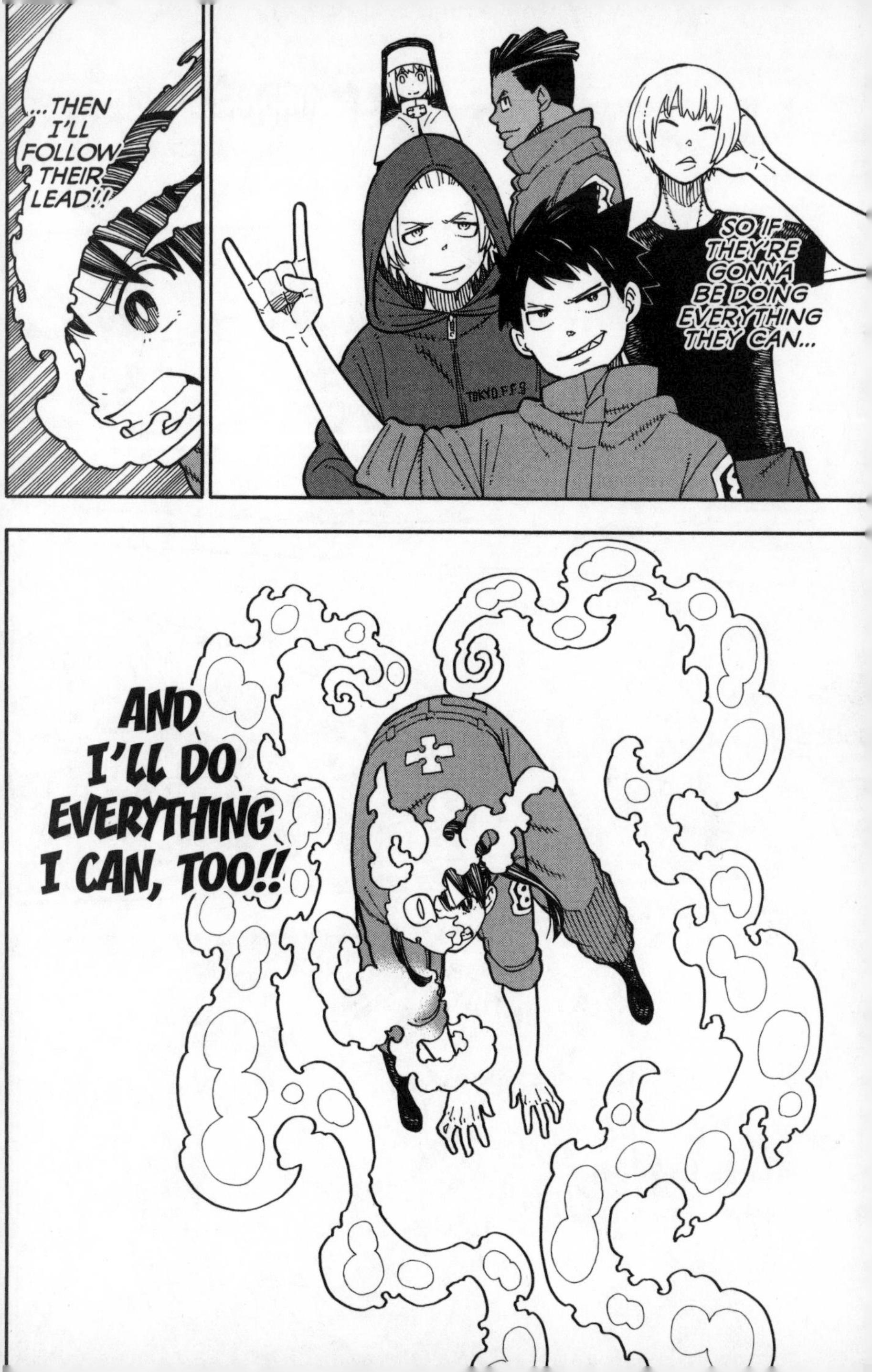
SO IF THEY'RE GONNA BE DOING EVERYTHING THEY CAN...
...THEN I'LL FOLLOW THEIR LEAD!!
AND I'LL DO EVERYTHING I CAN, TOO!!

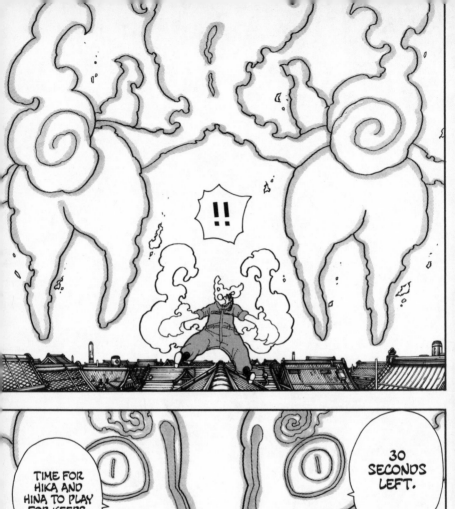

!!

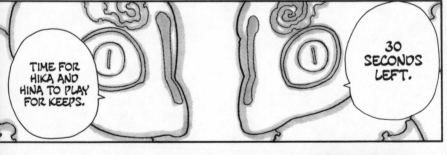

TIME FOR HIKA AND HINA TO PLAY FOR KEEPS.

30 SECONDS LEFT.

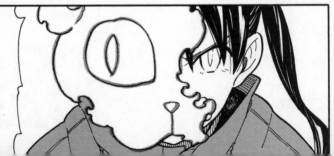

THERE'S NO WAY I'M GONNA LET YOU CATCH ME!!

FIRE FORCE

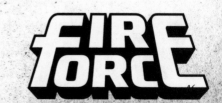

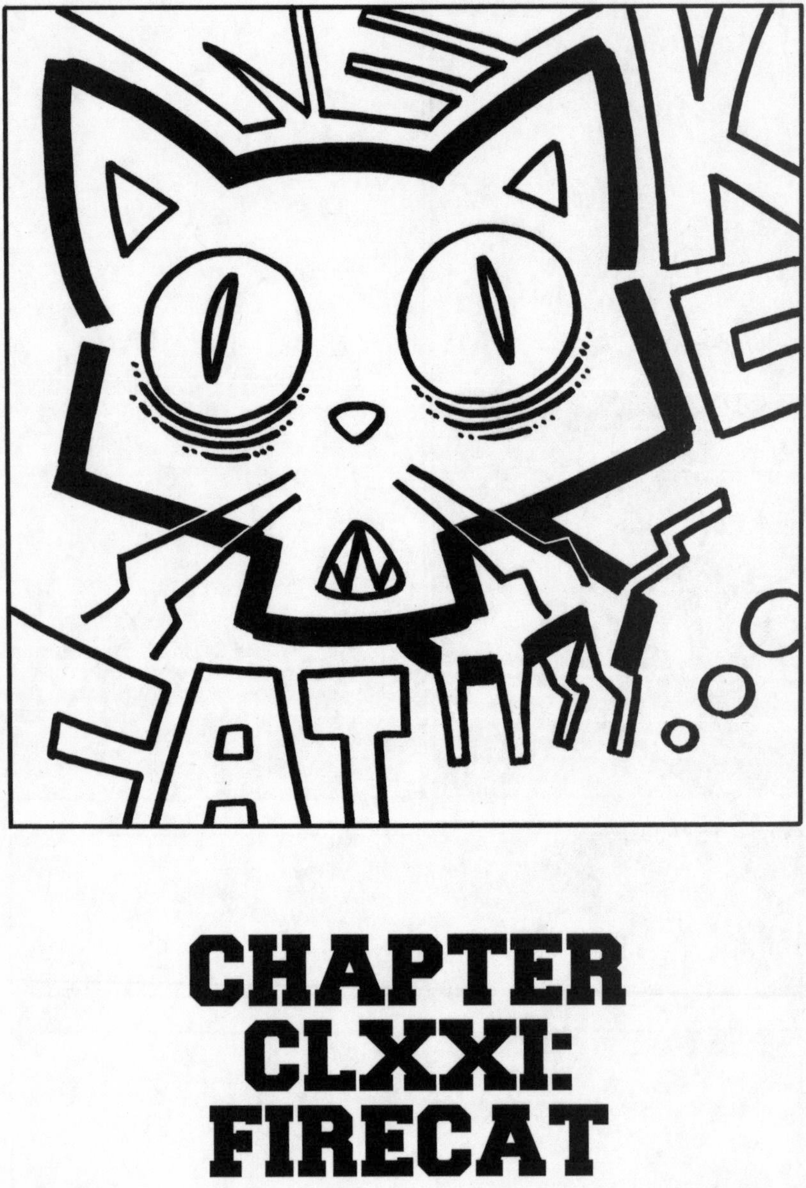

CHAPTER CLXXI: FIRECAT

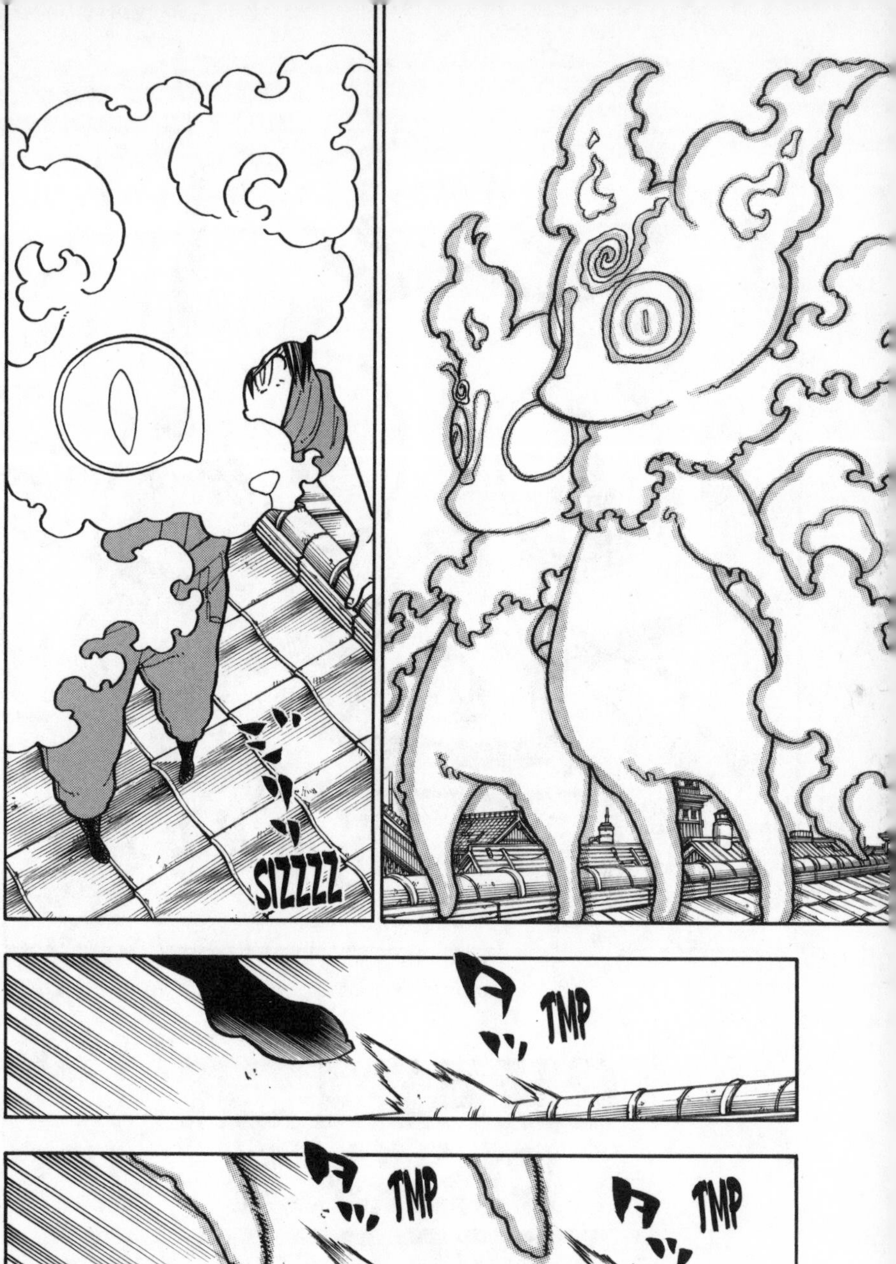
SIZZZZ
TMP
TMP
TMP

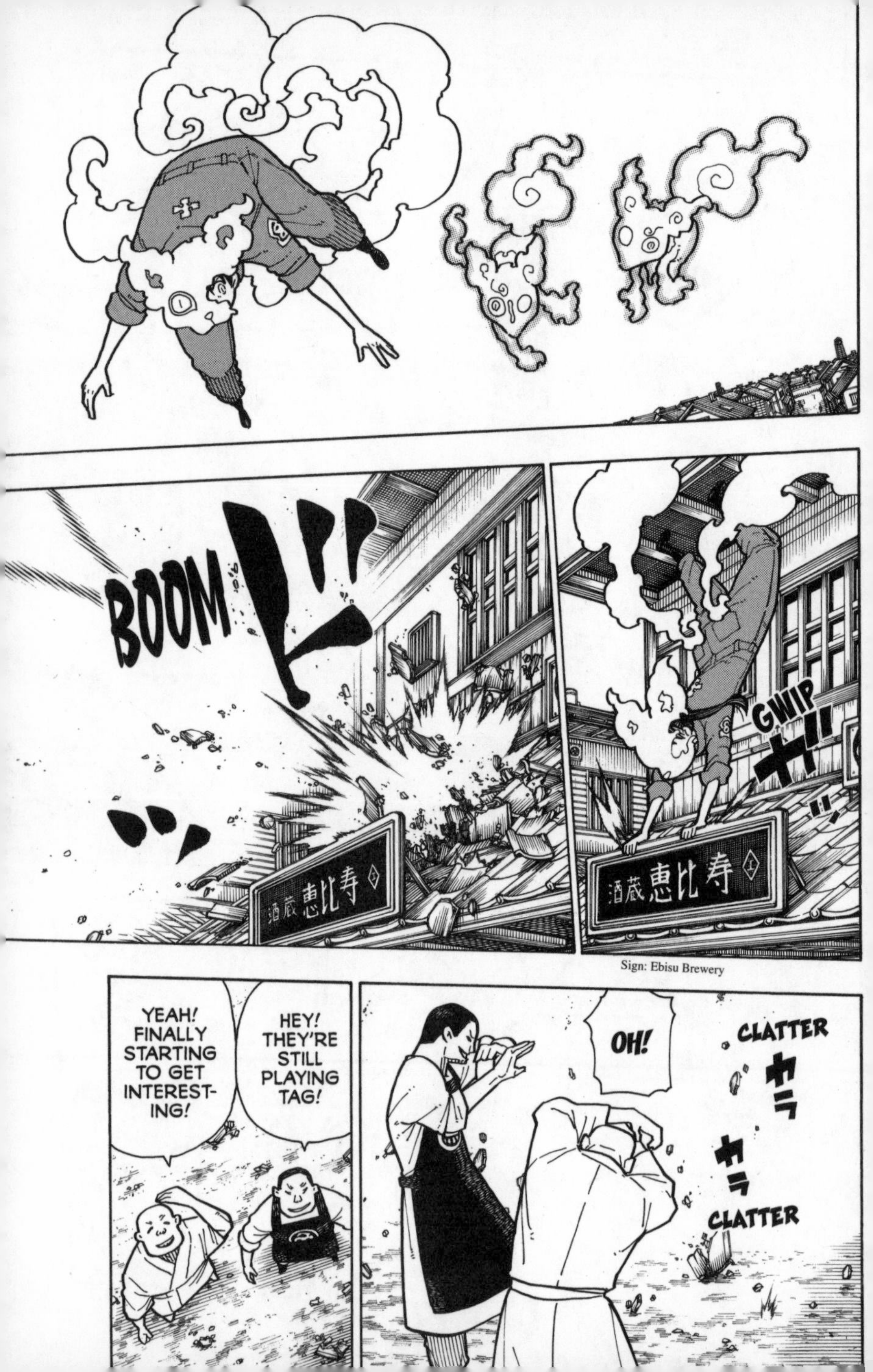
GWIP
酒蔵恵比寿
BOOM
酒蔵恵比寿
OH!
CLATTER
カラ
カラ
CLATTER
HEY! THEY'RE STILL PLAYING TAG!
YEAH! FINALLY STARTING TO GET INTEREST-ING!
Sign: Ebisu Brewery

Box: Instigator of the Kanazawa Curry Boom

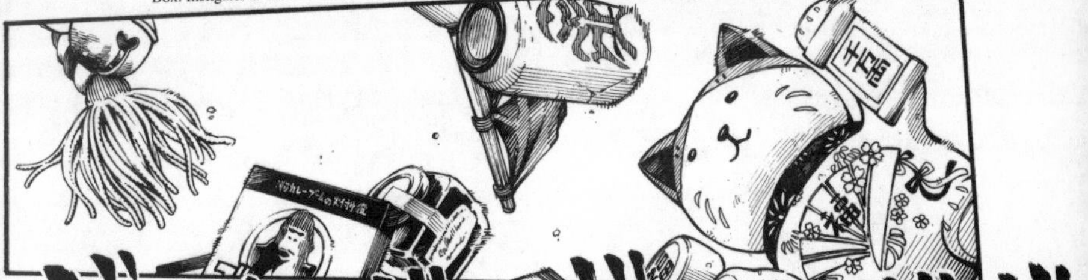

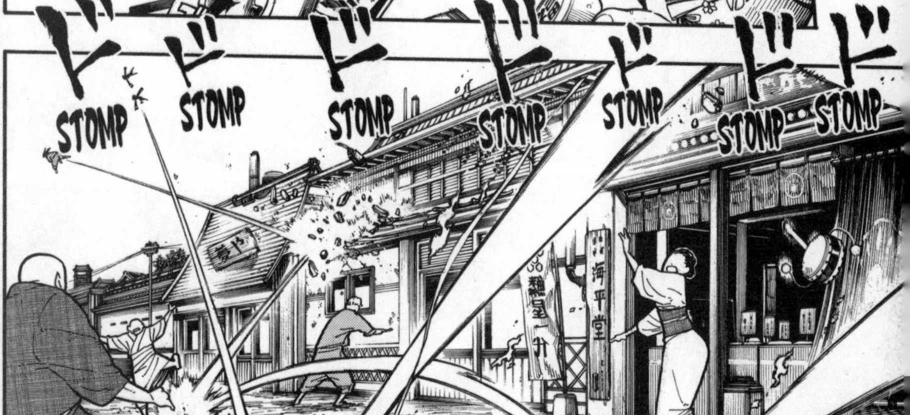
STOMP
STOMP
STOMP
STOMP
STOMP
STOMP
STOMP

Sign: Yumeya Sign: Urokoya Ichidai Sign: Kaiheido

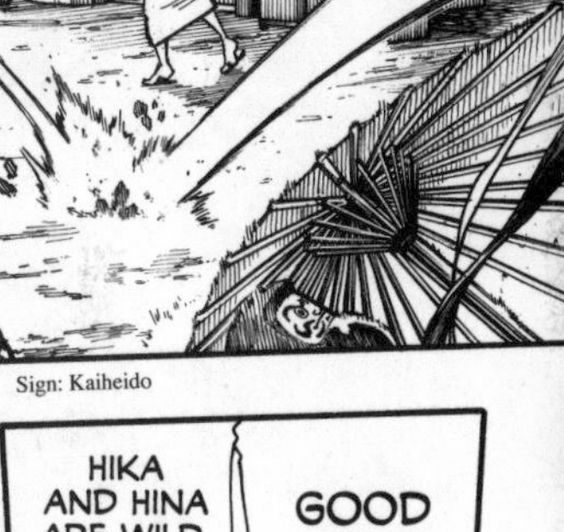
GOOD JOB!! GO, GO!!
HIKA AND HINA ARE WILD, CAT GIRL!! DON'T LET YOUR GUARD DOWN!!

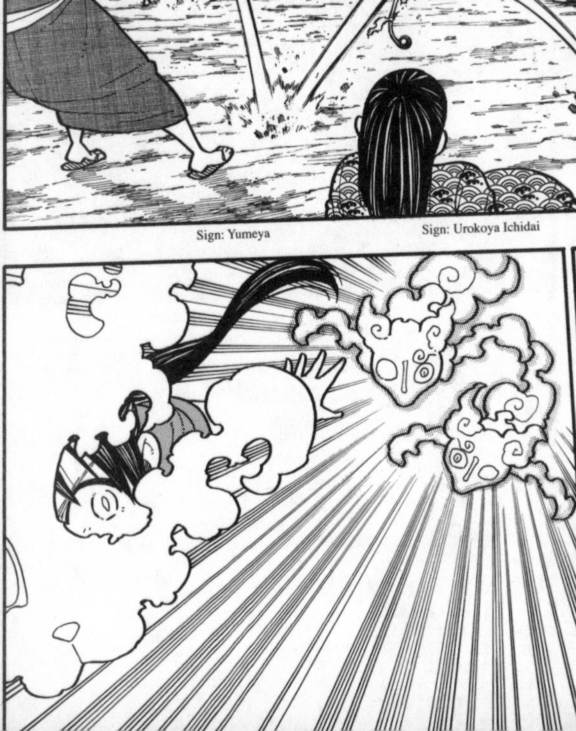

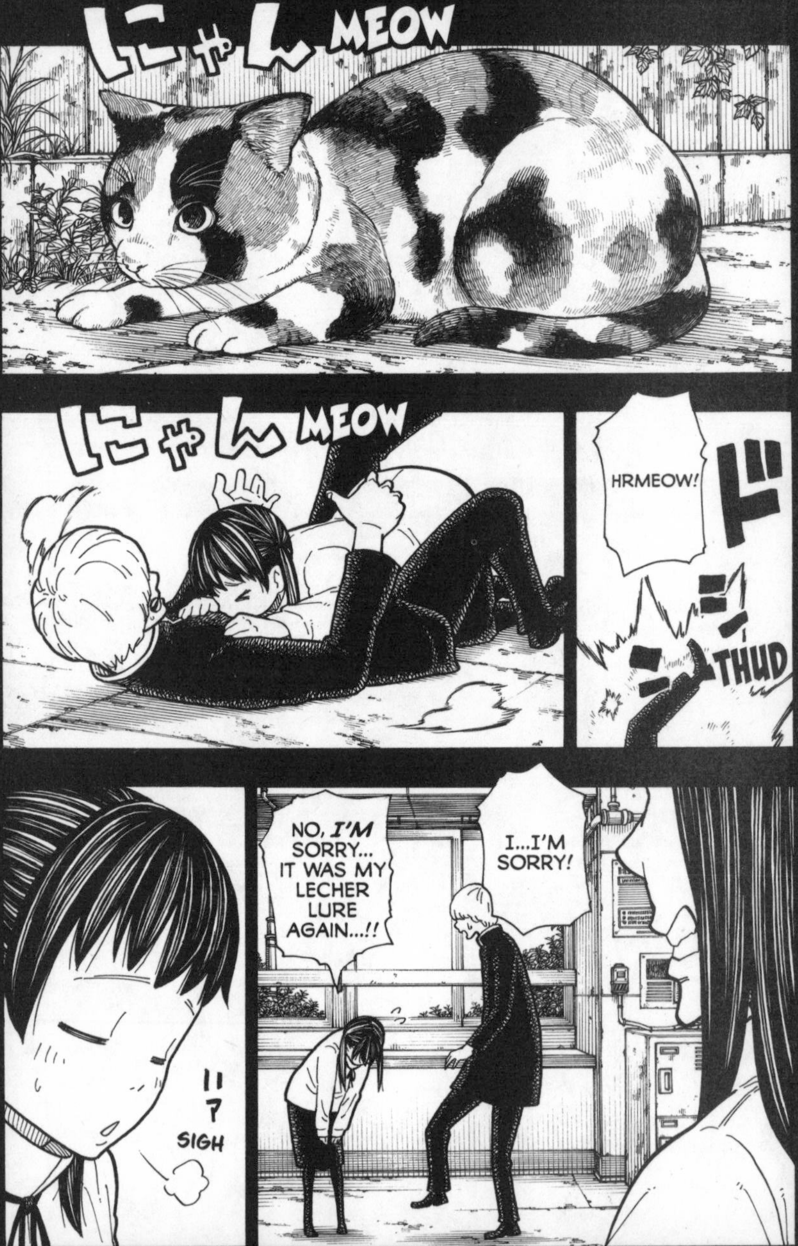
にゃん MEOW
HRMEOW!
ドン THUD
にゃん MEOW
I...I'M SORRY!
NO, *I'M* SORRY... IT WAS MY LECHER LURE AGAIN...!!
ハア SIGH

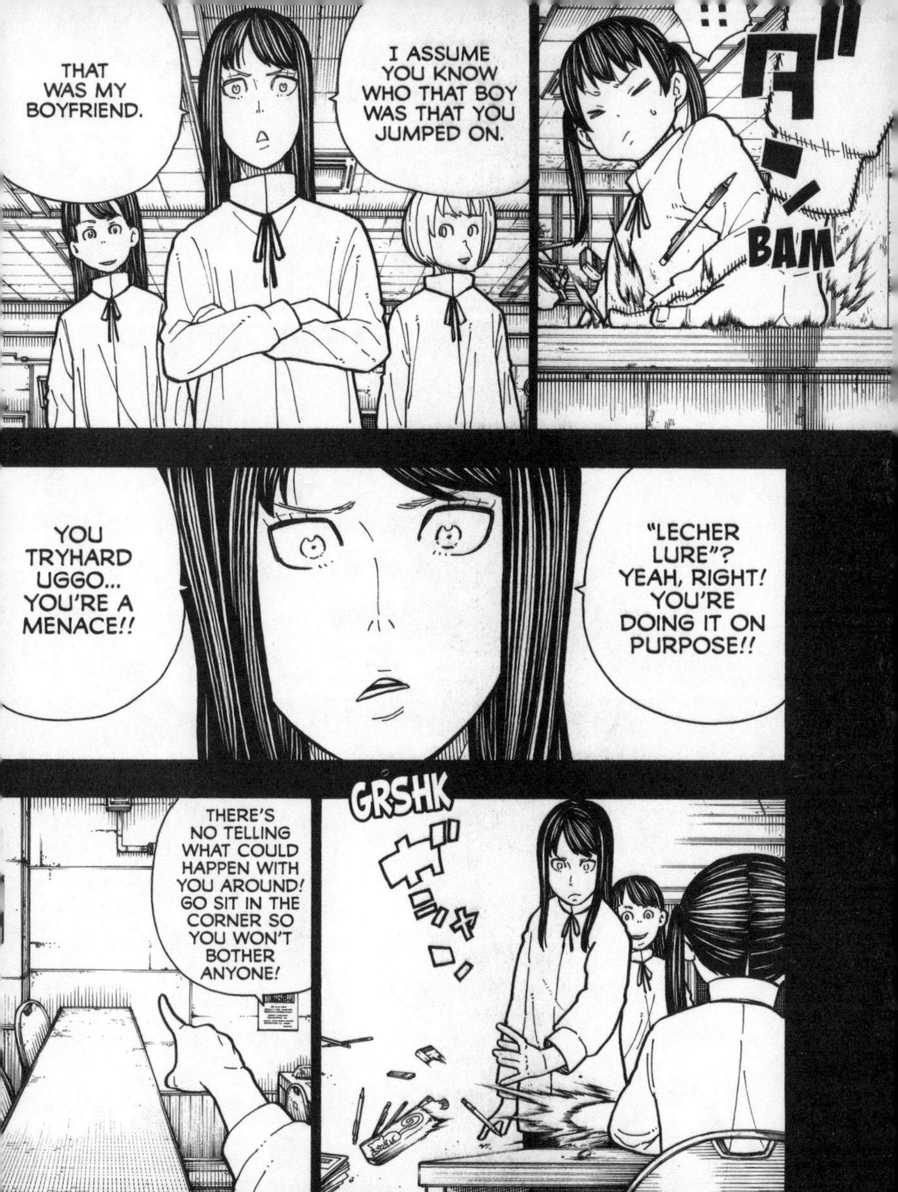
BAM
I ASSUME YOU KNOW WHO THAT BOY WAS THAT YOU JUMPED ON.
THAT WAS MY BOYFRIEND.
"LECHER LURE"? YEAH, RIGHT! YOU'RE DOING IT ON PURPOSE!!
YOU TRYHARD UGGO... YOU'RE A MENACE!!
GRSHK
THERE'S NO TELLING WHAT COULD HAPPEN WITH YOU AROUND! GO SIT IN THE CORNER SO YOU WON'T BOTHER ANYONE!

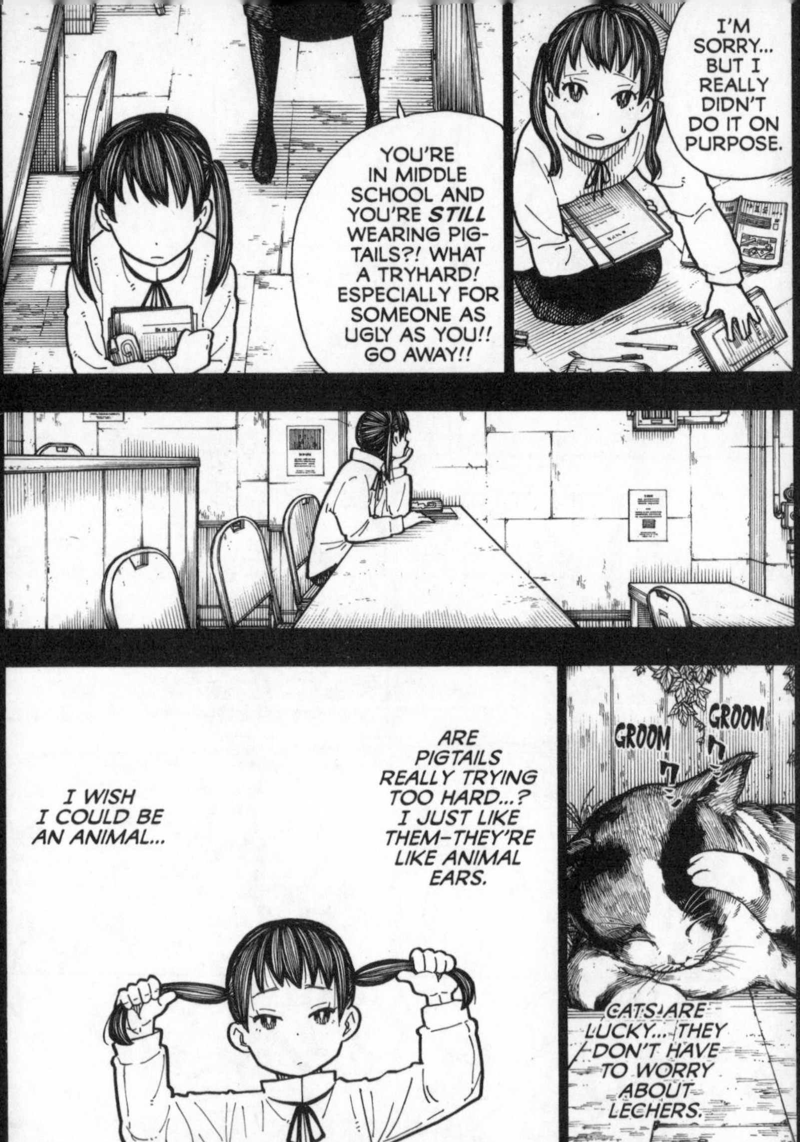
I'M SORRY... BUT I REALLY DIDN'T DO IT ON PURPOSE.
YOU'RE IN MIDDLE SCHOOL AND YOU'RE *STILL* WEARING PIG-TAILS?! WHAT A TRYHARD! ESPECIALLY FOR SOMEONE AS UGLY AS YOU!! GO AWAY!!
GROOM
GROOM
CATS ARE LUCKY... THEY DON'T HAVE TO WORRY ABOUT LECHERS.
ARE PIGTAILS REALLY TRYING TOO HARD...? I JUST LIKE THEM—THEY'RE LIKE ANIMAL EARS.
I WISH I COULD BE AN ANIMAL...

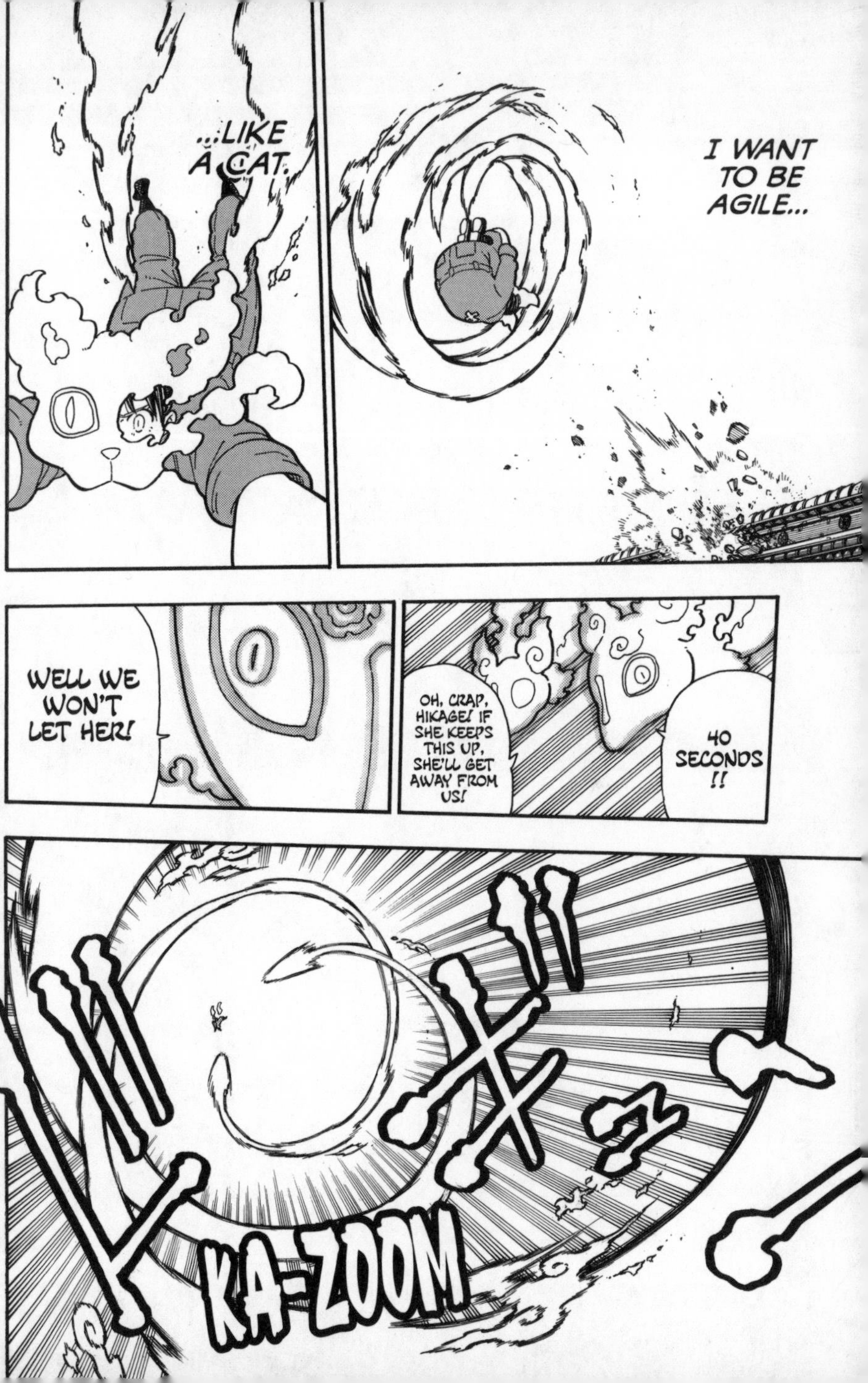
I WANT TO BE AGILE...
...LIKE A CAT.
40 SECONDS !!
OH, CRAP, HIKAGE! IF SHE KEEPS THIS UP, SHE'LL GET AWAY FROM US!
WELL WE WON'T LET HER!
KA-ZOOM

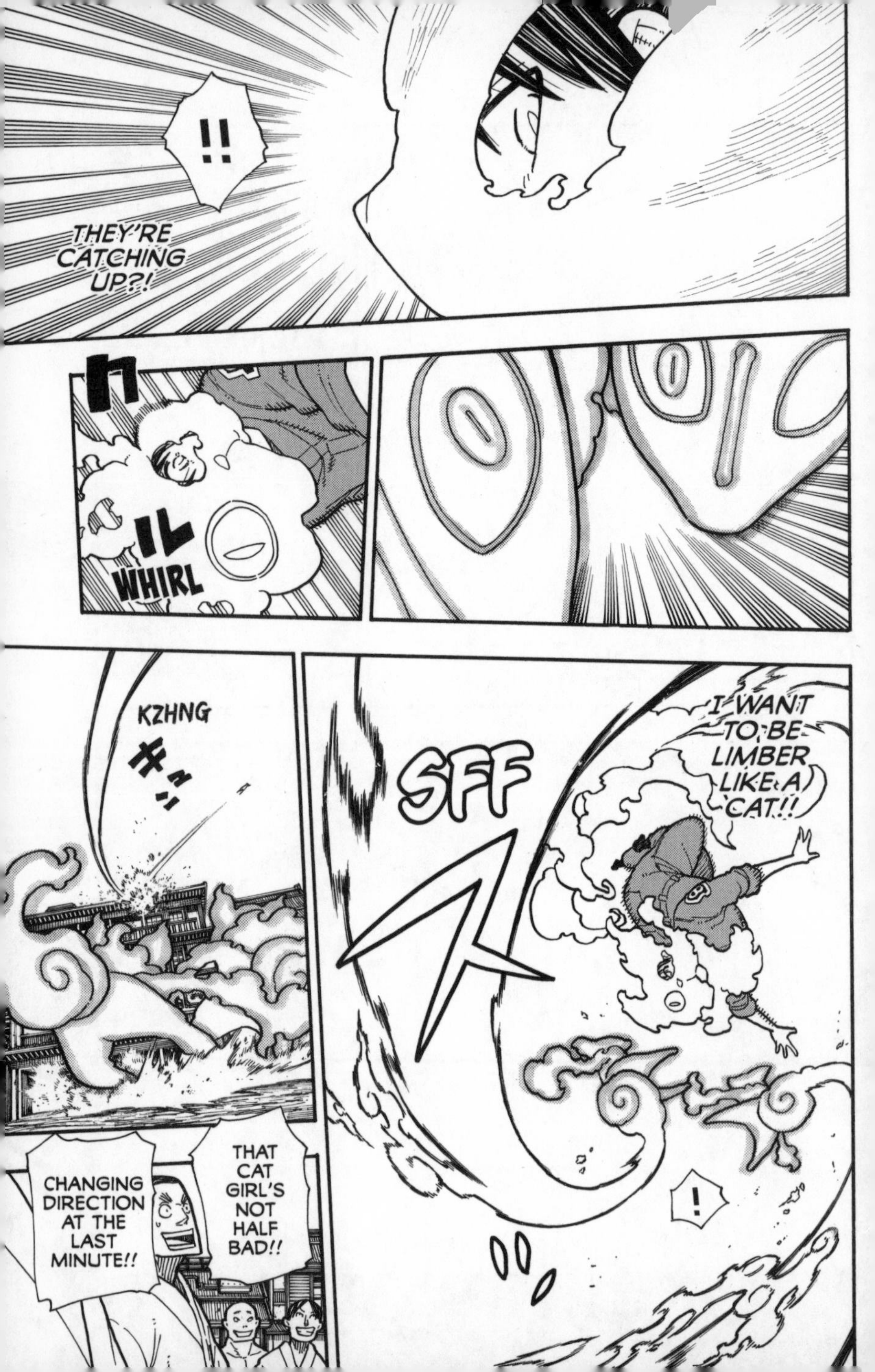
!!
THEY'RE CATCHING UP?!
WHIRL
SFF
I WANT TO BE LIMBER LIKE A CAT!!
!
KZHNG
THAT CAT GIRL'S NOT HALF BAD!!
CHANGING DIRECTION AT THE LAST MINUTE!!

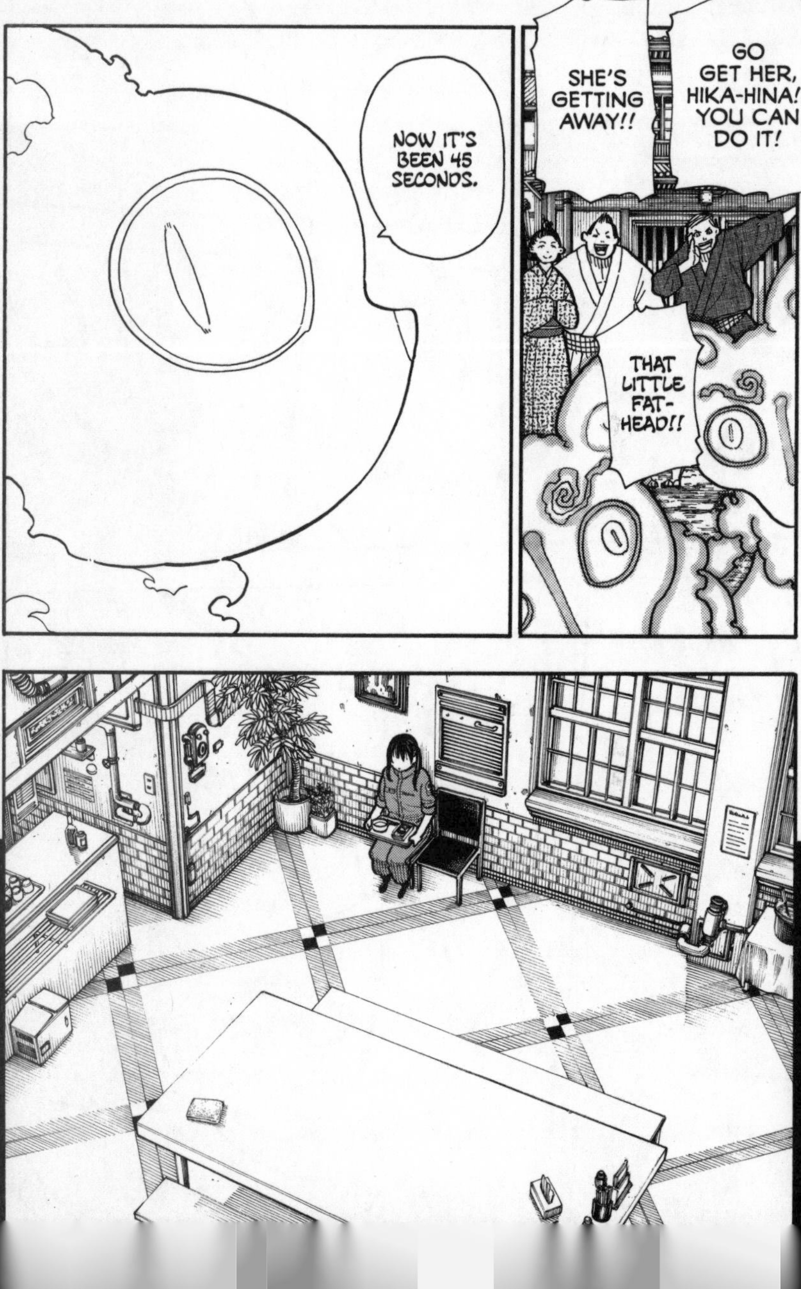
GO GET HER, HIKA-HINA!! YOU CAN DO IT!
SHE'S GETTING AWAY!!
THAT LITTLE FAT-HEAD!!
NOW IT'S BEEN 45 SECONDS.

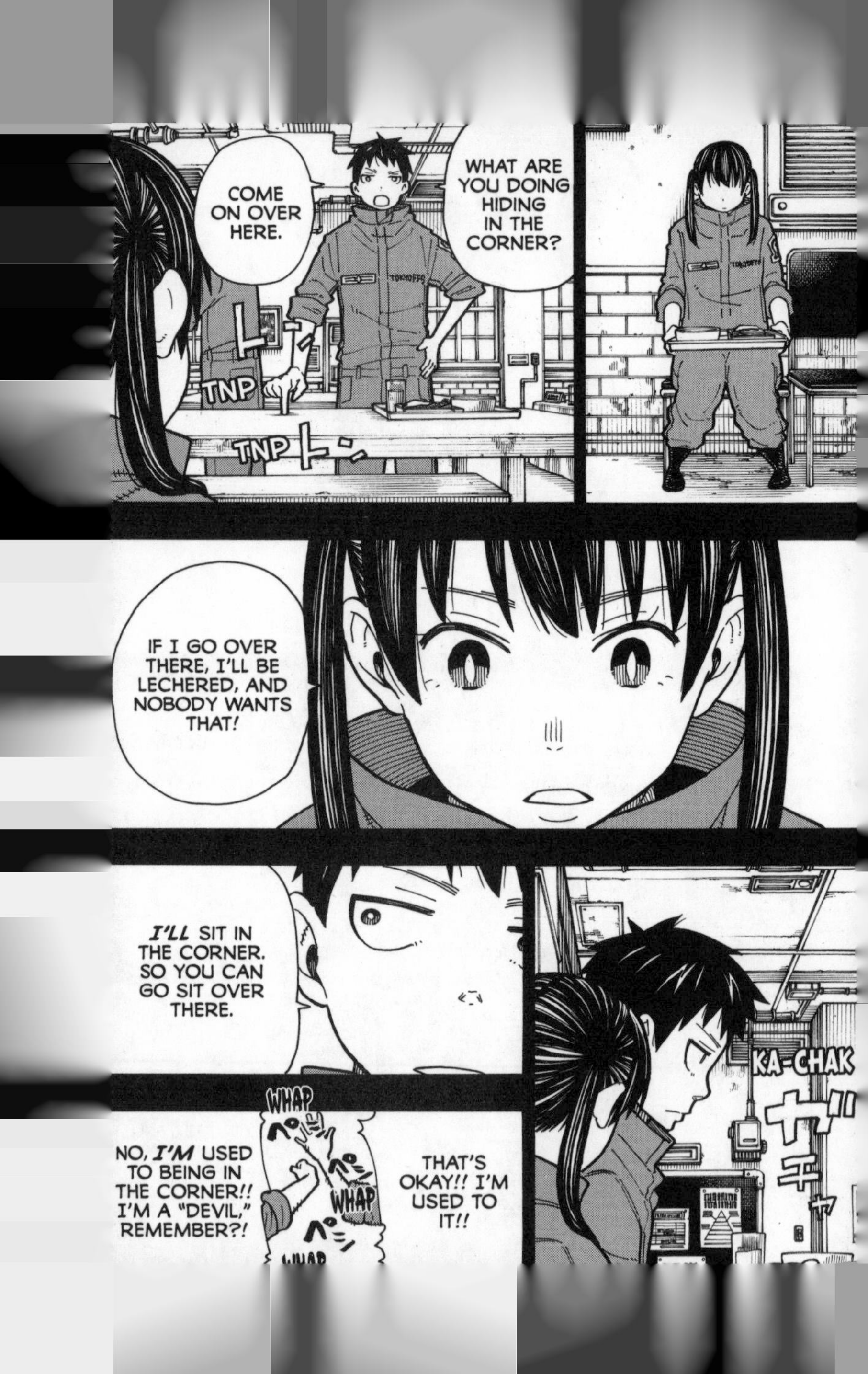
WHAT ARE YOU DOING HIDING IN THE CORNER?
COME ON OVER HERE.
TNP
TNP
IF I GO OVER THERE, I'LL BE LECHERED, AND NOBODY WANTS THAT!
KA-CHAK
I'LL SIT IN THE CORNER. SO YOU CAN GO SIT OVER THERE.
THAT'S OKAY!! I'M USED TO IT!!
WHAP
WHAP
NO, *I'M* USED TO BEING IN THE CORNER!! I'M A "DEVIL," REMEMBER?!

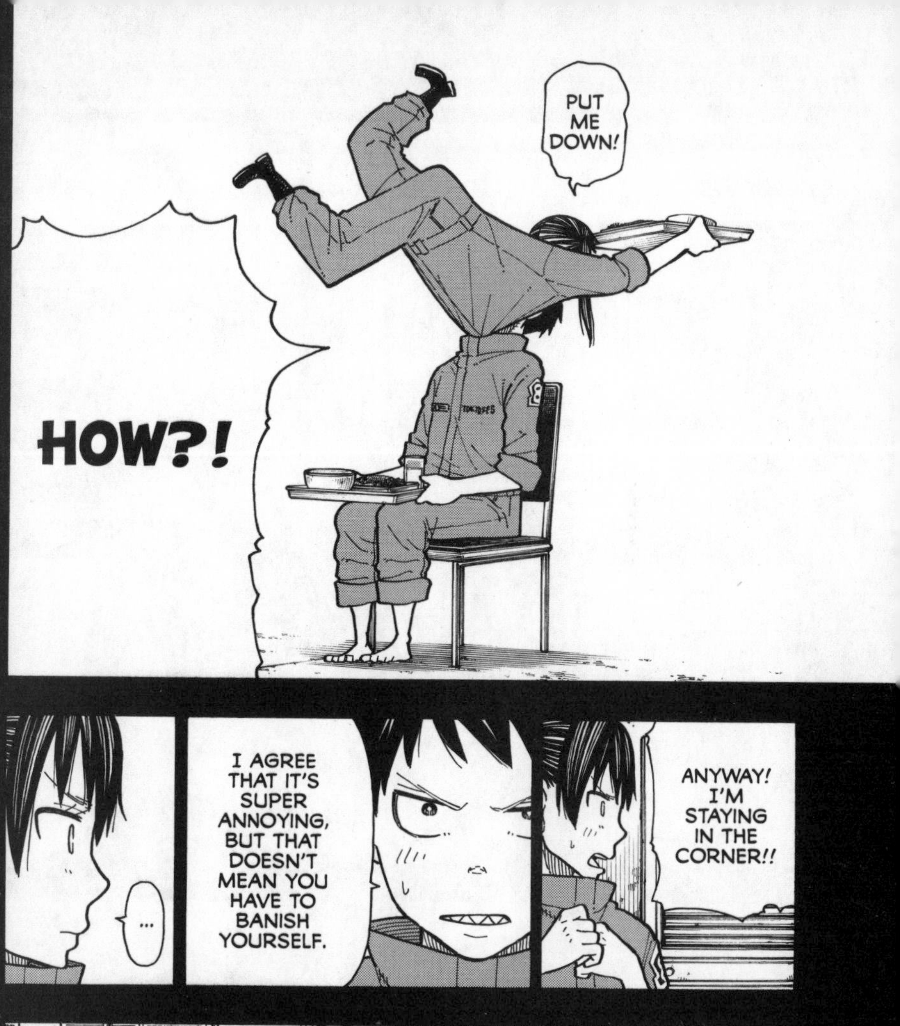
PUT ME DOWN!
HOW?!
ANYWAY! I'M STAYING IN THE CORNER!!
I AGREE THAT IT'S SUPER ANNOYING, BUT THAT DOESN'T MEAN YOU HAVE TO BANISH YOURSELF.
...
LOOK AT THAT LOSER. HE'S JUST A LOWLY GRUNT, BUT HE ALWAYS GOES STRAIGHT TO THE HEAD OF THE TABLE, LIKE HE OWNS THAT SPOT.
YOU SHOULD BE THAT CONFIDENT, TOO.

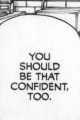

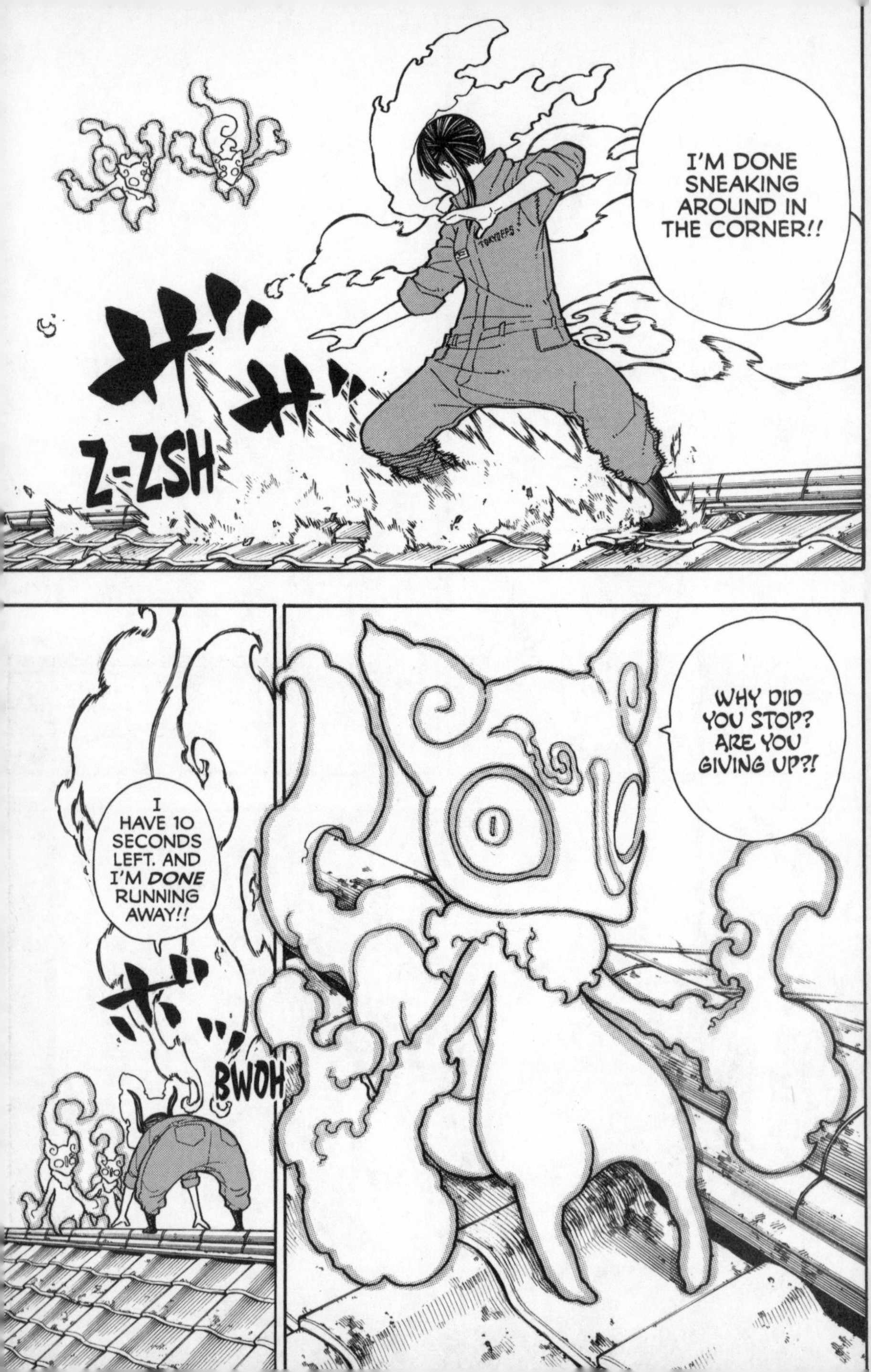

I'M DONE SNEAKING AROUND IN THE CORNER!!
Z-ZSH
WHY DID YOU STOP? ARE YOU GIVING UP?!
I HAVE 10 SECONDS LEFT. AND I'M *DONE* RUNNING AWAY!!
BWOH

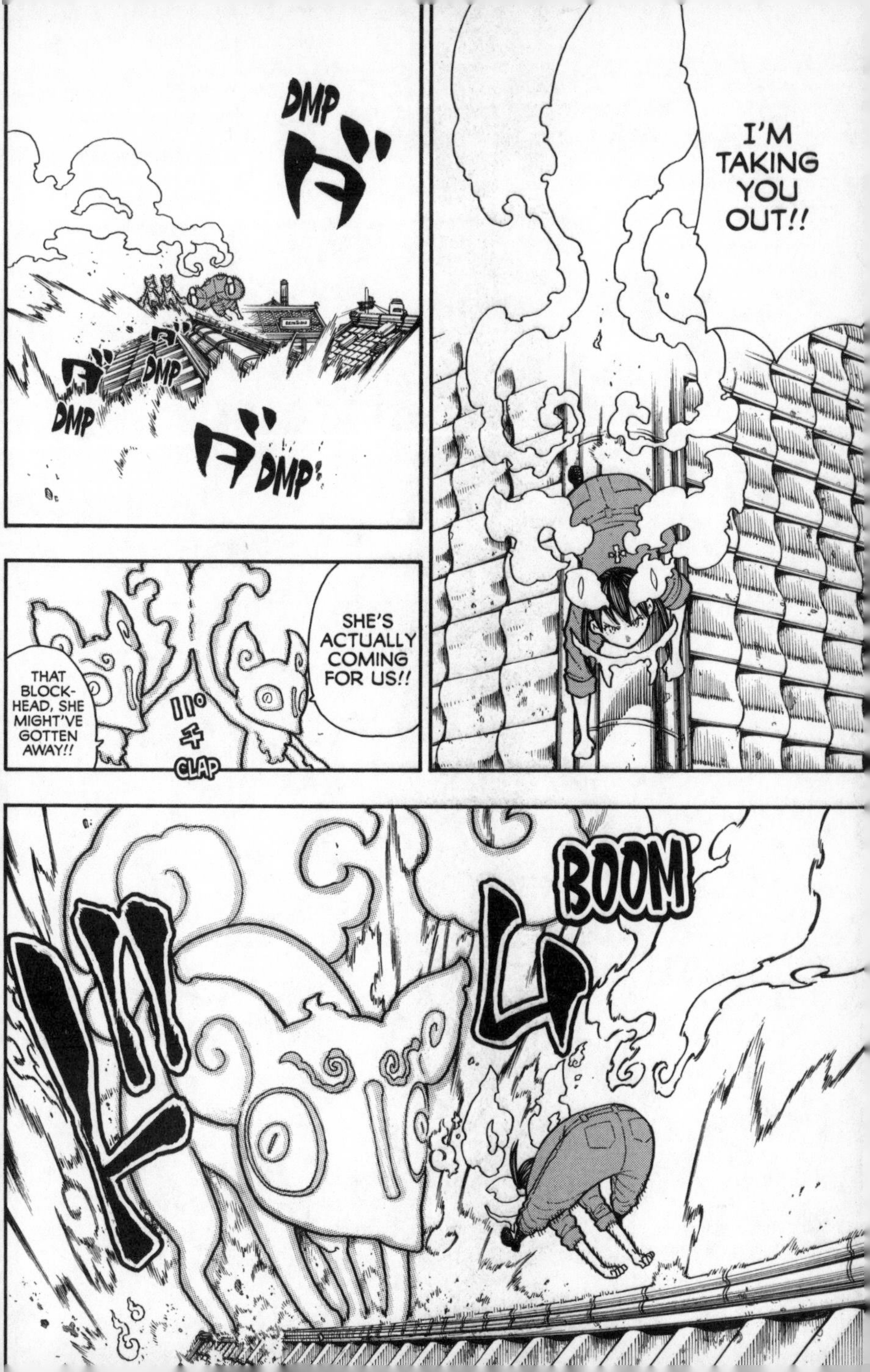
I'M TAKING YOU OUT!!
DMP
DMP
DMP
DMP
SHE'S ACTUALLY COMING FOR US!!
CLAP
THAT BLOCK-HEAD, SHE MIGHT'VE GOTTEN AWAY!!
BOOM

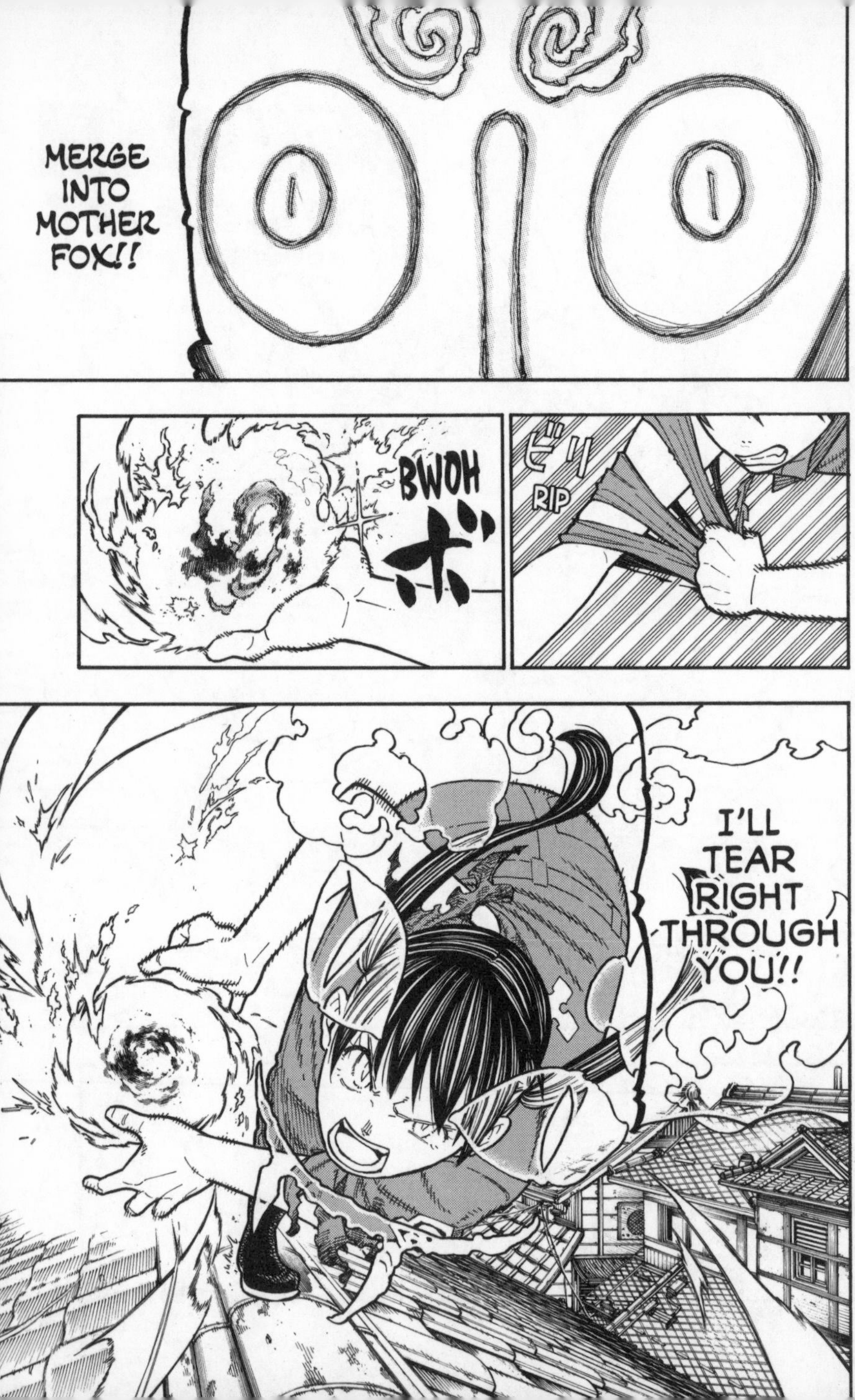
MERGE INTO MOTHER FOX!!
ビリ
RIP
BWOH
ボ
I'LL TEAR RIGHT THROUGH YOU!!

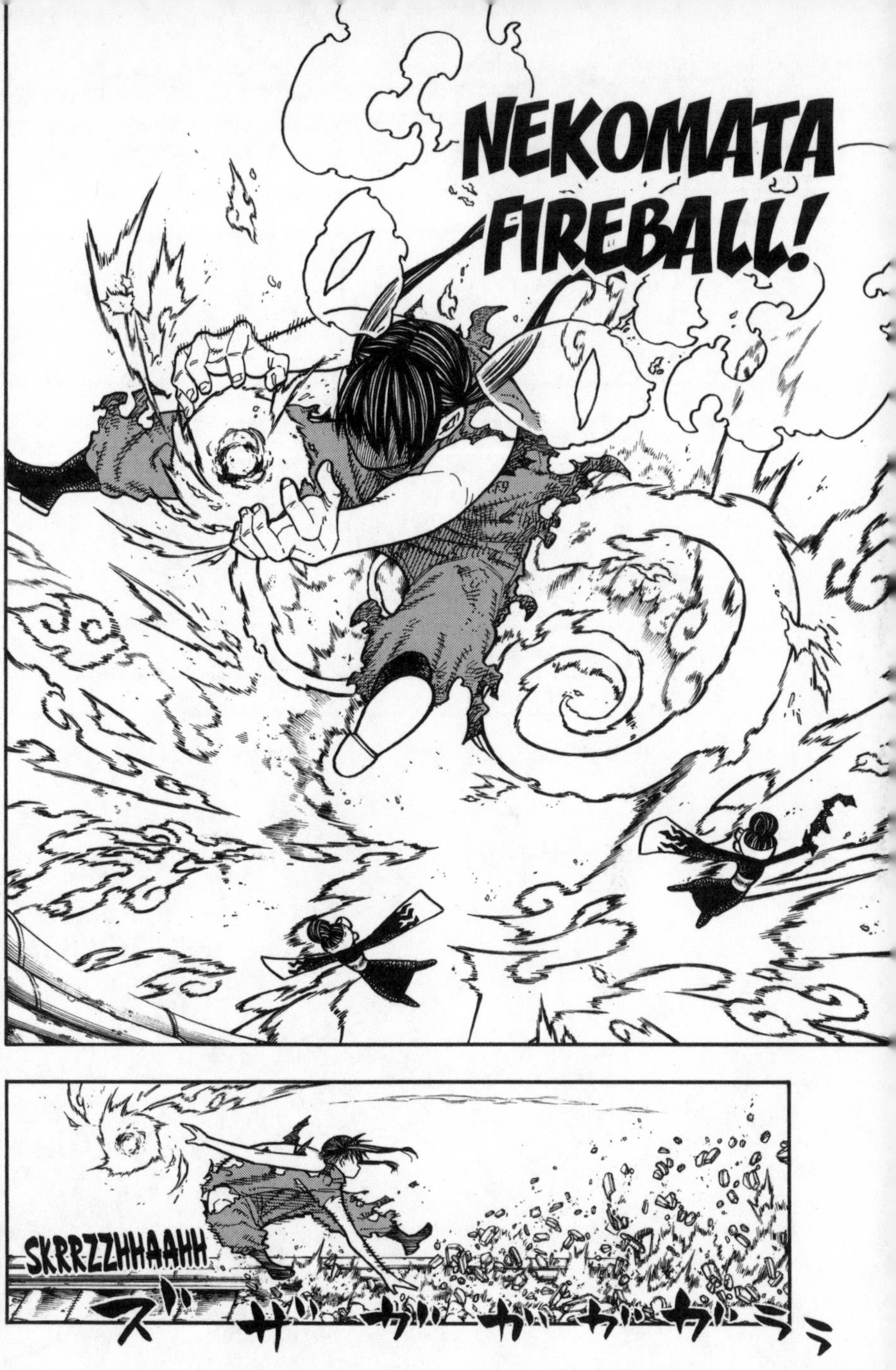
NEKOMATA FIREBALL!
SKRRZZHHAAHH

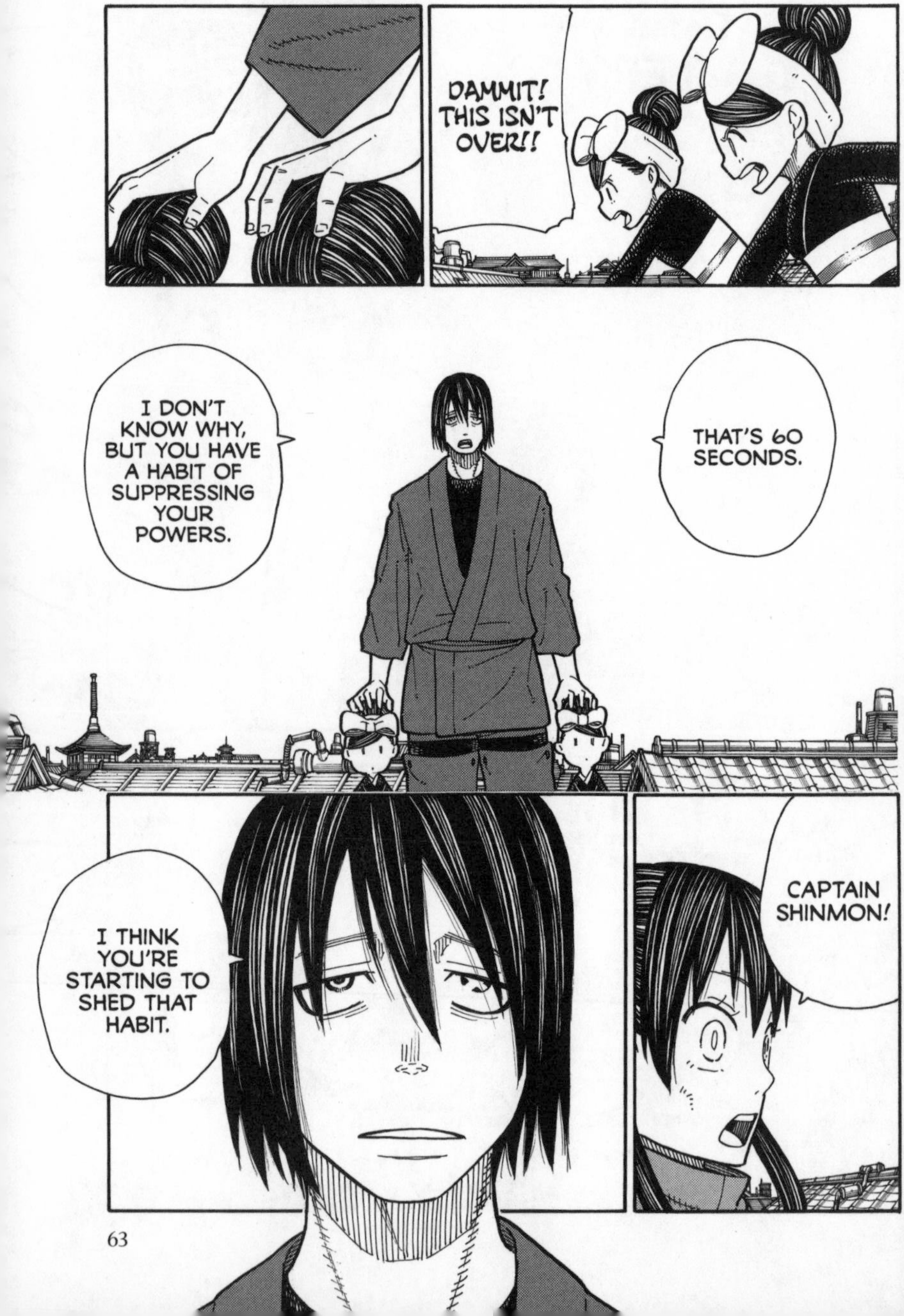
DAMMIT! THIS ISN'T OVER!!
THAT'S 60 SECONDS.
I DON'T KNOW WHY, BUT YOU HAVE A HABIT OF SUPPRESSING YOUR POWERS.
CAPTAIN SHINMON!
I THINK YOU'RE STARTING TO SHED THAT HABIT.

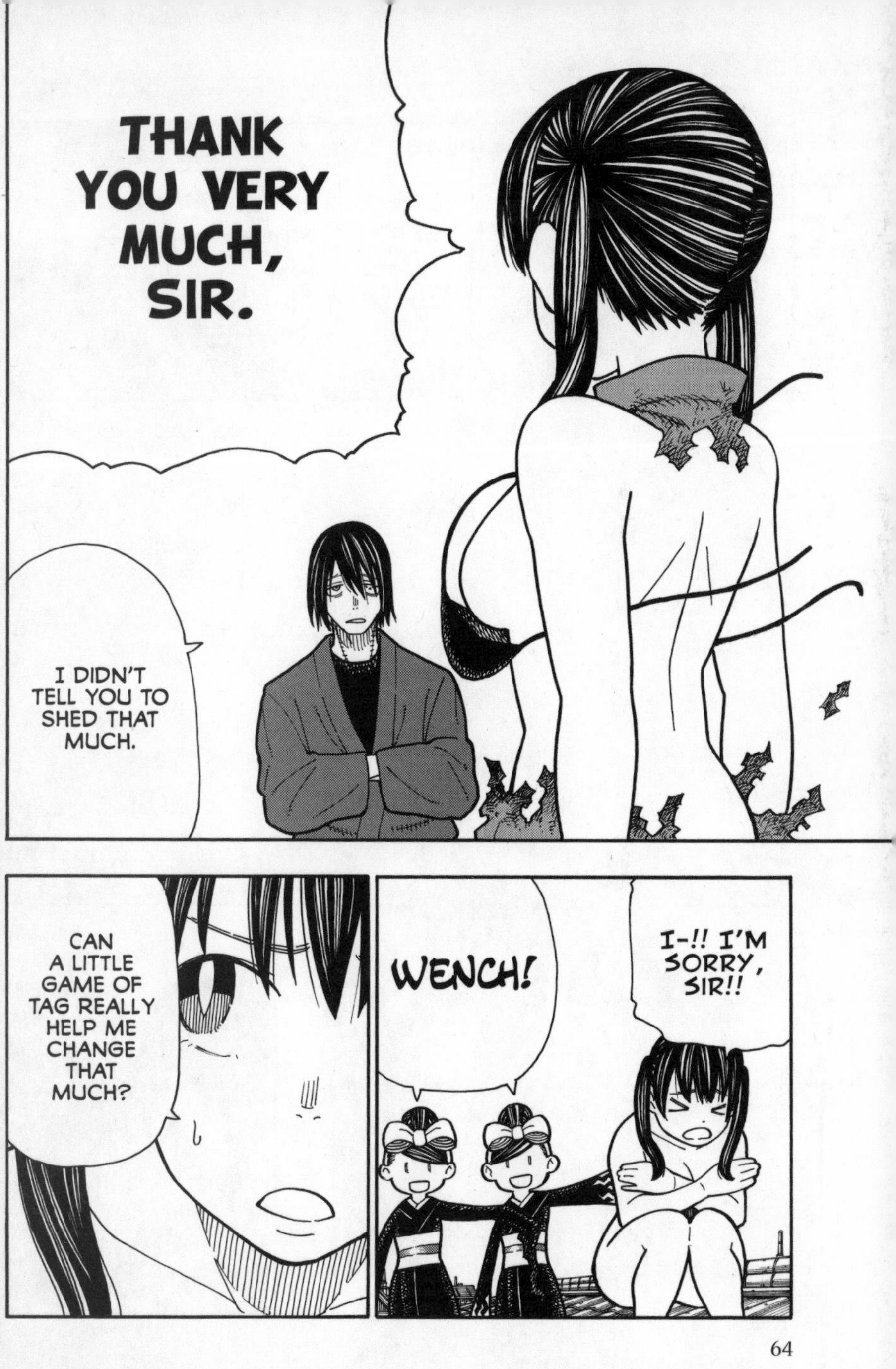
THANK YOU VERY MUCH, SIR.
I DIDN'T TELL YOU TO SHED THAT MUCH.
I-!! I'M SORRY, SIR!!
WENCH!
CAN A LITTLE GAME OF TAG REALLY HELP ME CHANGE THAT MUCH?

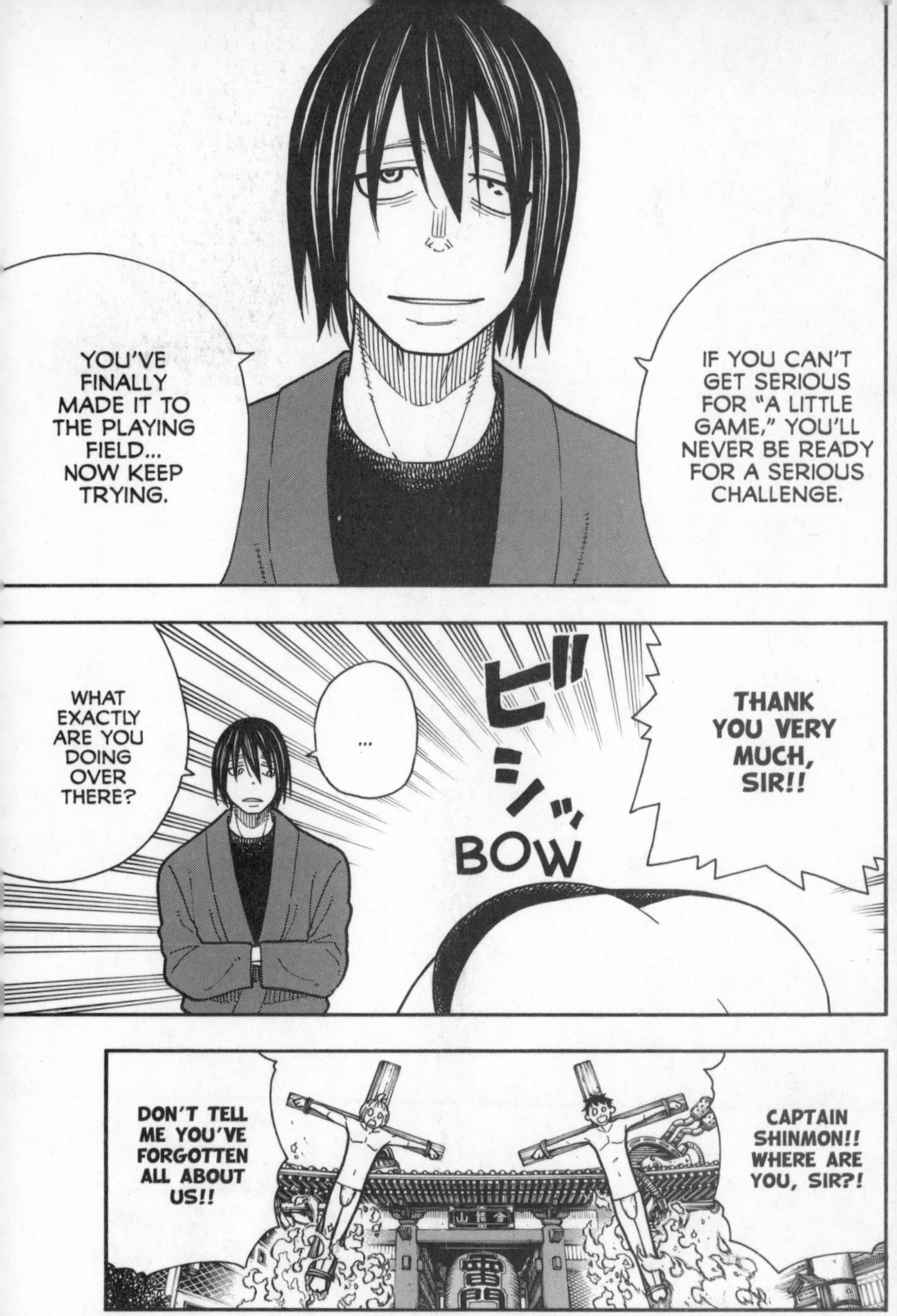
IF YOU CAN'T GET SERIOUS FOR "A LITTLE GAME," YOU'LL NEVER BE READY FOR A SERIOUS CHALLENGE.
YOU'VE FINALLY MADE IT TO THE PLAYING FIELD... NOW KEEP TRYING.
THANK YOU VERY MUCH, SIR!!
ビシッ
BOW
...
WHAT EXACTLY ARE YOU DOING OVER THERE?
CAPTAIN SHINMON!! WHERE ARE YOU, SIR?!
DON'T TELL ME YOU'VE FORGOTTEN ALL ABOUT US!!
雷門

FIRE FORCE

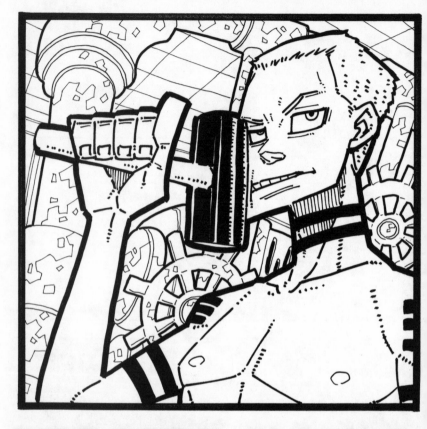

CHAPTER CLXXII: THE HYSTERICAL STRENGTH OF THE FIGHT-OR-FLIGHT RESPONSE

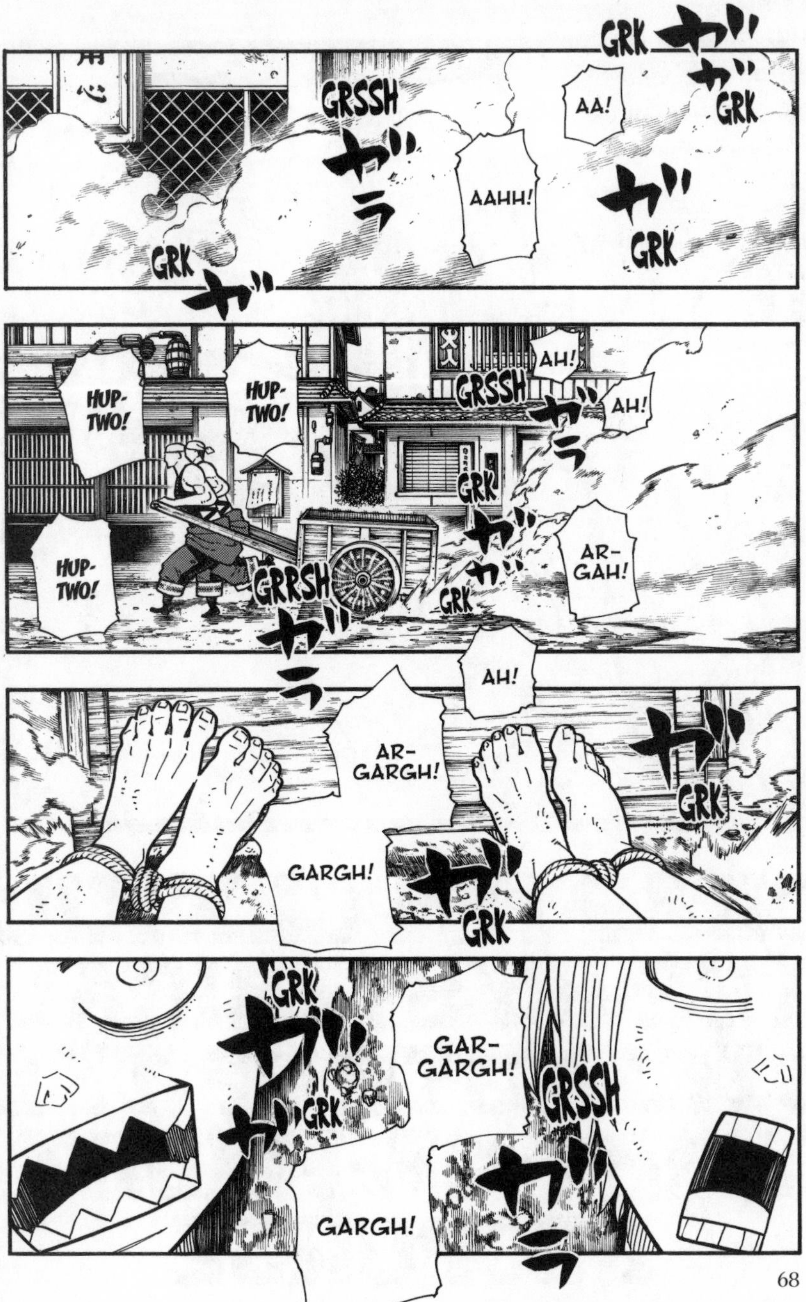
GRK
AA!
GRK
GRK
AAHH!
GRSSH
GRK
AH!
AH!
GRSSH
AR-GAH!
GRK
GRK
GRRSH
HUP-TWO!
HUP-TWO!
HUP-TWO!
AH!
GRK
AR-GARGH!
GARGH!
GRK
GRSSH
GAR-GARGH!
GRK
GRK
GARGH!

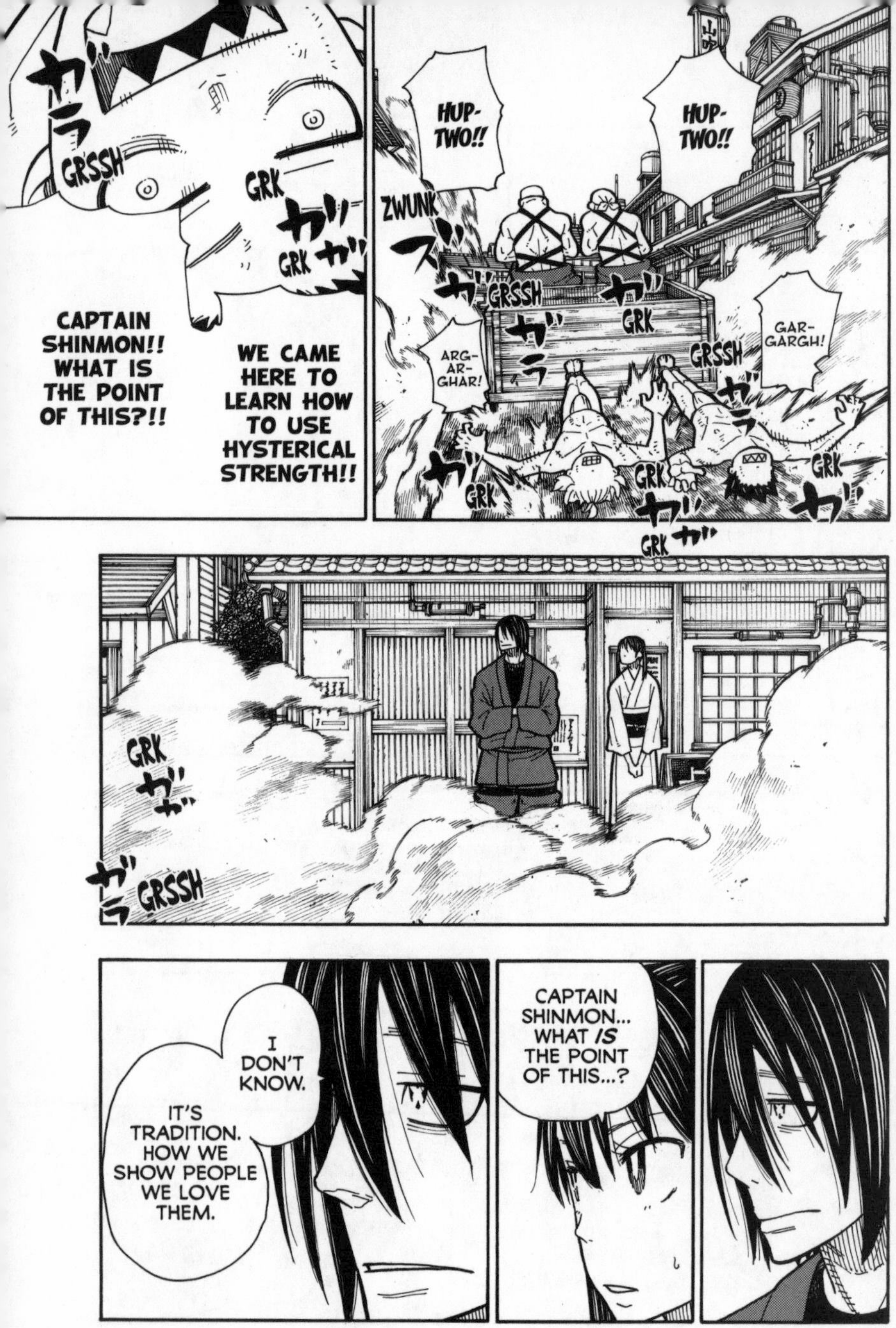
HUP-TWO!!
HUP-TWO!!
ZWUNK
GRSSH
GRK
GAR-GARGH!
GRSSH
ARG-AR-GHAR!
GRK
GRK
GRK
GRK
GRSSH
GRK
GRK
WE CAME HERE TO LEARN HOW TO USE HYSTERICAL STRENGTH!!
CAPTAIN SHINMON!! WHAT IS THE POINT OF THIS?!!
GRK
GRSSH
CAPTAIN SHINMON... WHAT *IS* THE POINT OF THIS...?
I DON'T KNOW.
IT'S TRADITION. HOW WE SHOW PEOPLE WE LOVE THEM.

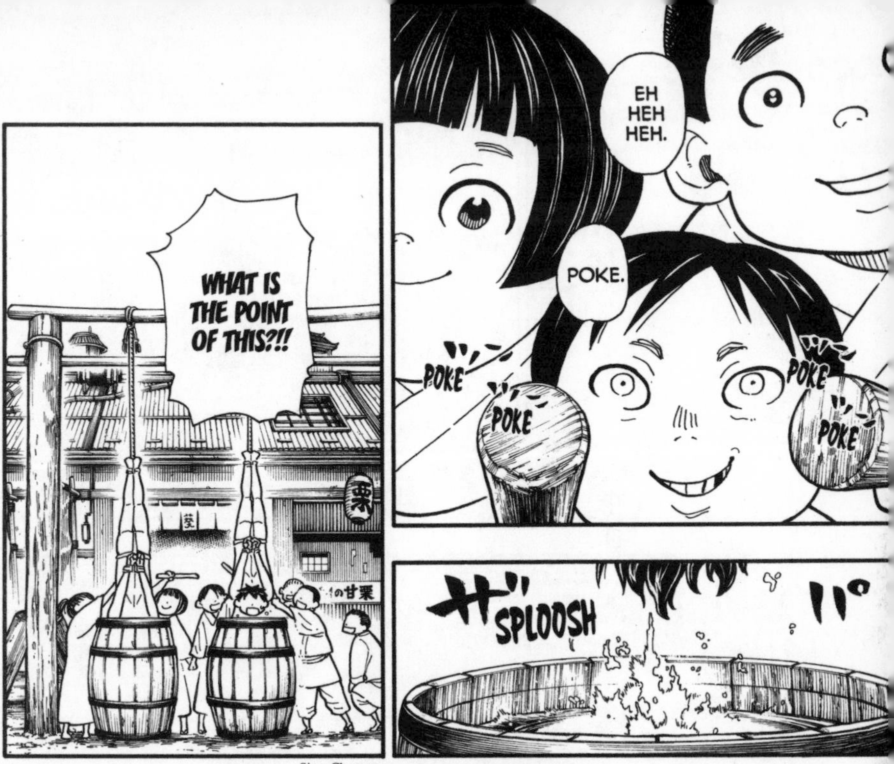
EH HEH HEH.
POKE.
POKE
POKE
POKE
POKE
SPLOOSH
WHAT IS THE POINT OF THIS?!!

Sign: Chestnuts

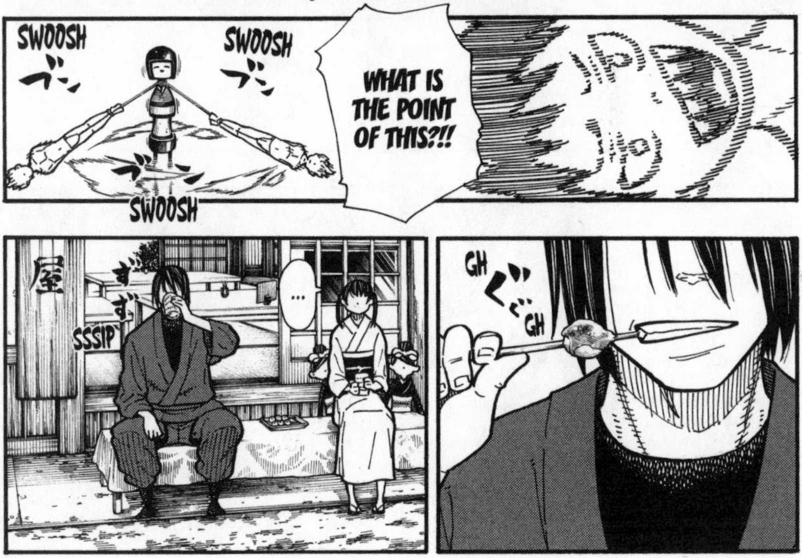
WHAT IS THE POINT OF THIS?!!
SWOOSH
SWOOSH
SWOOSH
GH
GH
...
SSSIP

Sign: Store

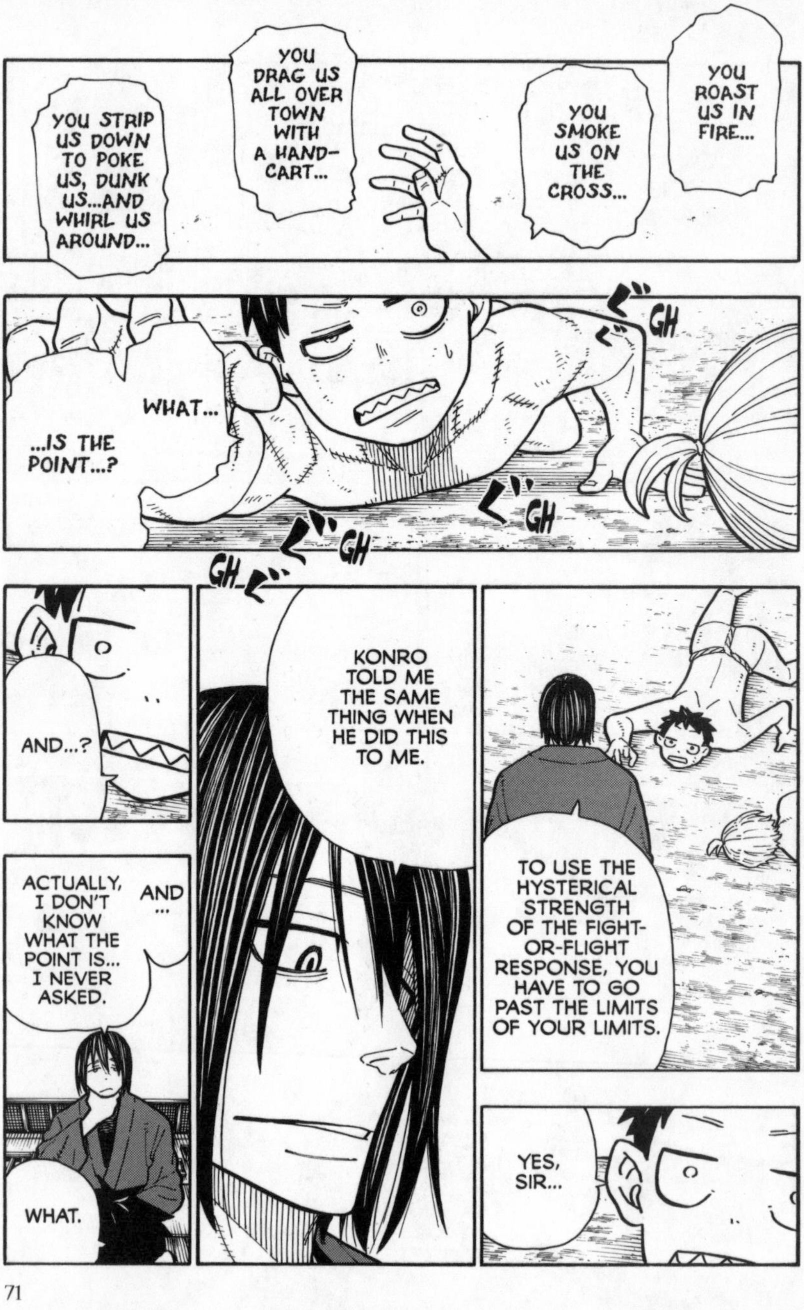
YOU ROAST US IN FIRE...
YOU SMOKE US ON THE CROSS...
YOU DRAG US ALL OVER TOWN WITH A HAND-CART...
YOU STRIP US DOWN TO POKE US, DUNK US...AND WHIRL US AROUND...
GH
WHAT...
...IS THE POINT...?
GH
GH
GH
TO USE THE HYSTERICAL STRENGTH OF THE FIGHT-OR-FLIGHT RESPONSE, YOU HAVE TO GO PAST THE LIMITS OF YOUR LIMITS.
YES, SIR...
KONRO TOLD ME THE SAME THING WHEN HE DID THIS TO ME.
AND...?
AND ...
ACTUALLY, I DON'T KNOW WHAT THE POINT IS... I NEVER ASKED.
WHAT.

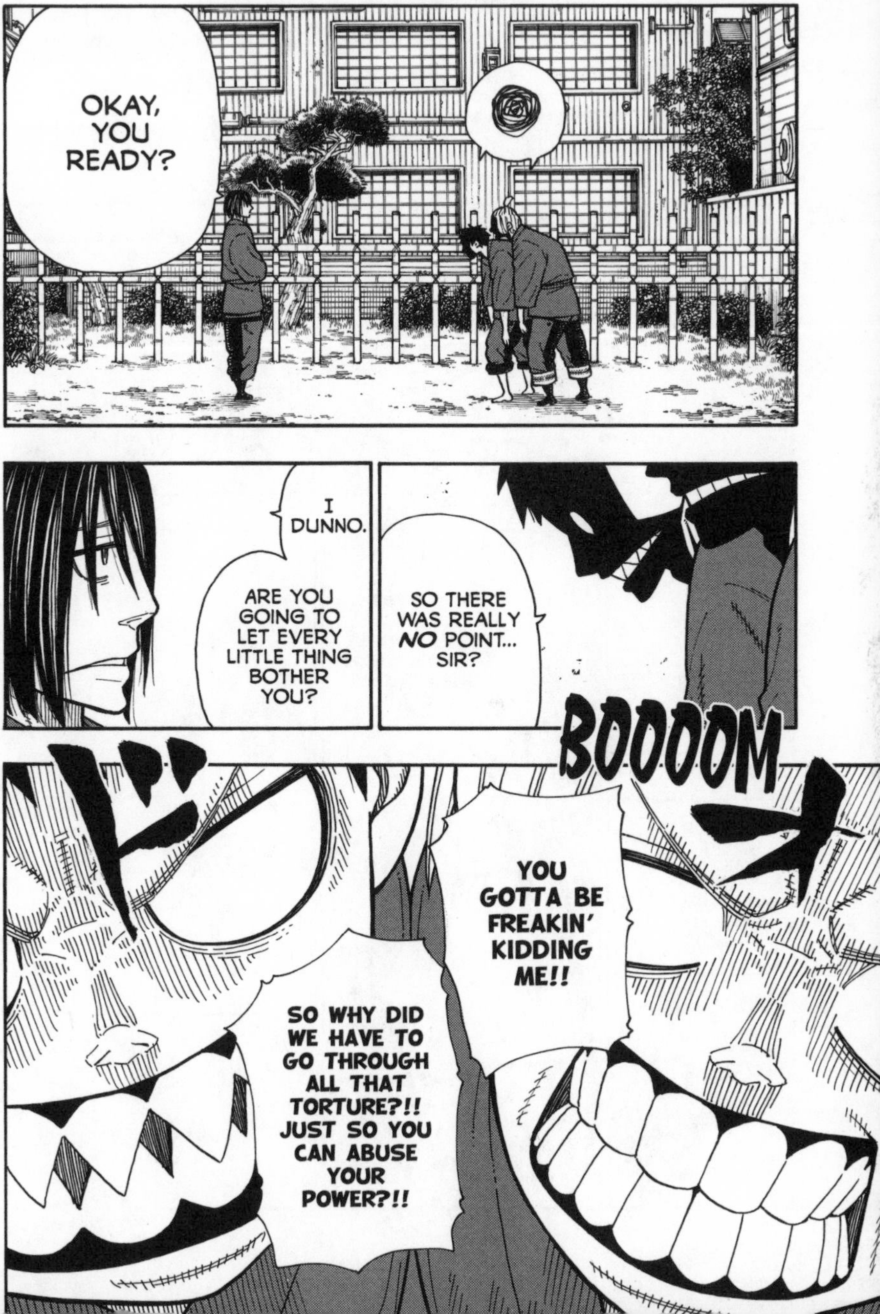
OKAY, YOU READY?
SO THERE WAS REALLY *NO* POINT... SIR?
I DUNNO.
ARE YOU GOING TO LET EVERY LITTLE THING BOTHER YOU?
BOOOOM
YOU GOTTA BE FREAKIN' KIDDING ME!!
SO WHY DID WE HAVE TO GO THROUGH ALL THAT TORTURE?!! JUST SO YOU CAN ABUSE YOUR POWER?!!

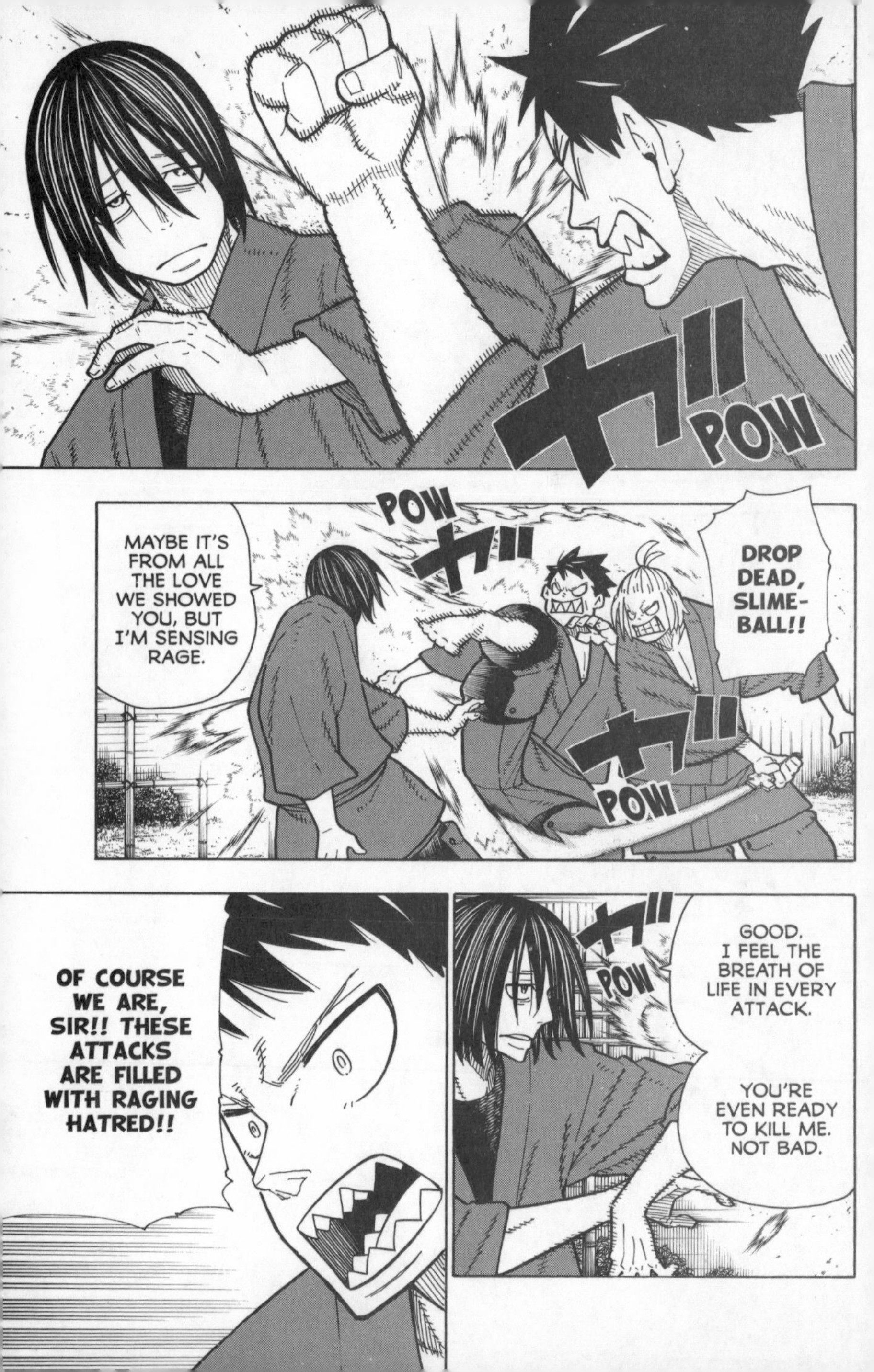
POW
DROP DEAD, SLIME-BALL!!
MAYBE IT'S FROM ALL THE LOVE WE SHOWED YOU, BUT I'M SENSING RAGE.
POW
POW
GOOD. I FEEL THE BREATH OF LIFE IN EVERY ATTACK.
POW
YOU'RE EVEN READY TO KILL ME. NOT BAD.
OF COURSE WE ARE, SIR!! THESE ATTACKS ARE FILLED WITH RAGING HATRED!!

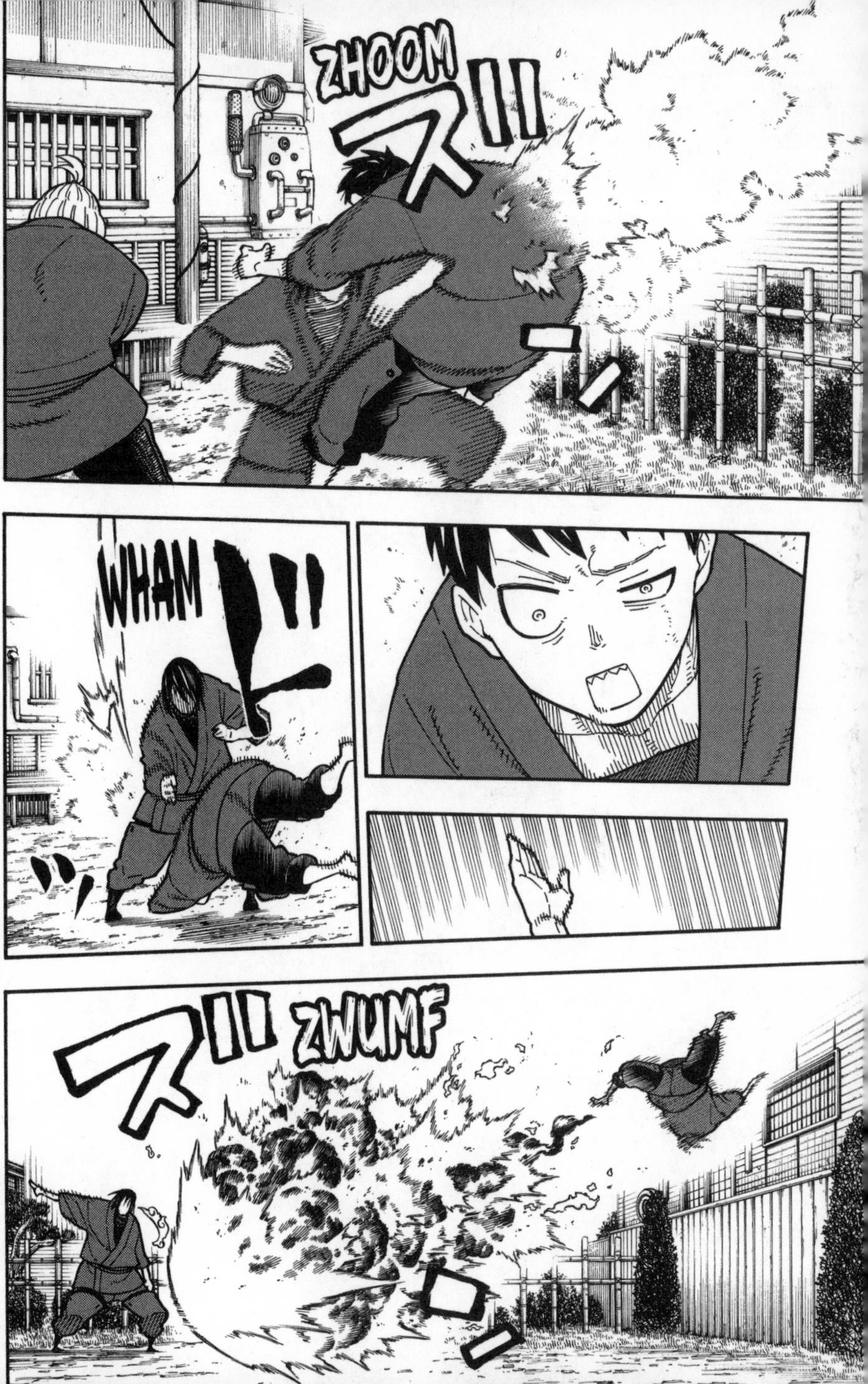
ZHOOM
WHAM
ZWUMF

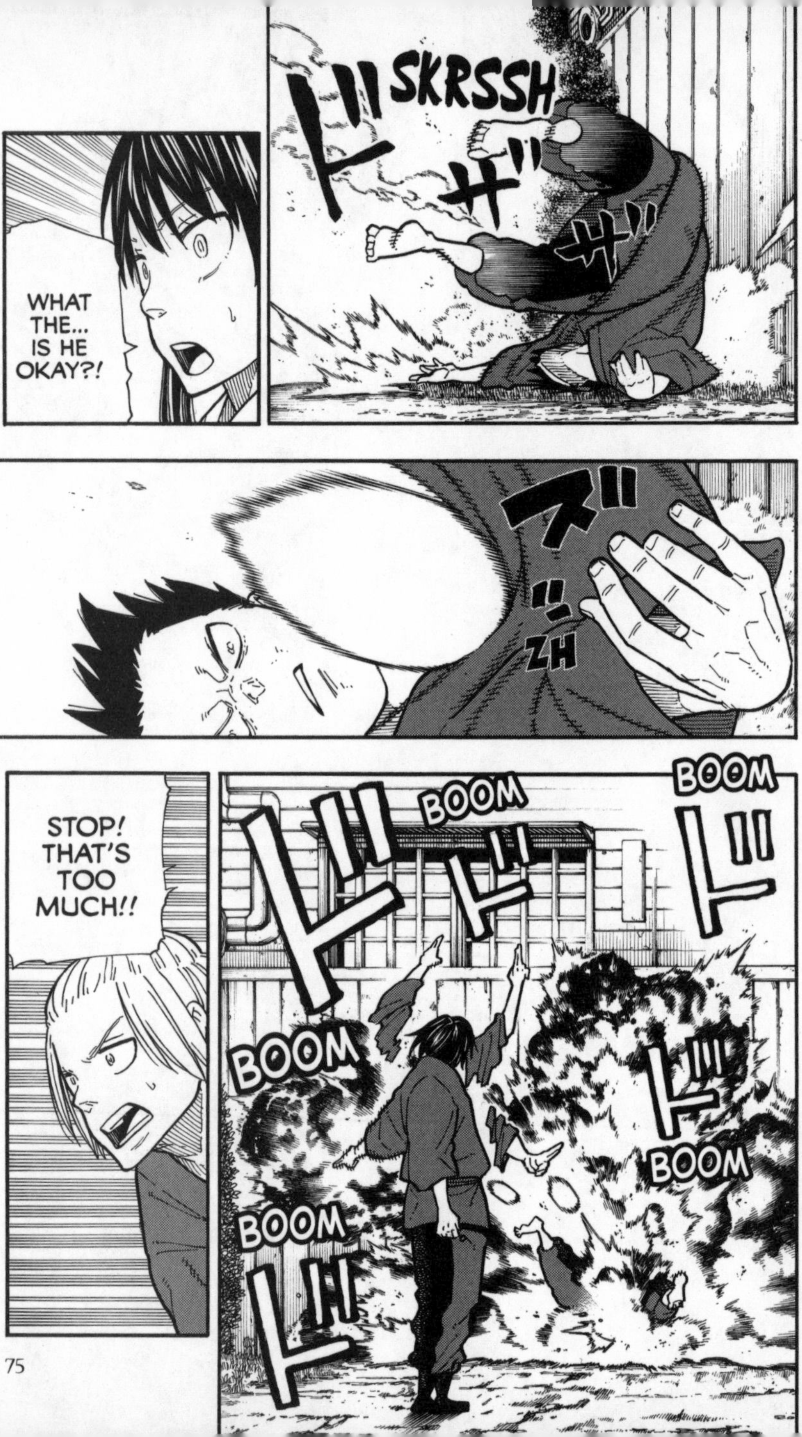
SKRSSH
WHAT THE... IS HE OKAY?!
ZH
BOOM
BOOM
BOOM
BOOM
BOOM
STOP! THAT'S TOO MUCH!!

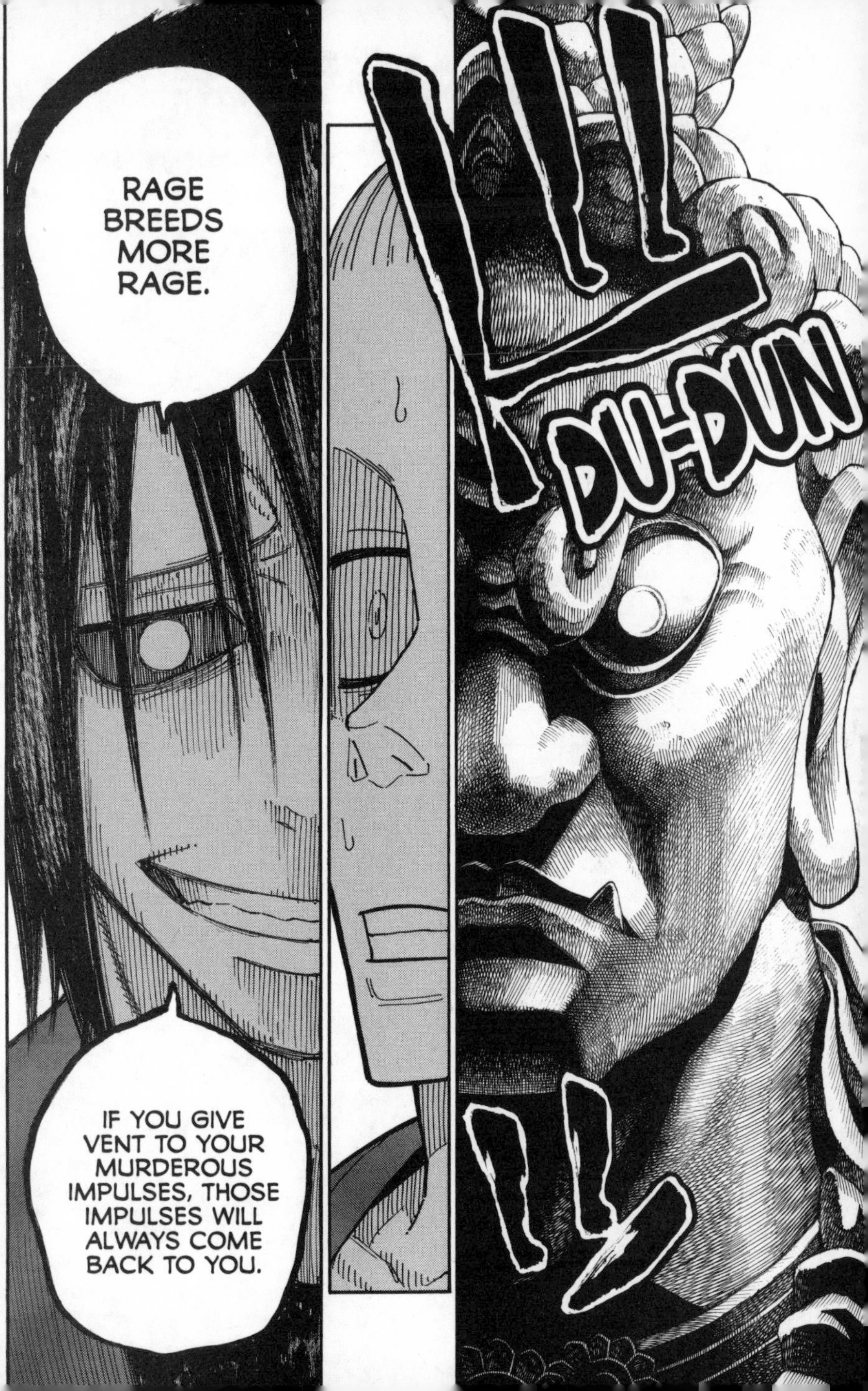
DU-DUN
RAGE BREEDS MORE RAGE.
IF YOU GIVE VENT TO YOUR MURDEROUS IMPULSES, THOSE IMPULSES WILL ALWAYS COME BACK TO YOU.

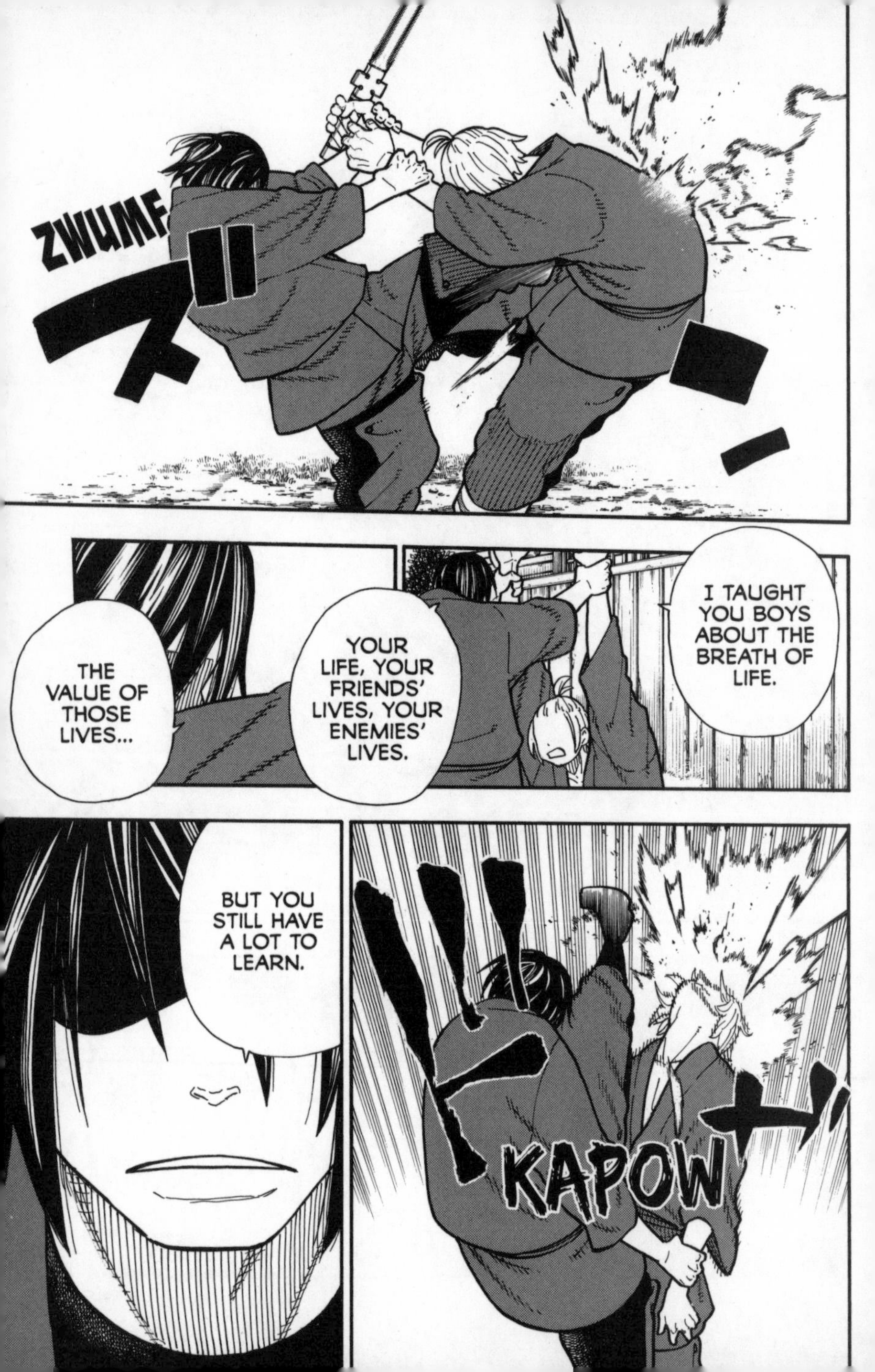
ZWUMF
I TAUGHT YOU BOYS ABOUT THE BREATH OF LIFE.
YOUR LIFE, YOUR FRIENDS' LIVES, YOUR ENEMIES' LIVES.
THE VALUE OF THOSE LIVES...
KAPOW
BUT YOU STILL HAVE A LOT TO LEARN.

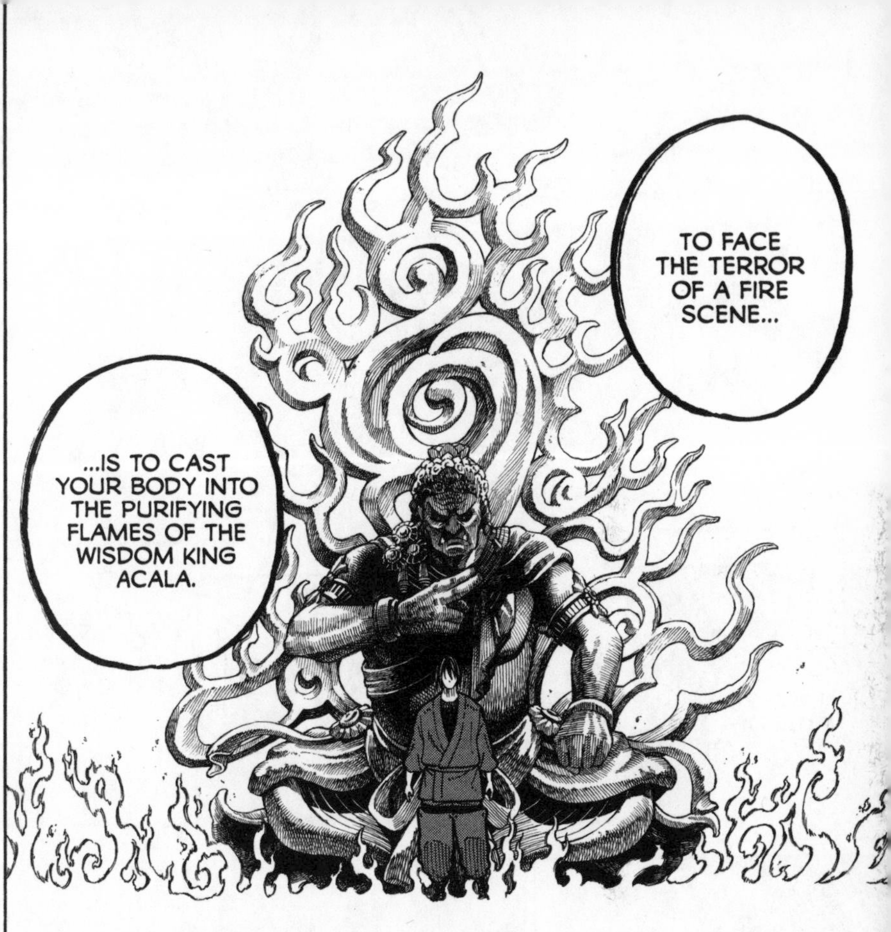
TO FACE THE TERROR OF A FIRE SCENE...
...IS TO CAST YOUR BODY INTO THE PURIFYING FLAMES OF THE WISDOM KING ACALA.

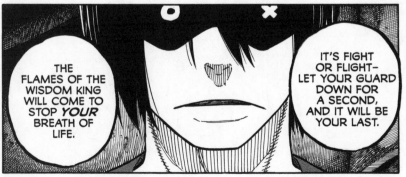

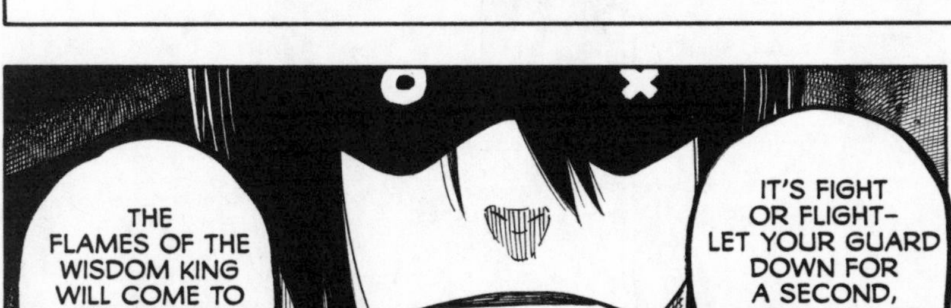
IT'S FIGHT OR FLIGHT– LET YOUR GUARD DOWN FOR A SECOND, AND IT WILL BE YOUR LAST.
THE FLAMES OF THE WISDOM KING WILL COME TO STOP ***YOUR*** BREATH OF LIFE.

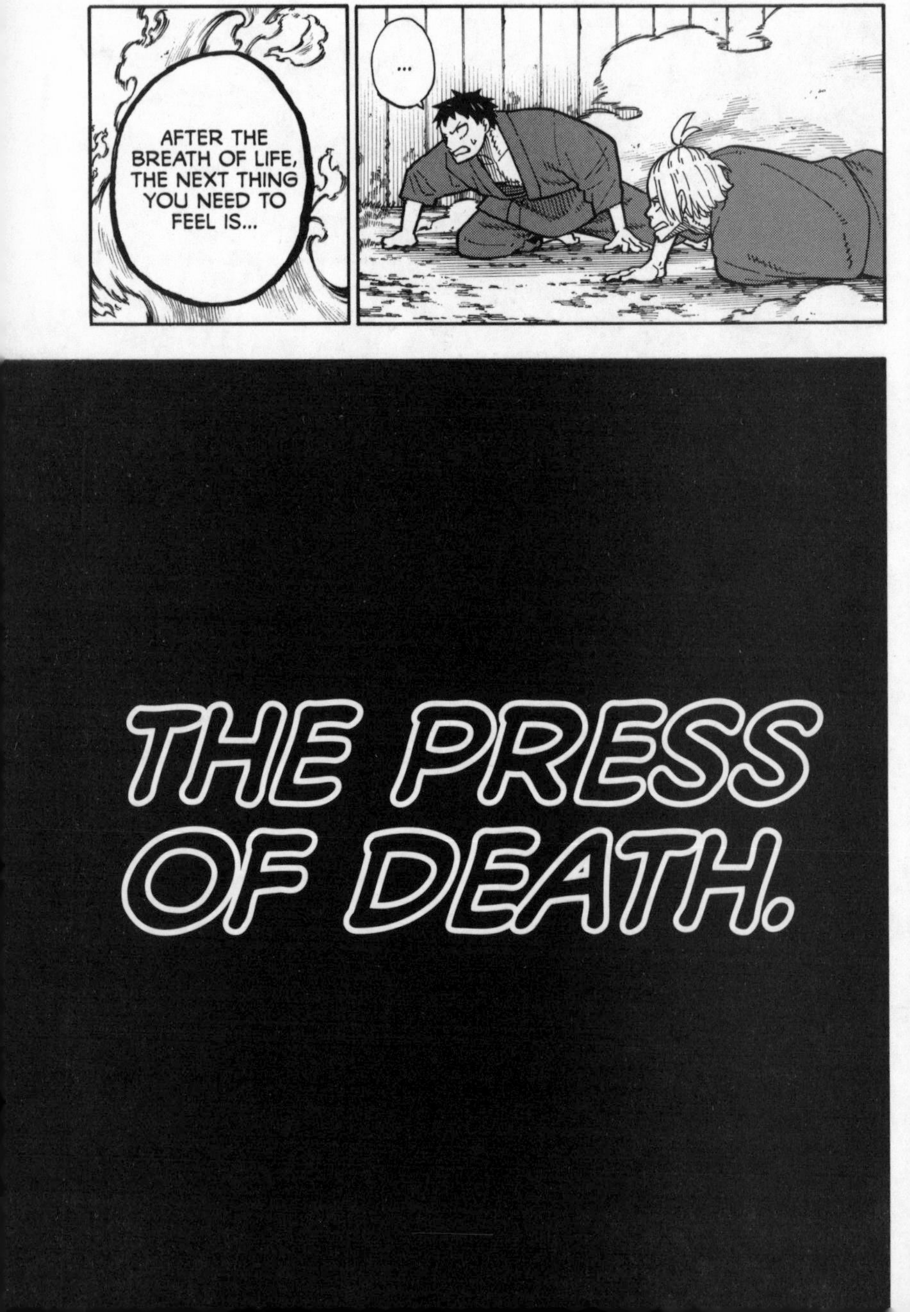
...
AFTER THE BREATH OF LIFE, THE NEXT THING YOU NEED TO FEEL IS...
THE PRESS OF DEATH.

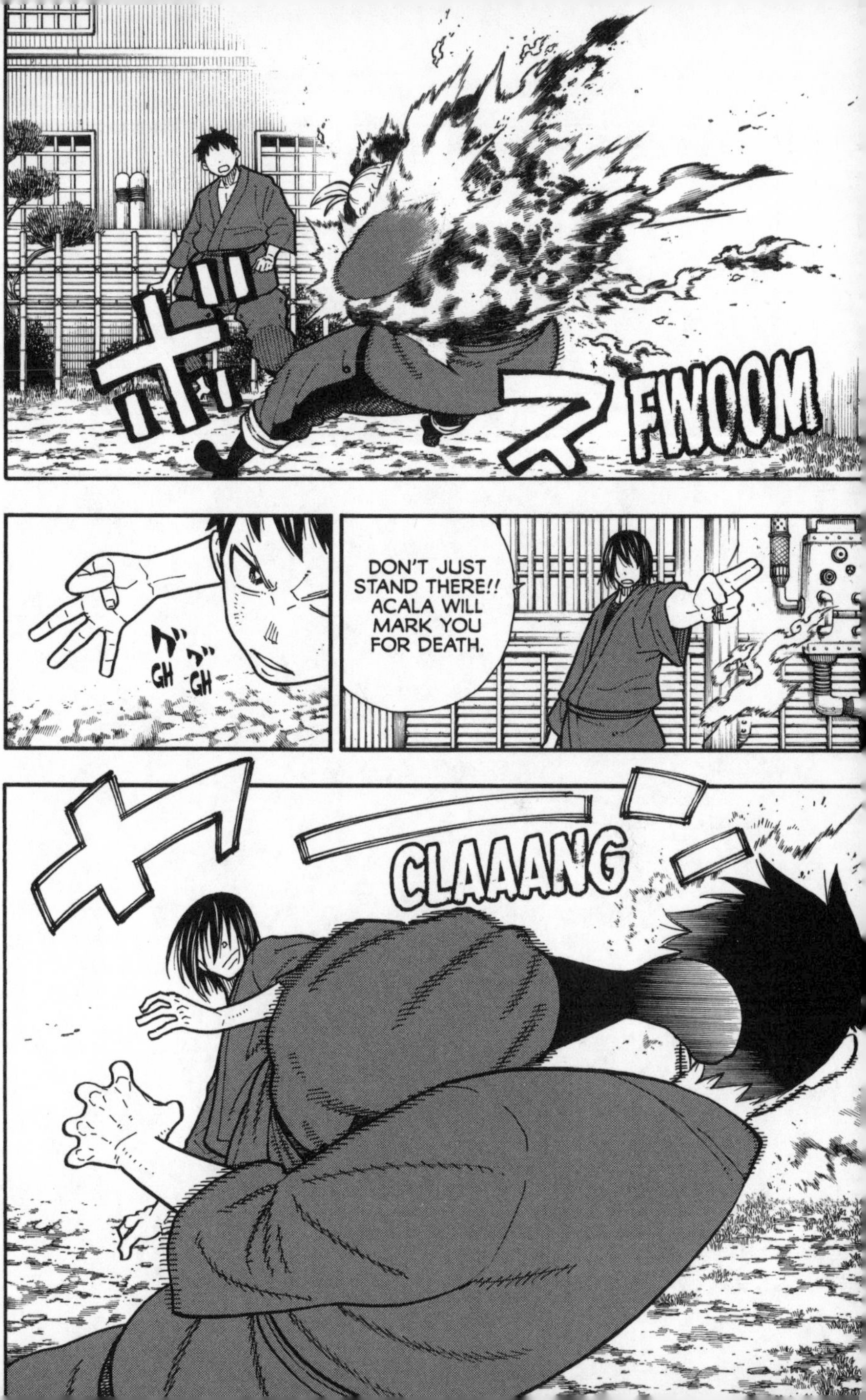
FWOOM
DON'T JUST STAND THERE!! ACALA WILL MARK YOU FOR DEATH.
GH GH
CLAAANG

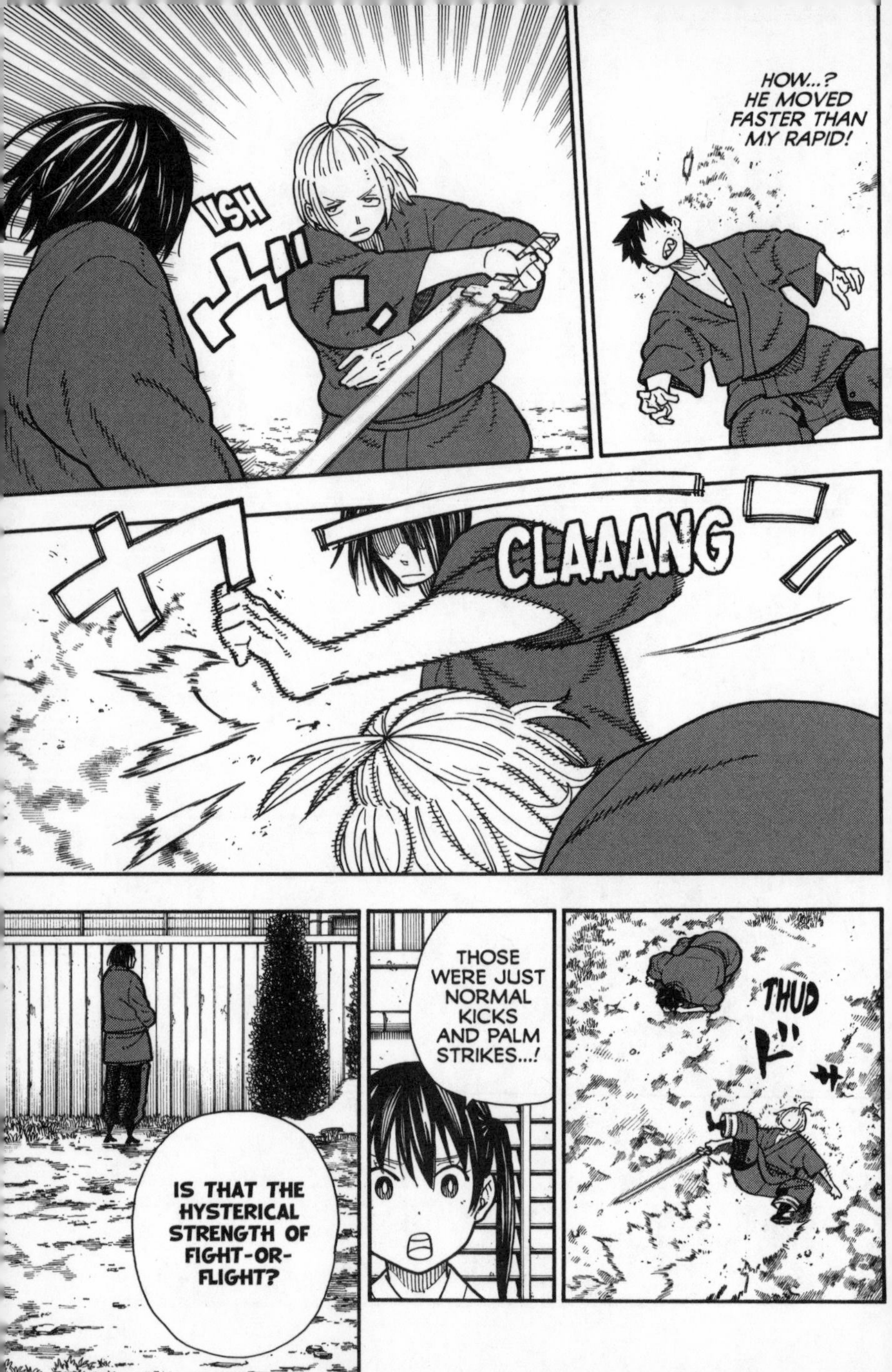
HOW...? HE MOVED FASTER THAN MY RAPID!
VSH
CLAAANG
THUD
THOSE WERE JUST NORMAL KICKS AND PALM STRIKES...!
IS THAT THE HYSTERICAL STRENGTH OF FIGHT-OR-FLIGHT?

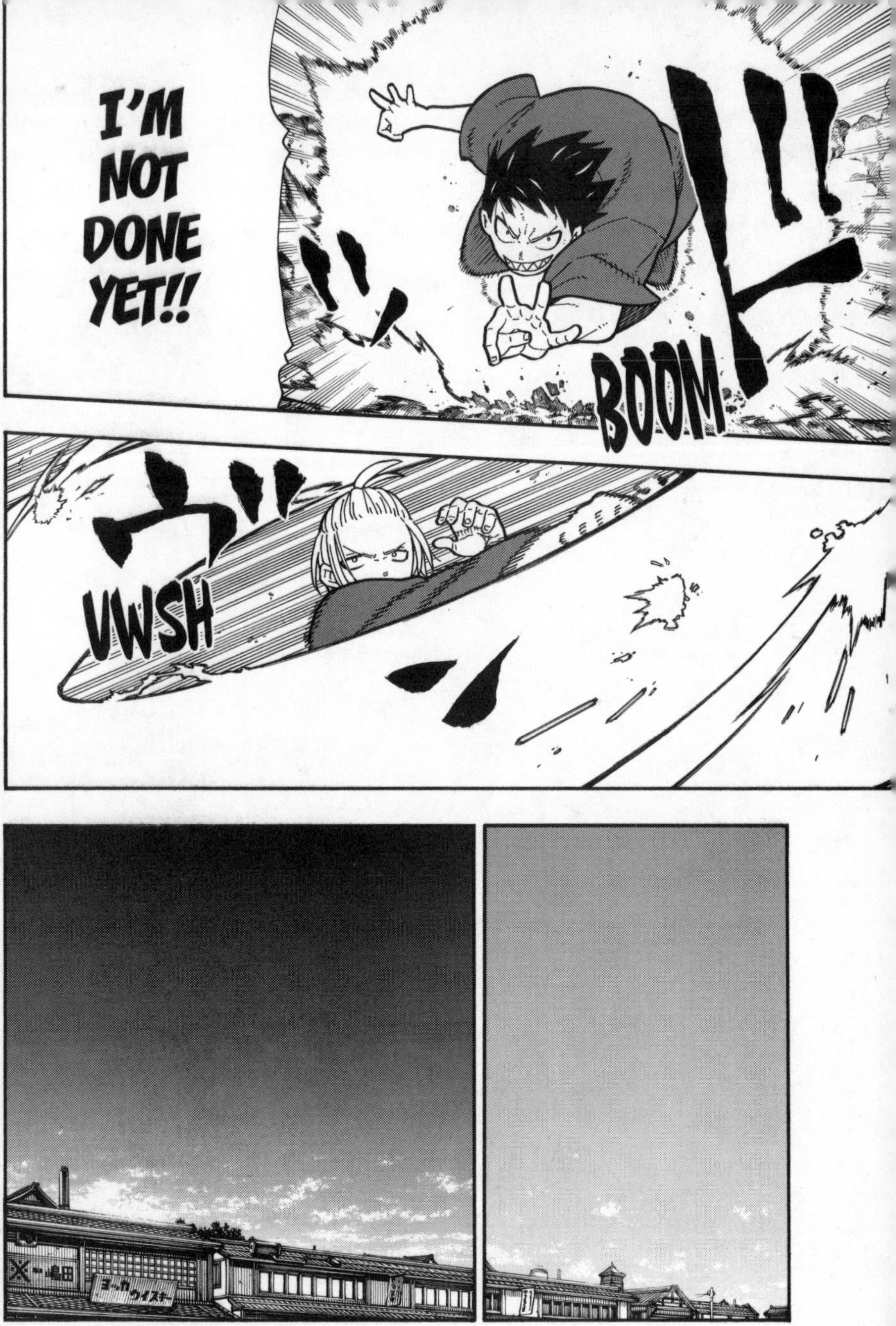
I'M NOT DONE YET!!
BOOM
UWSH

Sign: Shimada Sign: Yodka Whiskey

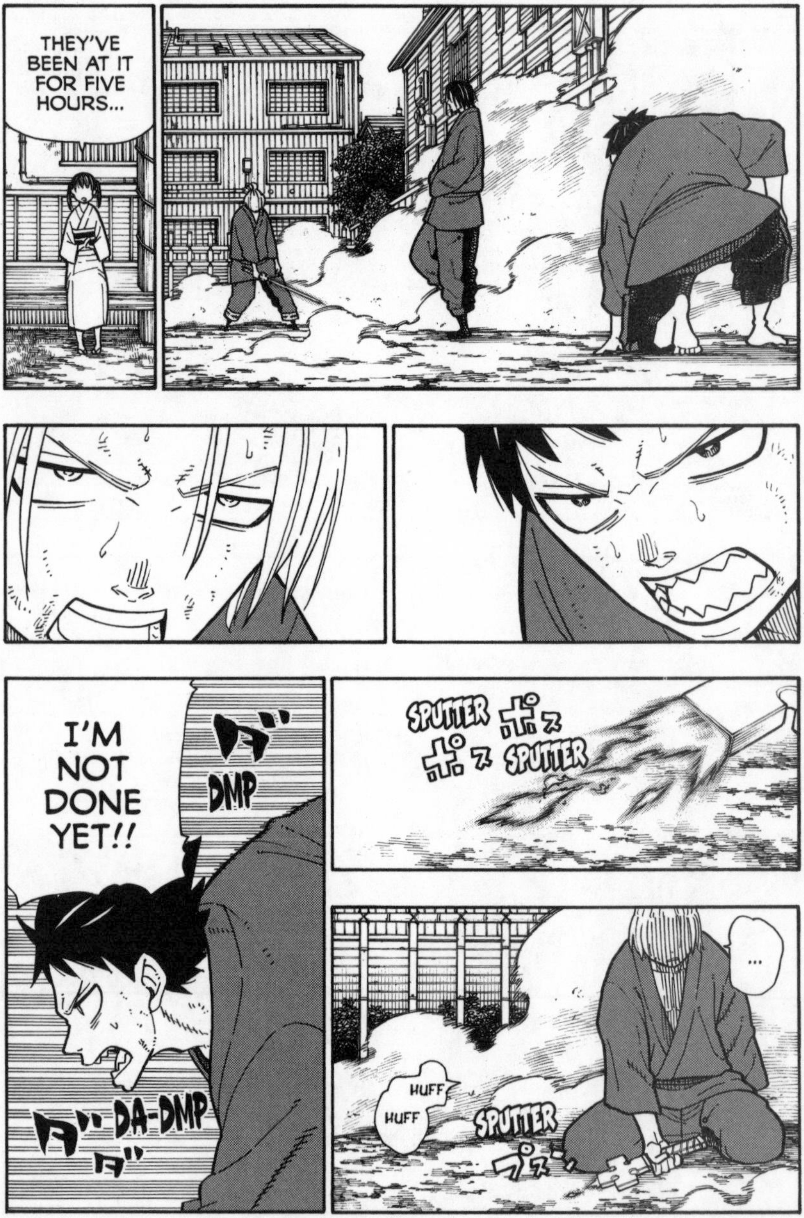
THEY'VE BEEN AT IT FOR FIVE HOURS...
SPUTTER
SPUTTER
...
HUFF
HUFF
SPUTTER
I'M NOT DONE YET!!
DMP
DA-DMP

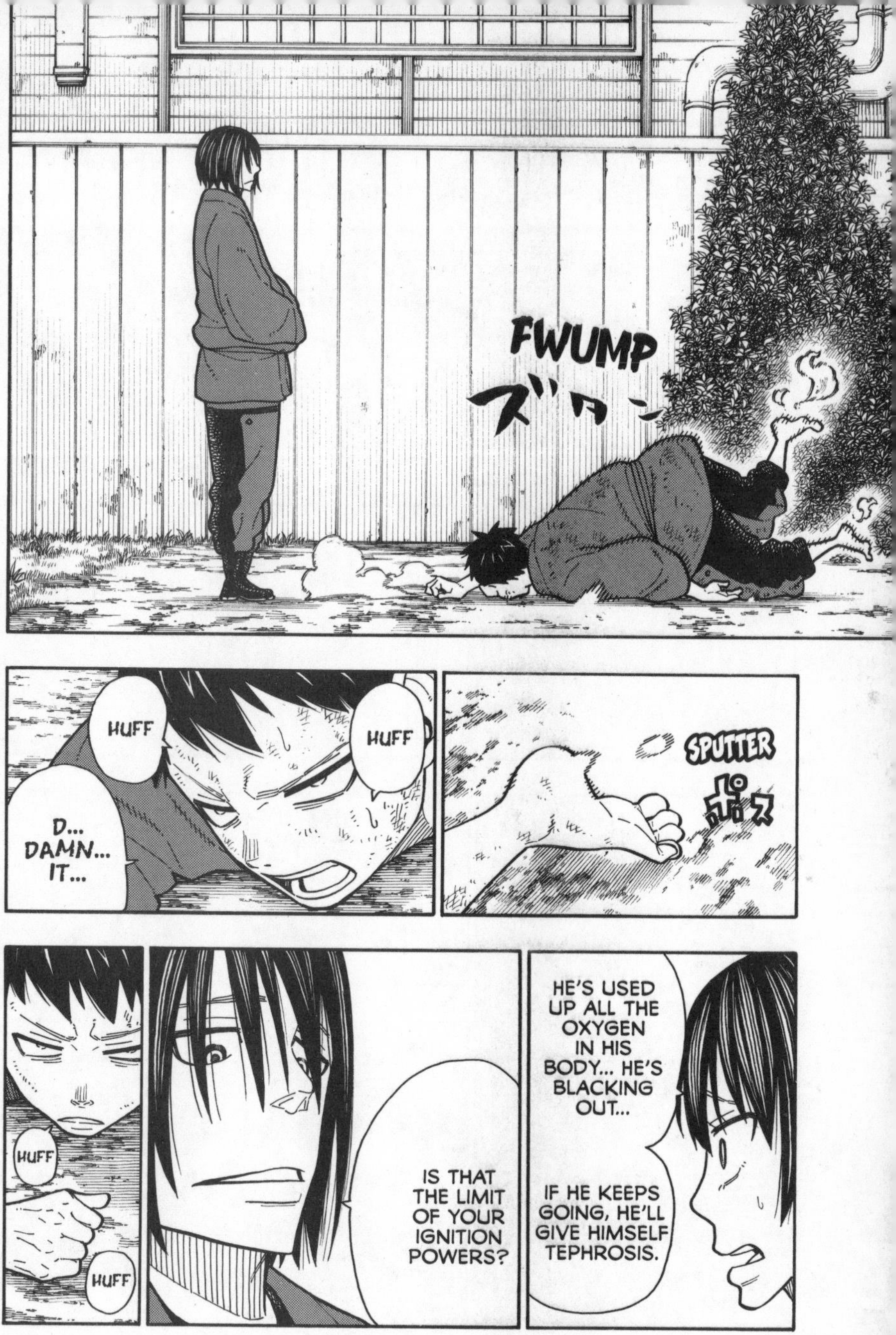
FWUMP
ズァー
SPUTTER
ポス
HUFF
HUFF
D... DAMN... IT...
HE'S USED UP ALL THE OXYGEN IN HIS BODY... HE'S BLACKING OUT...
IF HE KEEPS GOING, HE'LL GIVE HIMSELF TEPHROSIS.
IS THAT THE LIMIT OF YOUR IGNITION POWERS?
HUFF
HUFF

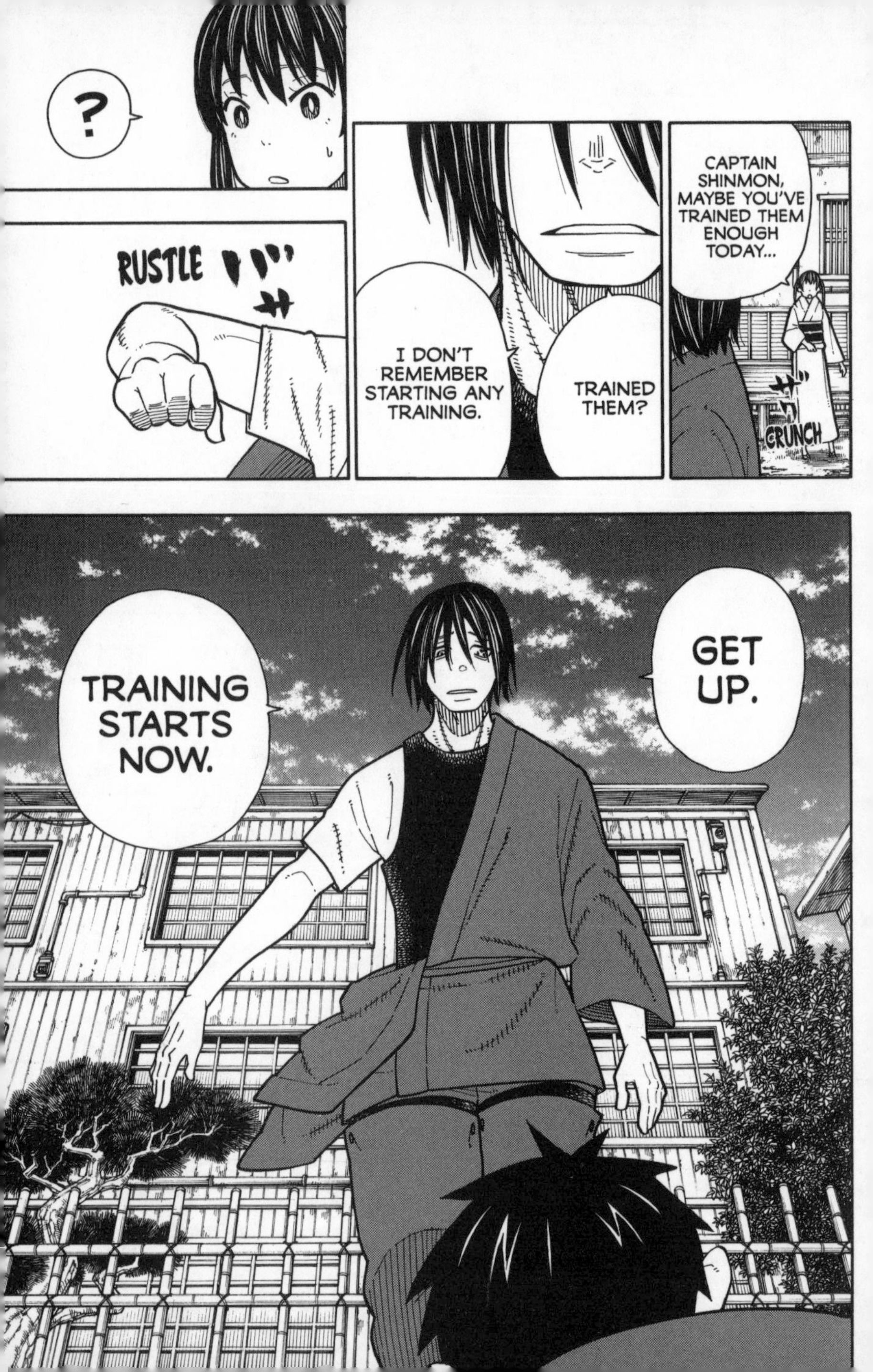
CAPTAIN SHINMON, MAYBE YOU'VE TRAINED THEM ENOUGH TODAY...
CRUNCH
TRAINED THEM?
I DON'T REMEMBER STARTING ANY TRAINING.
?
RUSTLE
GET UP.
TRAINING STARTS NOW.

FIRE FORCE

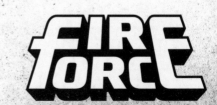

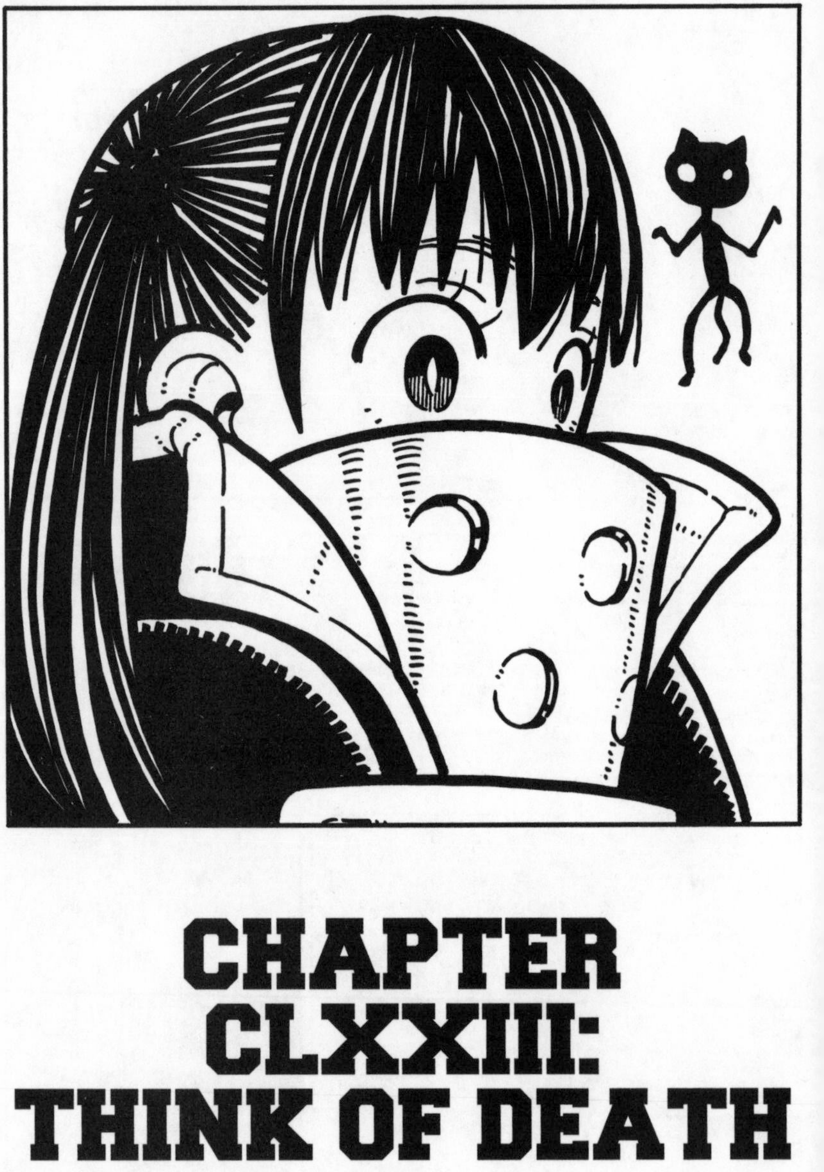

CHAPTER CLXXIII: THINK OF DEATH

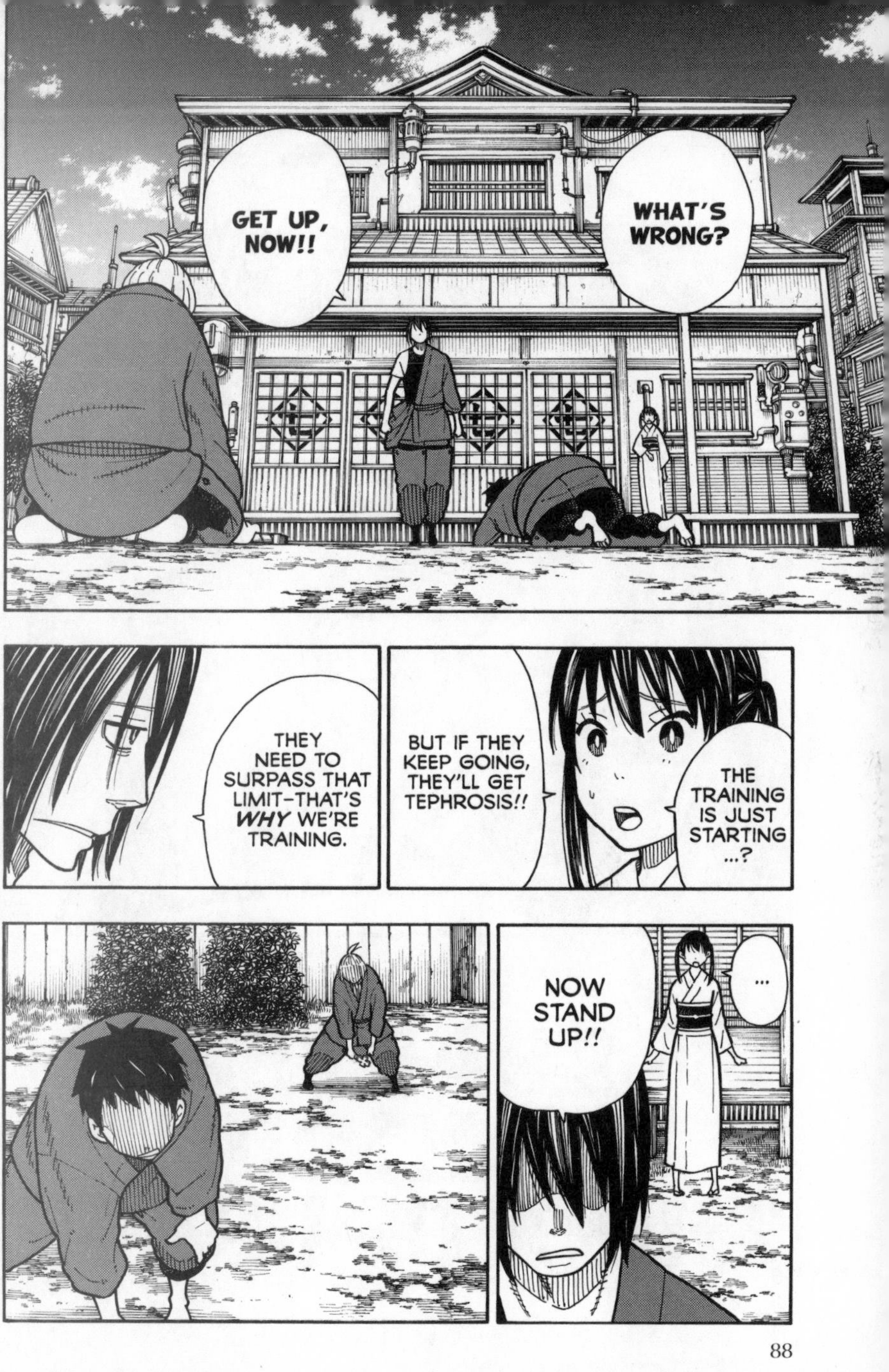
WHAT'S WRONG?
GET UP, NOW!!
THE TRAINING IS JUST STARTING ...?
BUT IF THEY KEEP GOING, THEY'LL GET TEPHROSIS!!
THEY NEED TO SURPASS THAT LIMIT–THAT'S *WHY* WE'RE TRAINING.
...
NOW STAND UP!!

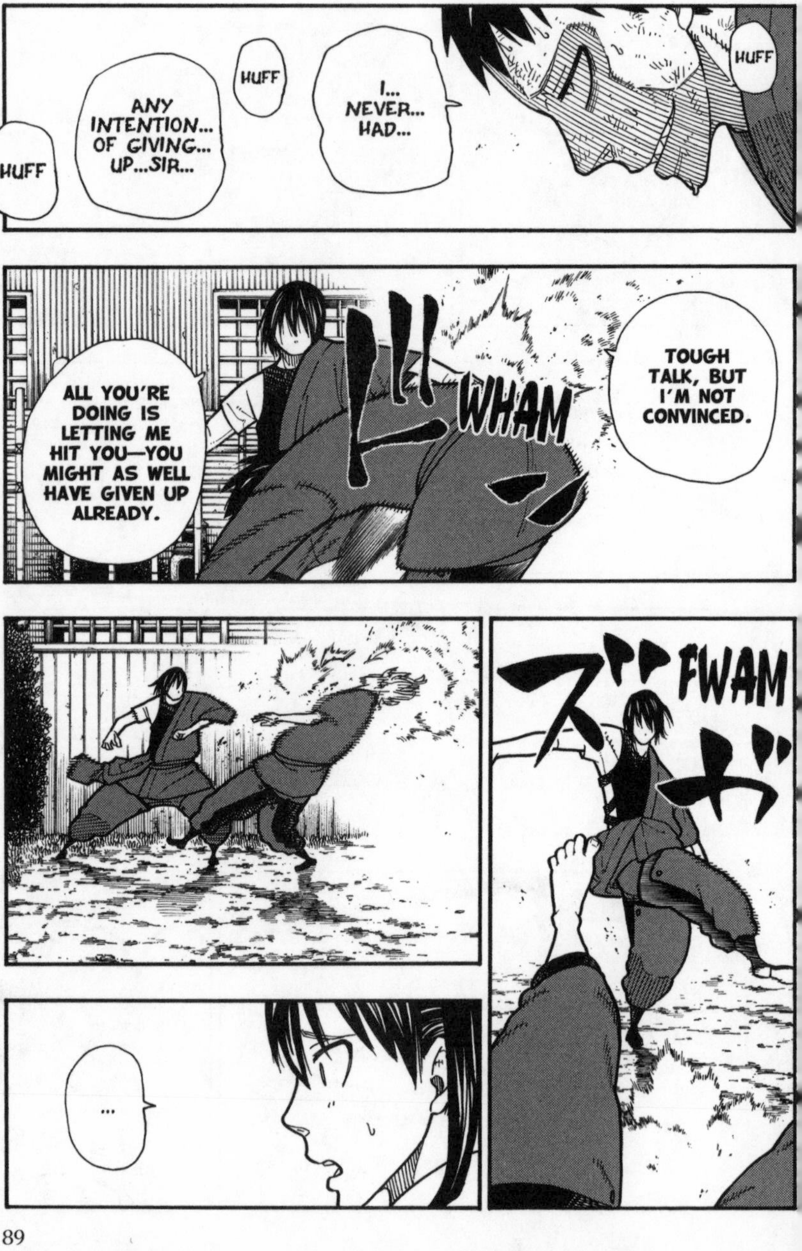
HUFF
I... NEVER... HAD...
HUFF
ANY INTENTION... OF GIVING... UP...SIR...
HUFF
TOUGH TALK, BUT I'M NOT CONVINCED.
WHAM
ALL YOU'RE DOING IS LETTING ME HIT YOU—YOU MIGHT AS WELL HAVE GIVEN UP ALREADY.
FWAM
...

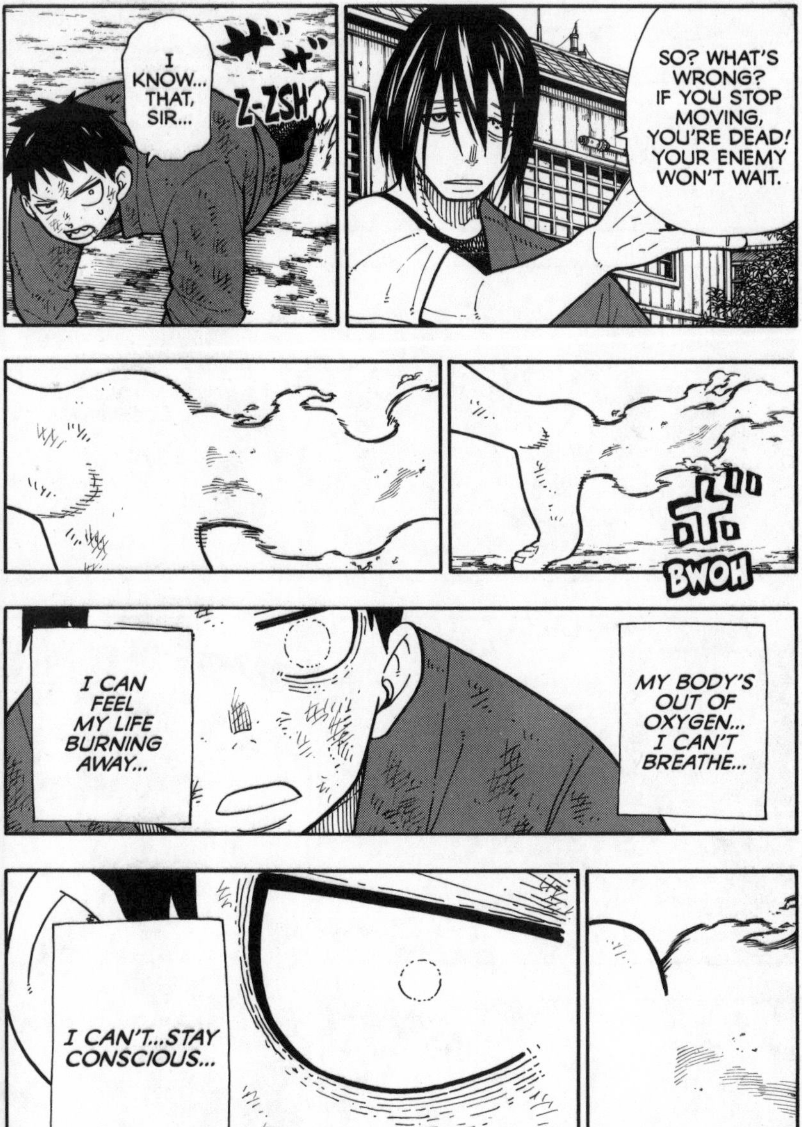
SO? WHAT'S WRONG? IF YOU STOP MOVING, YOU'RE DEAD! YOUR ENEMY WON'T WAIT.
Z-ZSH
I KNOW... THAT, SIR...
BWOH
MY BODY'S OUT OF OXYGEN... I CAN'T BREATHE...
I CAN FEEL MY LIFE BURNING AWAY...
I CAN'T...STAY CONSCIOUS...

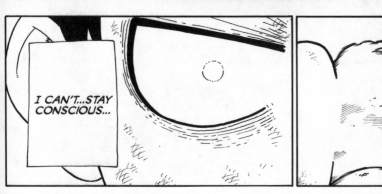

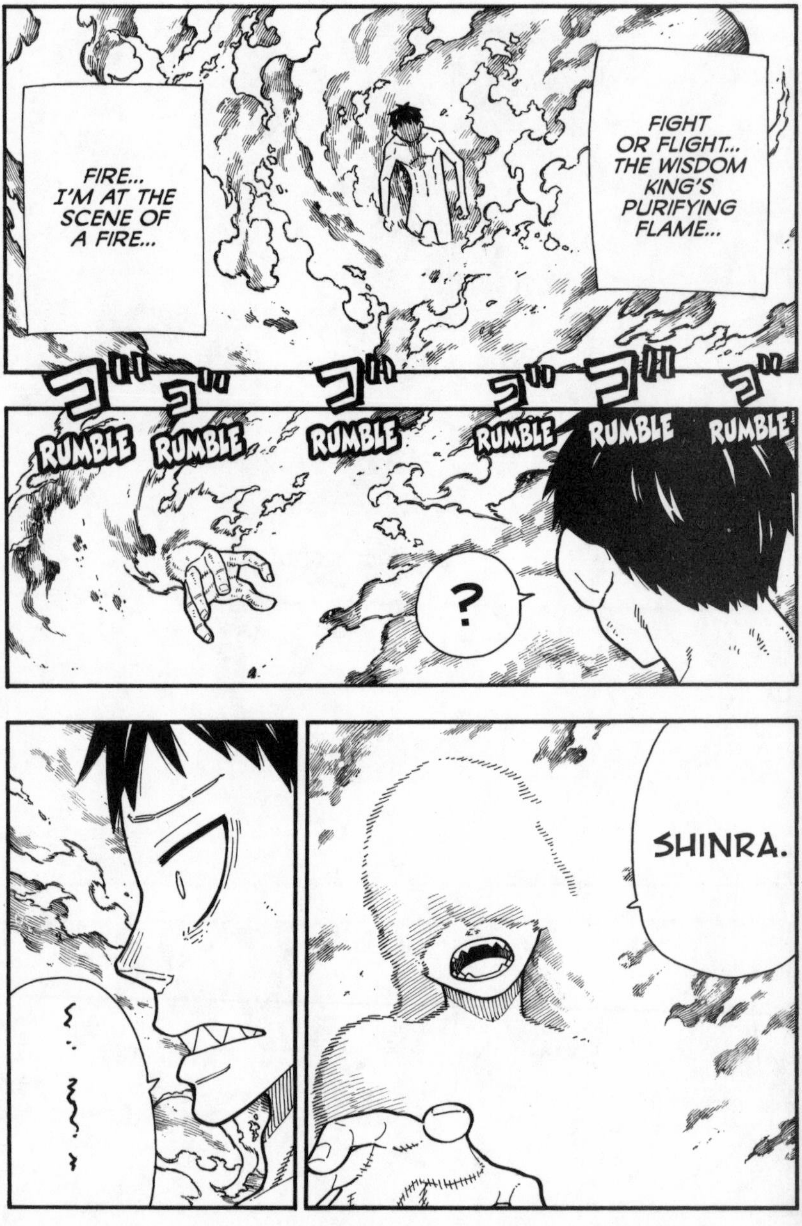
FIGHT OR FLIGHT... THE WISDOM KING'S PURIFYING FLAME...
FIRE... I'M AT THE SCENE OF A FIRE...
RUMBLE
RUMBLE
RUMBLE
RUMBLE
RUMBLE
RUMBLE
?
SHINRA.

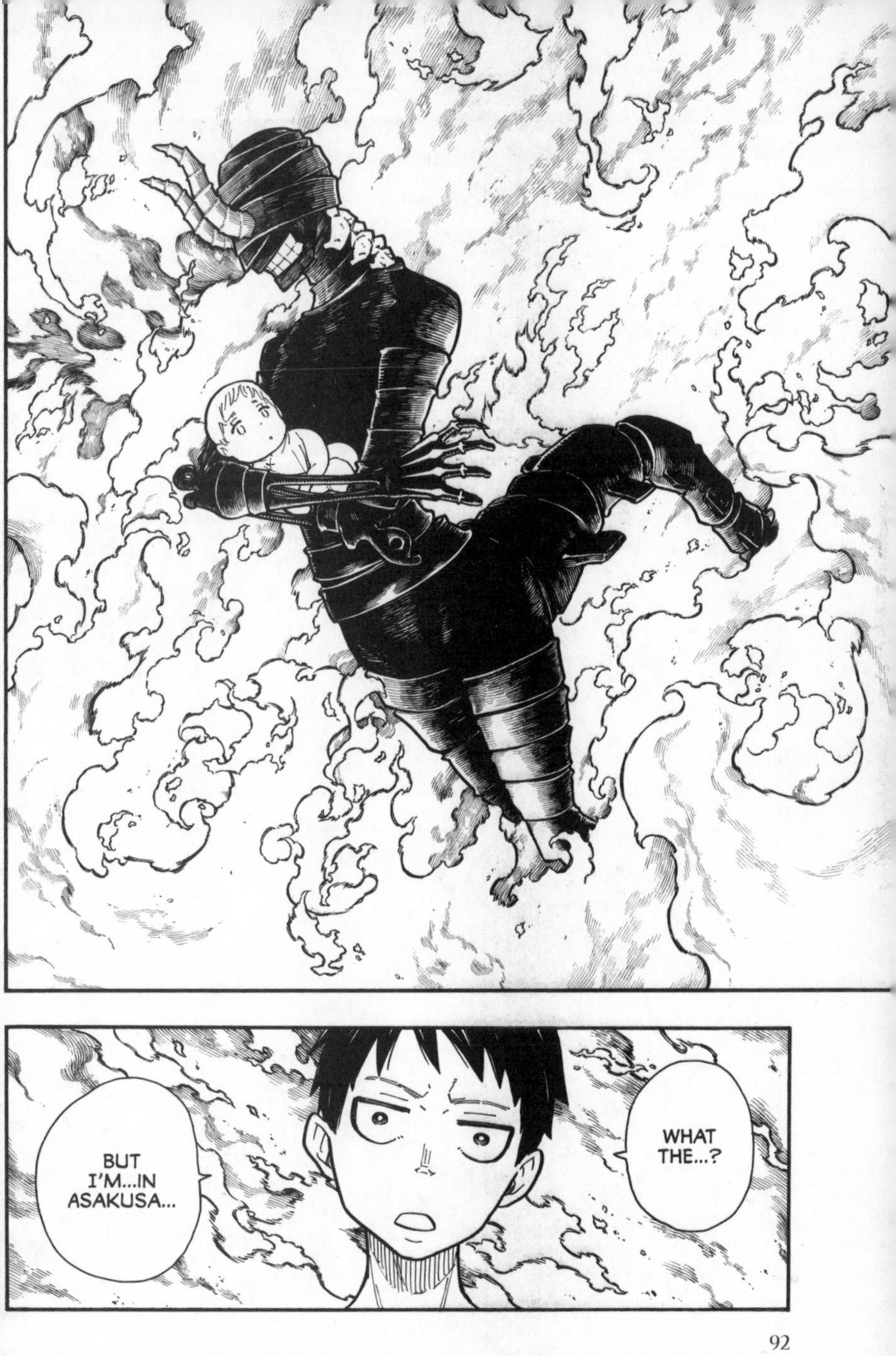
WHAT THE...?
BUT I'M...IN ASAKUSA...

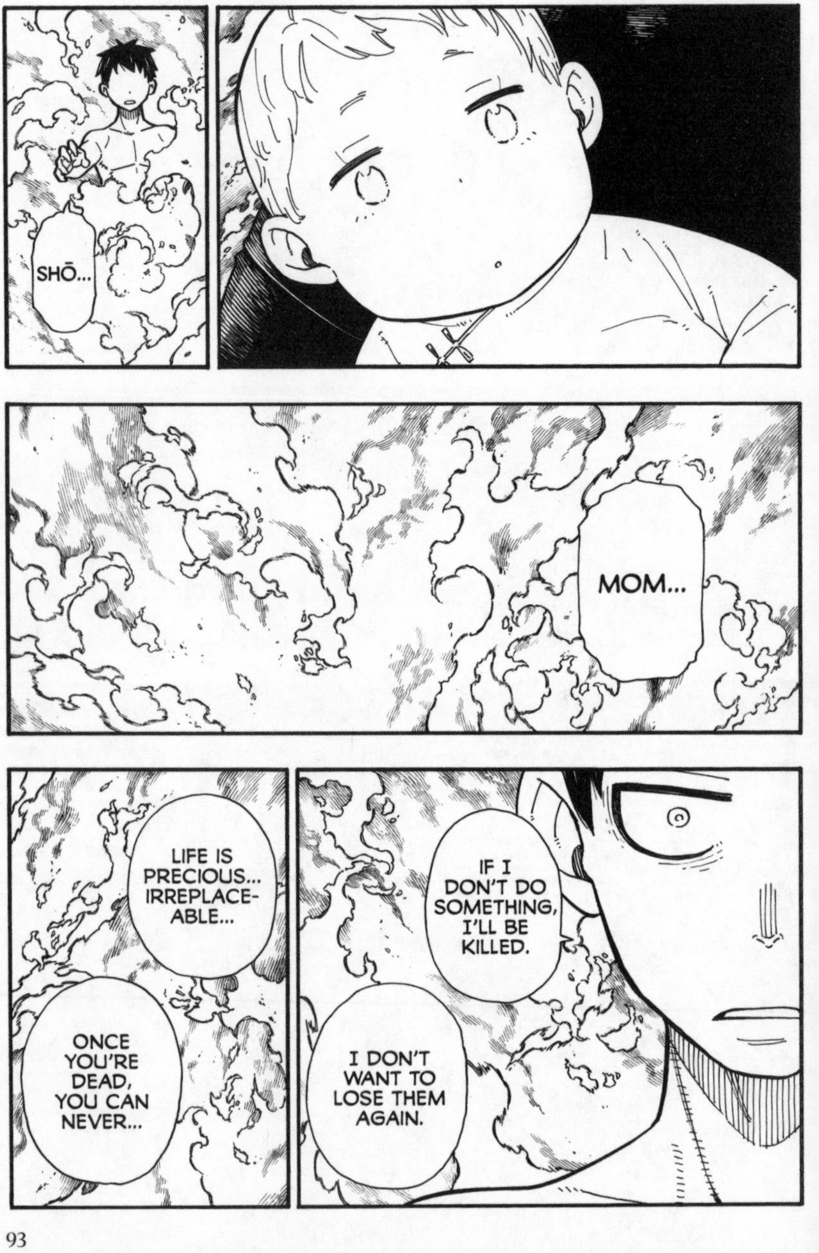
SHŌ...
MOM...
IF I DON'T DO SOMETHING, I'LL BE KILLED.
I DON'T WANT TO LOSE THEM AGAIN.
LIFE IS PRECIOUS... IRREPLACE-ABLE...
ONCE YOU'RE DEAD, YOU CAN NEVER...

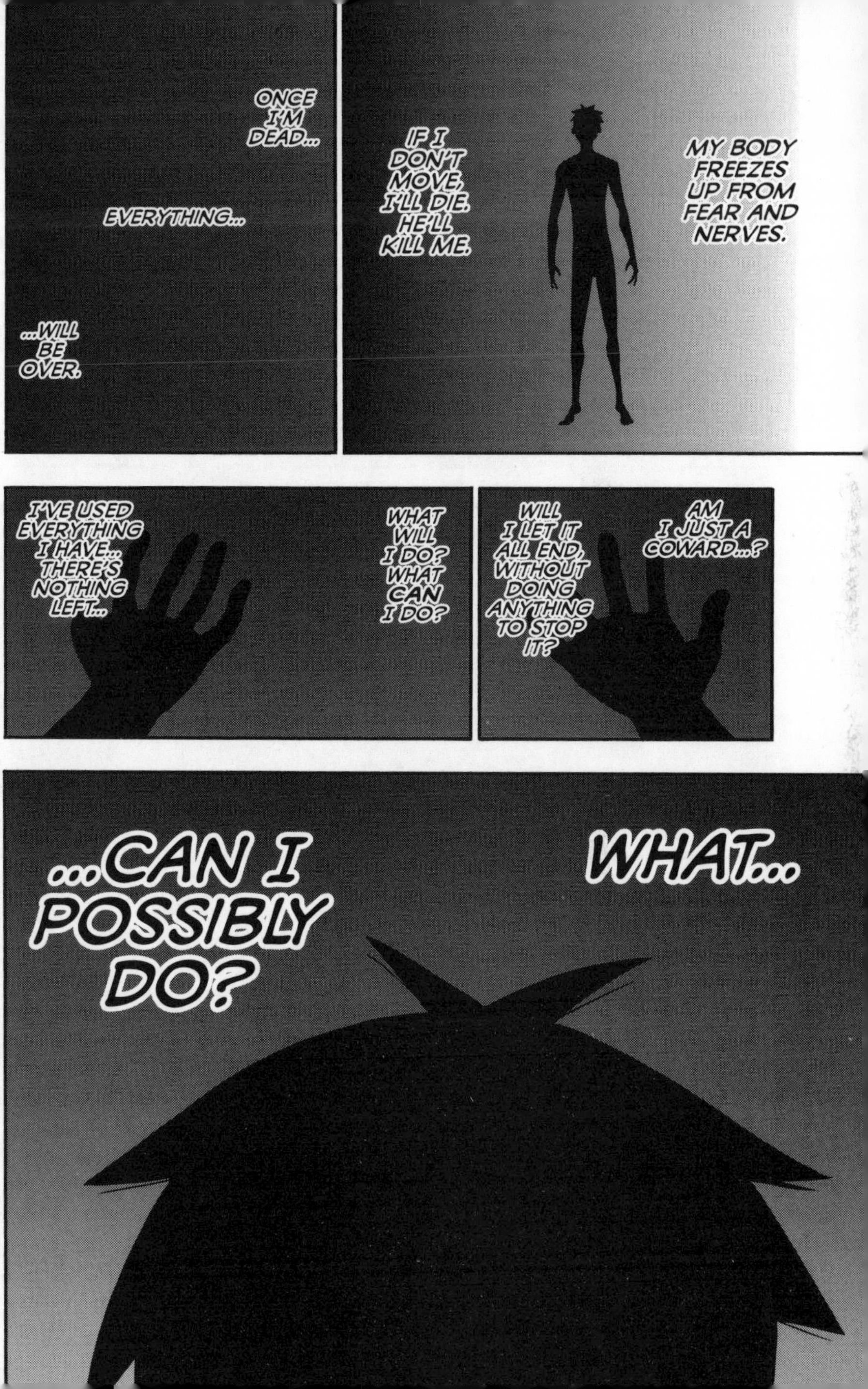
MY BODY FREEZES UP FROM FEAR AND NERVES.
IF I DON'T MOVE, I'LL DIE. HE'LL KILL ME.
ONCE I'M DEAD...
EVERYTHING...
...WILL BE OVER.
AM I JUST A COWARD...?
WILL I LET IT ALL END, WITHOUT DOING ANYTHING TO STOP IT?
WHAT WILL I DO? WHAT CAN I DO?
I'VE USED EVERYTHING I HAVE... THERE'S NOTHING LEFT...
WHAT...
...CAN I POSSIBLY DO?

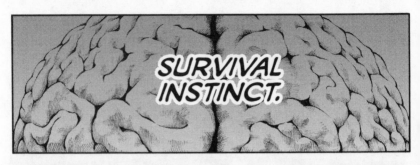

SURVIVAL INSTINCT.

...MY NERVES GIVE ME A SMILE.

IN THE FACE OF DEATH...

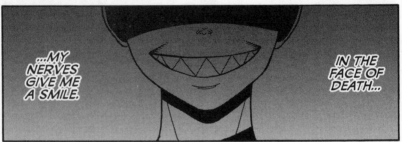

A PINCH OF ENERGY.

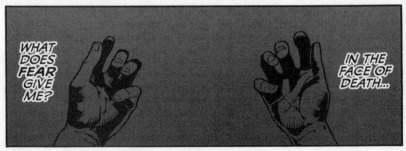

WHAT DOES FEAR GIVE ME?

IN THE FACE OF DEATH...

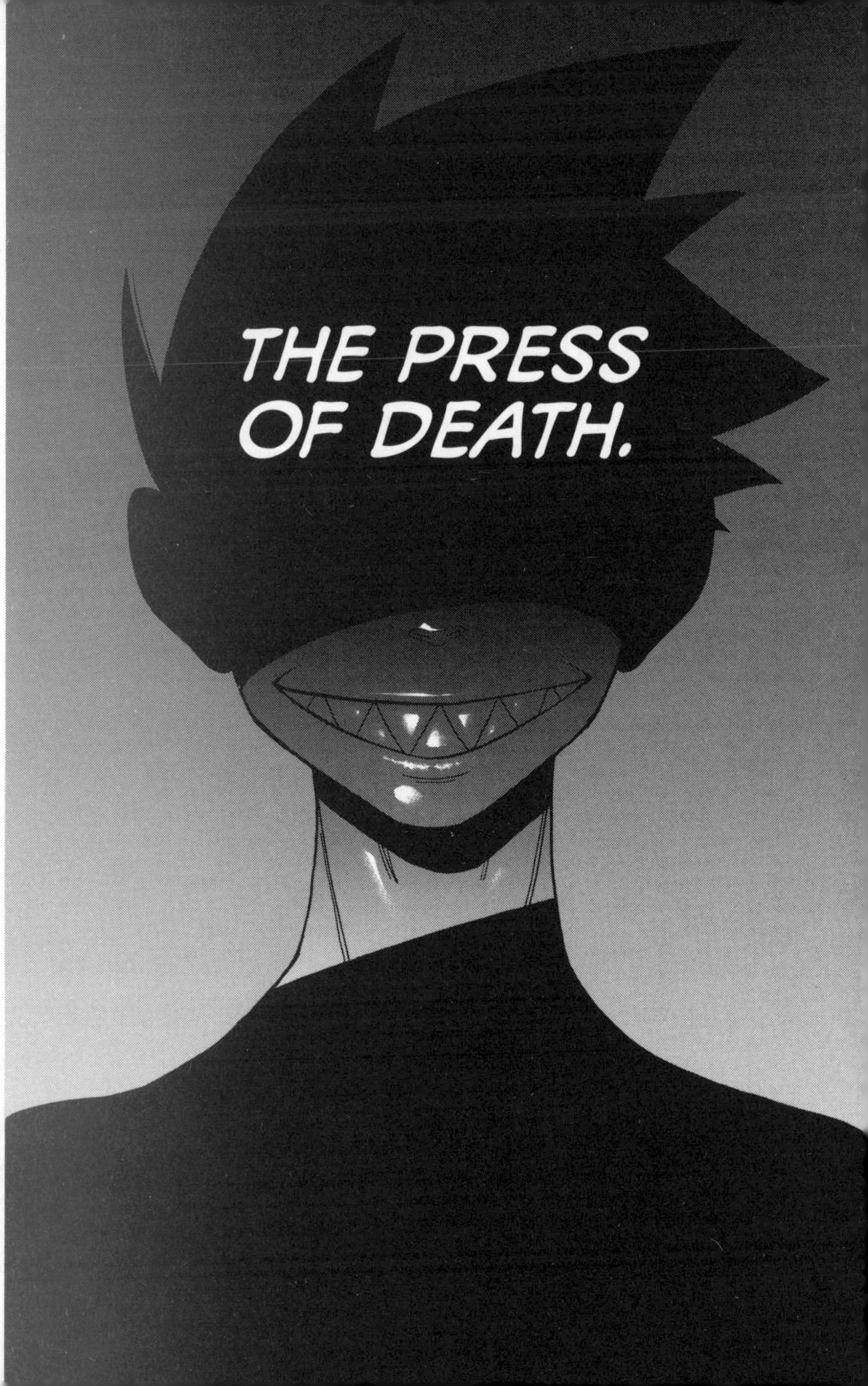
THE PRESS OF DEATH.

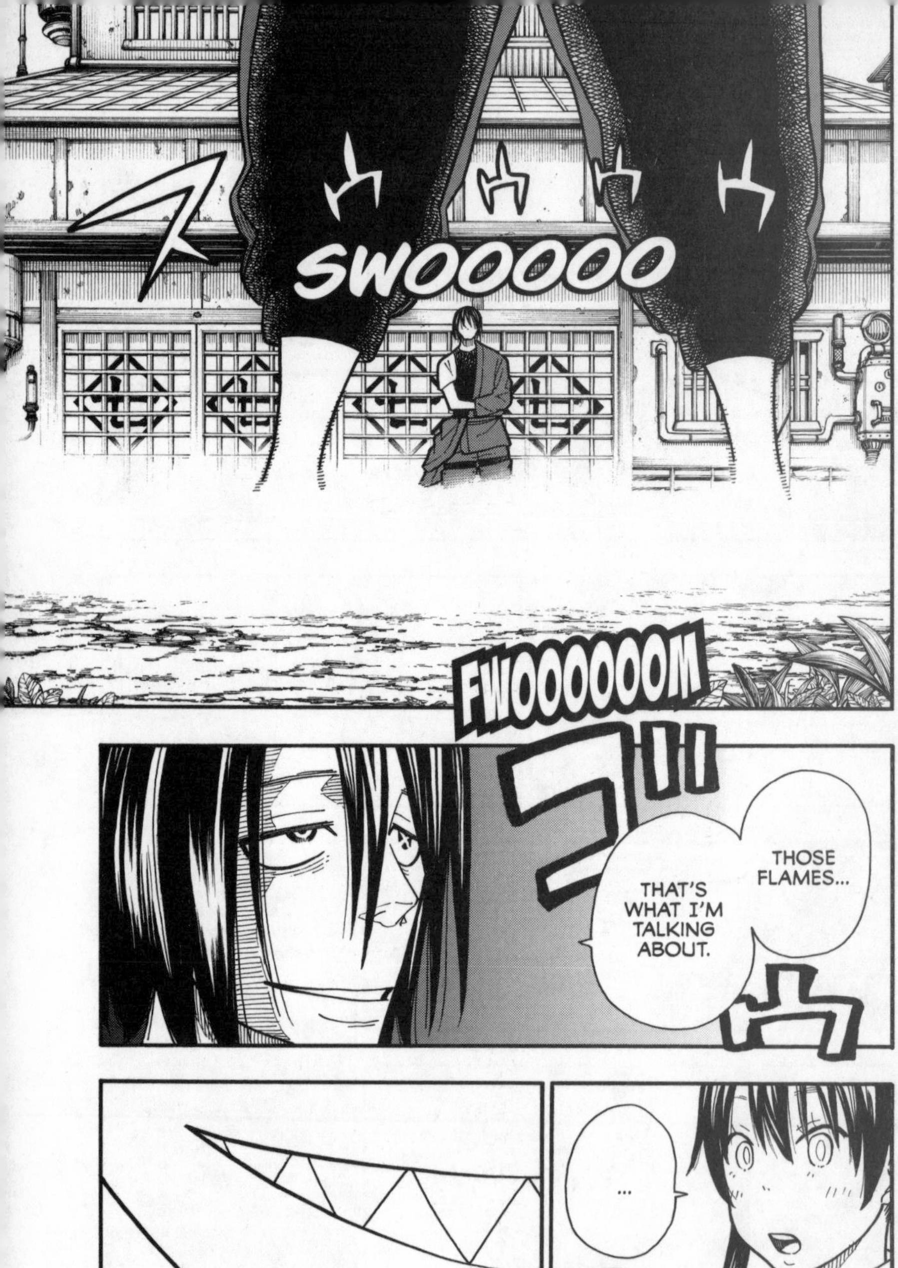
SWOOOOO
FWOOOOOM
THOSE FLAMES...
THAT'S WHAT I'M TALKING ABOUT.
...

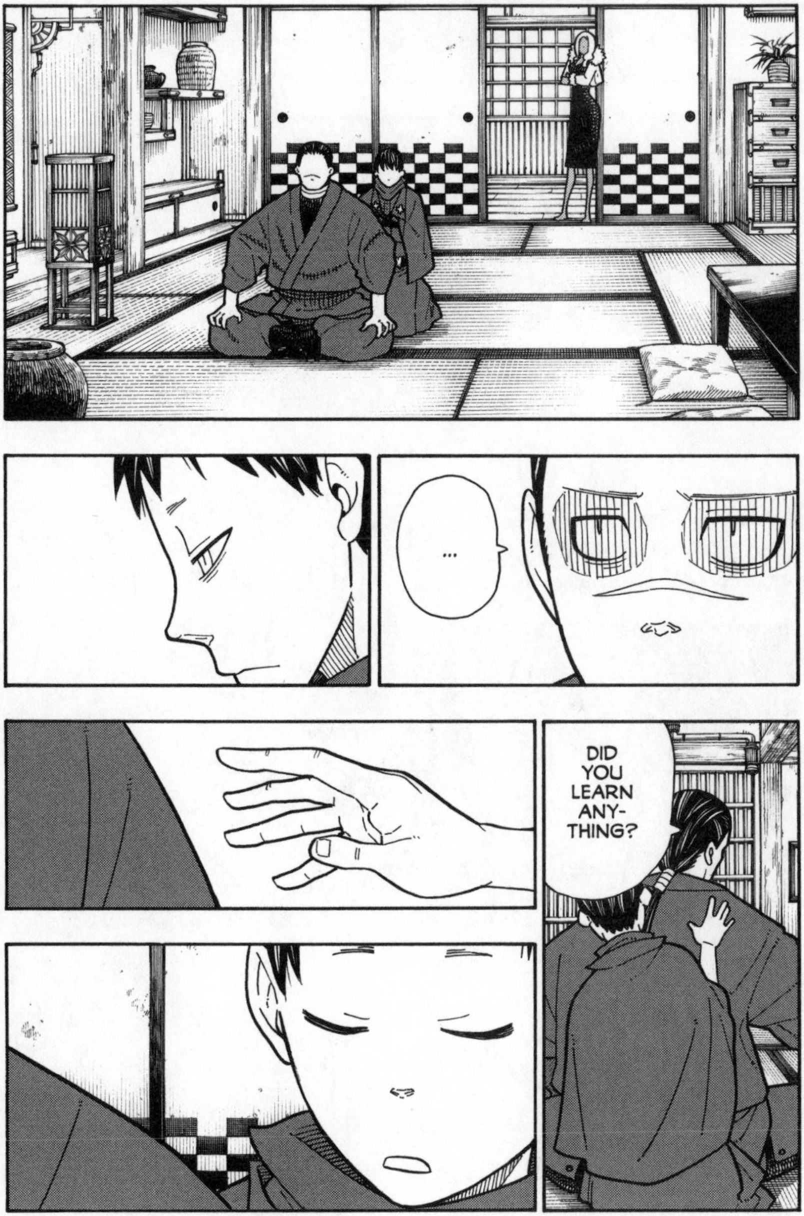
...
DID YOU LEARN ANY-THING?

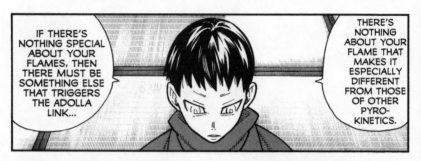

THERE'S NOTHING ABOUT YOUR FLAME THAT MAKES IT ESPECIALLY DIFFERENT FROM THOSE OF OTHER PYRO-KINETICS.
IF THERE'S NOTHING SPECIAL ABOUT YOUR FLAMES, THEN THERE MUST BE SOMETHING ELSE THAT TRIGGERS THE ADOLLA LINK...
LIEUTENANT KONRO, BOTH YOU AND COMPANY 4'S CAPTAIN HAGUE MADE YOUR ADOLLA LINKS DURING THE GREAT FIRE.
A LARGE CONFLAGRATION... THE DEATHS OF MANY... THOSE FACTORS MAY HAVE ACTIVATED SOMETHING.
KAYOKO-SAN. YOU SAID A MINUTE AGO THAT HIS FLAMES ARE JUST LIKE ANYONE ELSE'S.
HAVING TOUCHED ONE YOURSELF, IS THERE SOMETHING ABOUT AN ADOLLA BURST THAT MAKES IT DIFFERENT?

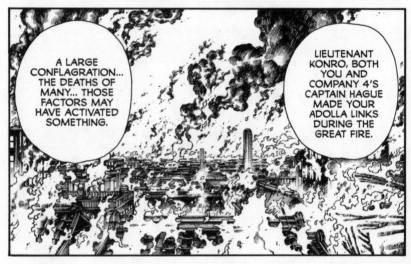

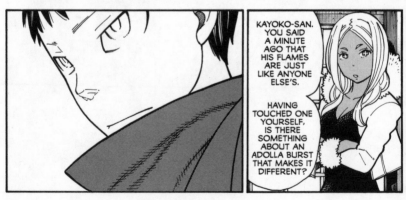

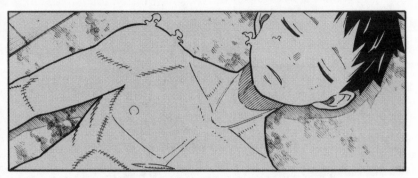

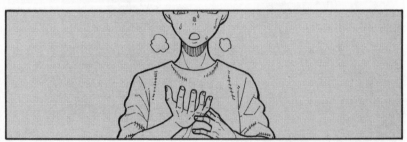

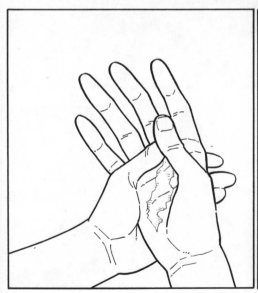

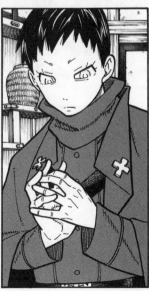

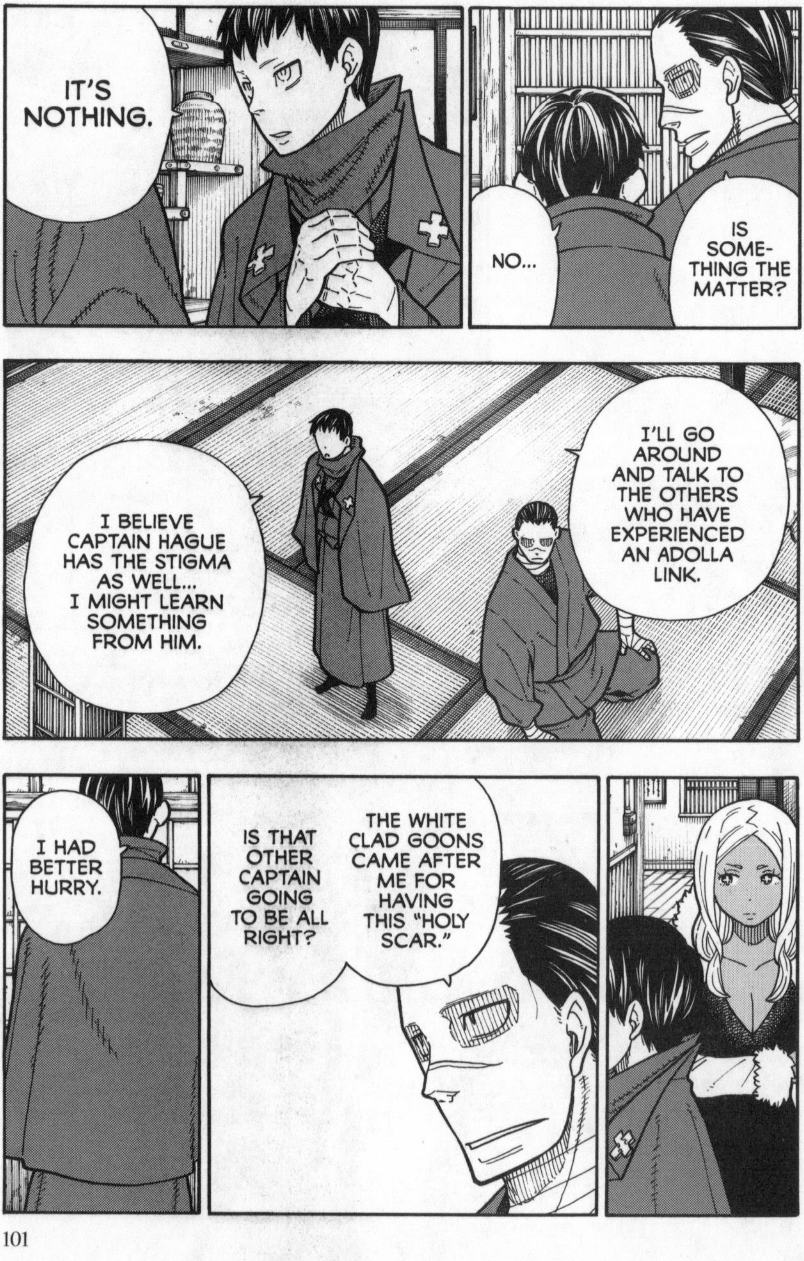
IS SOMETHING THE MATTER?
NO...
IT'S NOTHING.
I'LL GO AROUND AND TALK TO THE OTHERS WHO HAVE EXPERIENCED AN ADOLLA LINK.
I BELIEVE CAPTAIN HAGUE HAS THE STIGMA AS WELL... I MIGHT LEARN SOMETHING FROM HIM.
THE WHITE CLAD GOONS CAME AFTER ME FOR HAVING THIS "HOLY SCAR."
IS THAT OTHER CAPTAIN GOING TO BE ALL RIGHT?
I HAD BETTER HURRY.

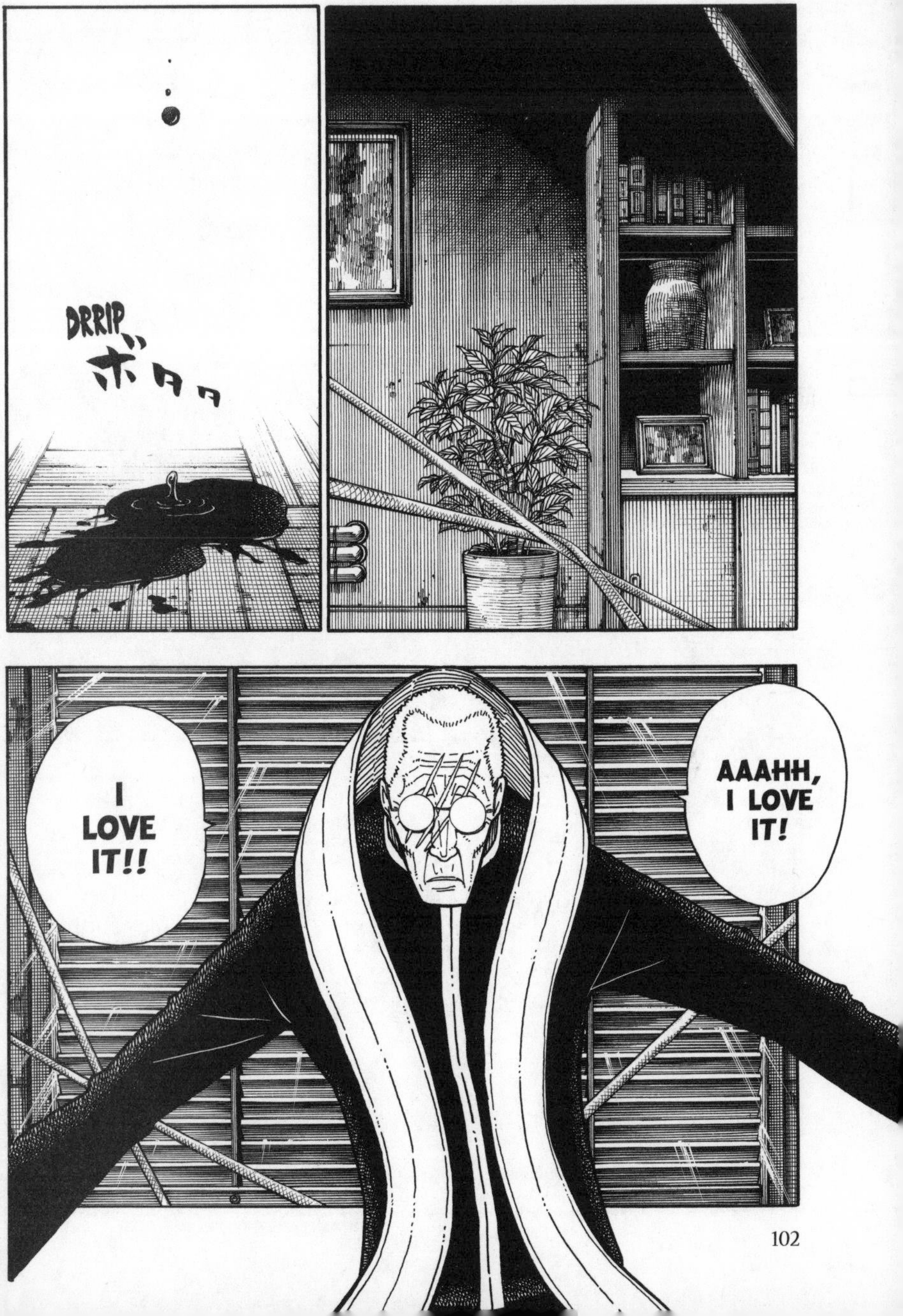
DRRIP
ボタタ
AAAHH, I LOVE IT!
I LOVE IT!!

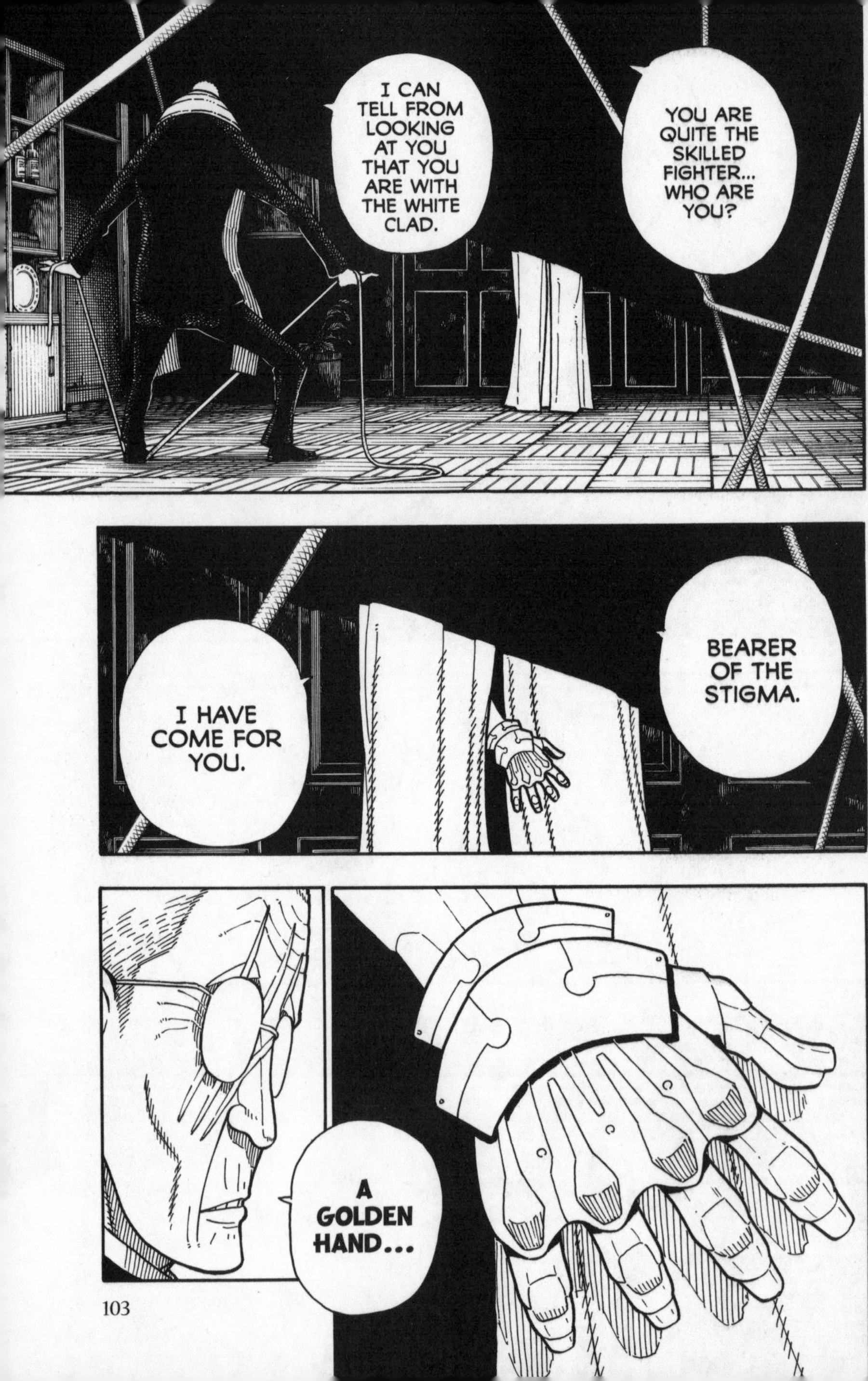
YOU ARE QUITE THE SKILLED FIGHTER... WHO ARE YOU?
I CAN TELL FROM LOOKING AT YOU THAT YOU ARE WITH THE WHITE CLAD.
BEARER OF THE STIGMA.
I HAVE COME FOR YOU.
A GOLDEN HAND...

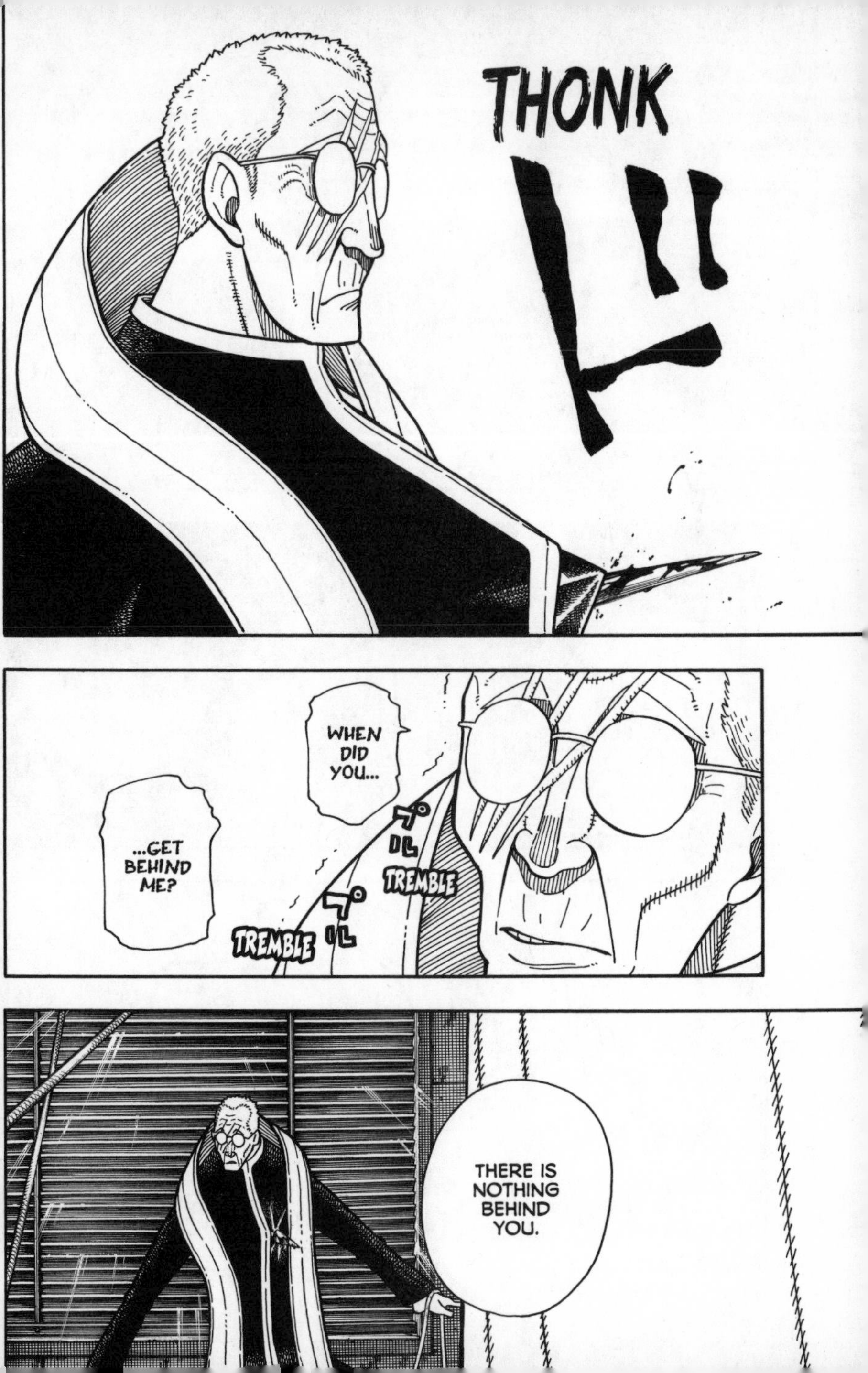
THONK
WHEN DID YOU...
TREMBLE
TREMBLE
...GET BEHIND ME?
THERE IS NOTHING BEHIND YOU.

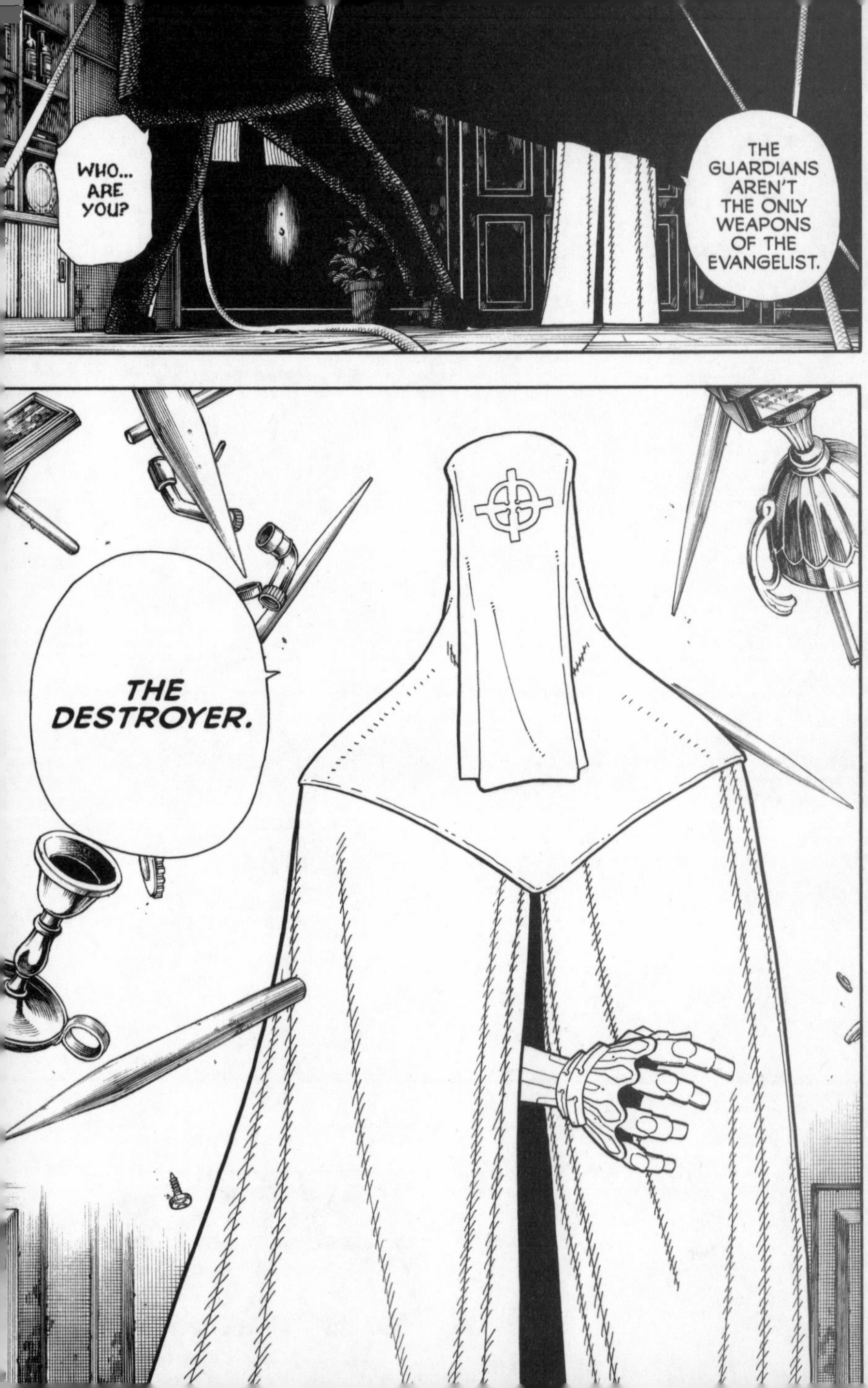
THE GUARDIANS AREN'T THE ONLY WEAPONS OF THE EVANGELIST.
WHO... ARE YOU?
THE DESTROYER.

FIRE FORCE

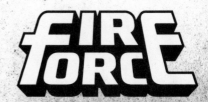

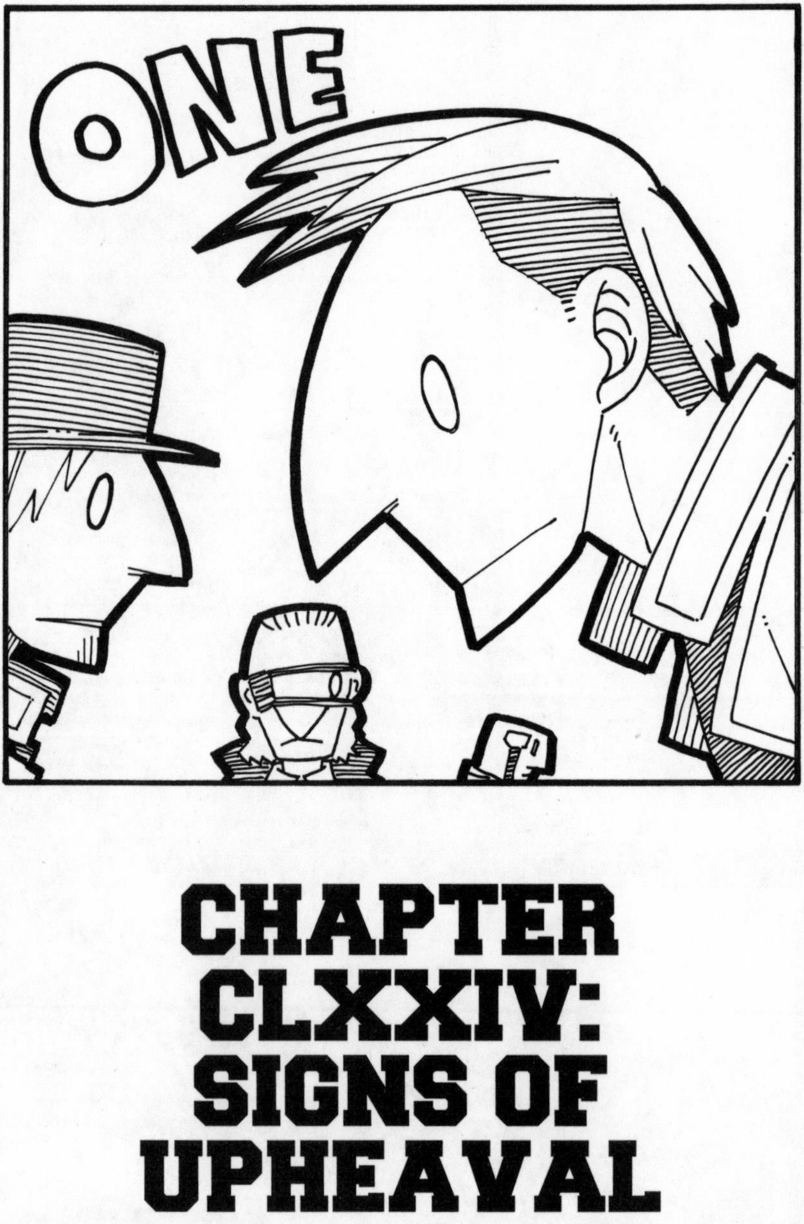
ONE

CHAPTER CLXXIV: SIGNS OF UPHEAVAL

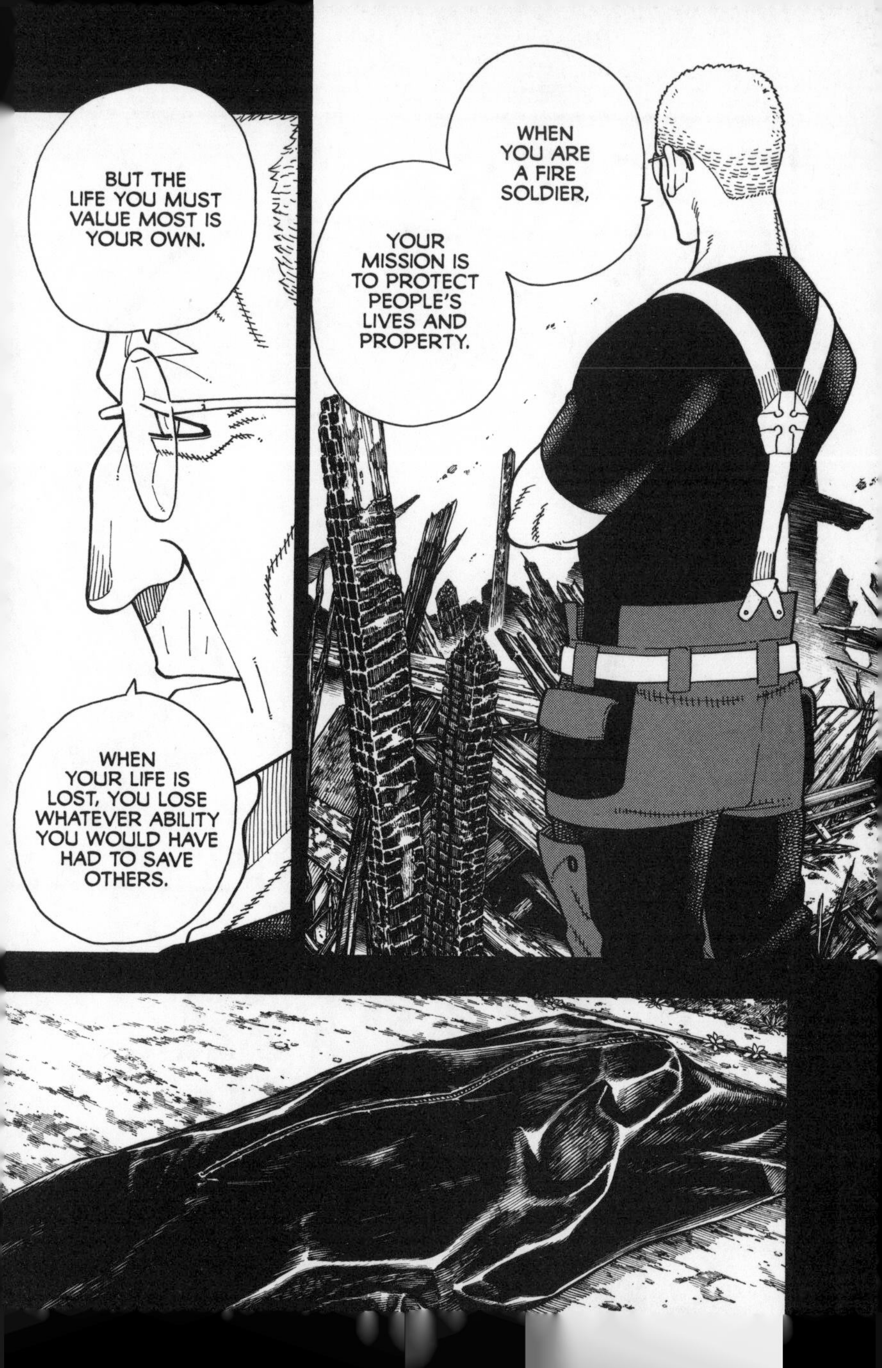
WHEN YOU ARE A FIRE SOLDIER,
YOUR MISSION IS TO PROTECT PEOPLE'S LIVES AND PROPERTY.
BUT THE LIFE YOU MUST VALUE MOST IS YOUR OWN.
WHEN YOUR LIFE IS LOST, YOU LOSE WHATEVER ABILITY YOU WOULD HAVE HAD TO SAVE OTHERS.

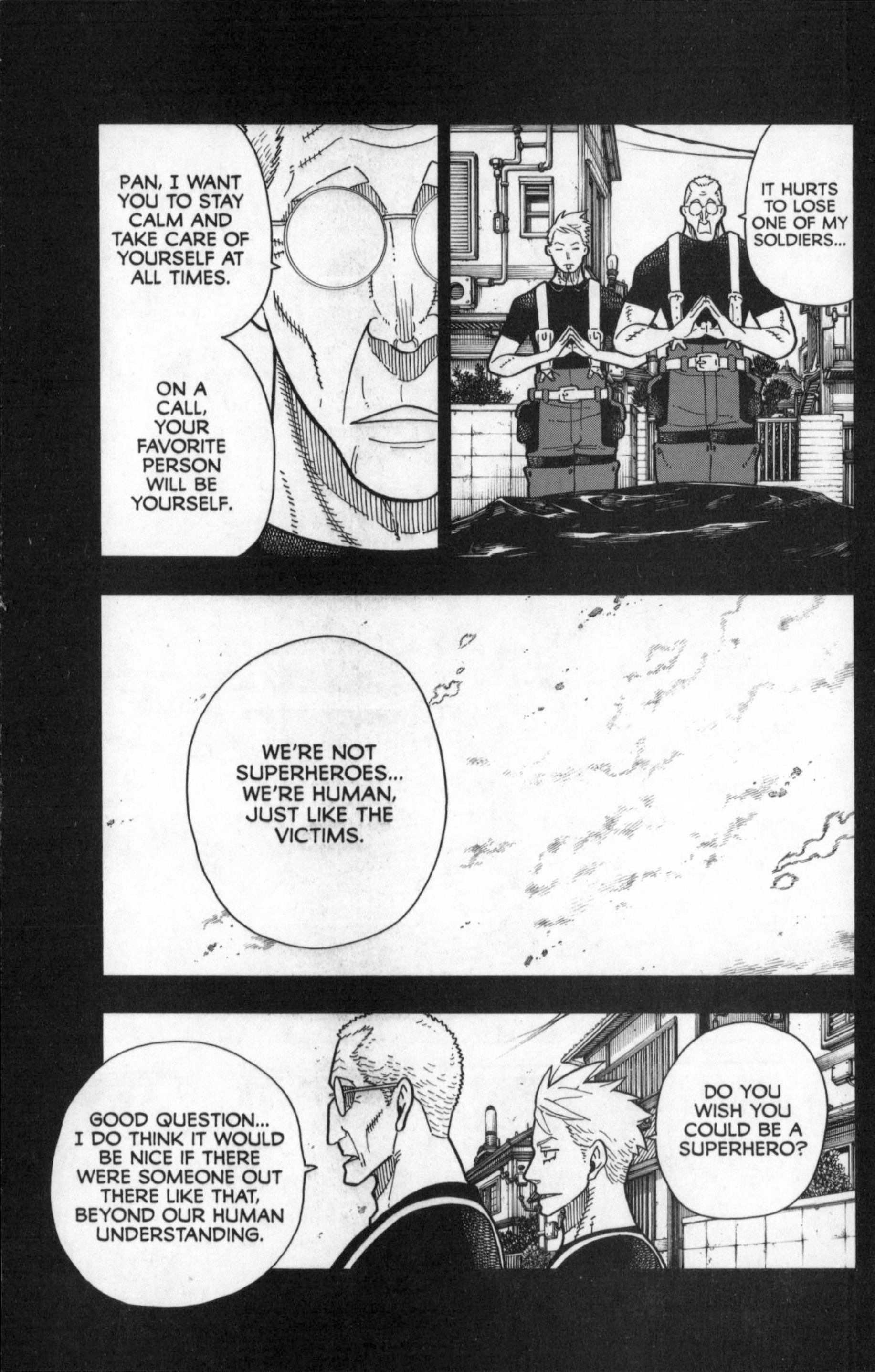
IT HURTS TO LOSE ONE OF MY SOLDIERS...
PAN, I WANT YOU TO STAY CALM AND TAKE CARE OF YOURSELF AT ALL TIMES.
ON A CALL, YOUR FAVORITE PERSON WILL BE YOURSELF.
WE'RE NOT SUPERHEROES... WE'RE HUMAN, JUST LIKE THE VICTIMS.
DO YOU WISH YOU COULD BE A SUPERHERO?
GOOD QUESTION... I DO THINK IT WOULD BE NICE IF THERE WERE SOMEONE OUT THERE LIKE THAT, BEYOND OUR HUMAN UNDERSTANDING.

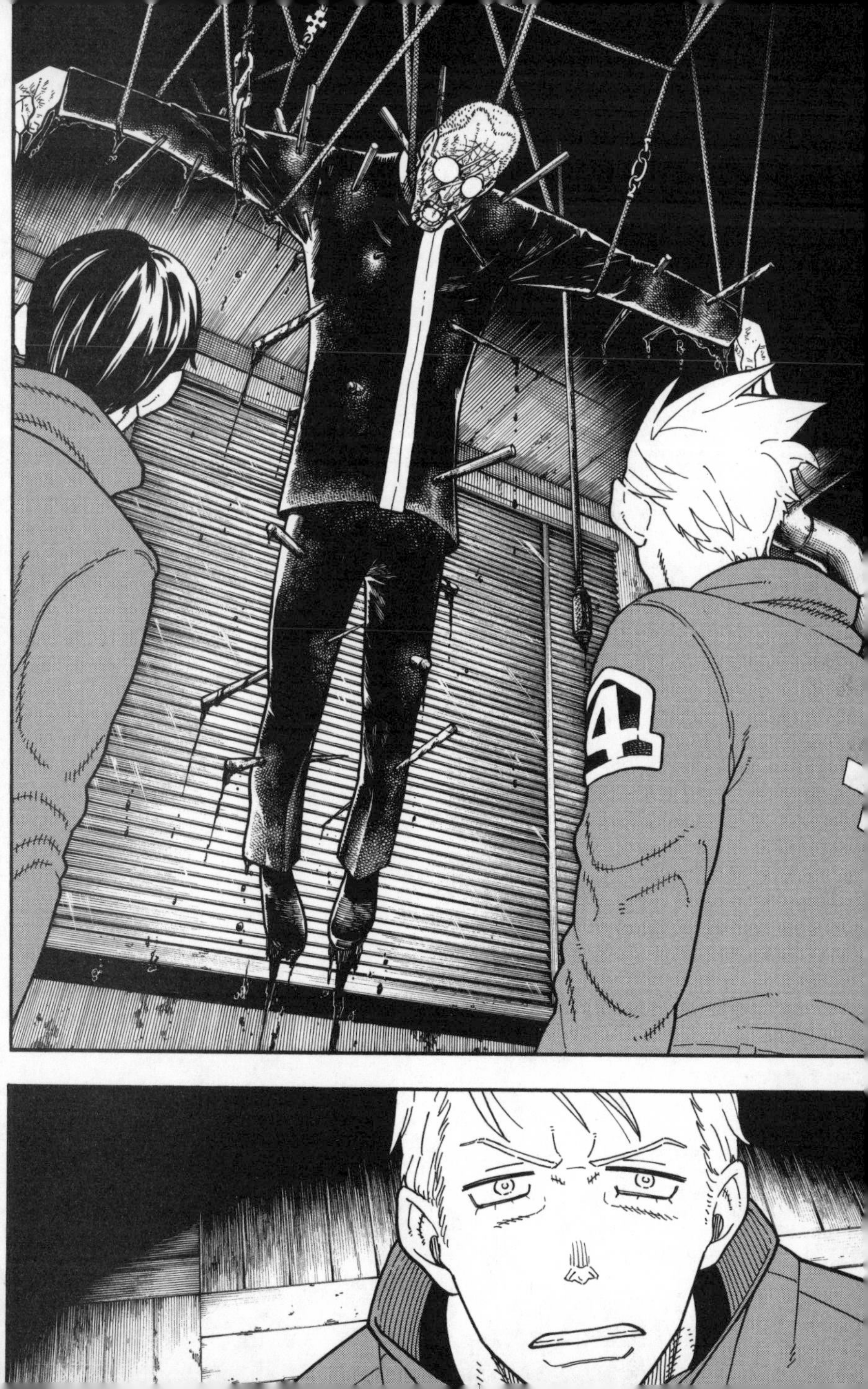

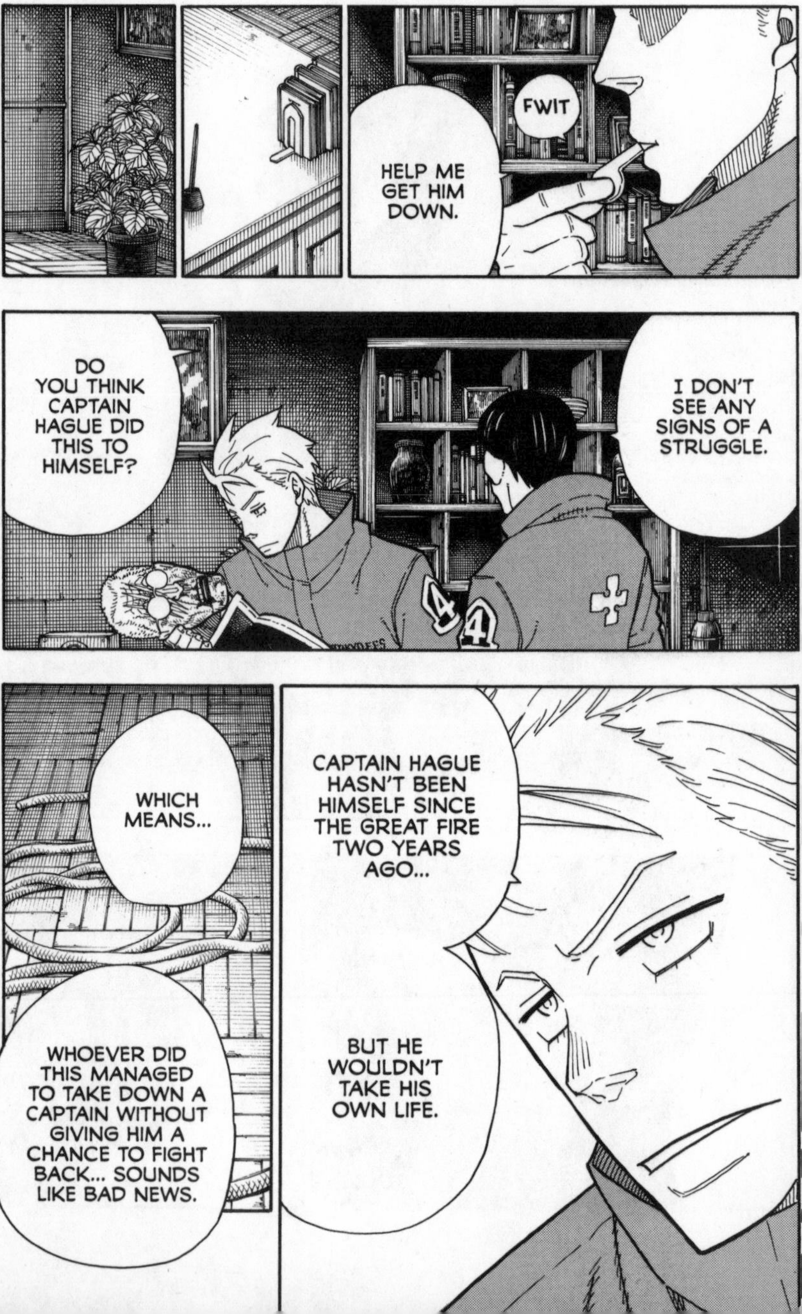
FWIT
HELP ME GET HIM DOWN.
I DON'T SEE ANY SIGNS OF A STRUGGLE.
DO YOU THINK CAPTAIN HAGUE DID THIS TO HIMSELF?
CAPTAIN HAGUE HASN'T BEEN HIMSELF SINCE THE GREAT FIRE TWO YEARS AGO...
BUT HE WOULDN'T TAKE HIS OWN LIFE.
WHICH MEANS...
WHOEVER DID THIS MANAGED TO TAKE DOWN A CAPTAIN WITHOUT GIVING HIM A CHANCE TO FIGHT BACK... SOUNDS LIKE BAD NEWS.

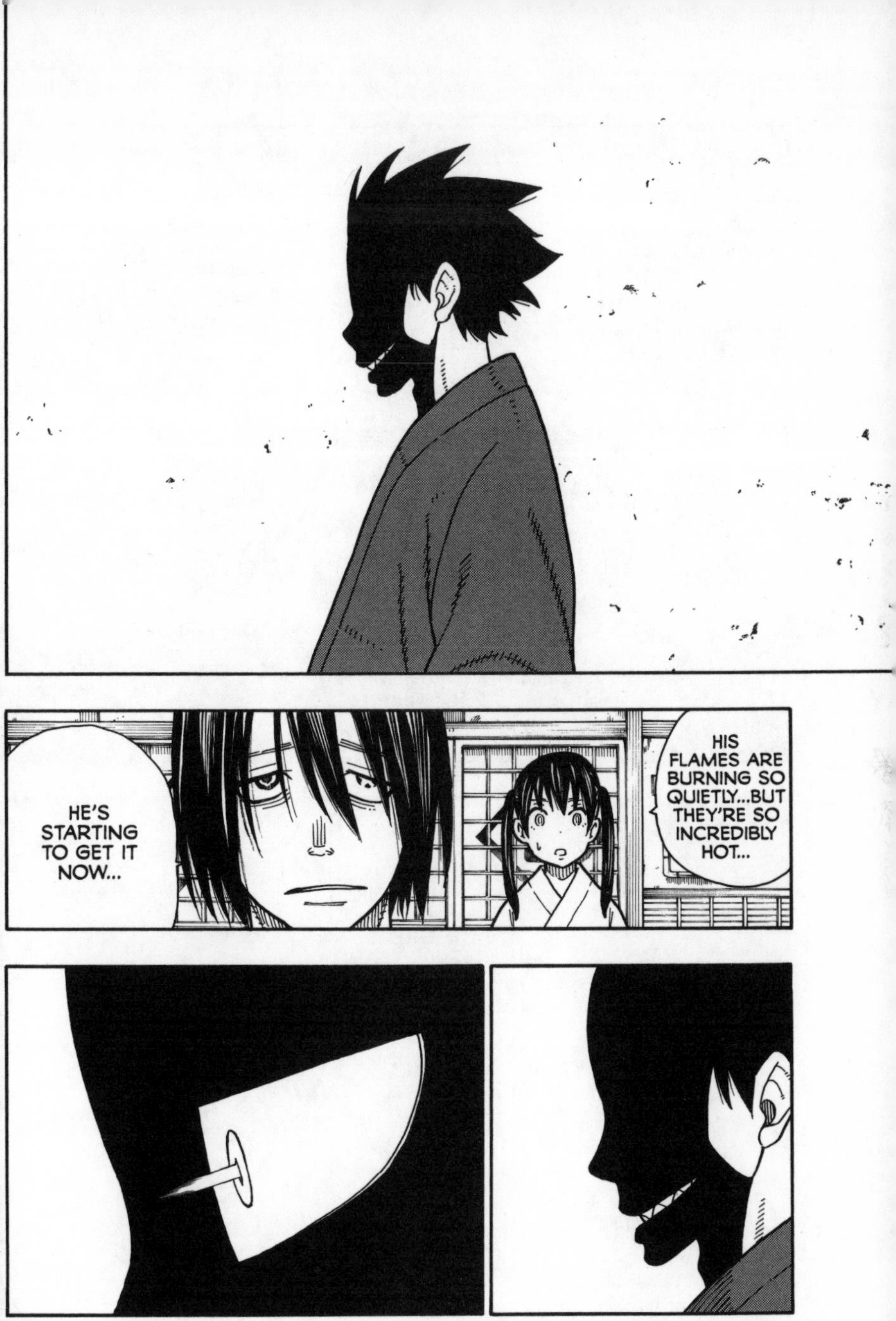
HIS FLAMES ARE BURNING SO QUIETLY...BUT THEY'RE SO INCREDIBLY HOT...
HE'S STARTING TO GET IT NOW...

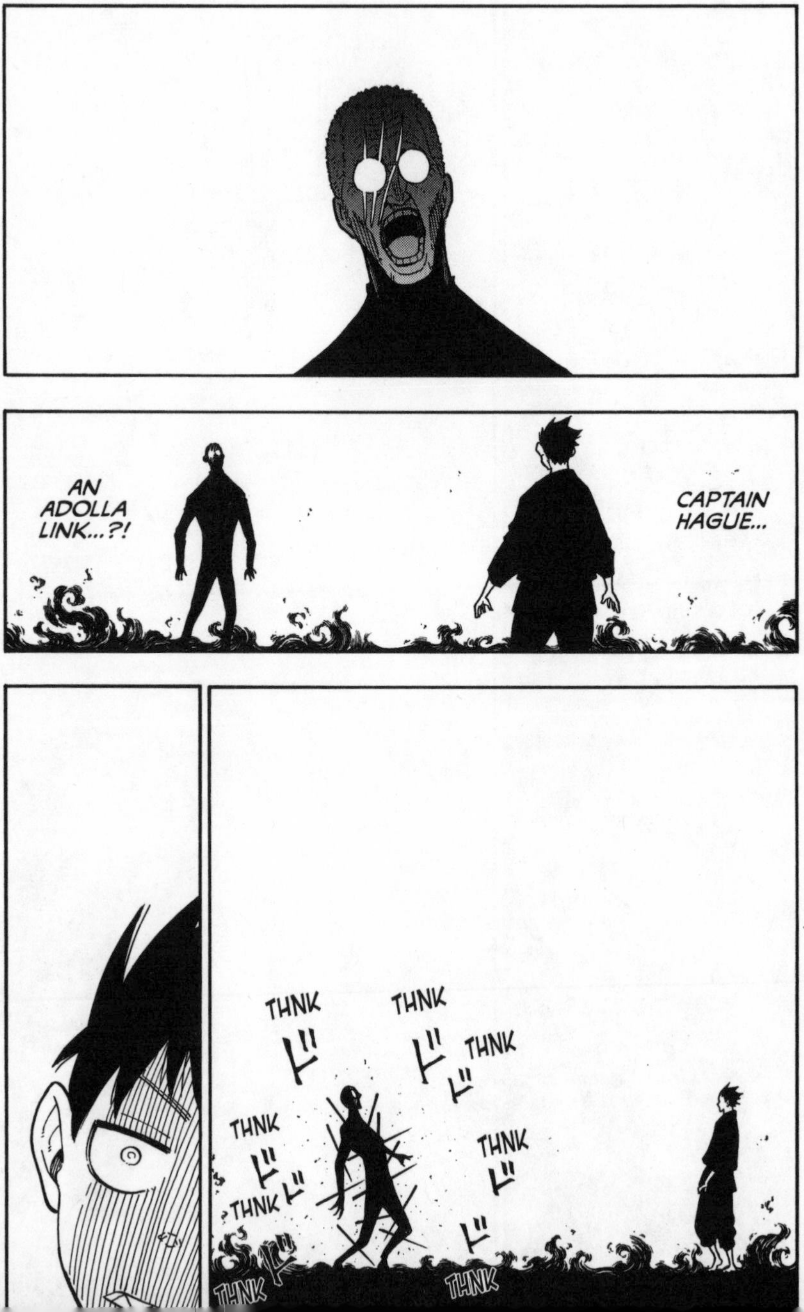
CAPTAIN HAGUE...
AN ADOLLA LINK...?!
THNK
ド
THNK
ド
THNK
ド
THNK
ド
ド
THNK
ド
THNK
ド
THNK
ド
THNK
THNK

RATTLE
カタ
カタ
RATTLE
RATTLE
カタ
カタ
RATTLE
NOT YET.
NOT YET.
NOT YET.
UH
UH
UH
UH
UH
UH
UH

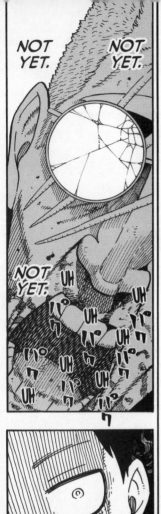

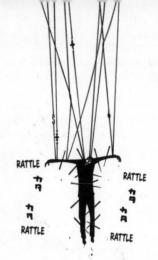

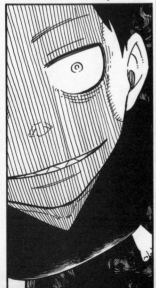

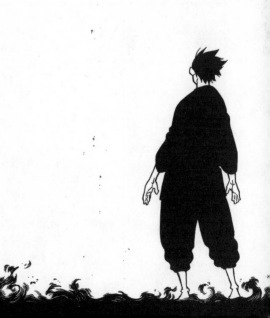

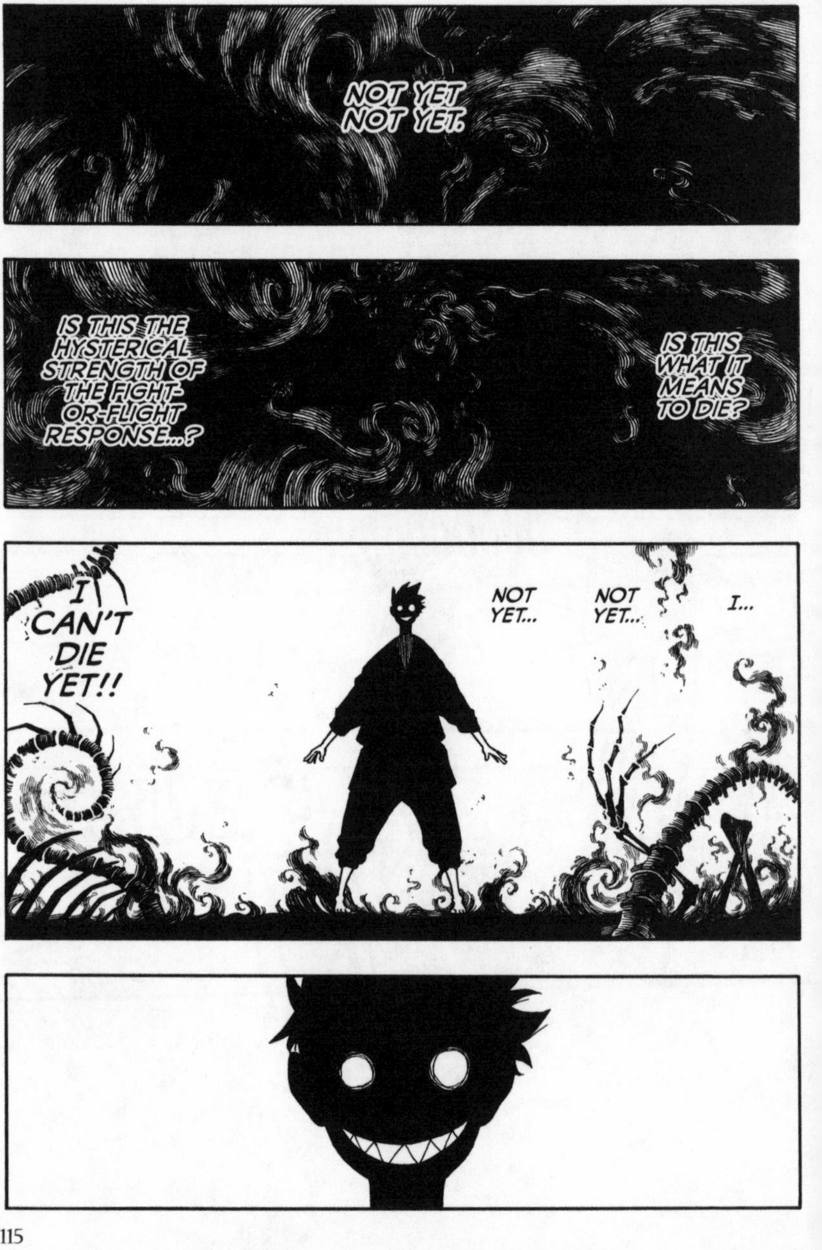
NOT YET NOT YET.
IS THIS WHAT IT MEANS TO DIE?
IS THIS THE HYSTERICAL STRENGTH OF THE FIGHT-OR-FLIGHT RESPONSE...?
I...
NOT YET...
NOT YET...
I CAN'T DIE YET!!

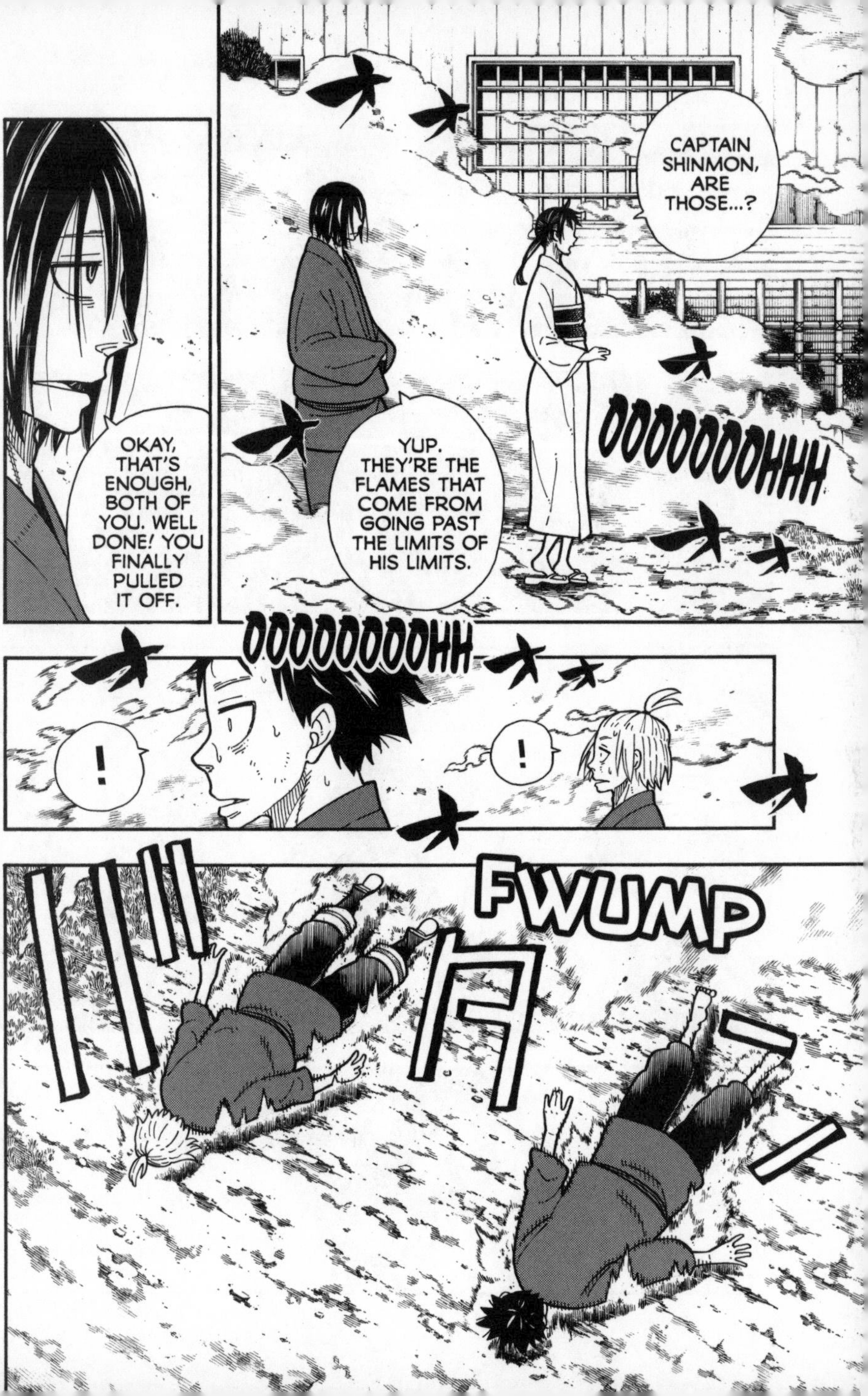
CAPTAIN SHINMON, ARE THOSE...?
OOOOOOOHHH
YUP. THEY'RE THE FLAMES THAT COME FROM GOING PAST THE LIMITS OF HIS LIMITS.
OKAY, THAT'S ENOUGH, BOTH OF YOU. WELL DONE! YOU FINALLY PULLED IT OFF.
OOOOOOOOHH
!
!
FWUMP

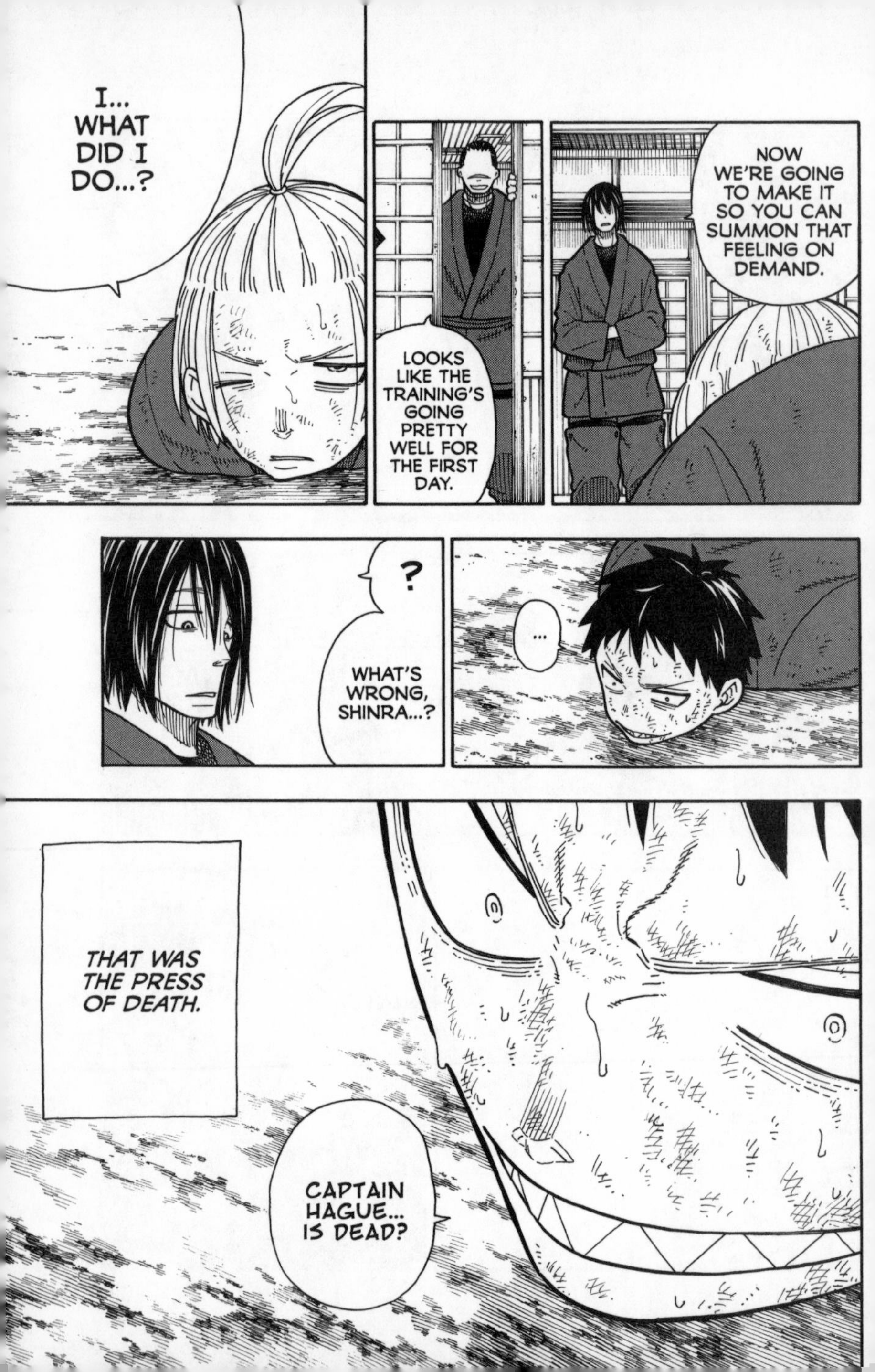
NOW WE'RE GOING TO MAKE IT SO YOU CAN SUMMON THAT FEELING ON DEMAND.
LOOKS LIKE THE TRAINING'S GOING PRETTY WELL FOR THE FIRST DAY.
I... WHAT DID I DO...?
...
?
WHAT'S WRONG, SHINRA...?
THAT WAS THE PRESS OF DEATH.
CAPTAIN HAGUE... IS DEAD?

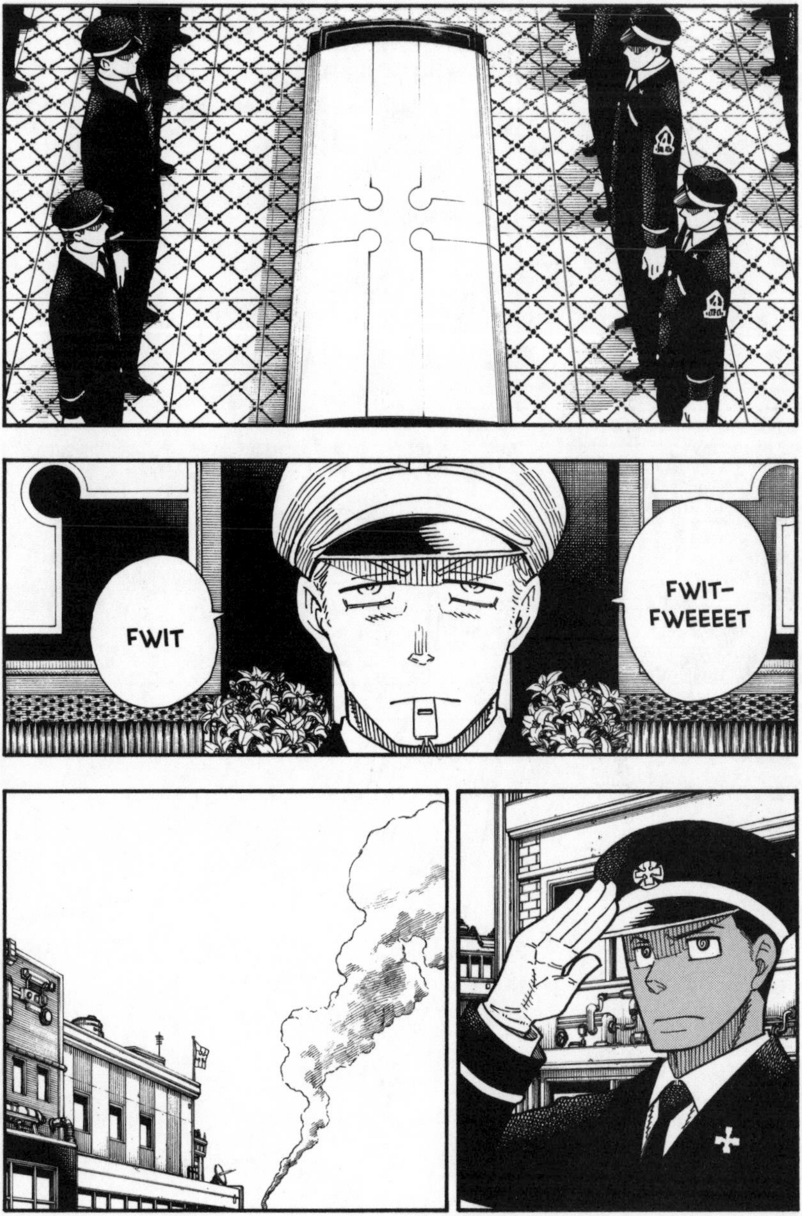
FWIT-
FWEEEET
FWIT

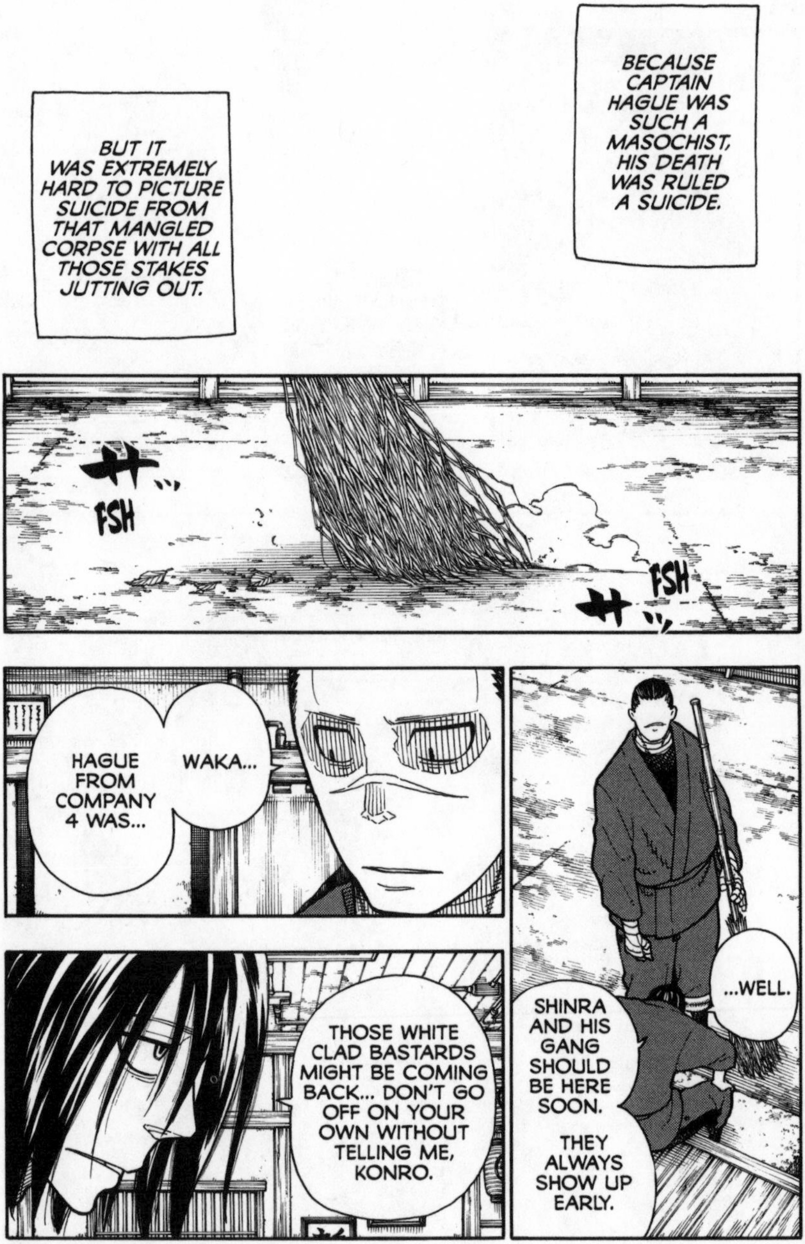
BECAUSE CAPTAIN HAGUE WAS SUCH A MASOCHIST, HIS DEATH WAS RULED A SUICIDE.
BUT IT WAS EXTREMELY HARD TO PICTURE SUICIDE FROM THAT MANGLED CORPSE WITH ALL THOSE STAKES JUTTING OUT.
FSH
FSH
...WELL.
SHINRA AND HIS GANG SHOULD BE HERE SOON.
THEY ALWAYS SHOW UP EARLY.
WAKA...
HAGUE FROM COMPANY 4 WAS...
THOSE WHITE CLAD BASTARDS MIGHT BE COMING BACK... DON'T GO OFF ON YOUR OWN WITHOUT TELLING ME, KONRO.

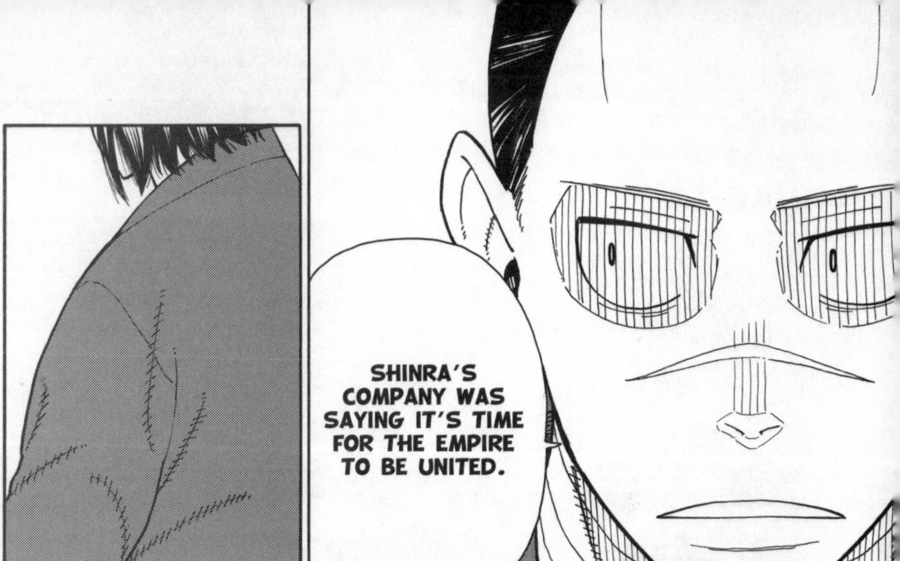
SHINRA'S COMPANY WAS SAYING IT'S TIME FOR THE EMPIRE TO BE UNITED.

Lantern: Seven. Sign: Beware of Fire.

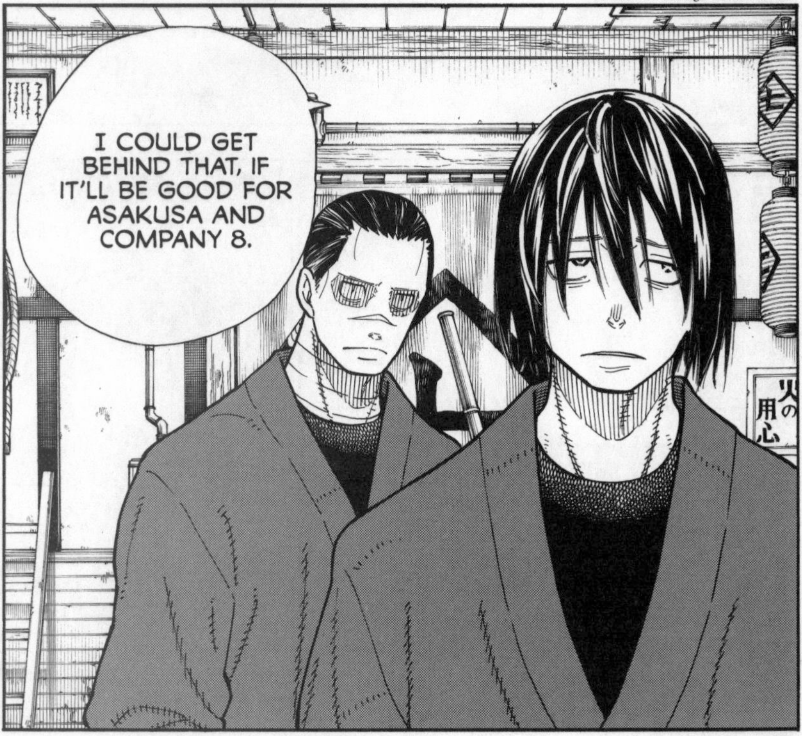
I COULD GET BEHIND THAT, IF IT'LL BE GOOD FOR ASAKUSA AND COMPANY 8.
火の用心

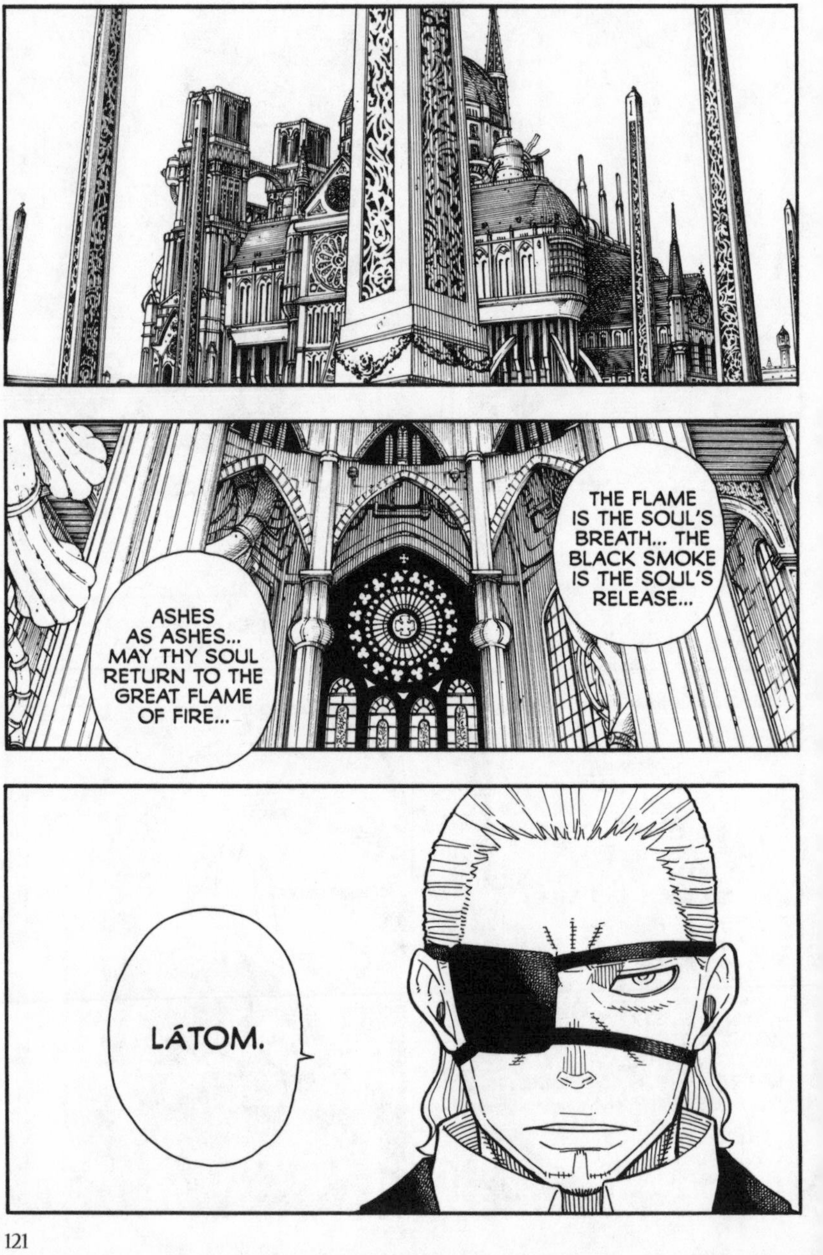
THE FLAME IS THE SOUL'S BREATH... THE BLACK SMOKE IS THE SOUL'S RELEASE...
ASHES AS ASHES... MAY THY SOUL RETURN TO THE GREAT FLAME OF FIRE...
LÁTOM.

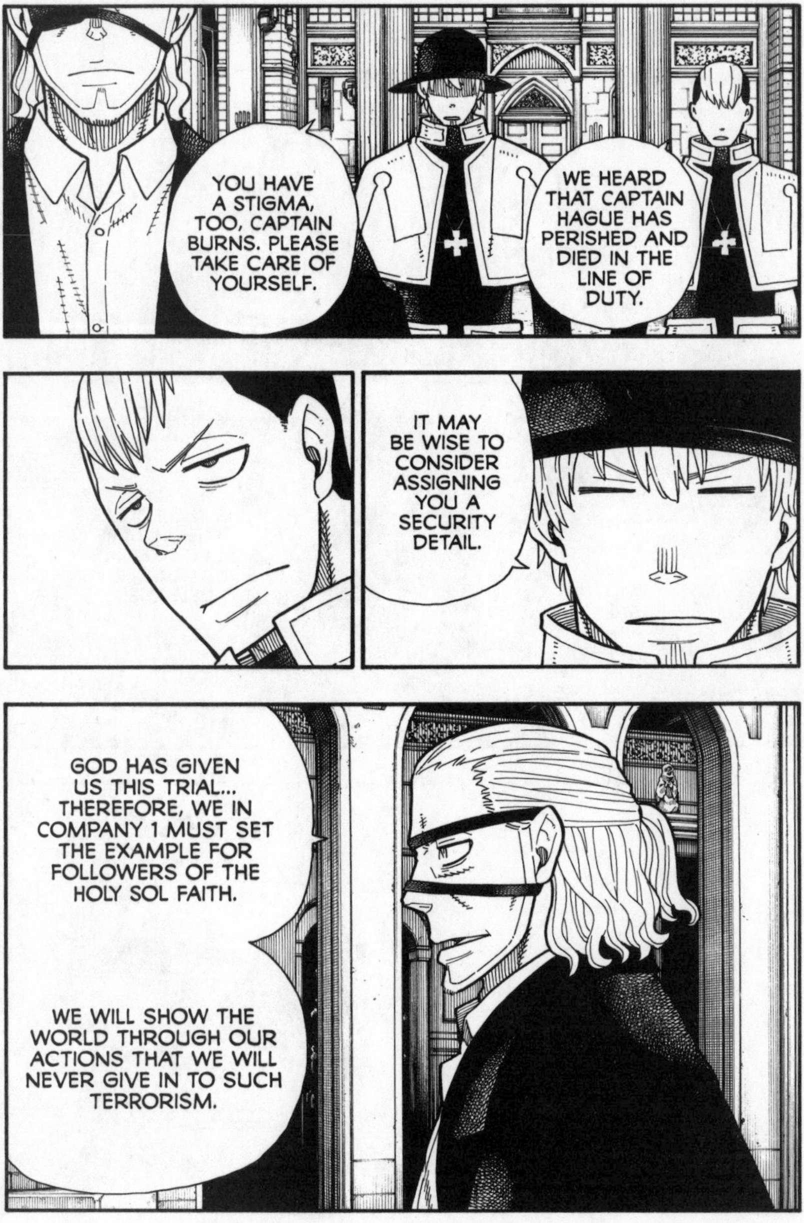
WE HEARD THAT CAPTAIN HAGUE HAS PERISHED AND DIED IN THE LINE OF DUTY.
YOU HAVE A STIGMA, TOO, CAPTAIN BURNS. PLEASE TAKE CARE OF YOURSELF.
IT MAY BE WISE TO CONSIDER ASSIGNING YOU A SECURITY DETAIL.
GOD HAS GIVEN US THIS TRIAL... THEREFORE, WE IN COMPANY 1 MUST SET THE EXAMPLE FOR FOLLOWERS OF THE HOLY SOL FAITH.
WE WILL SHOW THE WORLD THROUGH OUR ACTIONS THAT WE WILL NEVER GIVE IN TO SUCH TERRORISM.

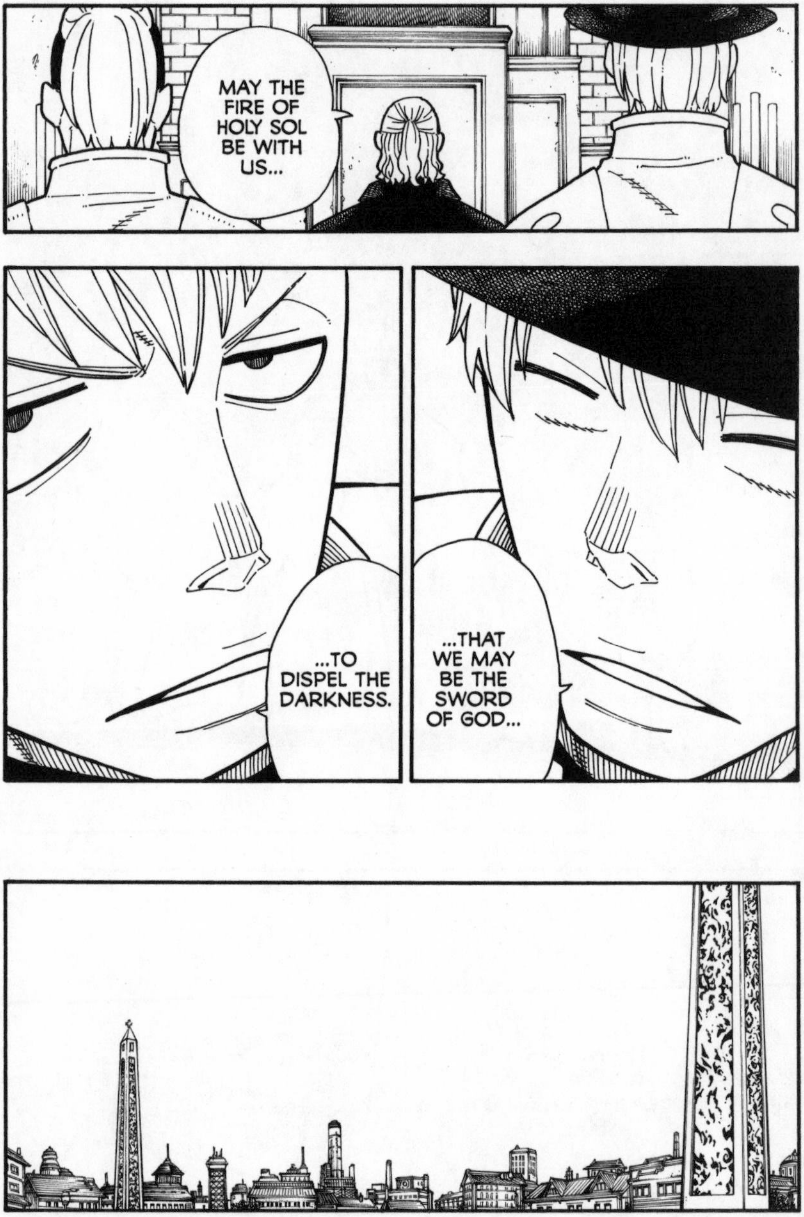
MAY THE FIRE OF HOLY SOL BE WITH US...
...THAT WE MAY BE THE SWORD OF GOD...
...TO DISPEL THE DARKNESS.

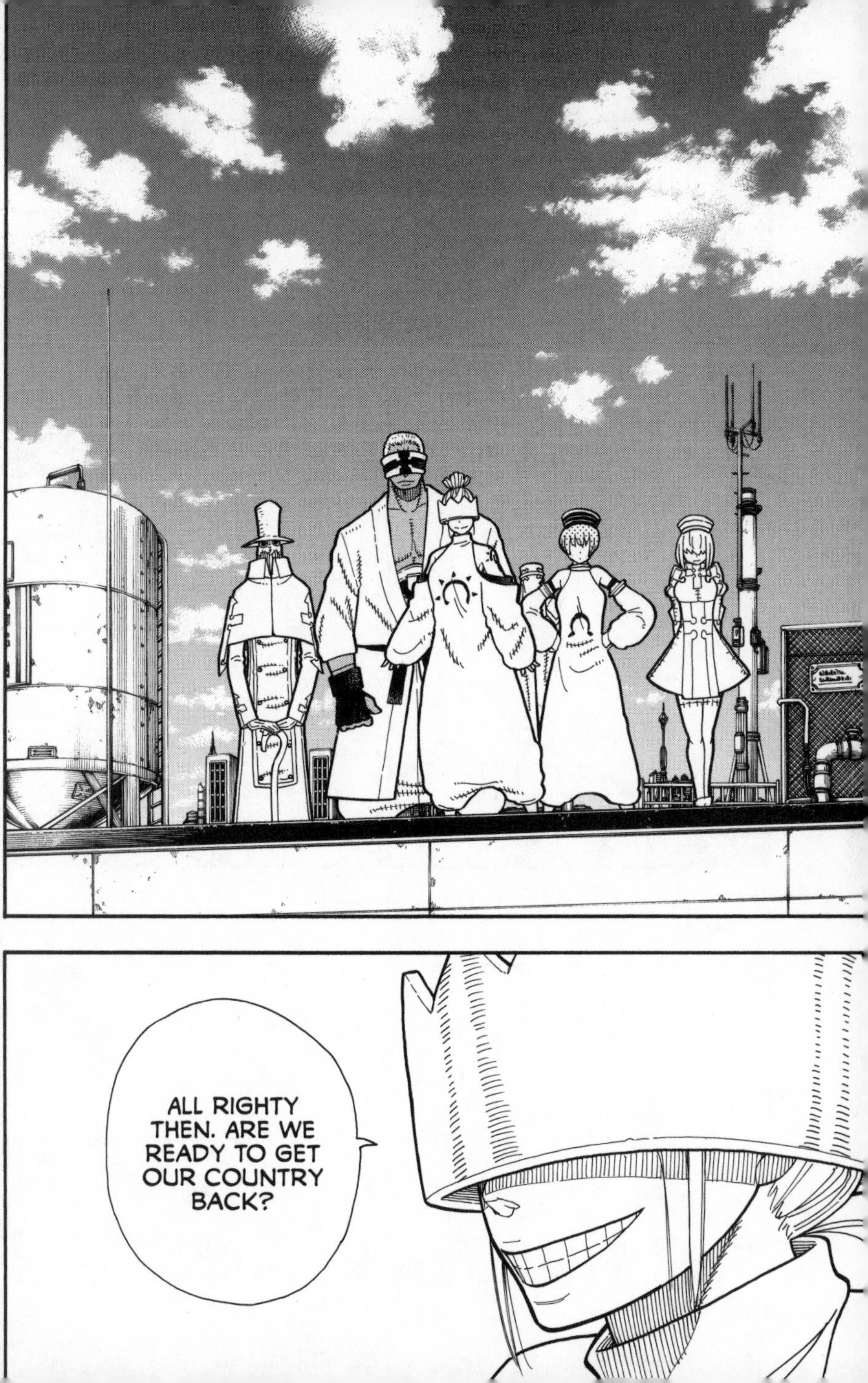
ALL RIGHTY THEN. ARE WE READY TO GET OUR COUNTRY BACK?

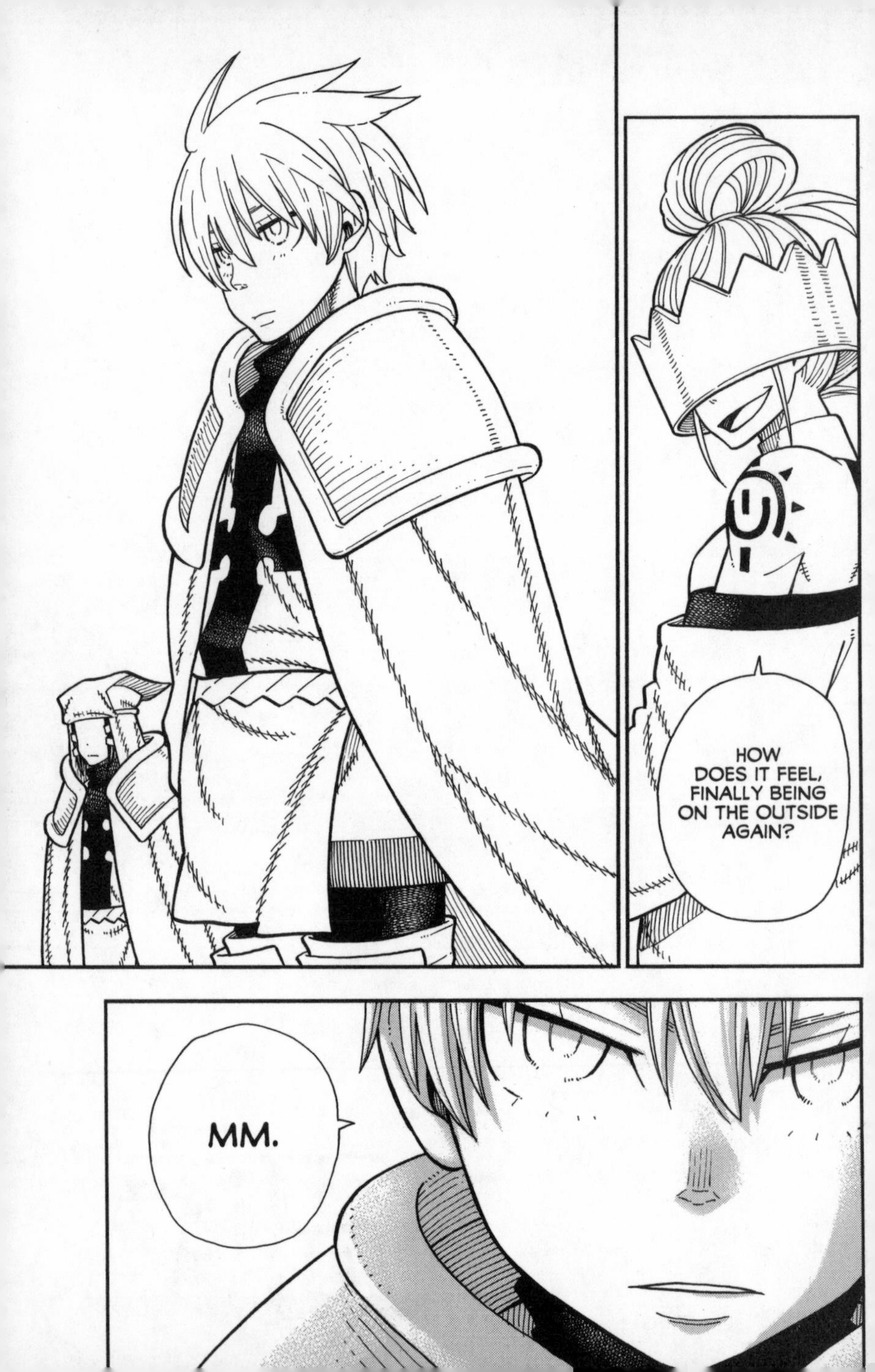
HOW DOES IT FEEL, FINALLY BEING ON THE OUTSIDE AGAIN?
MM.

FIRE FORCE

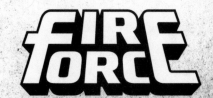

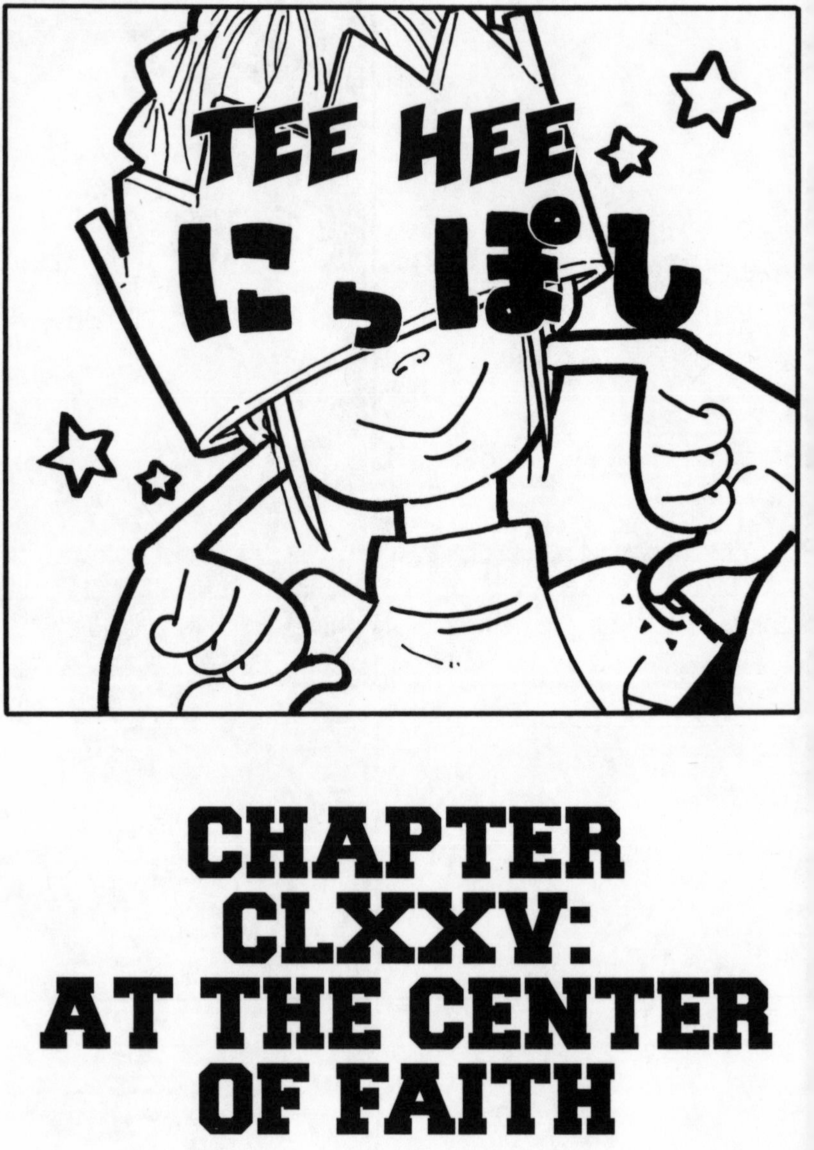
TEE HEE
にっぽし

CHAPTER CLXXV: AT THE CENTER OF FAITH

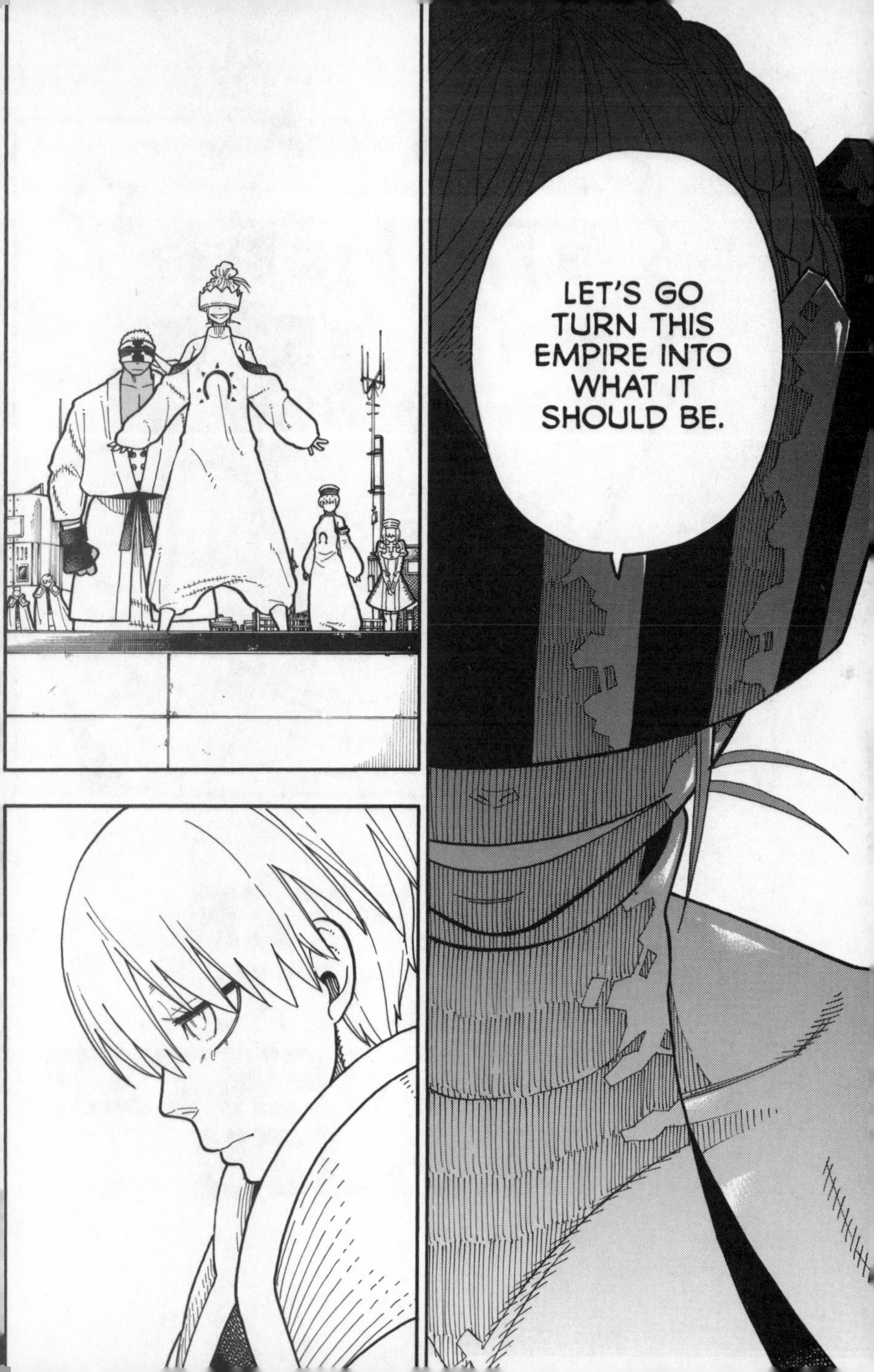
LET'S GO TURN THIS EMPIRE INTO WHAT IT SHOULD BE.

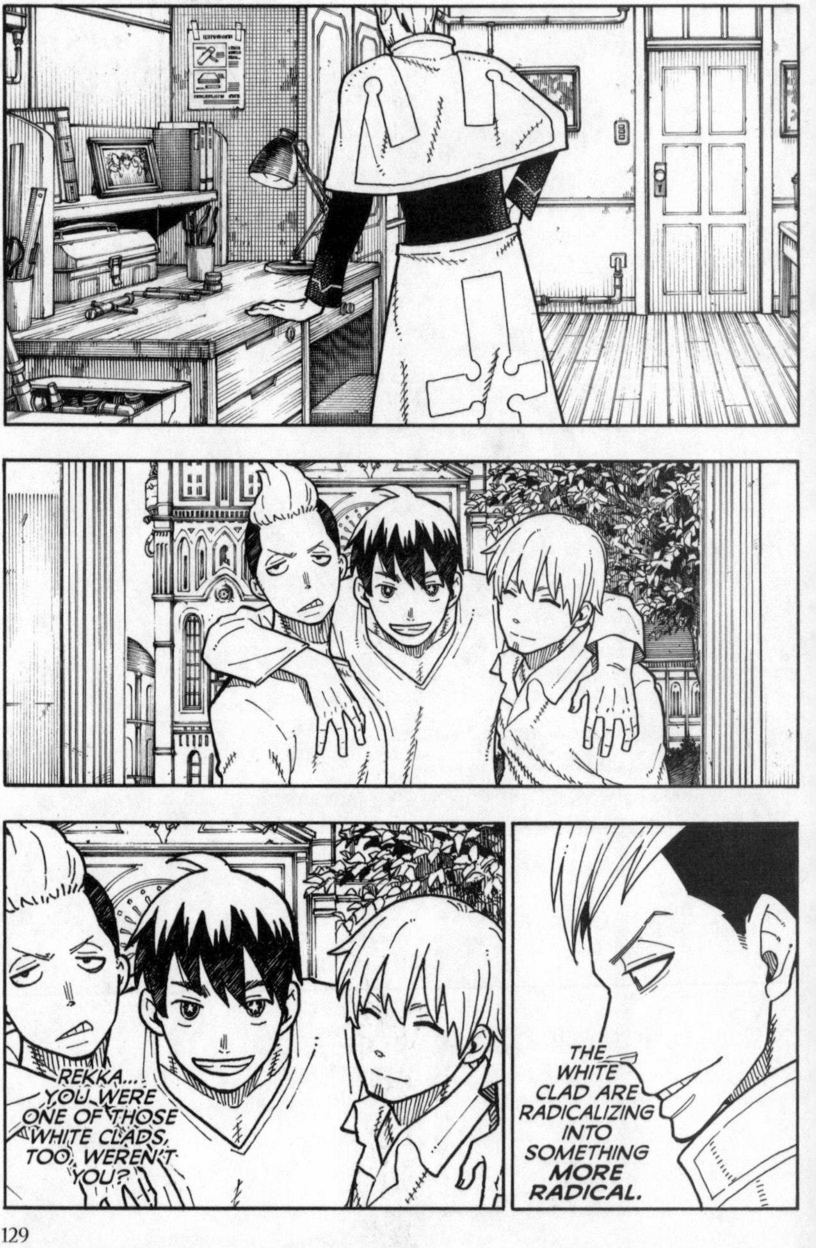
THE WHITE CLAD ARE RADICALIZING INTO SOMETHING MORE RADICAL.
REKKA... YOU WERE ONE OF THOSE WHITE CLADS, TOO, WEREN'T YOU?

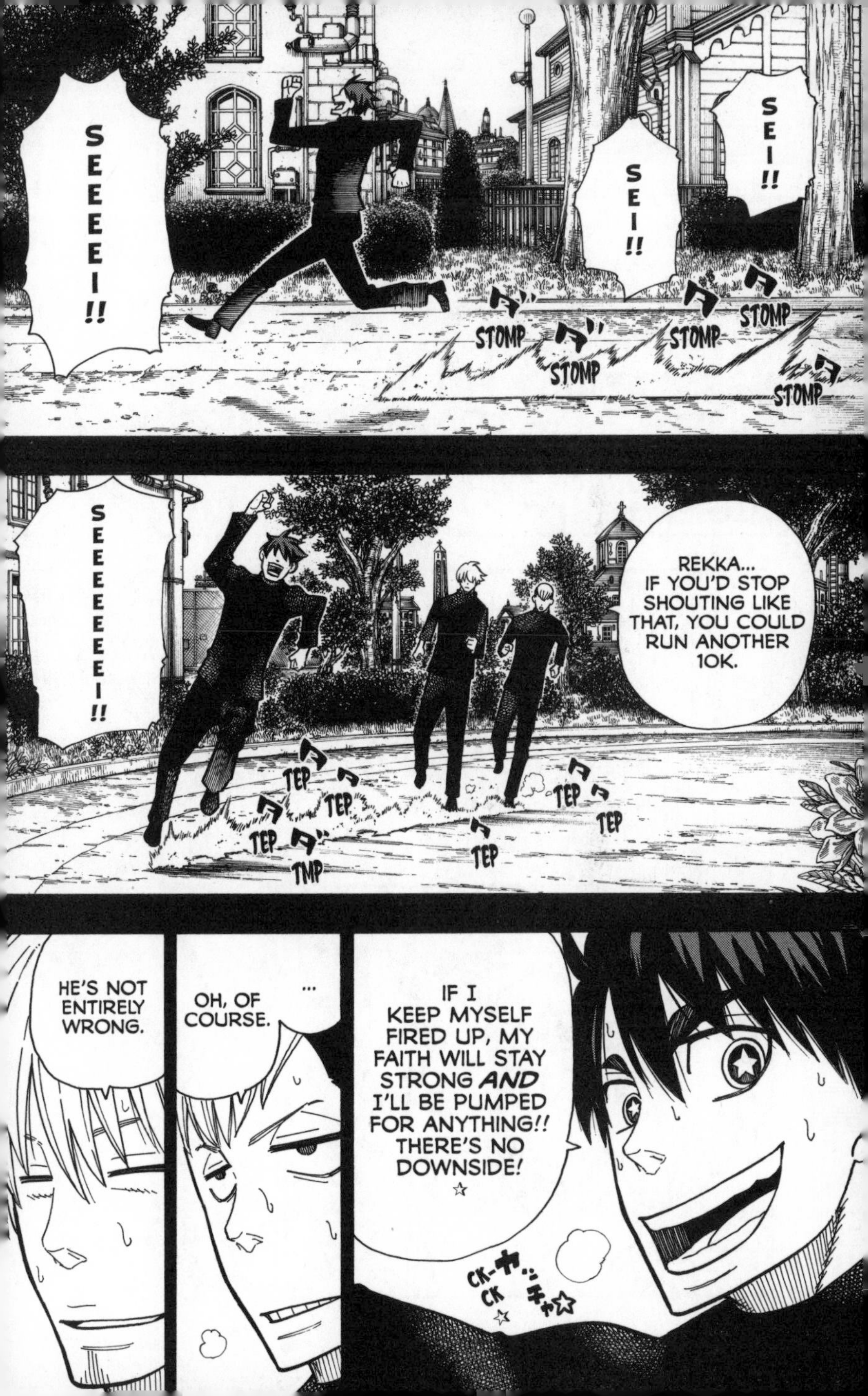
SEI!!
SEI!!
STOMP
STOMP
STOMP
STOMP
STOMP
SEEEEI!!
REKKA... IF YOU'D STOP SHOUTING LIKE THAT, YOU COULD RUN ANOTHER 10K.
TEP
TEP
TEP
TEP
TEP
TEP
TMP
SEEEEEEEI!!
IF I KEEP MYSELF FIRED UP, MY FAITH WILL STAY STRONG *AND* I'LL BE PUMPED FOR ANYTHING!! THERE'S NO DOWNSIDE! ☆
CK-CK ☆
...
OH, OF COURSE.
HE'S NOT ENTIRELY WRONG.

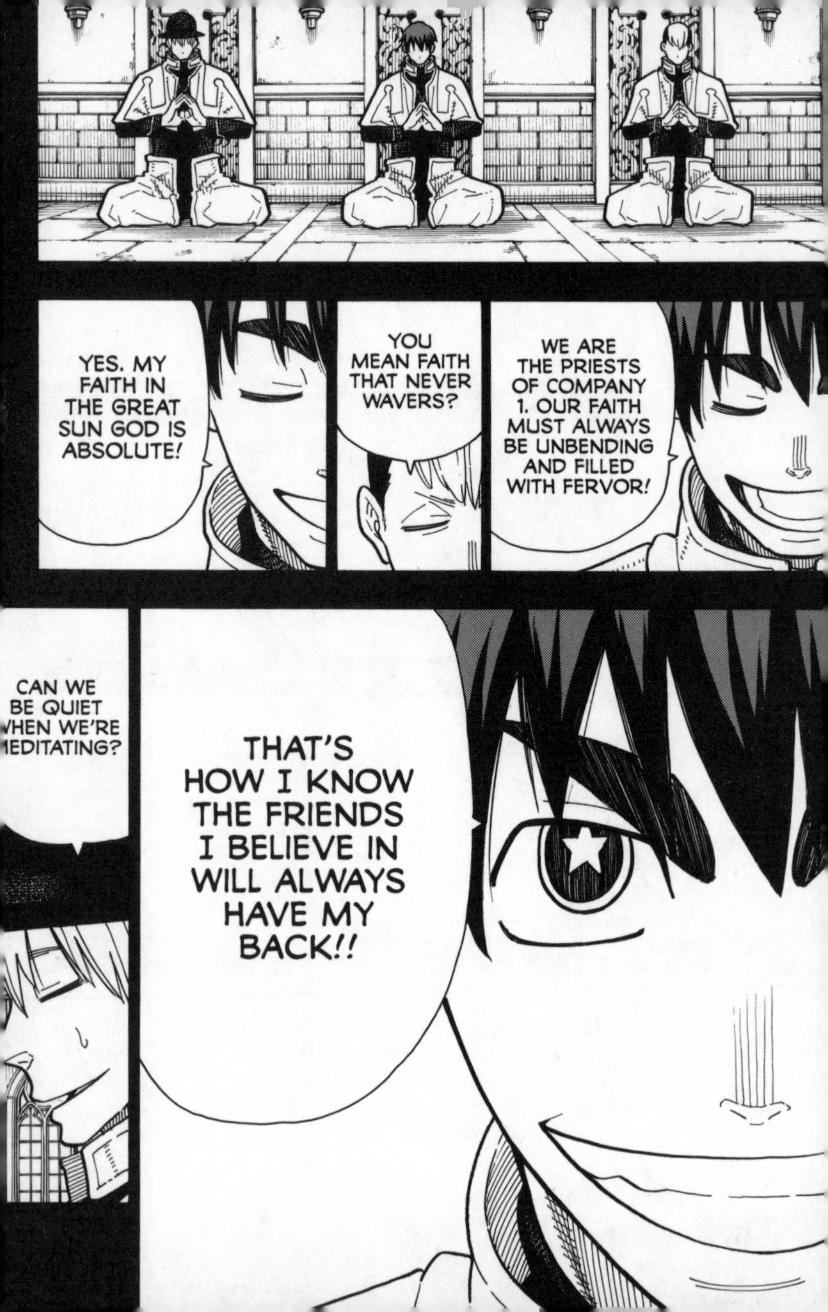
WE ARE THE PRIESTS OF COMPANY 1. OUR FAITH MUST ALWAYS BE UNBENDING AND FILLED WITH FERVOR!
YOU MEAN FAITH THAT NEVER WAVERS?
YES. MY FAITH IN THE GREAT SUN GOD IS ABSOLUTE!
THAT'S HOW I KNOW THE FRIENDS I BELIEVE IN WILL ALWAYS HAVE MY BACK!!
CAN WE BE QUIET HEN WE'RE EDITATING?

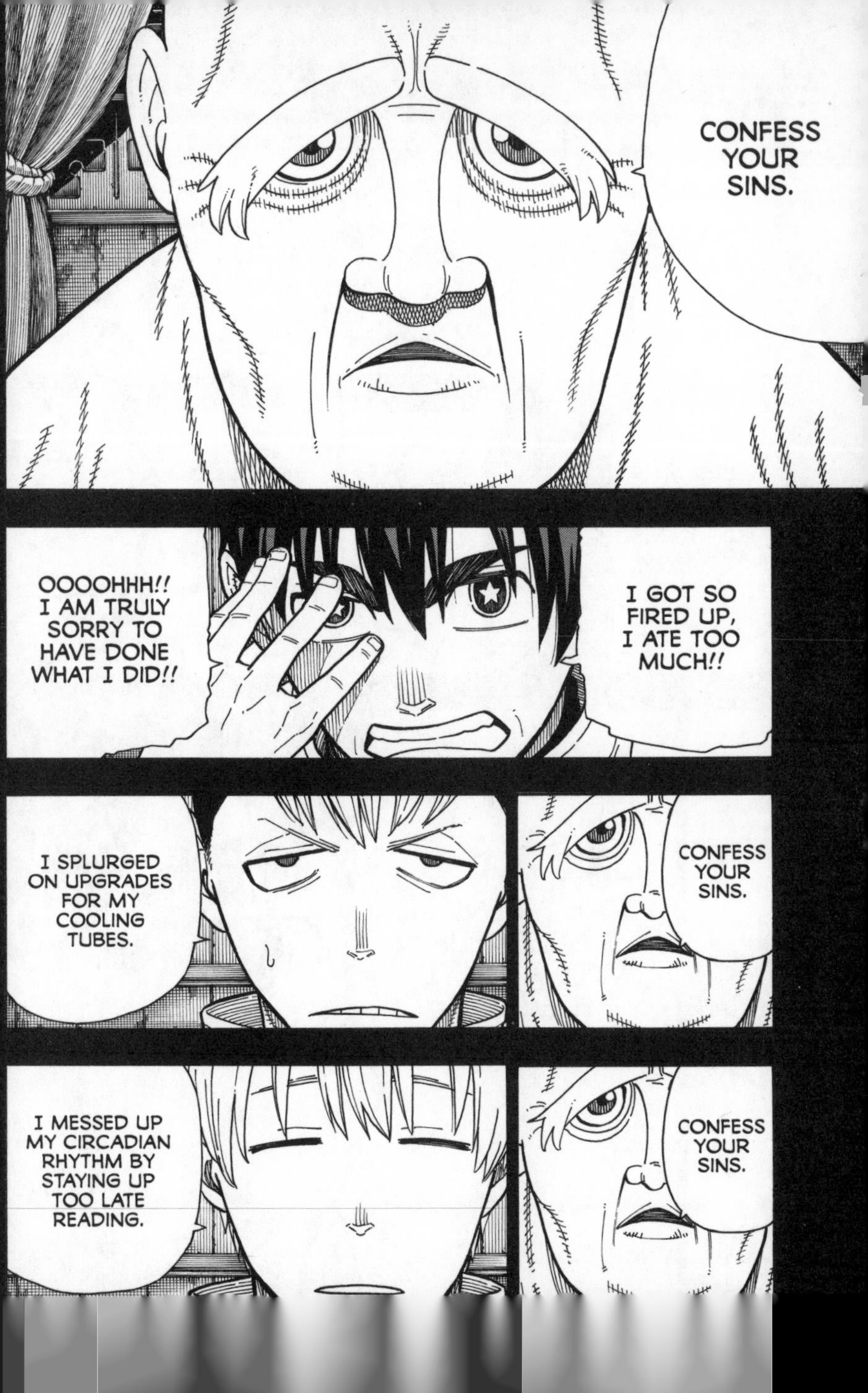
CONFESS YOUR SINS.
I GOT SO FIRED UP, I ATE TOO MUCH!!
OOOOHHH!! I AM TRULY SORRY TO HAVE DONE WHAT I DID!!
CONFESS YOUR SINS.
I SPLURGED ON UPGRADES FOR MY COOLING TUBES.
CONFESS YOUR SINS.
I MESSED UP MY CIRCADIAN RHYTHM BY STAYING UP TOO LATE READING.

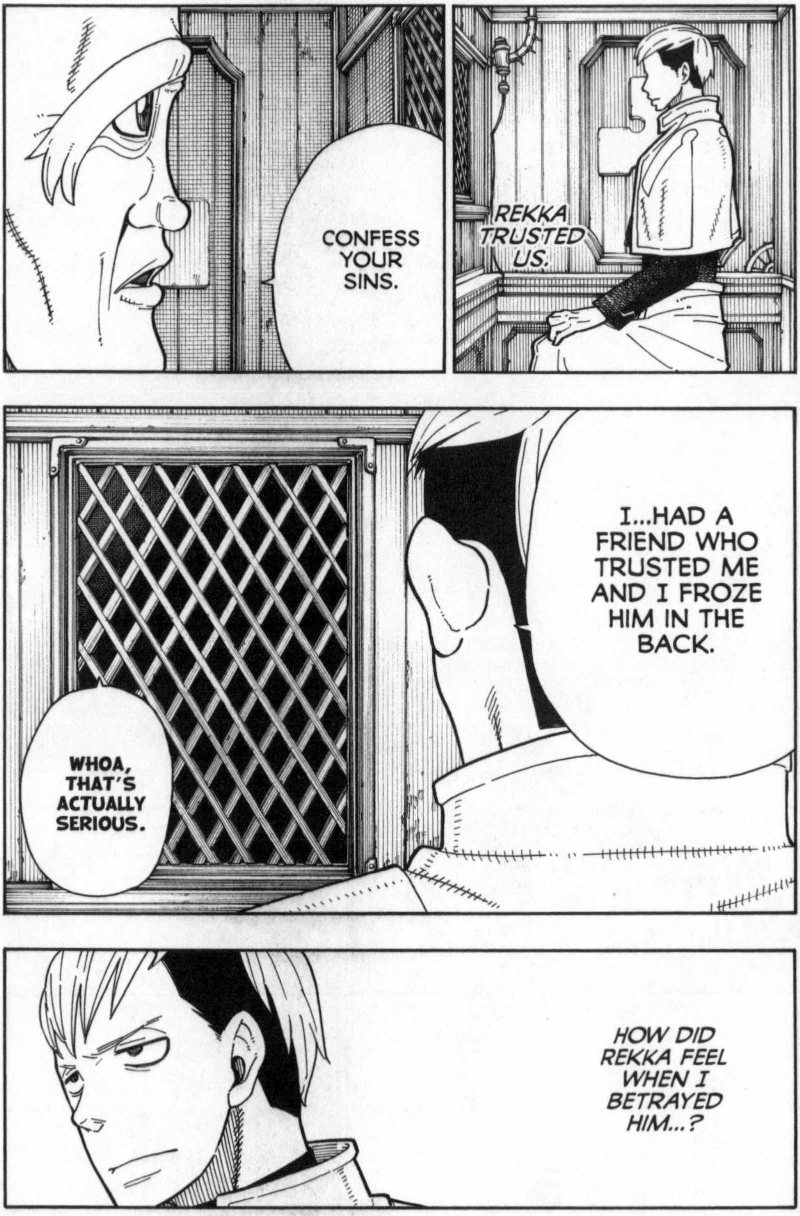
REKKA TRUSTED US.
CONFESS YOUR SINS.
I...HAD A FRIEND WHO TRUSTED ME AND I FROZE HIM IN THE BACK.
WHOA, THAT'S ACTUALLY SERIOUS.
HOW DID REKKA FEEL WHEN I BETRAYED HIM...?

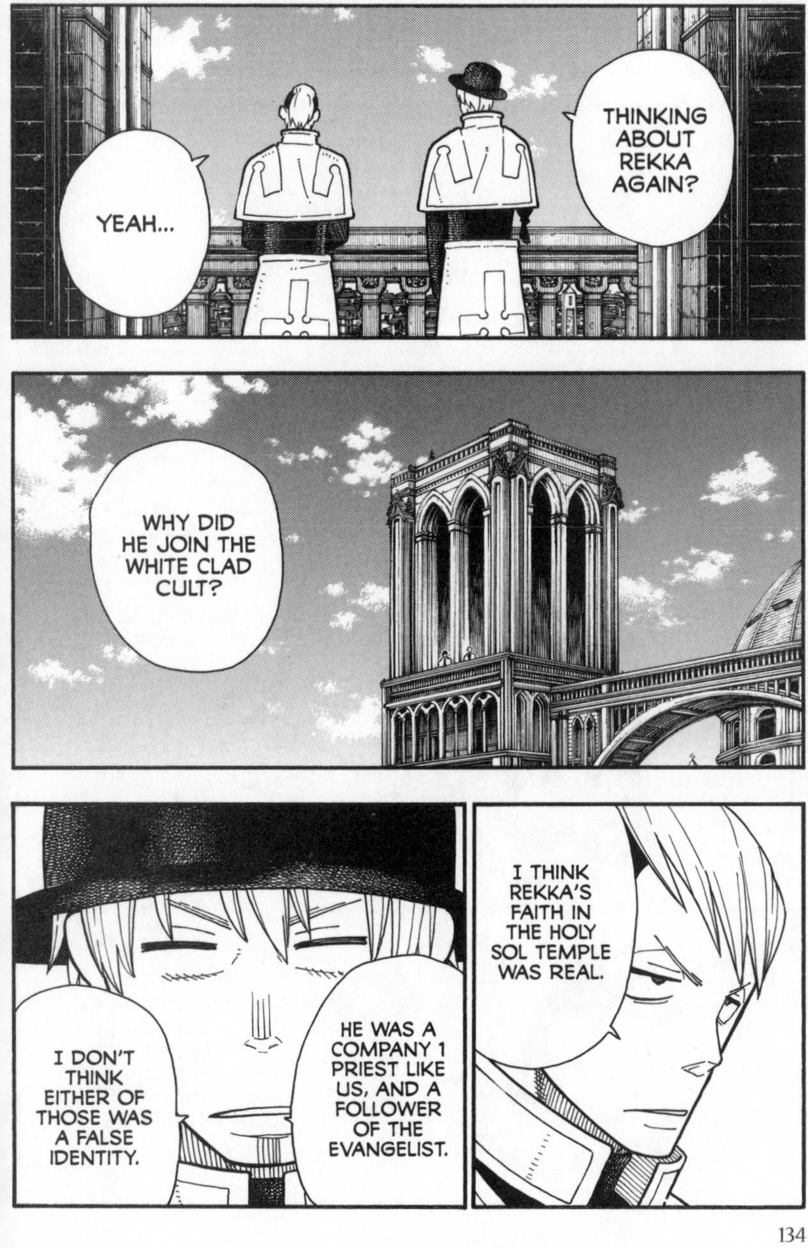
THINKING ABOUT REKKA AGAIN?
YEAH...
WHY DID HE JOIN THE WHITE CLAD CULT?
I THINK REKKA'S FAITH IN THE HOLY SOL TEMPLE WAS REAL.
HE WAS A COMPANY 1 PRIEST LIKE US, AND A FOLLOWER OF THE EVANGELIST.
I DON'T THINK EITHER OF THOSE WAS A FALSE IDENTITY.

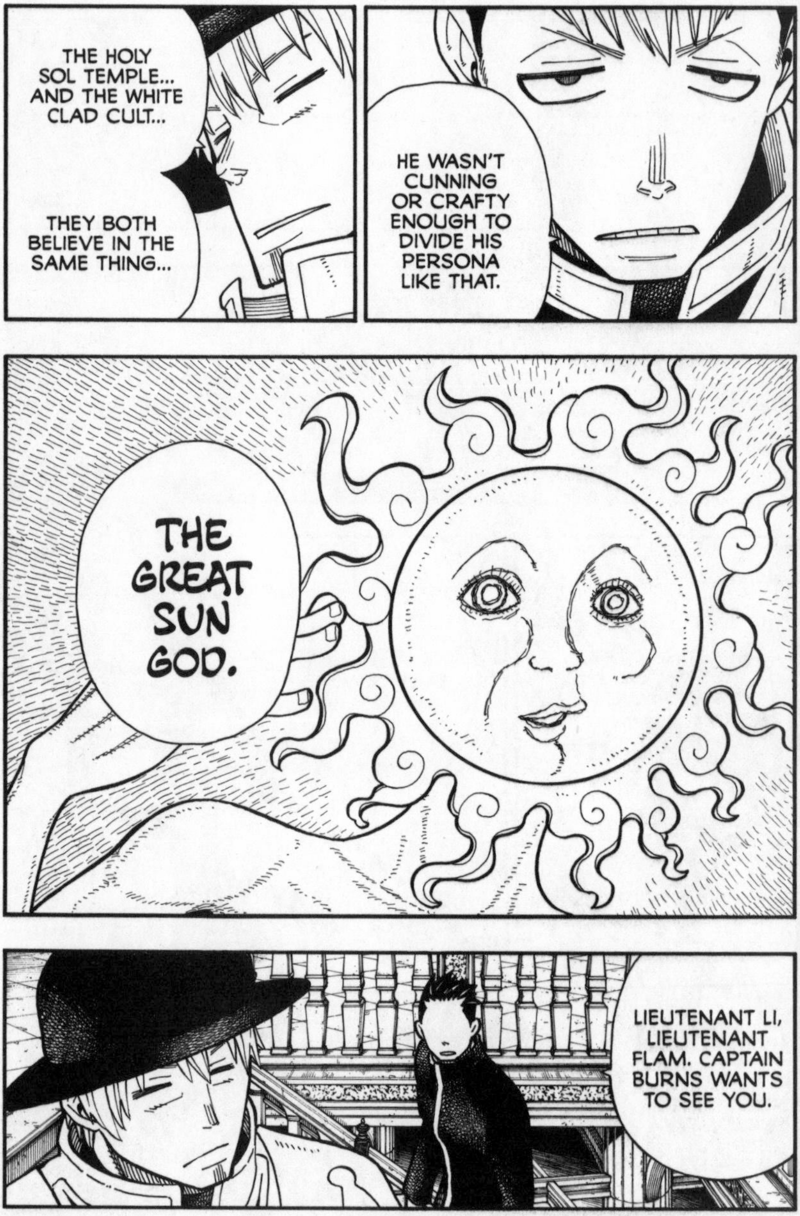
HE WASN'T CUNNING OR CRAFTY ENOUGH TO DIVIDE HIS PERSONA LIKE THAT.
THE HOLY SOL TEMPLE... AND THE WHITE CLAD CULT...
THEY BOTH BELIEVE IN THE SAME THING...
THE GREAT SUN GOD.
LIEUTENANT LI, LIEUTENANT FLAM. CAPTAIN BURNS WANTS TO SEE YOU.

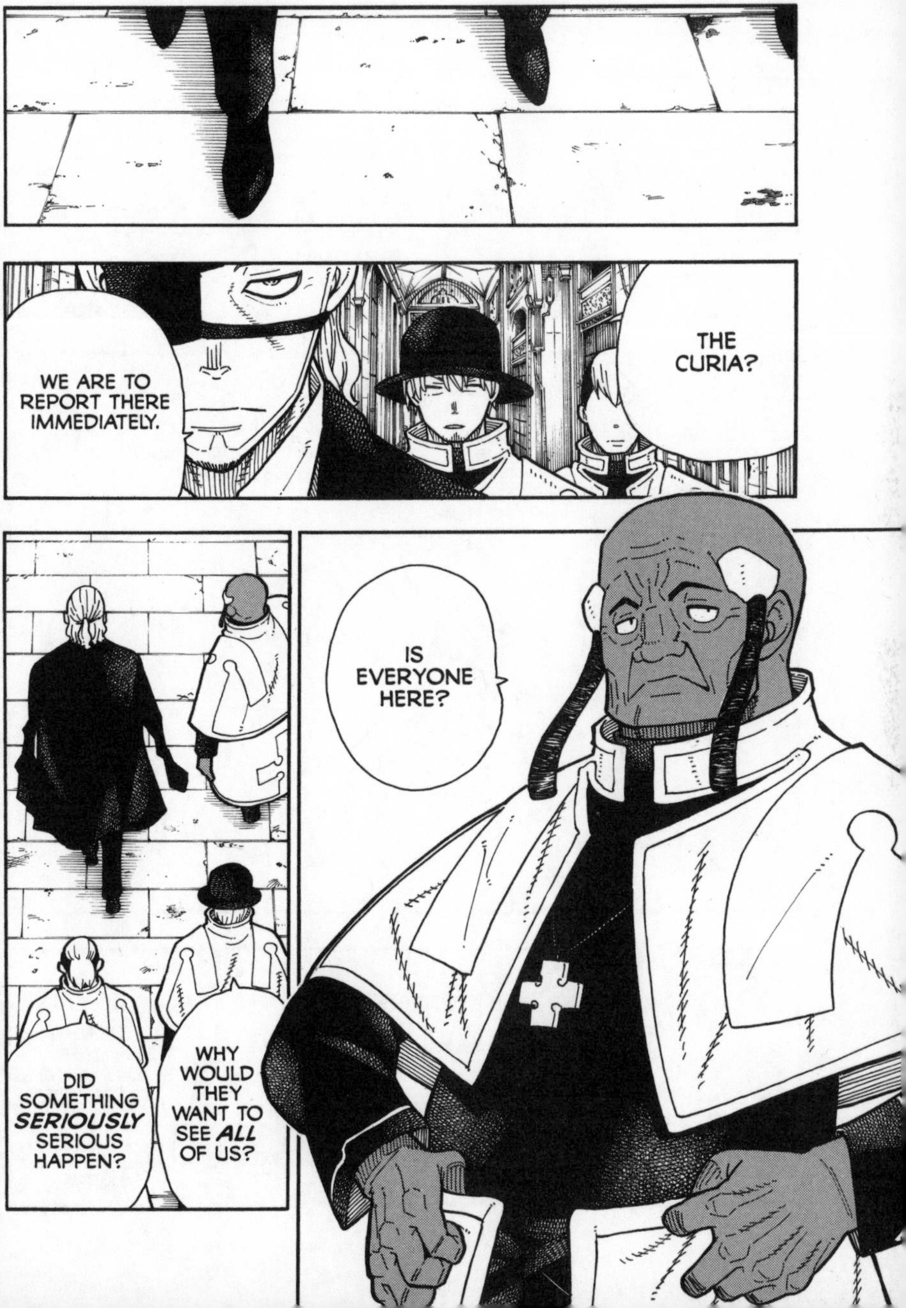
THE CURIA?
WE ARE TO REPORT THERE IMMEDIATELY.
IS EVERYONE HERE?
WHY WOULD THEY WANT TO SEE ***ALL*** OF US?
DID SOMETHING ***SERIOUSLY*** SERIOUS HAPPEN?

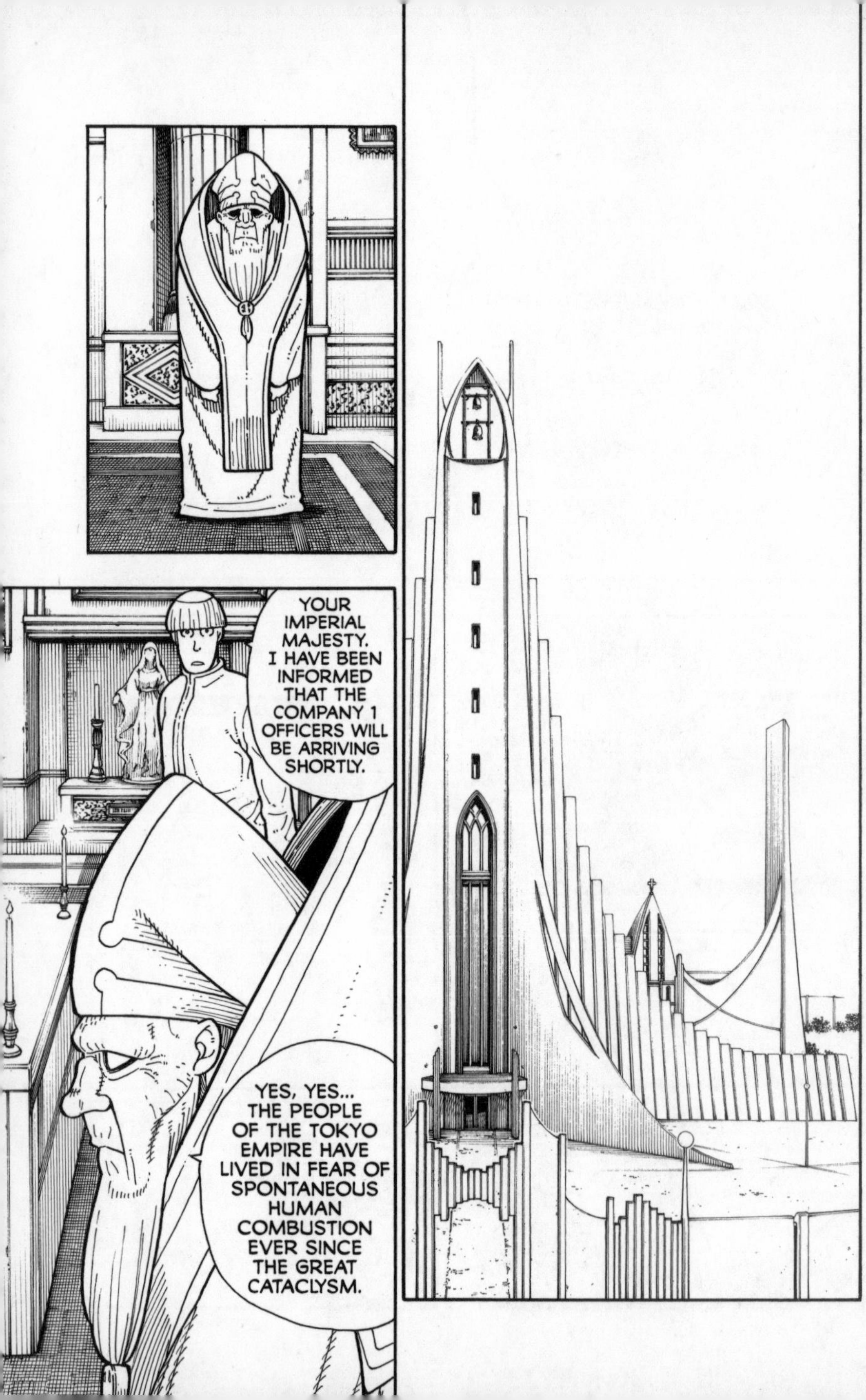
YOUR IMPERIAL MAJESTY. I HAVE BEEN INFORMED THAT THE COMPANY 1 OFFICERS WILL BE ARRIVING SHORTLY.
YES, YES... THE PEOPLE OF THE TOKYO EMPIRE HAVE LIVED IN FEAR OF SPONTANEOUS HUMAN COMBUSTION EVER SINCE THE GREAT CATACLYSM.

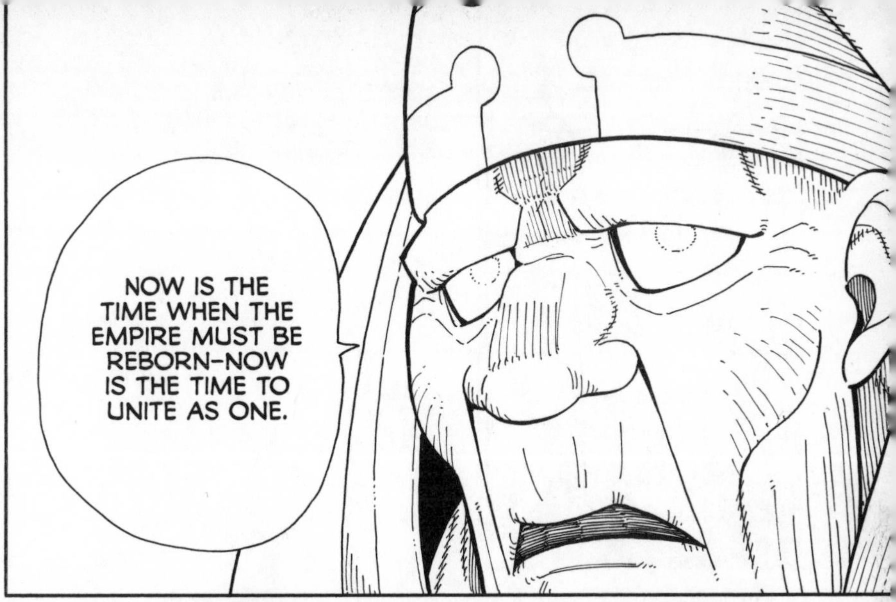
NOW IS THE TIME WHEN THE EMPIRE MUST BE REBORN—NOW IS THE TIME TO UNITE AS ONE.

Hat: Fish Beat

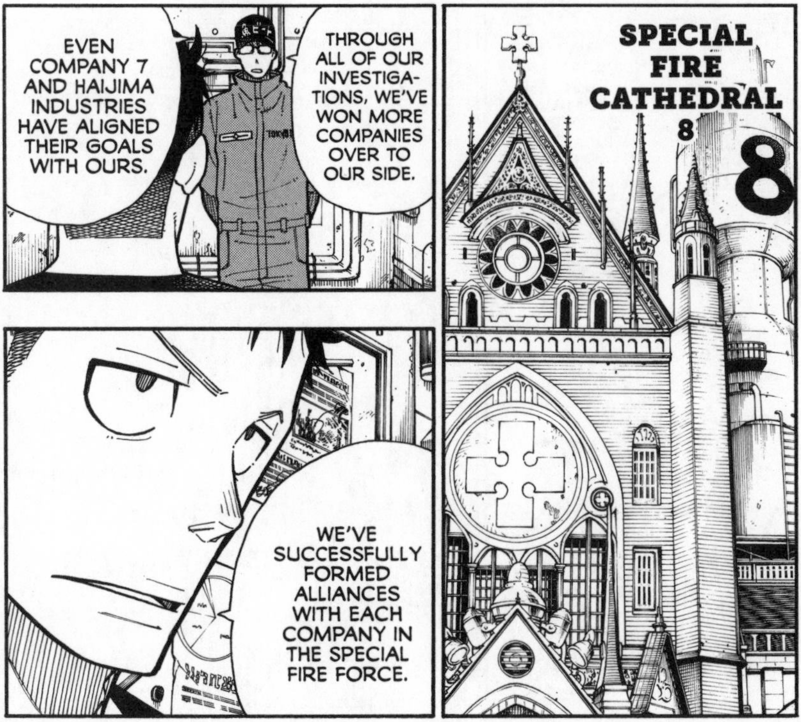
SPECIAL FIRE CATHEDRAL 8
8
THROUGH ALL OF OUR INVESTIGA-TIONS, WE'VE WON MORE COMPANIES OVER TO OUR SIDE.
EVEN COMPANY 7 AND HAIJIMA INDUSTRIES HAVE ALIGNED THEIR GOALS WITH OURS.
WE'VE SUCCESSFULLY FORMED ALLIANCES WITH EACH COMPANY IN THE SPECIAL FIRE FORCE.

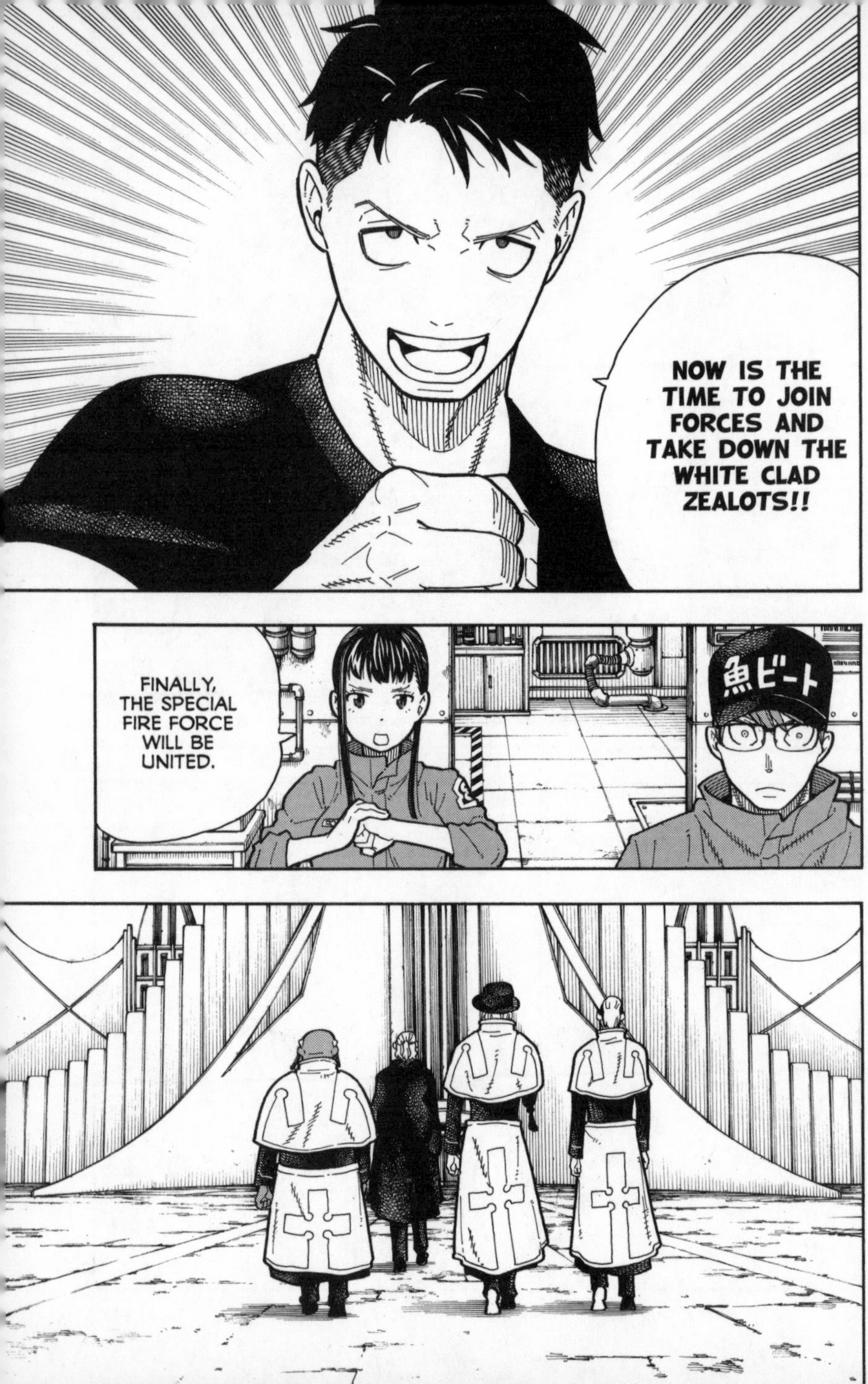
NOW IS THE TIME TO JOIN FORCES AND TAKE DOWN THE WHITE CLAD ZEALOTS!!
魚ビート
FINALLY, THE SPECIAL FIRE FORCE WILL BE UNITED.

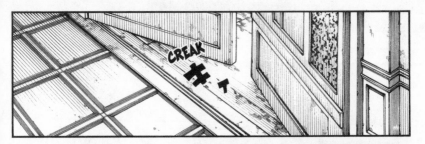

CREAK
キィ
I'VE BEEN EXPECTING YOU.
CAPTAIN LEONARD BURNS.
YOU WANTED TO SEE ME, YOUR IMPERIAL MAJESTY?
TOO MANY POWERS HAVE BEEN AT PLAY IN THE EMPIRE, AND AS A RESULT, OUR NATION HAS BEEN ALL BUT DIVIDED.
HOWEVER, IT IS NOW IMPERATIVE THAT WE TRULY BECOME ***ONE.***

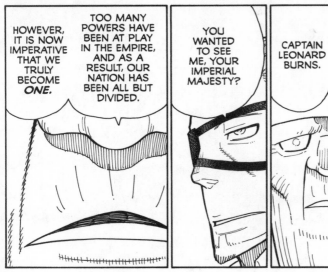

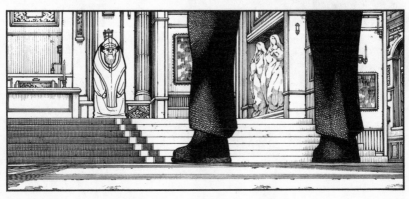

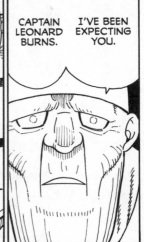

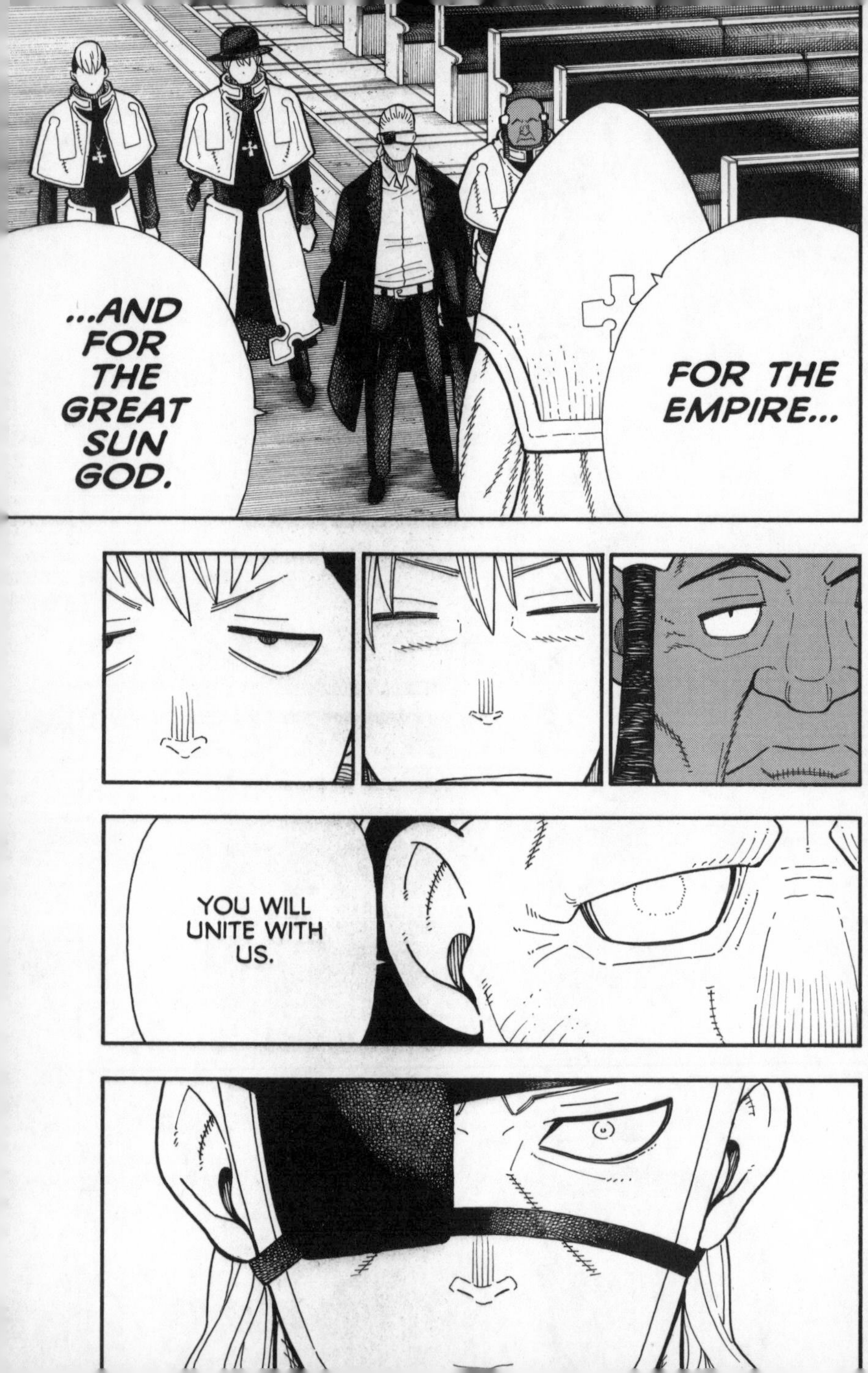
FOR THE EMPIRE...
...AND FOR THE GREAT SUN GOD.
YOU WILL UNITE WITH US.

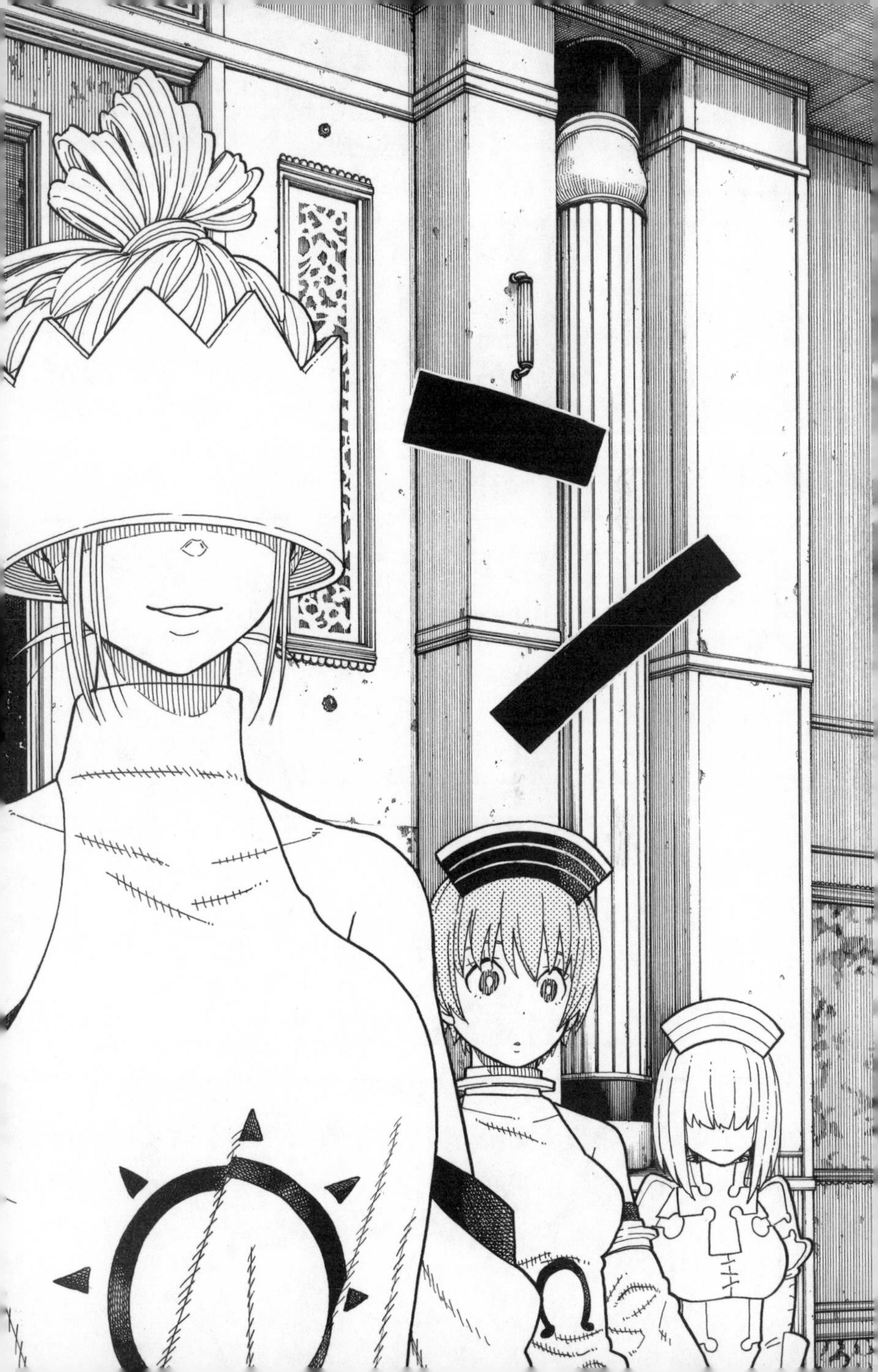

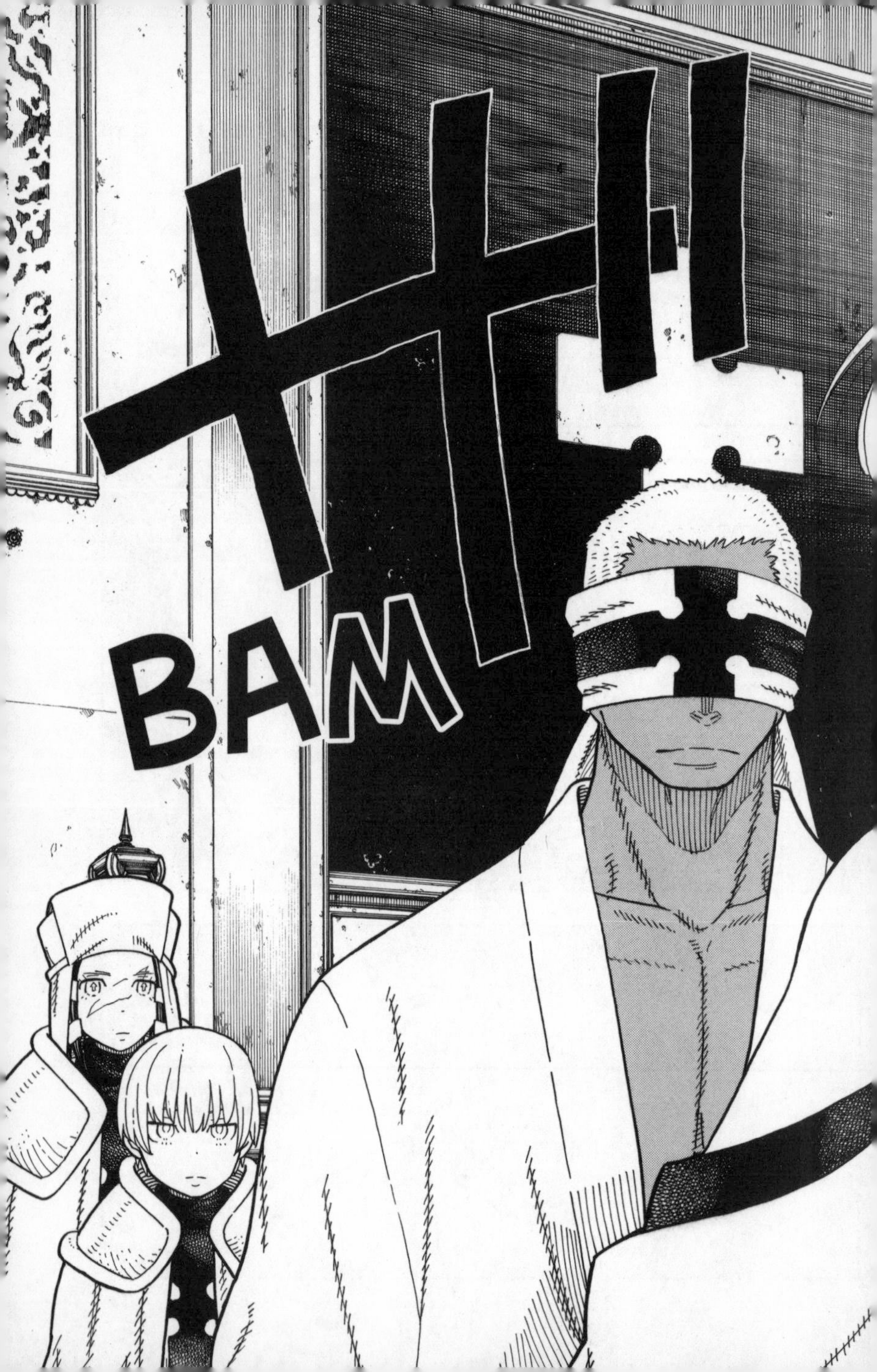
BAM

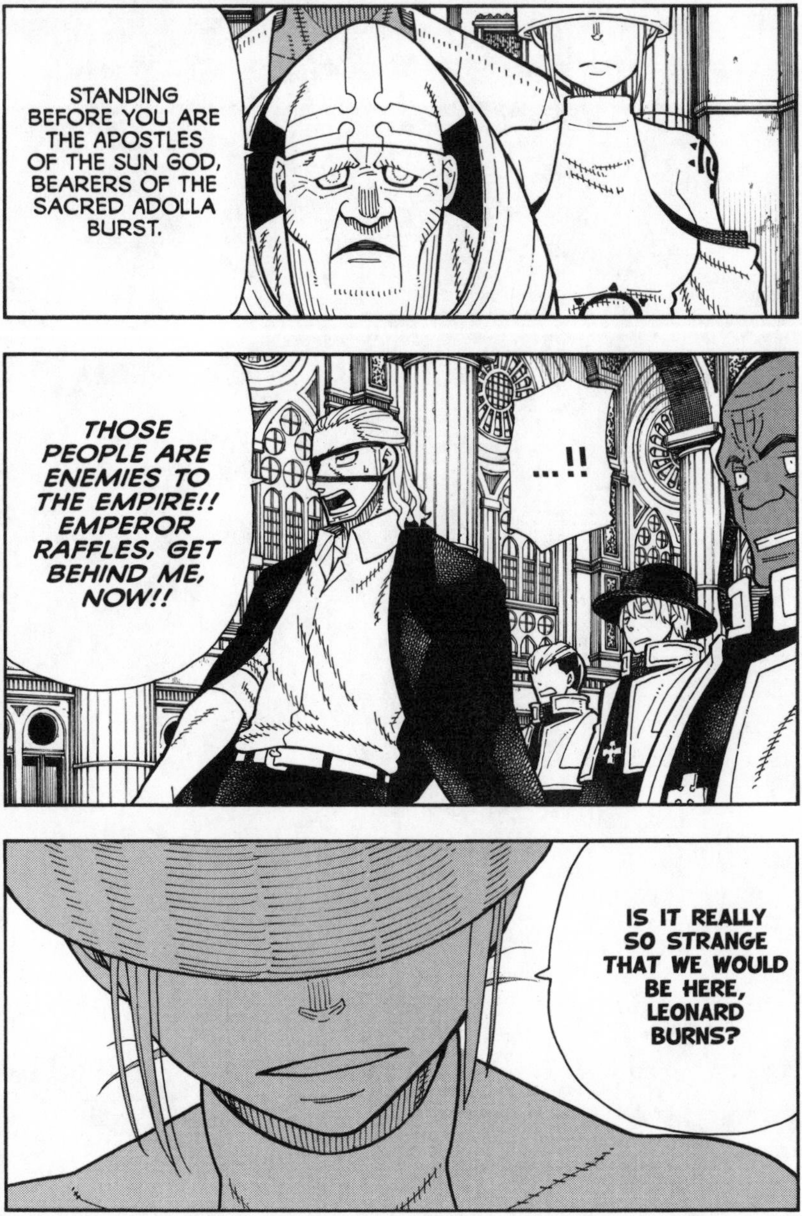
STANDING BEFORE YOU ARE THE APOSTLES OF THE SUN GOD, BEARERS OF THE SACRED ADOLLA BURST.
THOSE PEOPLE ARE ENEMIES TO THE EMPIRE!! EMPEROR RAFFLES, GET BEHIND ME, NOW!!
...!!
IS IT REALLY SO STRANGE THAT WE WOULD BE HERE, LEONARD BURNS?

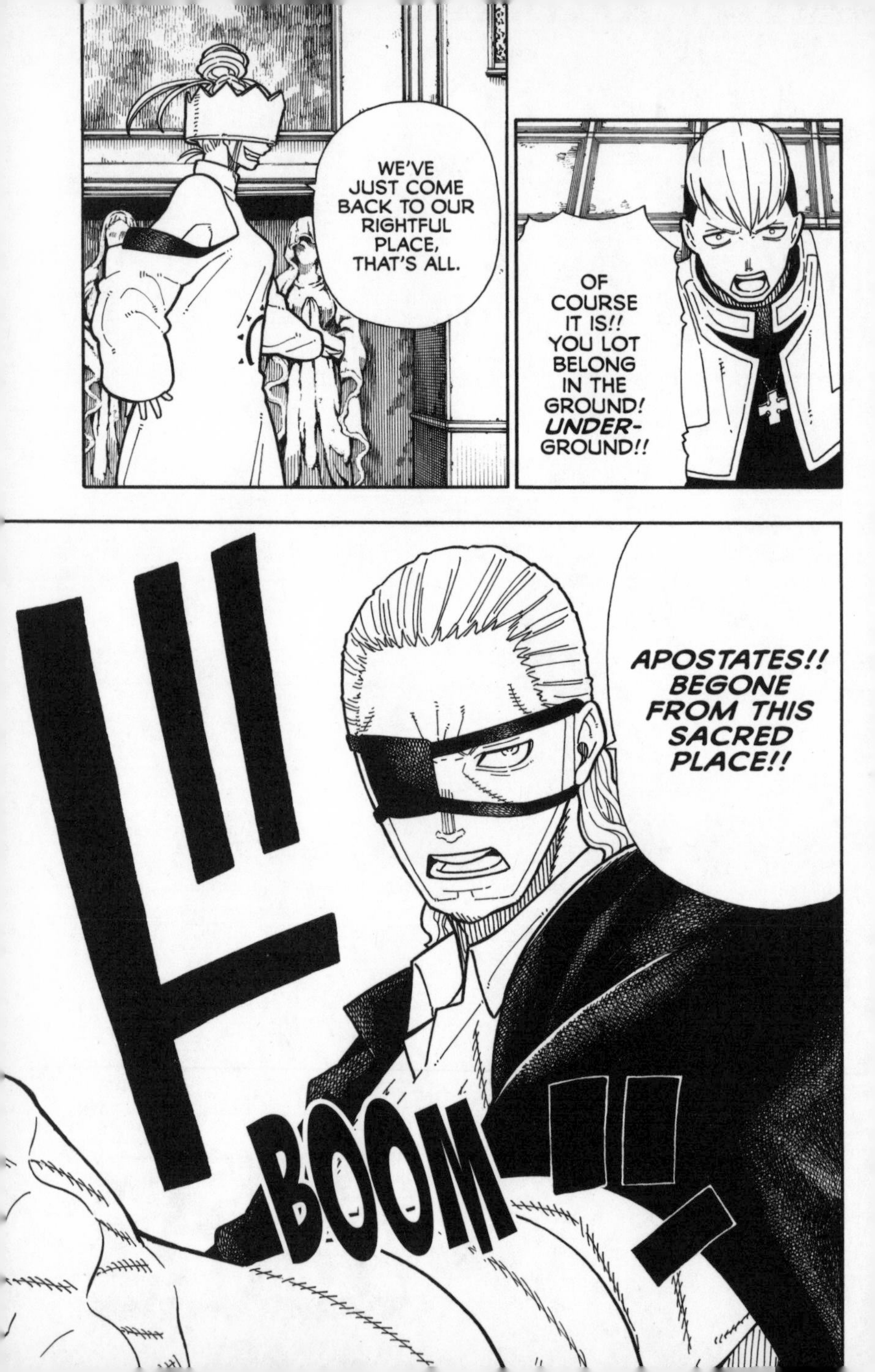
OF COURSE IT IS!! YOU LOT BELONG IN THE GROUND! UNDER-GROUND!!
WE'VE JUST COME BACK TO OUR RIGHTFUL PLACE, THAT'S ALL.
APOSTATES!! BEGONE FROM THIS SACRED PLACE!!
BOOM

FIRE FORCE

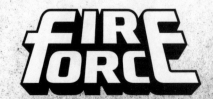

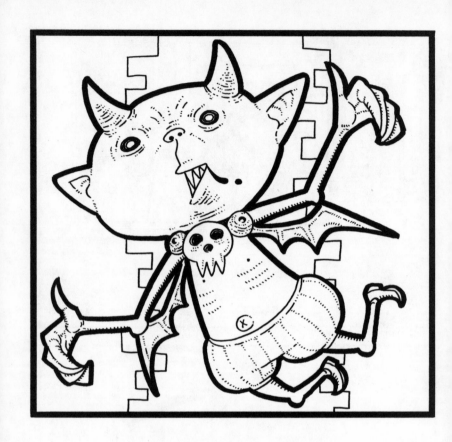

CHAPTER CLXXVI: TRIAL OF FAITH

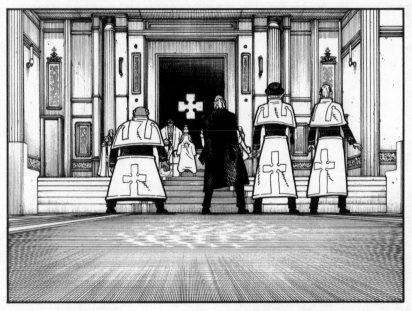

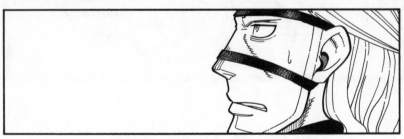

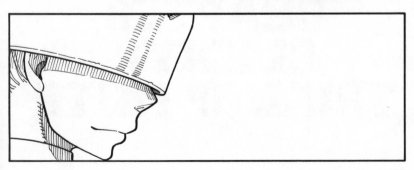

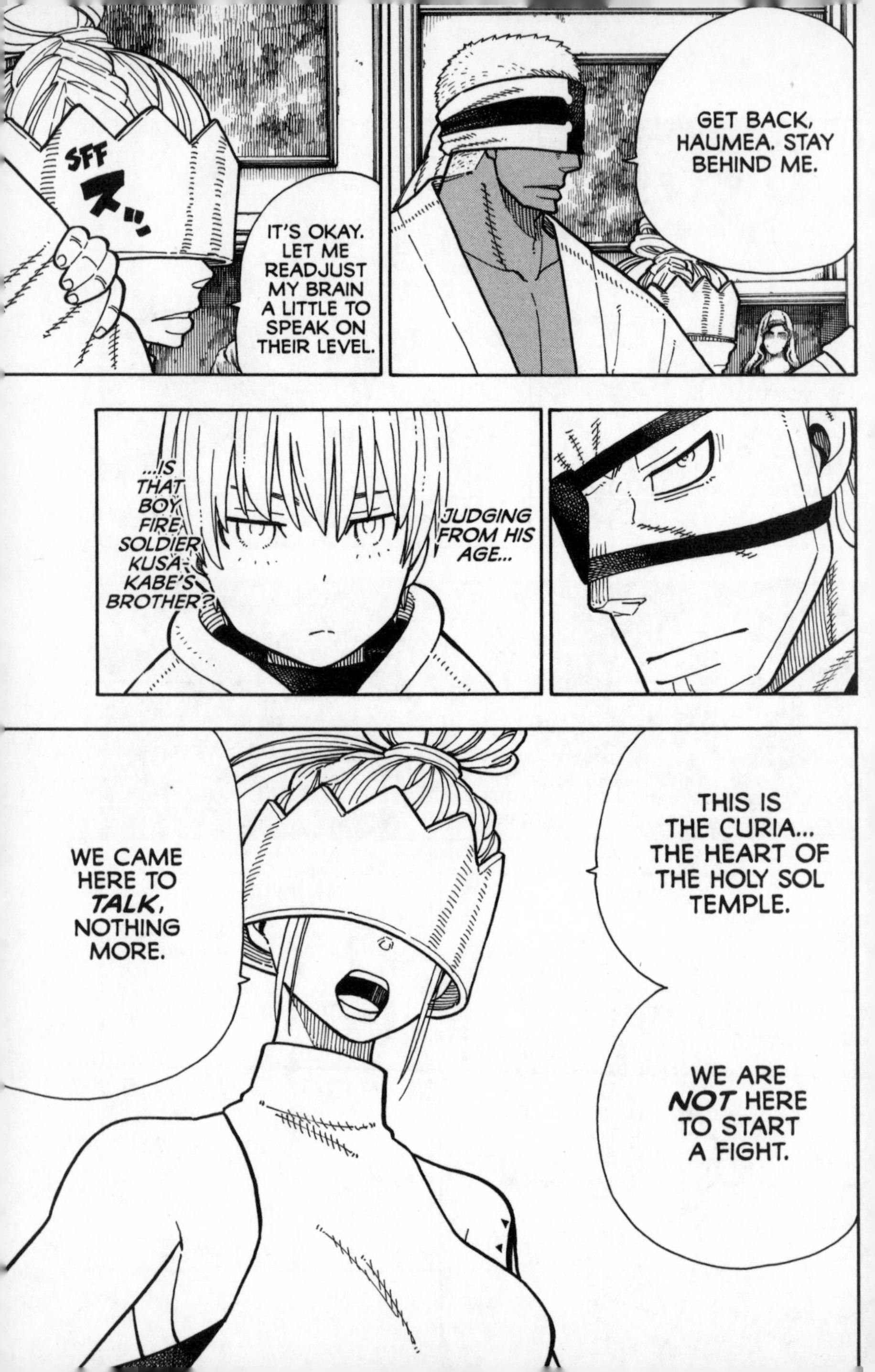
GET BACK, HAUMEA. STAY BEHIND ME.
SFF
IT'S OKAY. LET ME READJUST MY BRAIN A LITTLE TO SPEAK ON THEIR LEVEL.
JUDGING FROM HIS AGE...
...IS THAT BOY FIRE SOLDIER KUSAKABE'S BROTHER?
THIS IS THE CURIA... THE HEART OF THE HOLY SOL TEMPLE.
WE ARE ***NOT*** HERE TO START A FIGHT.
WE CAME HERE TO ***TALK***, NOTHING MORE.

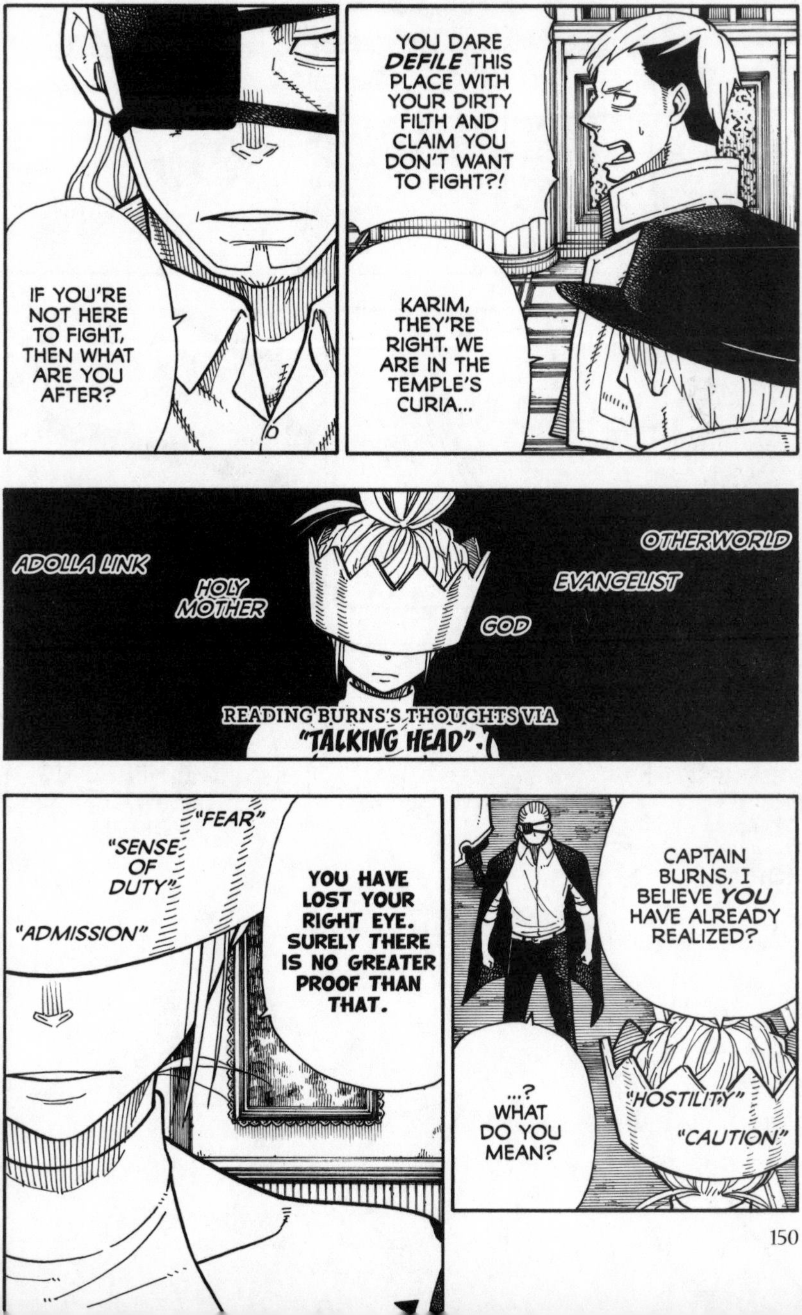
YOU DARE DEFILE THIS PLACE WITH YOUR DIRTY FILTH AND CLAIM YOU DON'T WANT TO FIGHT?!
KARIM, THEY'RE RIGHT. WE ARE IN THE TEMPLE'S CURIA...
IF YOU'RE NOT HERE TO FIGHT, THEN WHAT ARE YOU AFTER?
OTHERWORLD
ADOLLA LINK
EVANGELIST
HOLY MOTHER
GOD
READING BURNS'S THOUGHTS VIA "TALKING HEAD".
CAPTAIN BURNS, I BELIEVE YOU HAVE ALREADY REALIZED?
...? WHAT DO YOU MEAN?
"HOSTILITY"
"CAUTION"
"FEAR"
"SENSE OF DUTY"
YOU HAVE LOST YOUR RIGHT EYE. SURELY THERE IS NO GREATER PROOF THAN THAT.
"ADMISSION"

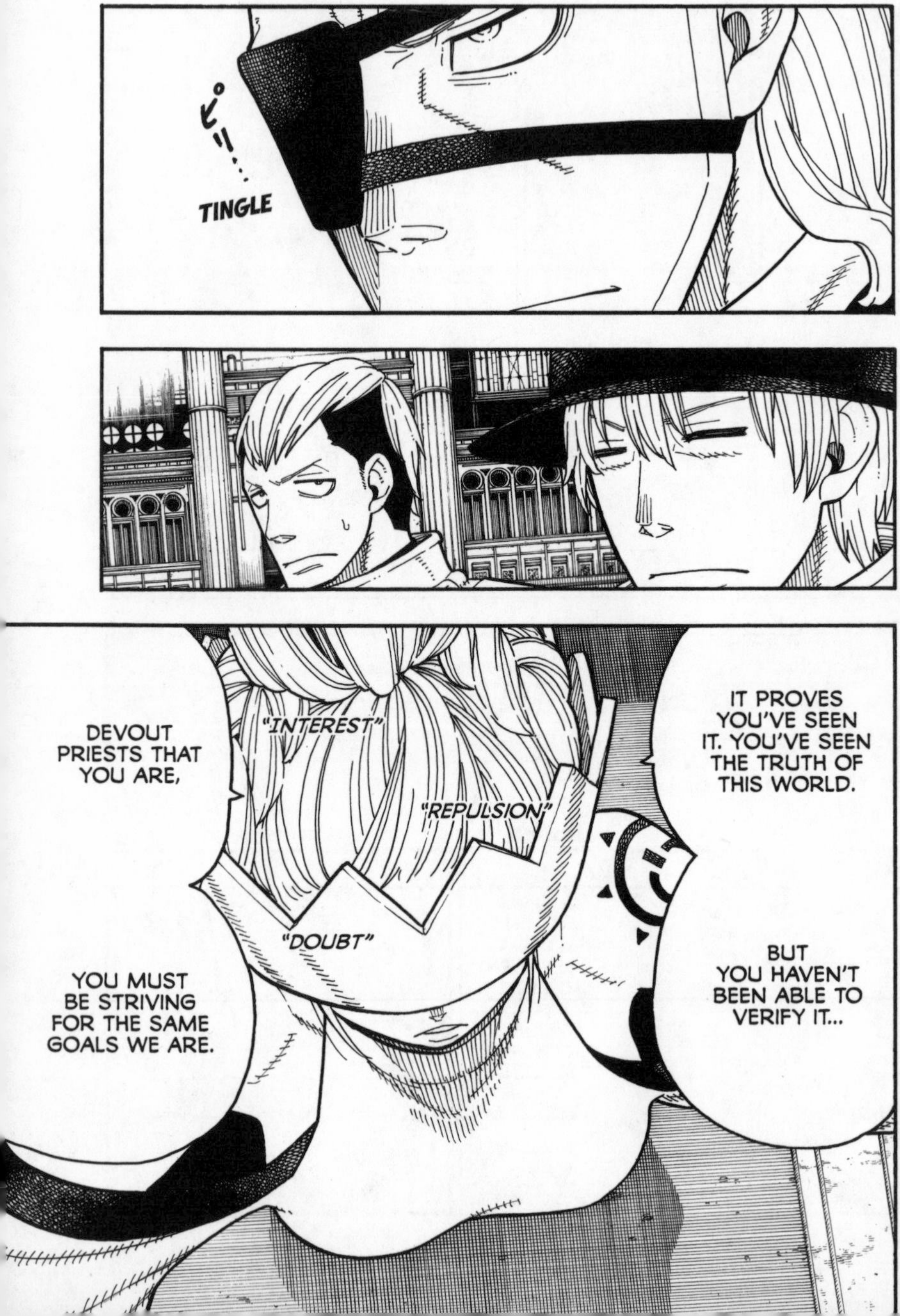
ピリ…
TINGLE
IT PROVES YOU'VE SEEN IT. YOU'VE SEEN THE TRUTH OF THIS WORLD.
DEVOUT PRIESTS THAT YOU ARE,
"INTEREST"
"REPULSION"
"DOUBT"
BUT YOU HAVEN'T BEEN ABLE TO VERIFY IT...
YOU MUST BE STRIVING FOR THE SAME GOALS WE ARE.

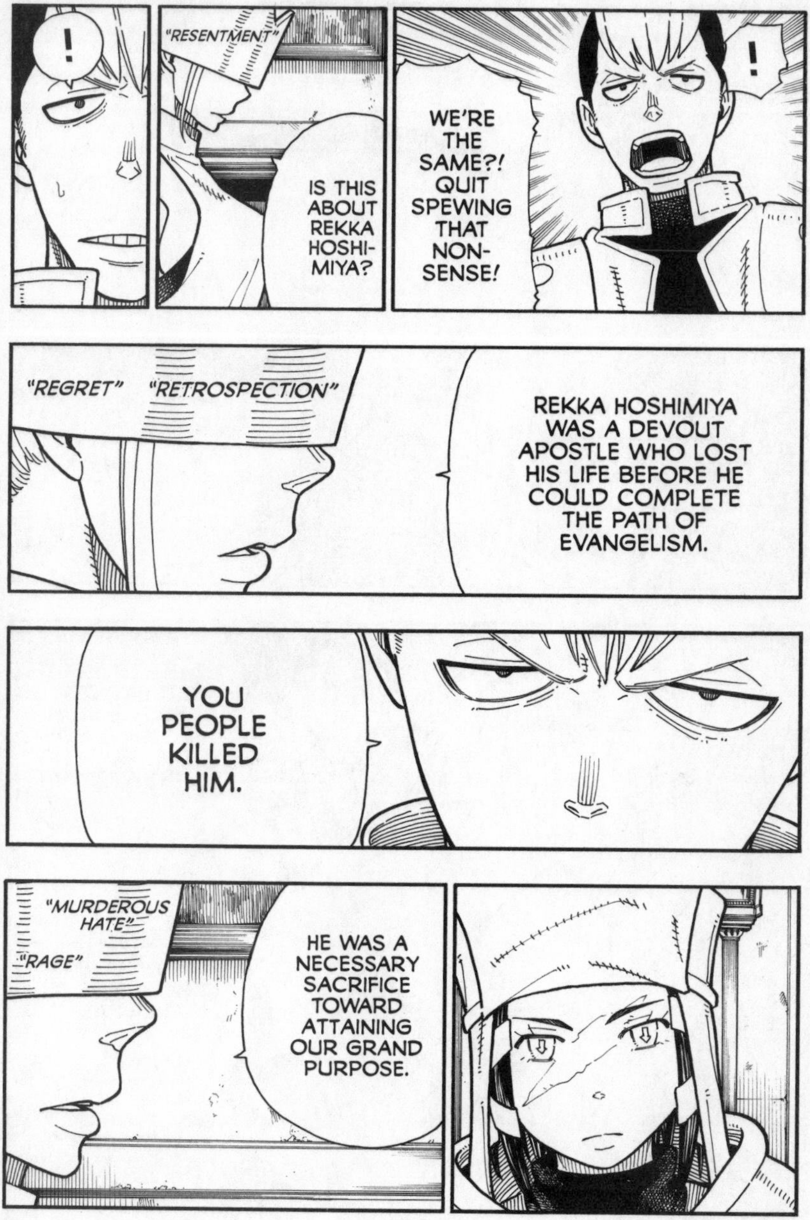
!
WE'RE THE SAME?! QUIT SPEWING THAT NONSENSE!
"RESENTMENT"
IS THIS ABOUT REKKA HOSHIMIYA?
!
REKKA HOSHIMIYA WAS A DEVOUT APOSTLE WHO LOST HIS LIFE BEFORE HE COULD COMPLETE THE PATH OF EVANGELISM.
"RETROSPECTION"
"REGRET"
YOU PEOPLE KILLED HIM.
HE WAS A NECESSARY SACRIFICE TOWARD ATTAINING OUR GRAND PURPOSE.
"MURDEROUS HATE"
"RAGE"

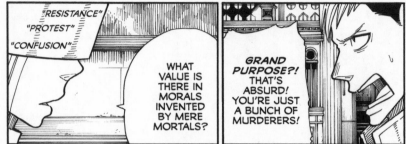

GRAND PURPOSE?! THAT'S ABSURD! YOU'RE JUST A BUNCH OF MURDERERS!
"RESISTANCE"
"PROTEST"
"CONFUSION"
WHAT VALUE IS THERE IN MORALS INVENTED BY MERE MORTALS?
...ARE YOU TRYING TO TELL ME IT WAS SOME REVELATION FROM GOD?
THAT'S JUST A BUNCH OF YOUR FANATICAL NON-SENSE!
"CONSIDERATION"
"RECOLLECTION"
"ANALYSIS"
BUT DON'T YOU FEEL IT IN THE WORDS WE SPEAK?
YOU SHOULD SENSE WITHIN THEM A FRAGMENT OF THE GRAND WILL OF THE UNIVERSE.
WITH MY WORDS, I SPEAK FOR GOD.

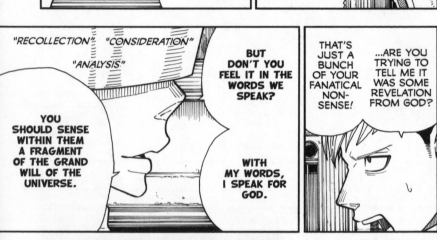

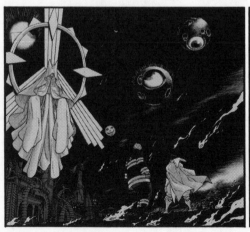

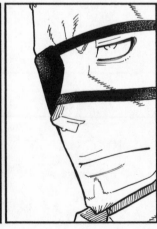

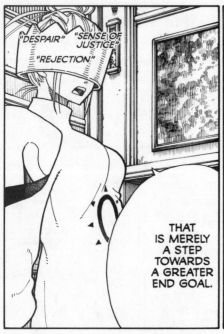

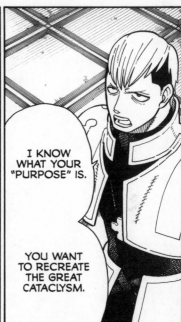

I KNOW WHAT YOUR "PURPOSE" IS.
YOU WANT TO RECREATE THE GREAT CATACLYSM.
"SENSE OF JUSTICE"
"DESPAIR"
"REJECTION"
THAT IS MERELY A STEP TOWARDS A GREATER END GOAL.
IN THE HOLY SOL TEMPLE, WE MERELY SUBMIT TO THE WILL OF THE GREAT SUN GOD.
SO THE GREAT CATACLYSM ISN'T THE END GOAL...
DO YOU MEAN TO TELL US THAT THIS IS WHAT THE SUN GOD WISHES?

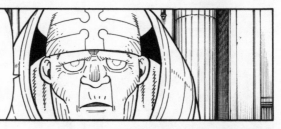

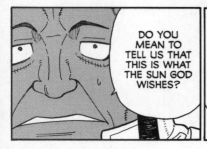

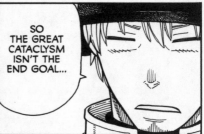

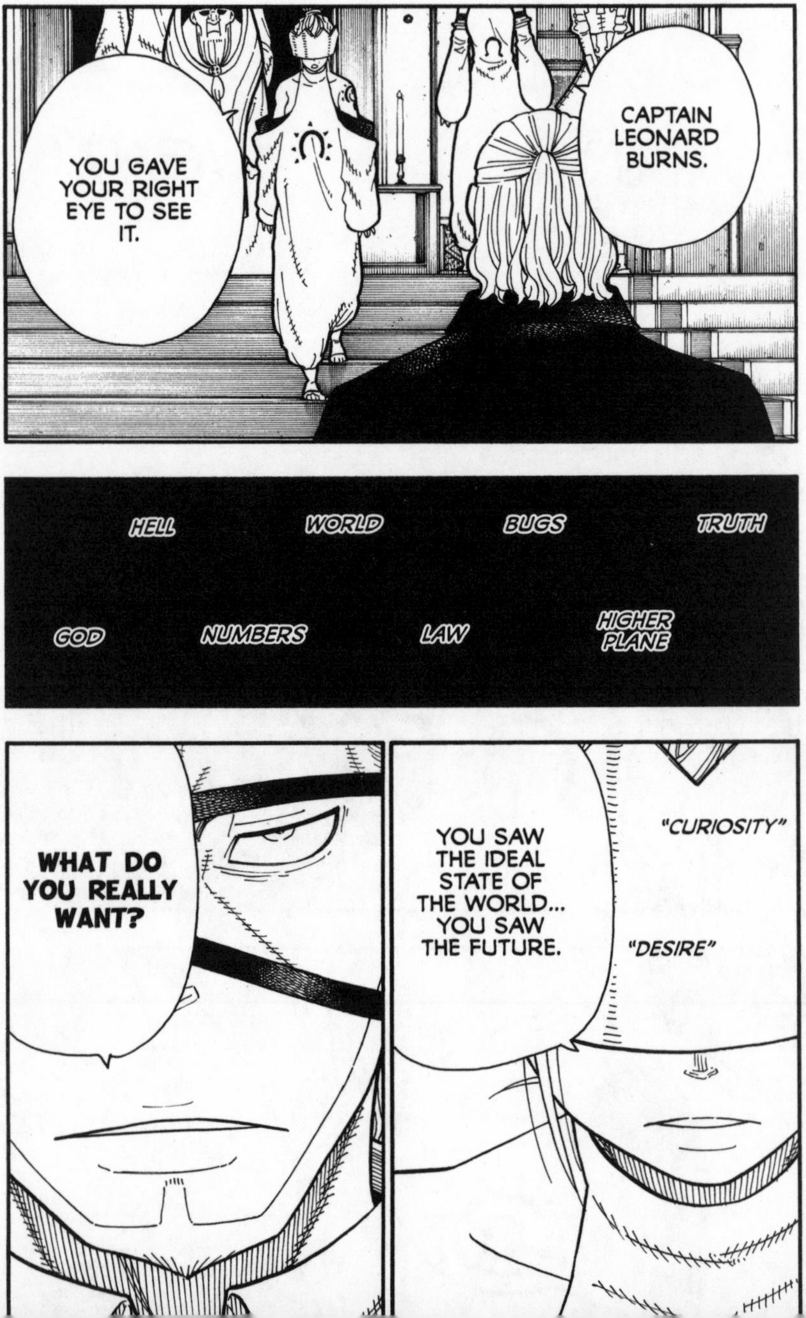
CAPTAIN LEONARD BURNS.
YOU GAVE YOUR RIGHT EYE TO SEE IT.
TRUTH
BUGS
WORLD
HELL
HIGHER PLANE
LAW
NUMBERS
GOD
"CURIOSITY"
YOU SAW THE IDEAL STATE OF THE WORLD... YOU SAW THE FUTURE.
"DESIRE"
WHAT DO YOU REALLY WANT?

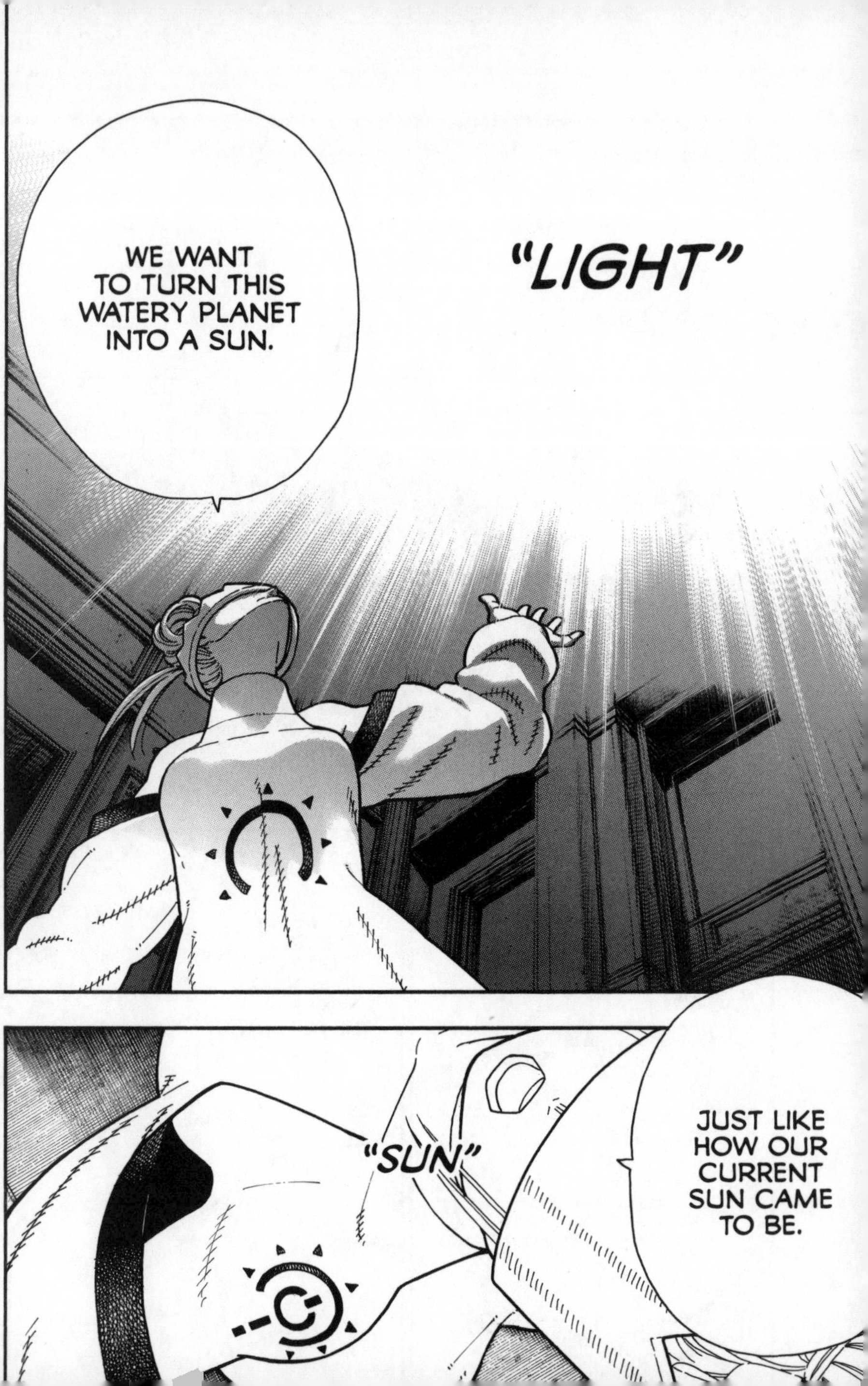
"LIGHT"
WE WANT TO TURN THIS WATERY PLANET INTO A SUN.
JUST LIKE HOW OUR CURRENT SUN CAME TO BE.
"SUN"

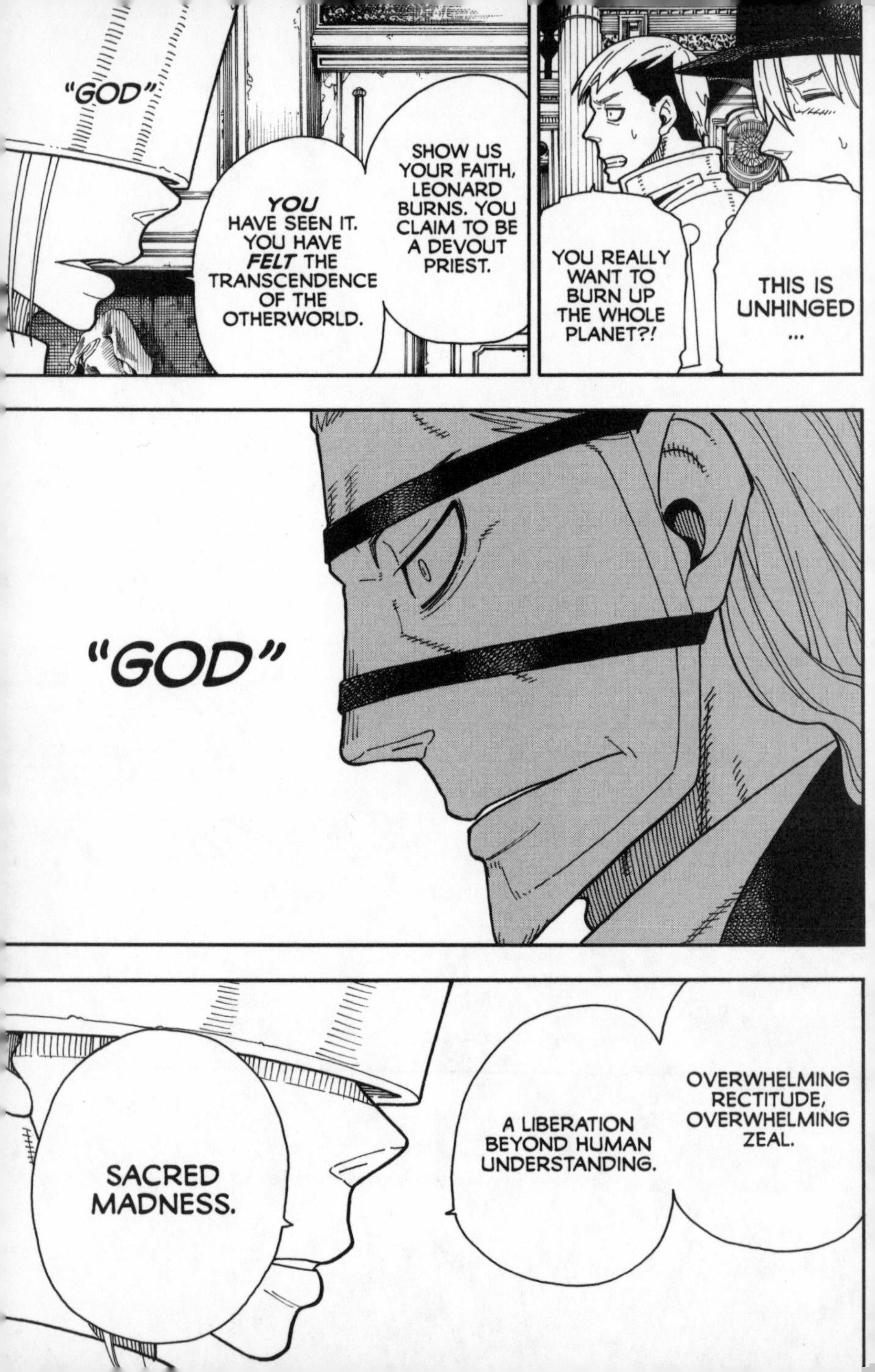
THIS IS UNHINGED ...
YOU REALLY WANT TO BURN UP THE WHOLE PLANET?!
SHOW US YOUR FAITH, LEONARD BURNS. YOU CLAIM TO BE A DEVOUT PRIEST.
YOU HAVE SEEN IT. YOU HAVE FELT THE TRANSCENDENCE OF THE OTHERWORLD.
"GOD"
"GOD"
OVERWHELMING RECTITUDE, OVERWHELMING ZEAL.
A LIBERATION BEYOND HUMAN UNDERSTANDING.
SACRED MADNESS.

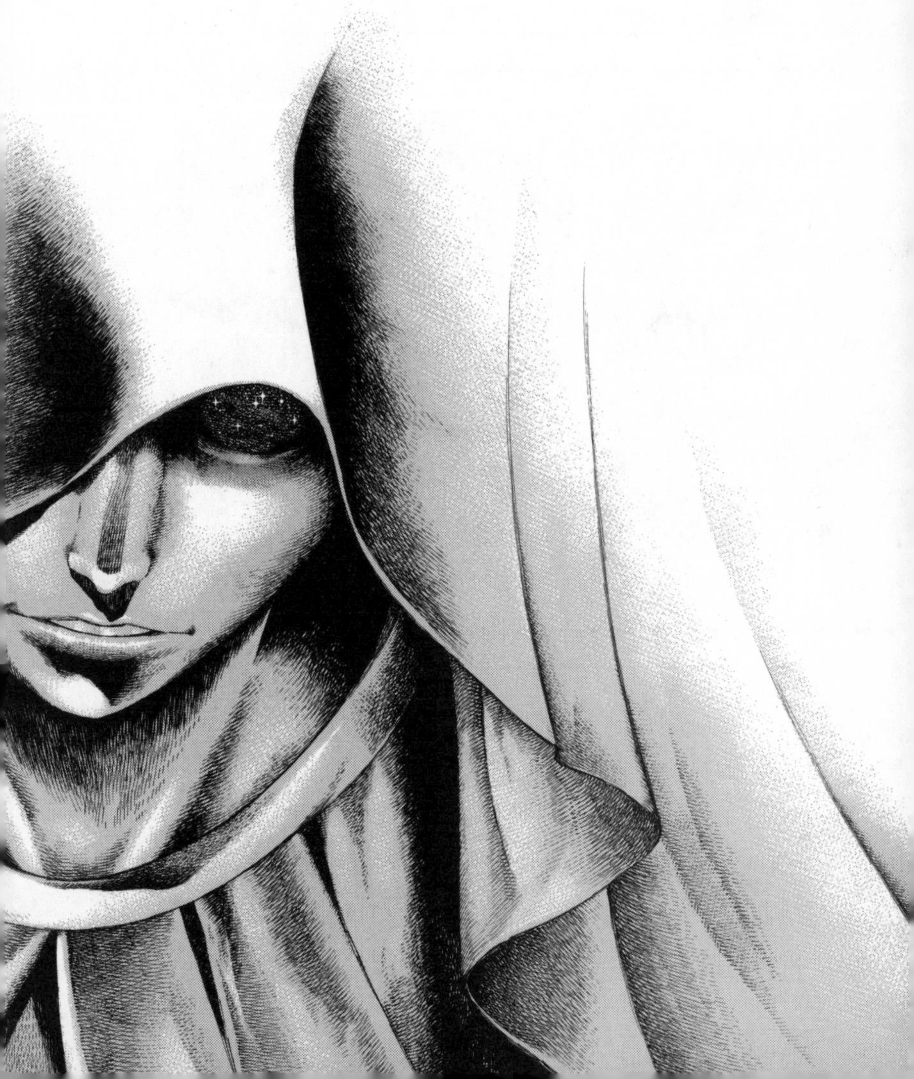

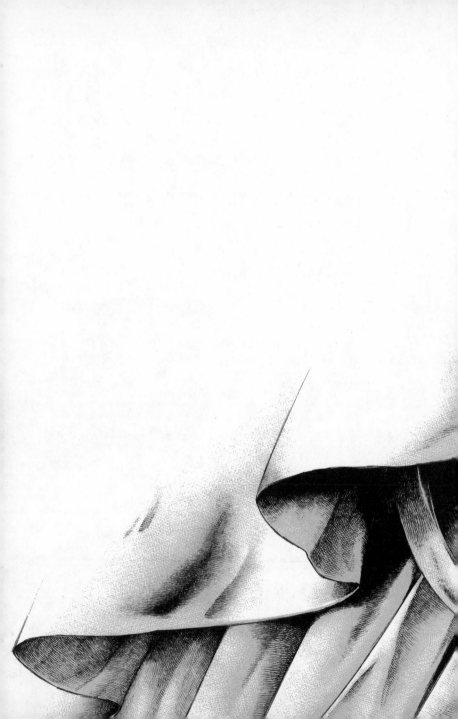

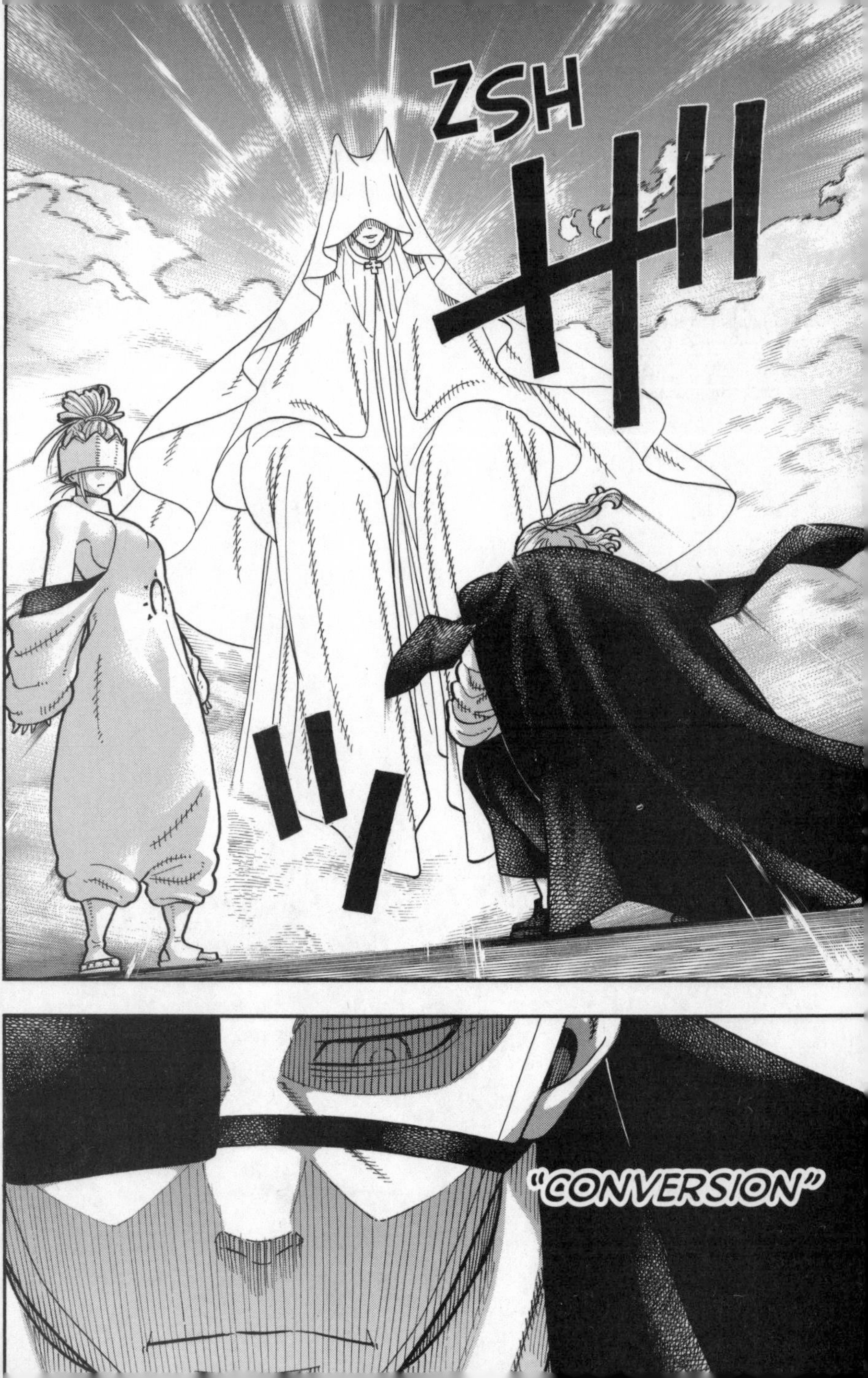
ZSH
"CONVERSION"

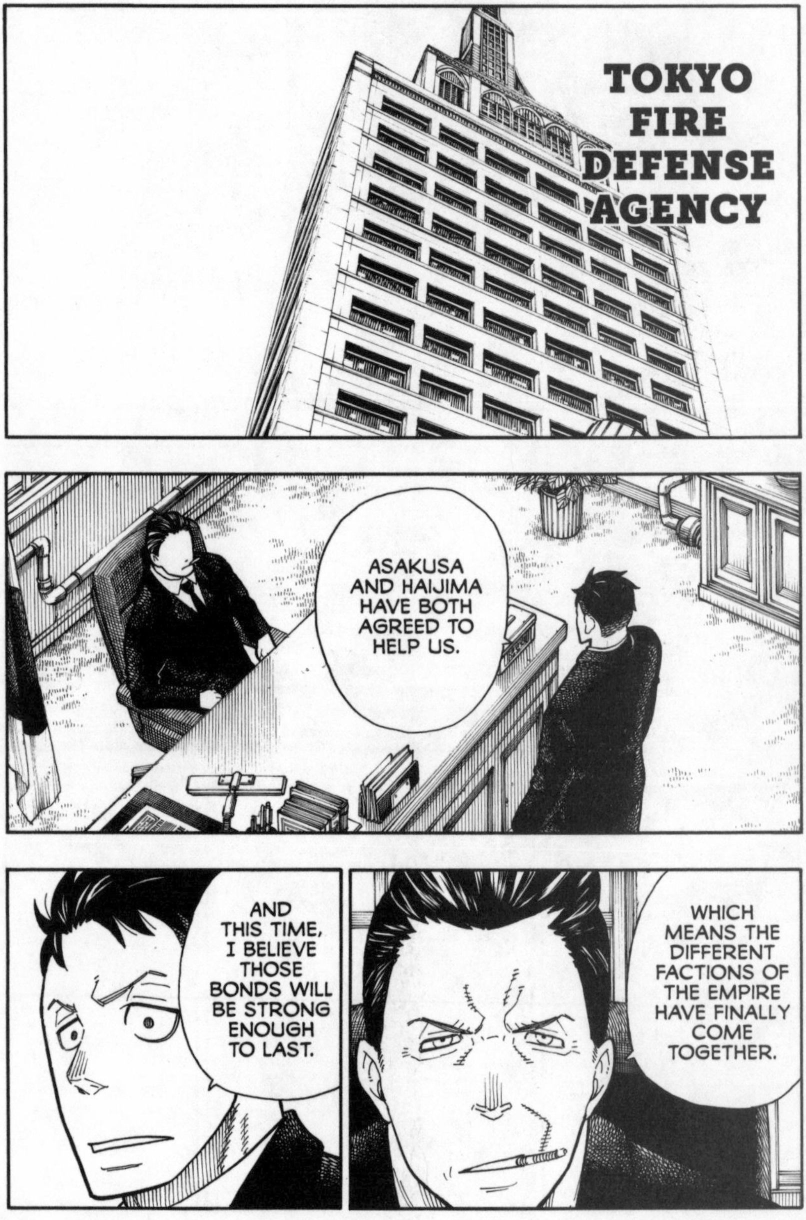
TOKYO FIRE DEFENSE AGENCY
ASAKUSA AND HAIJIMA HAVE BOTH AGREED TO HELP US.
WHICH MEANS THE DIFFERENT FACTIONS OF THE EMPIRE HAVE FINALLY COME TOGETHER.
AND THIS TIME, I BELIEVE THOSE BONDS WILL BE STRONG ENOUGH TO LAST.

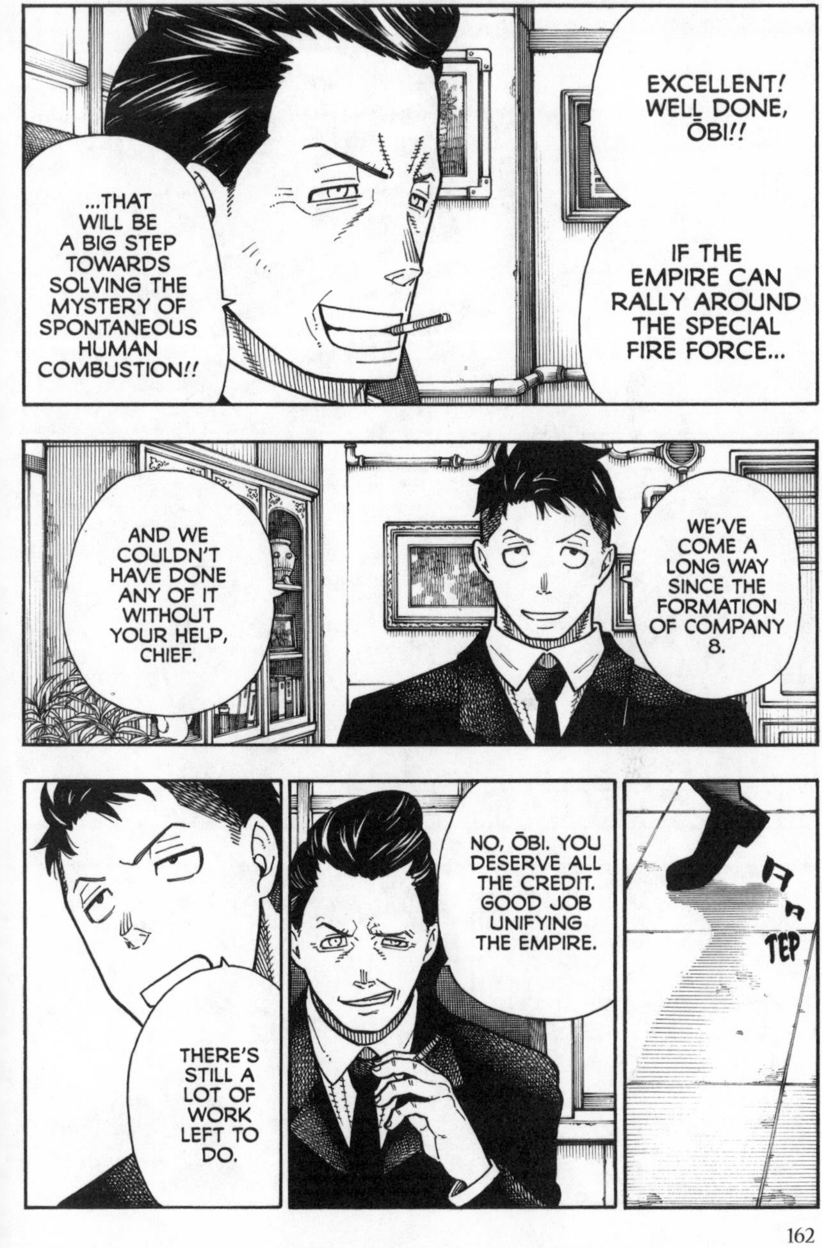
EXCELLENT! WELL DONE, ŌBI!!
IF THE EMPIRE CAN RALLY AROUND THE SPECIAL FIRE FORCE...
...THAT WILL BE A BIG STEP TOWARDS SOLVING THE MYSTERY OF SPONTANEOUS HUMAN COMBUSTION!!
WE'VE COME A LONG WAY SINCE THE FORMATION OF COMPANY 8.
AND WE COULDN'T HAVE DONE ANY OF IT WITHOUT YOUR HELP, CHIEF.
TEP
NO, ŌBI. YOU DESERVE ALL THE CREDIT. GOOD JOB UNIFYING THE EMPIRE.
THERE'S STILL A LOT OF WORK LEFT TO DO.

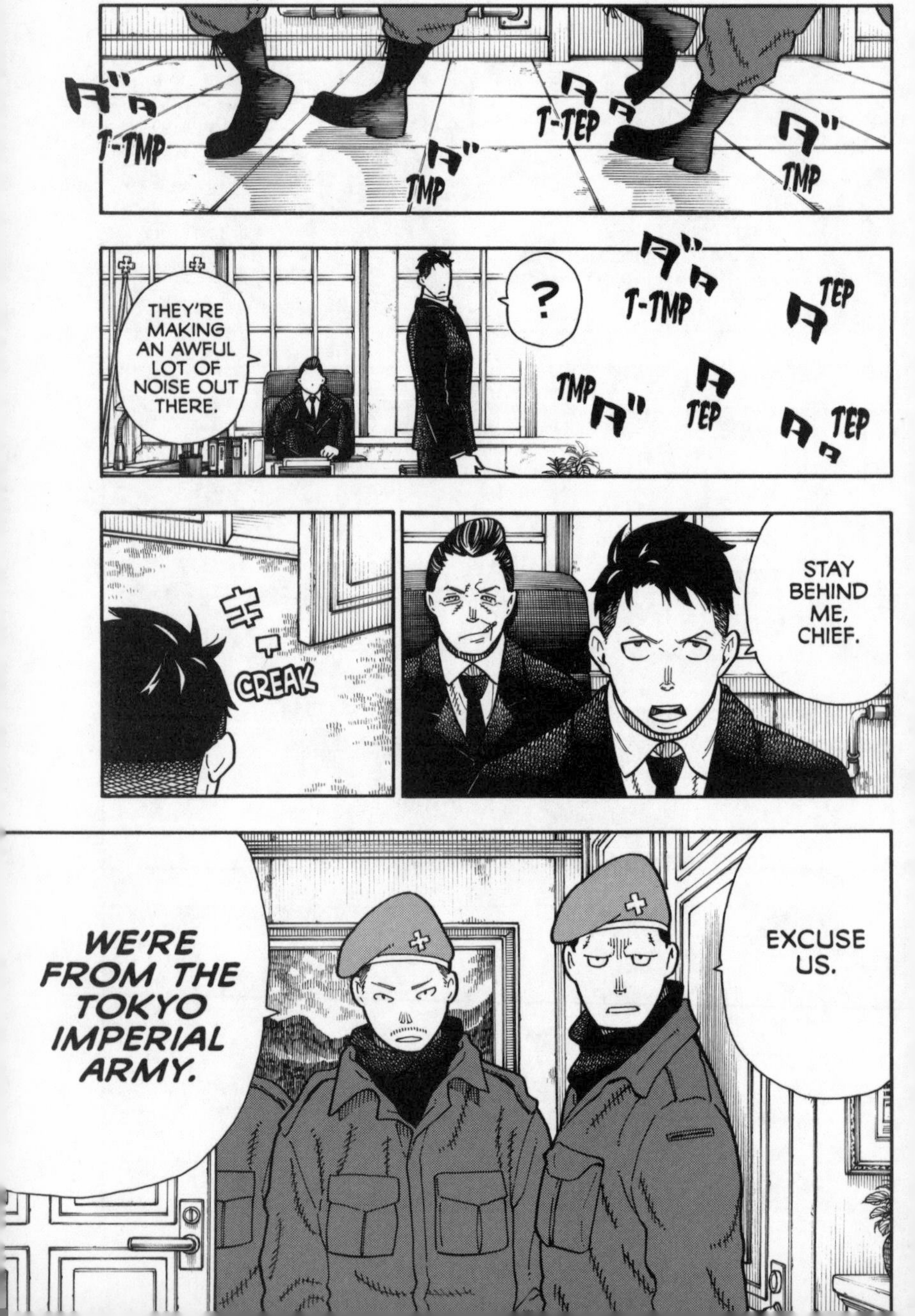
TMP
T-TEP
TMP
T-TMP
TEP
TEP
TEP
T-TMP
TMP
?
THEY'RE MAKING AN AWFUL LOT OF NOISE OUT THERE.
STAY BEHIND ME, CHIEF.
CREAK
EXCUSE US.
WE'RE FROM THE TOKYO IMPERIAL ARMY.

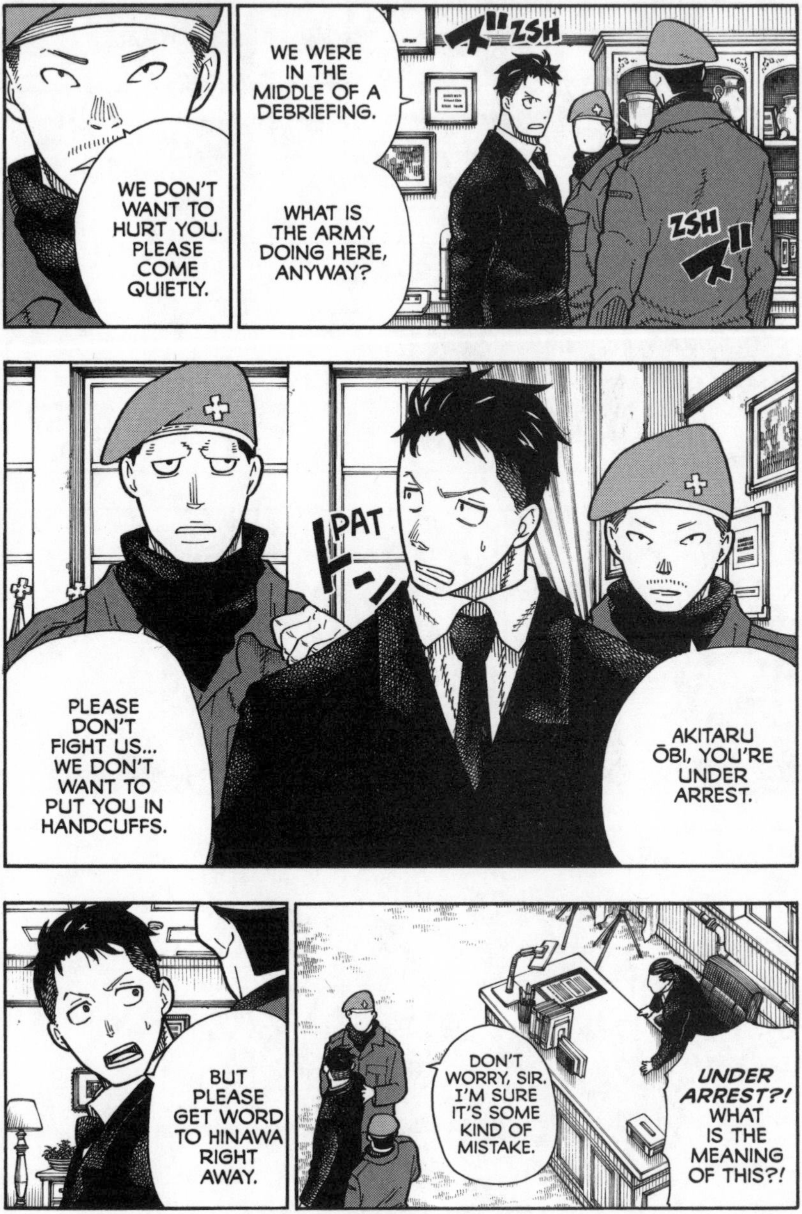
ZSH
WE WERE IN THE MIDDLE OF A DEBRIEFING.
WHAT IS THE ARMY DOING HERE, ANYWAY?
ZSH
WE DON'T WANT TO HURT YOU. PLEASE COME QUIETLY.
AKITARU ŌBI, YOU'RE UNDER ARREST.
PAT
PLEASE DON'T FIGHT US... WE DON'T WANT TO PUT YOU IN HANDCUFFS.
UNDER ARREST?! WHAT IS THE MEANING OF THIS?!
DON'T WORRY, SIR. I'M SURE IT'S SOME KIND OF MISTAKE.
BUT PLEASE GET WORD TO HINAWA RIGHT AWAY.

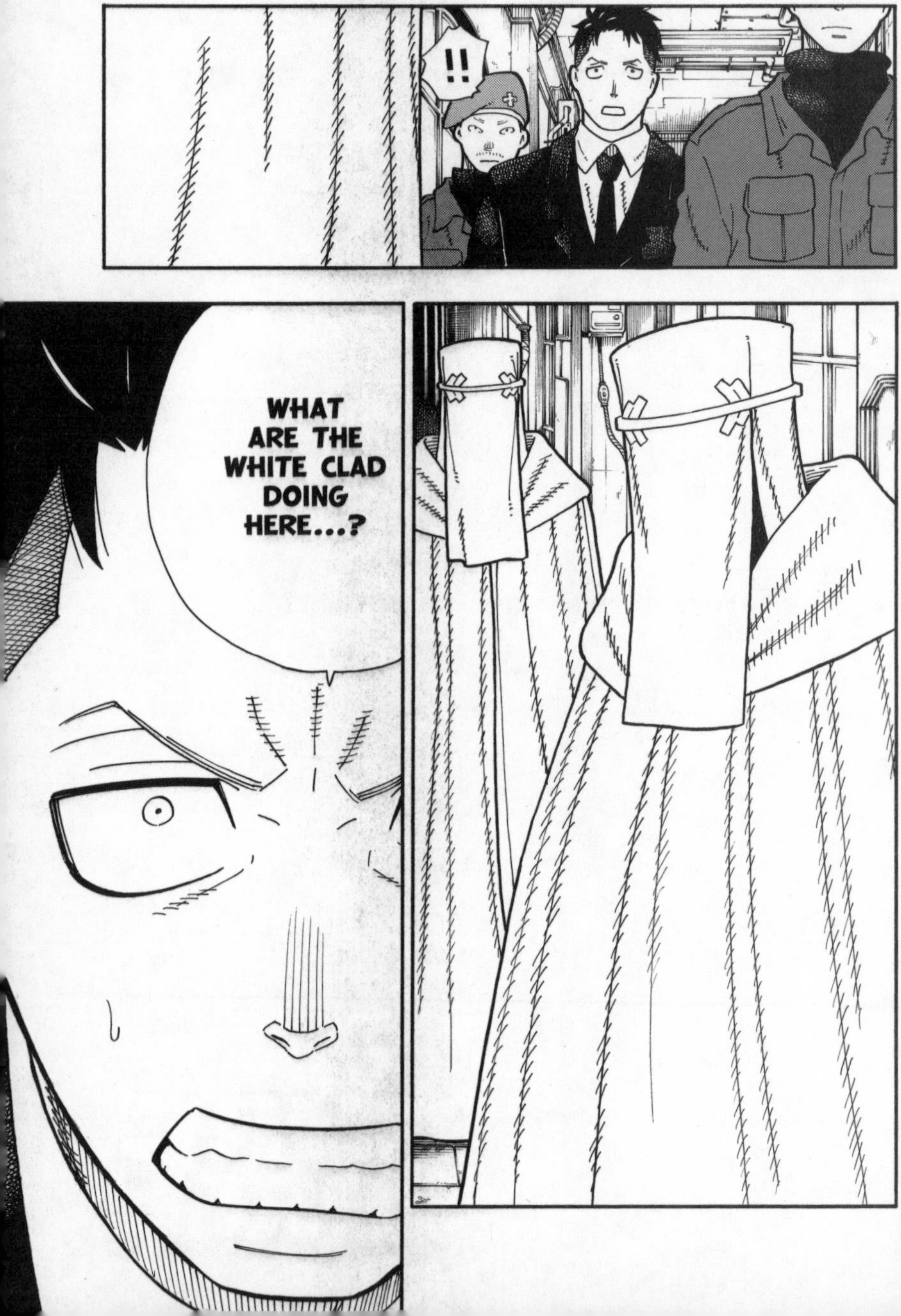
!!
WHAT ARE THE WHITE CLAD DOING HERE...?

FIRE FORCE

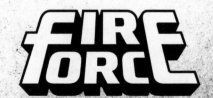

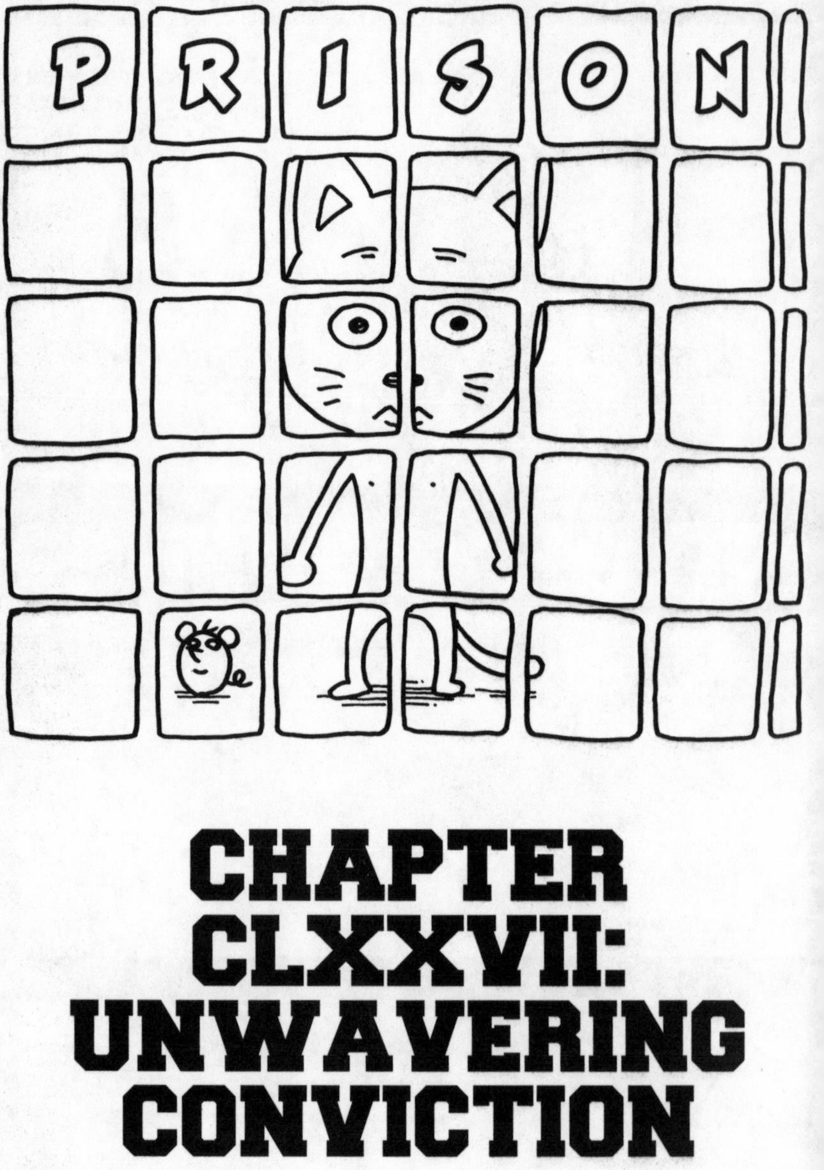
PRISON

CHAPTER CLXXVII: UNWAVERING CONVICTION

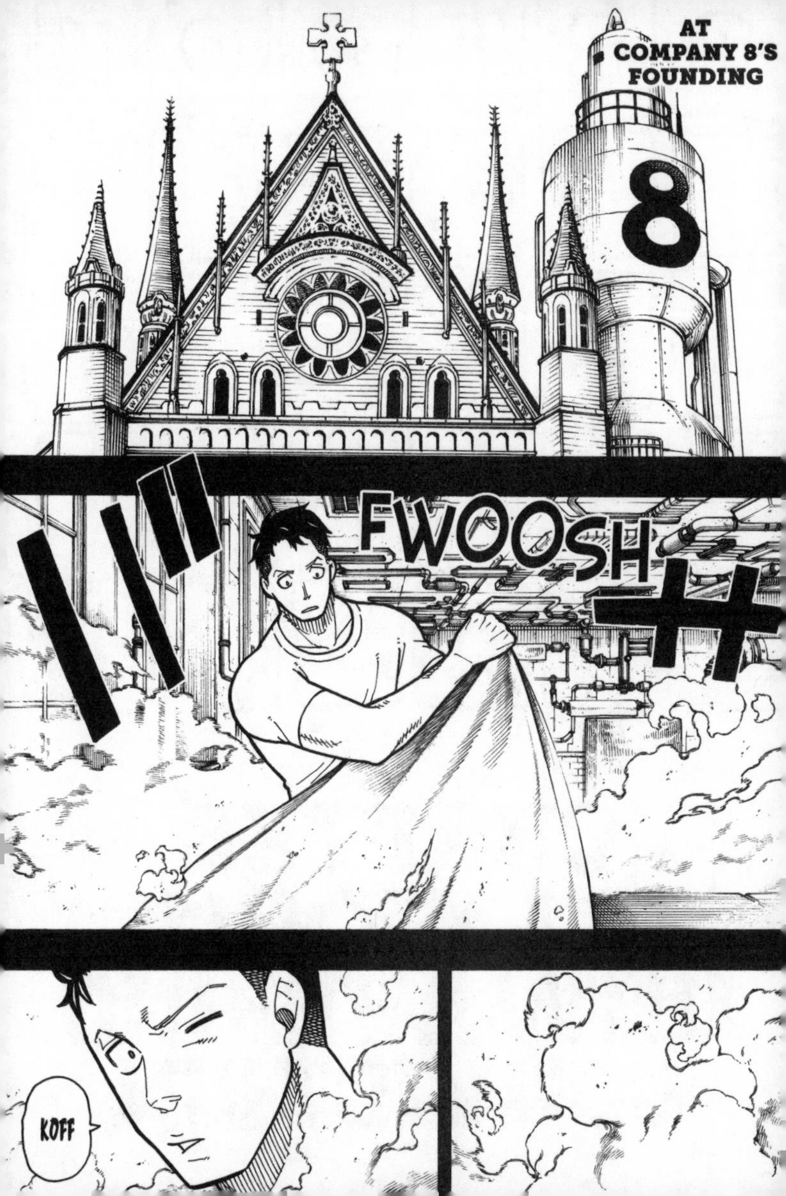
AT COMPANY 8'S FOUNDING
8
FWOOSH
KOFF

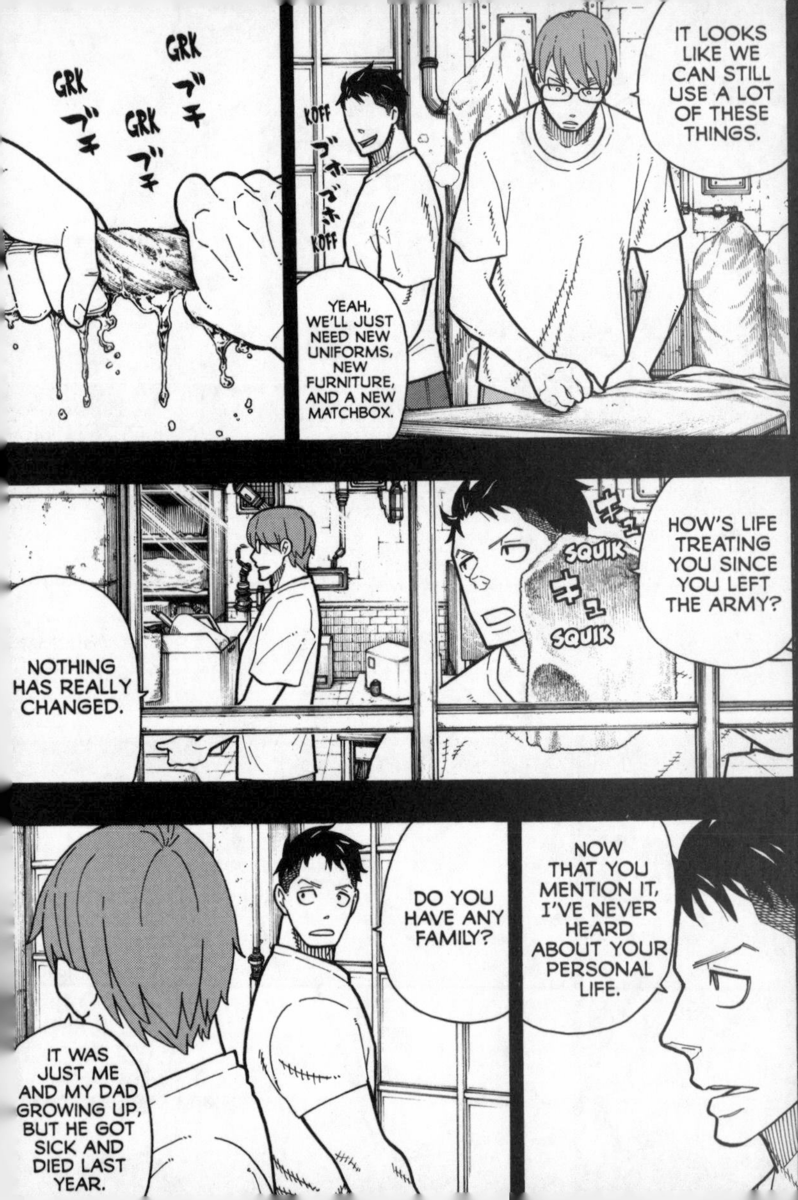
IT LOOKS LIKE WE CAN STILL USE A LOT OF THESE THINGS.
KOFF ゴホ
ゴホ KOFF
YEAH, WE'LL JUST NEED NEW UNIFORMS, NEW FURNITURE, AND A NEW MATCHBOX.
GRK ブチ
GRK ブチ
GRK ブチ
HOW'S LIFE TREATING YOU SINCE YOU LEFT THE ARMY?
キュ SQUIK
キュ SQUIK
NOTHING HAS REALLY CHANGED.
NOW THAT YOU MENTION IT, I'VE NEVER HEARD ABOUT YOUR PERSONAL LIFE.
DO YOU HAVE ANY FAMILY?
IT WAS JUST ME AND MY DAD GROWING UP, BUT HE GOT SICK AND DIED LAST YEAR.

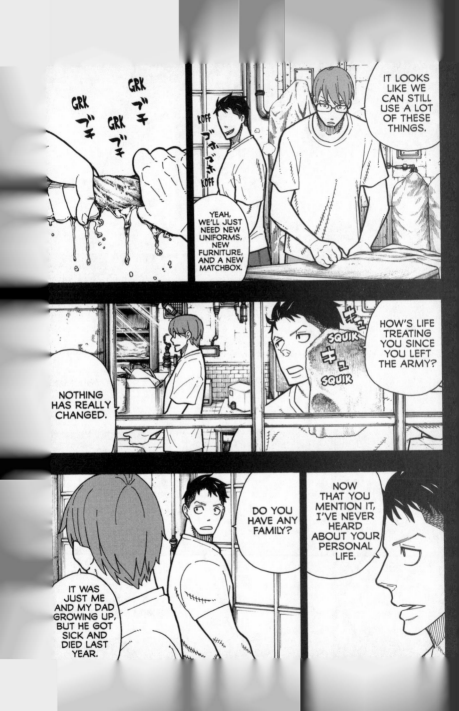

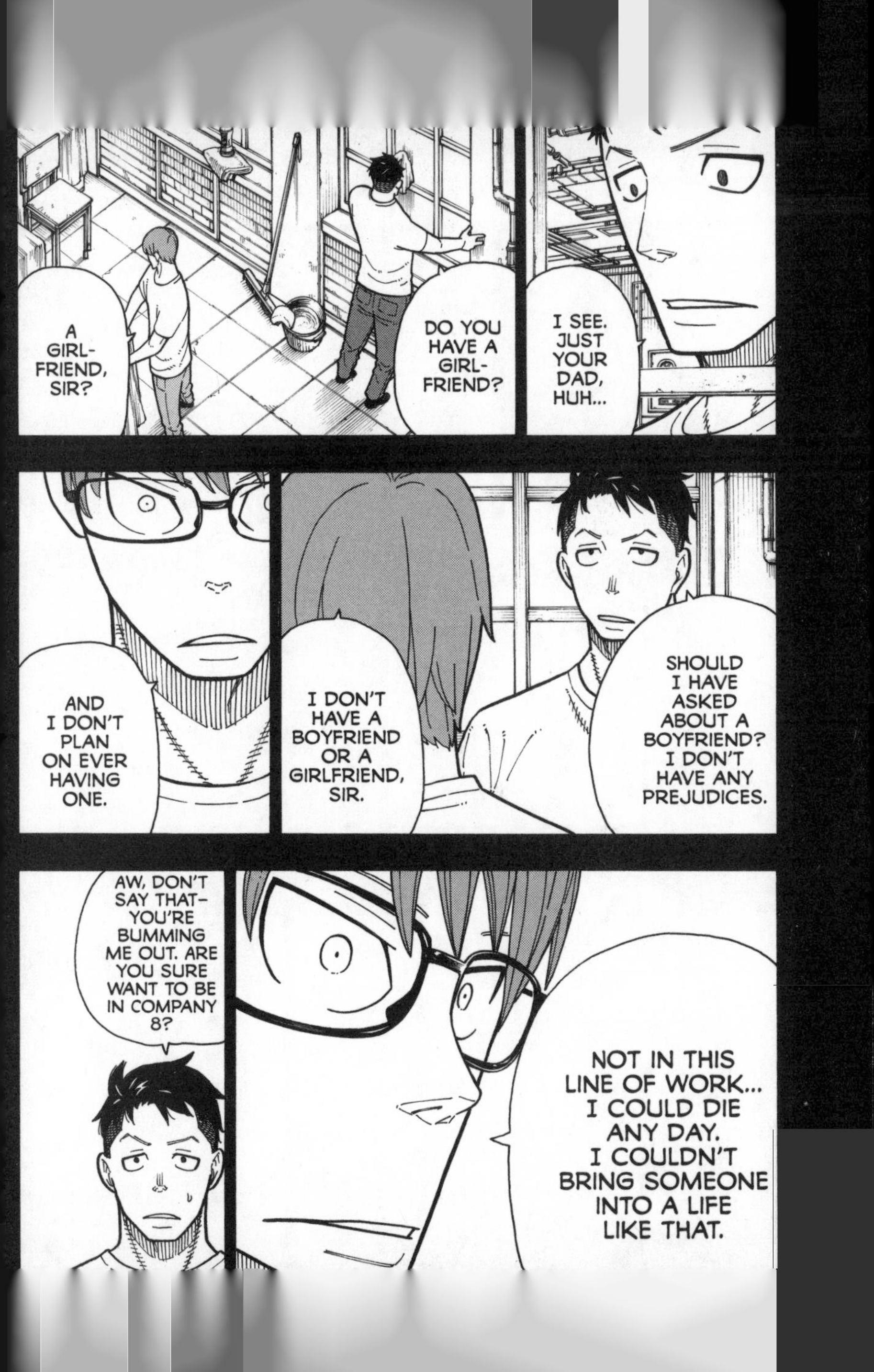
I SEE. JUST YOUR DAD, HUH...
DO YOU HAVE A GIRLFRIEND?
A GIRLFRIEND, SIR?
SHOULD I HAVE ASKED ABOUT A BOYFRIEND? I DON'T HAVE ANY PREJUDICES.
I DON'T HAVE A BOYFRIEND OR A GIRLFRIEND, SIR.
AND I DON'T PLAN ON EVER HAVING ONE.
NOT IN THIS LINE OF WORK... I COULD DIE ANY DAY. I COULDN'T BRING SOMEONE INTO A LIFE LIKE THAT.
AW, DON'T SAY THAT– YOU'RE BUMMING ME OUT. ARE YOU SURE WANT TO BE IN COMPANY 8?

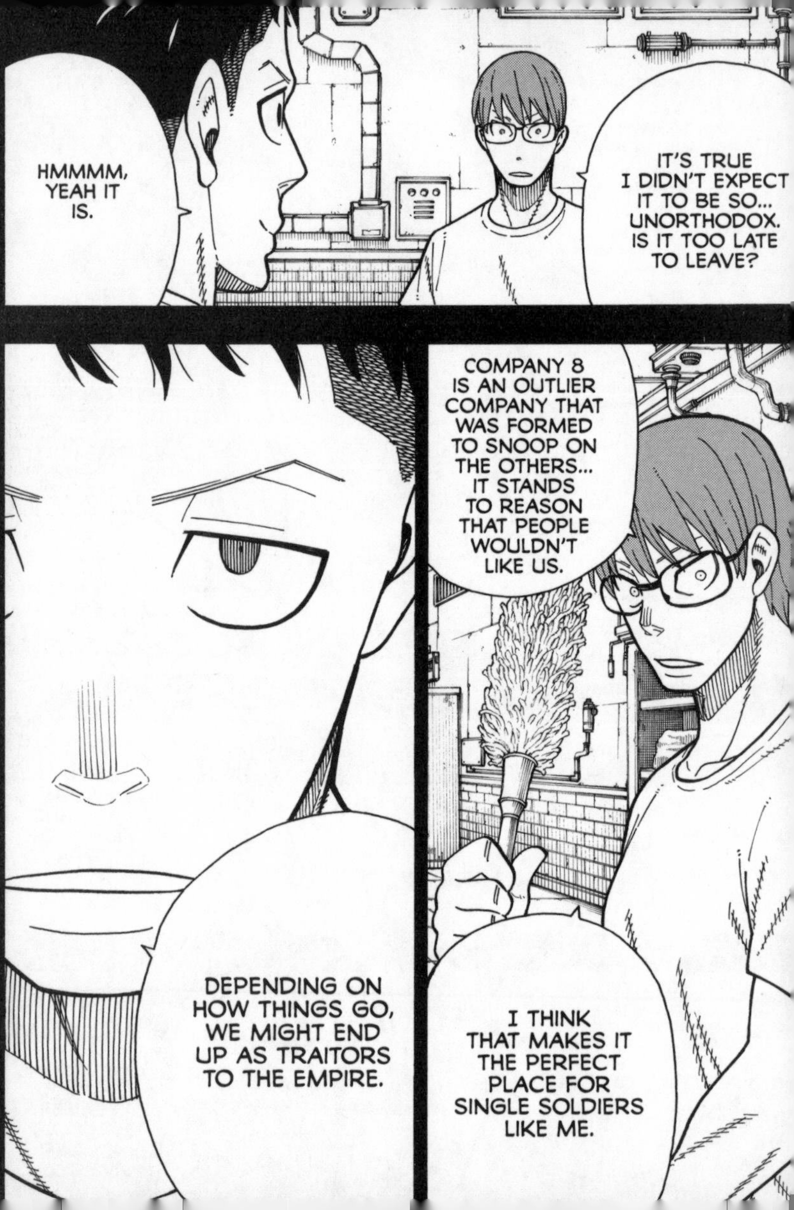

IT'S TRUE I DIDN'T EXPECT IT TO BE SO... UNORTHODOX. IS IT TOO LATE TO LEAVE?
HMMMM, YEAH IT IS.
COMPANY 8 IS AN OUTLIER COMPANY THAT WAS FORMED TO SNOOP ON THE OTHERS... IT STANDS TO REASON THAT PEOPLE WOULDN'T LIKE US.
I THINK THAT MAKES IT THE PERFECT PLACE FOR SINGLE SOLDIERS LIKE ME.
DEPENDING ON HOW THINGS GO, WE MIGHT END UP AS TRAITORS TO THE EMPIRE.

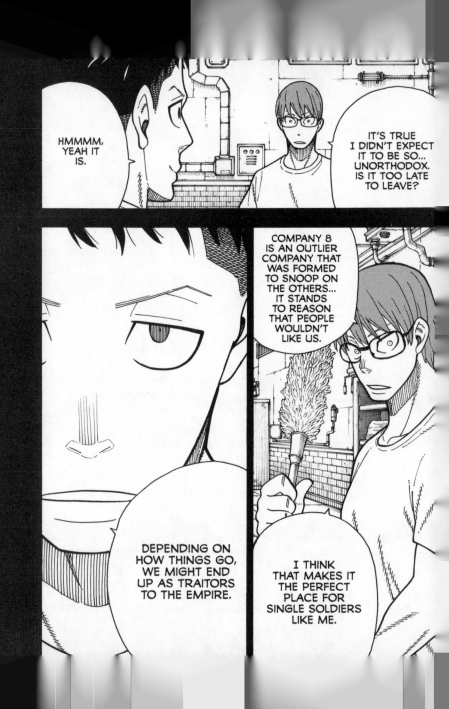

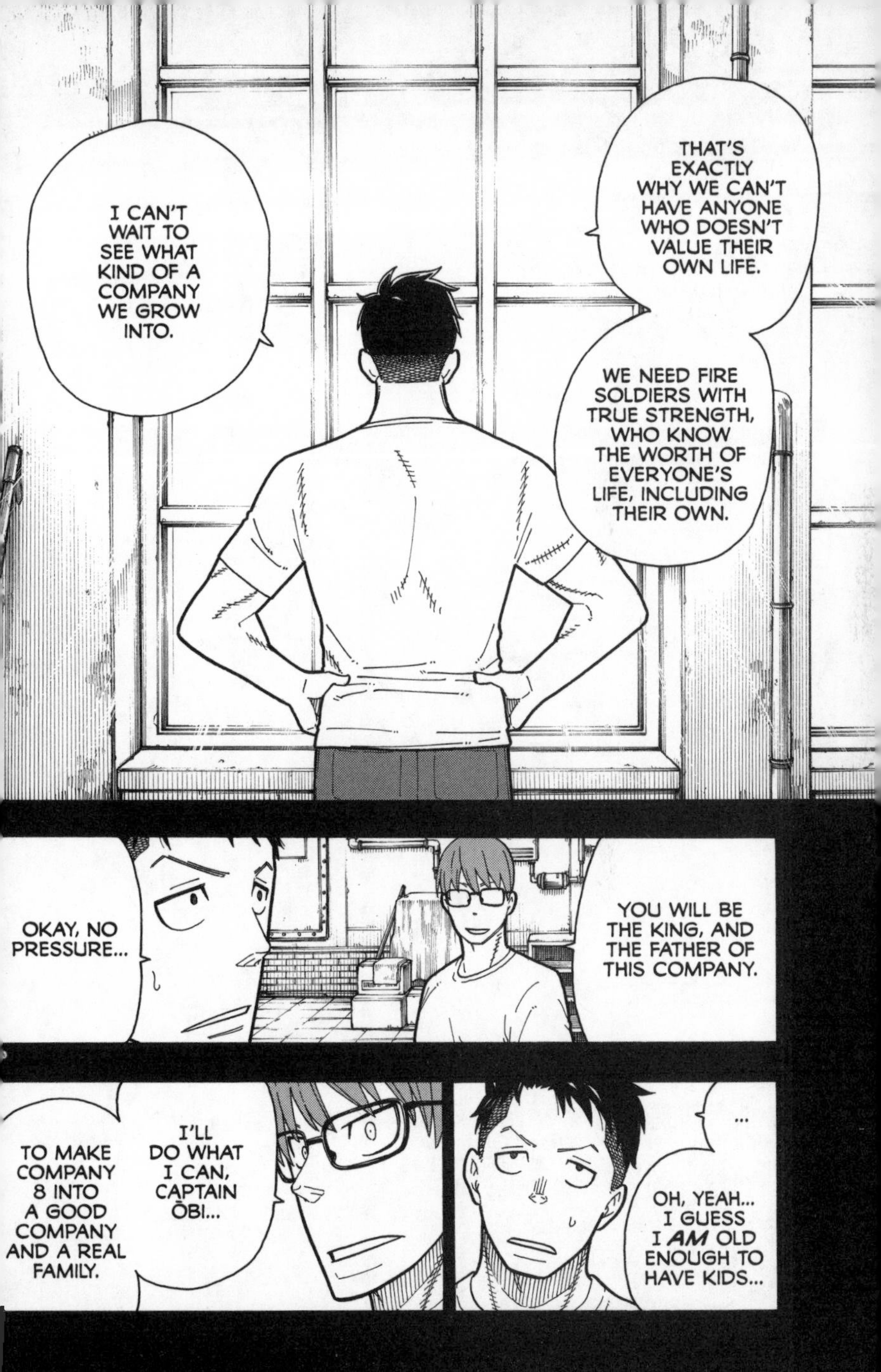
THAT'S EXACTLY WHY WE CAN'T HAVE ANYONE WHO DOESN'T VALUE THEIR OWN LIFE.
WE NEED FIRE SOLDIERS WITH TRUE STRENGTH, WHO KNOW THE WORTH OF EVERYONE'S LIFE, INCLUDING THEIR OWN.
I CAN'T WAIT TO SEE WHAT KIND OF A COMPANY WE GROW INTO.
YOU WILL BE THE KING, AND THE FATHER OF THIS COMPANY.
OKAY, NO PRESSURE...
...
OH, YEAH... I GUESS I *AM* OLD ENOUGH TO HAVE KIDS...
I'LL DO WHAT I CAN, CAPTAIN ŌBI...
TO MAKE COMPANY 8 INTO A GOOD COMPANY AND A REAL FAMILY.

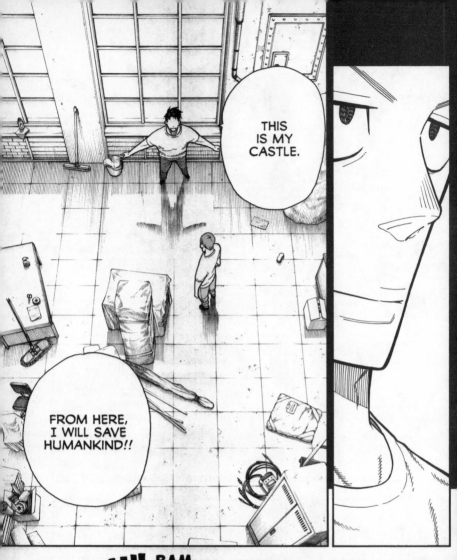

THIS IS MY CASTLE.

FROM HERE, I WILL SAVE HUMANKIND!!

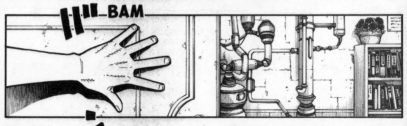

BAM

173

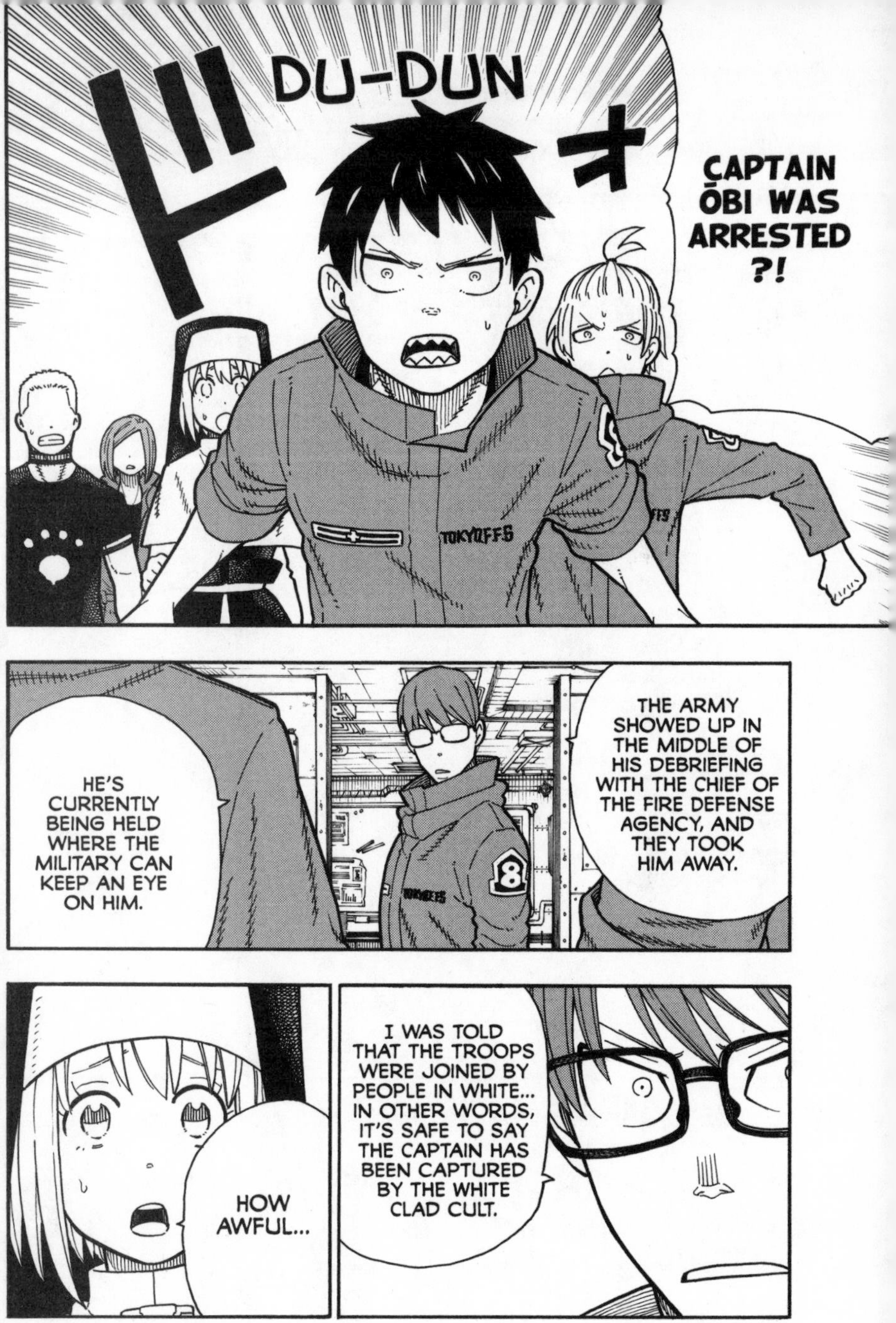
CAPTAIN ŌBI WAS ARRESTED ?!
ドォ
DU-DUN
THE ARMY SHOWED UP IN THE MIDDLE OF HIS DEBRIEFING WITH THE CHIEF OF THE FIRE DEFENSE AGENCY, AND THEY TOOK HIM AWAY.
HE'S CURRENTLY BEING HELD WHERE THE MILITARY CAN KEEP AN EYE ON HIM.
I WAS TOLD THAT THE TROOPS WERE JOINED BY PEOPLE IN WHITE... IN OTHER WORDS, IT'S SAFE TO SAY THE CAPTAIN HAS BEEN CAPTURED BY THE WHITE CLAD CULT.
HOW AWFUL...

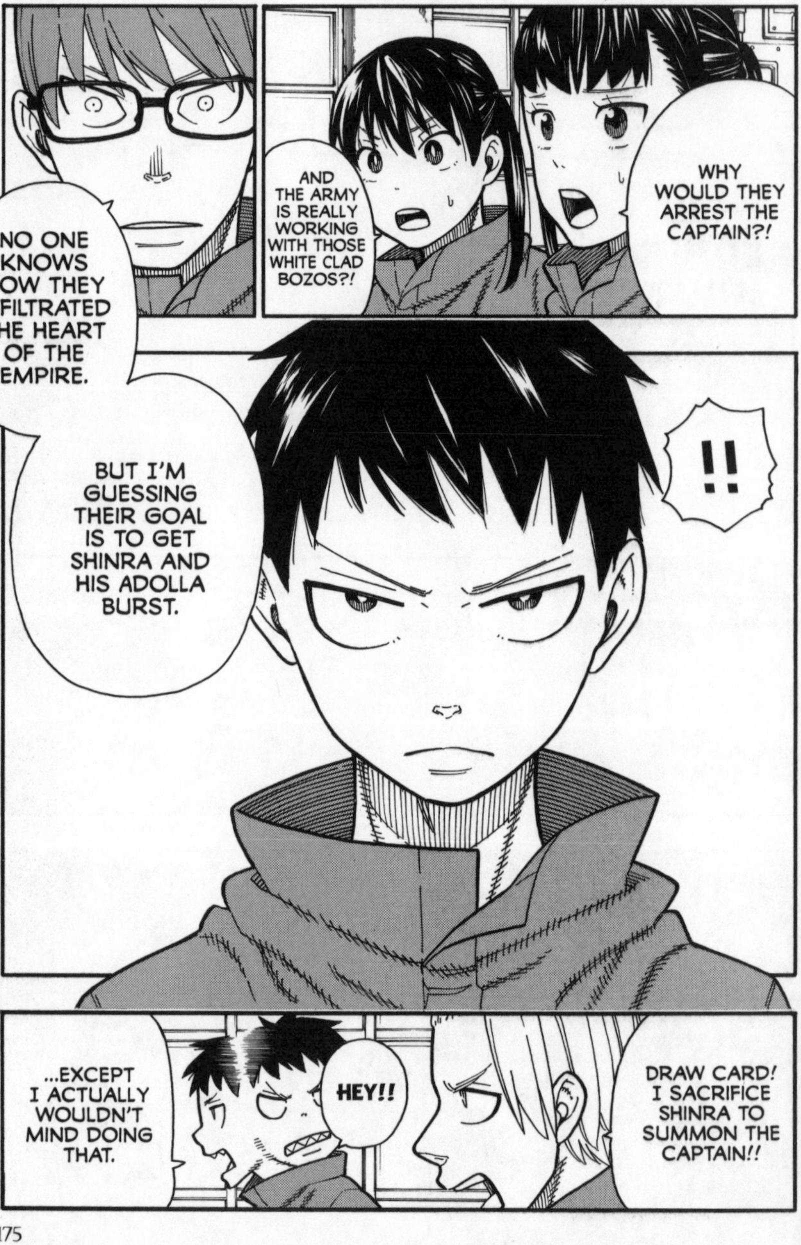
WHY WOULD THEY ARREST THE CAPTAIN?!
AND THE ARMY IS REALLY WORKING WITH THOSE WHITE CLAD BOZOS?!
NO ONE KNOWS HOW THEY INFILTRATED THE HEART OF THE EMPIRE.
BUT I'M GUESSING THEIR GOAL IS TO GET SHINRA AND HIS ADOLLA BURST.
!!
DRAW CARD! I SACRIFICE SHINRA TO SUMMON THE CAPTAIN!!
HEY!!
...EXCEPT I ACTUALLY WOULDN'T MIND DOING THAT.

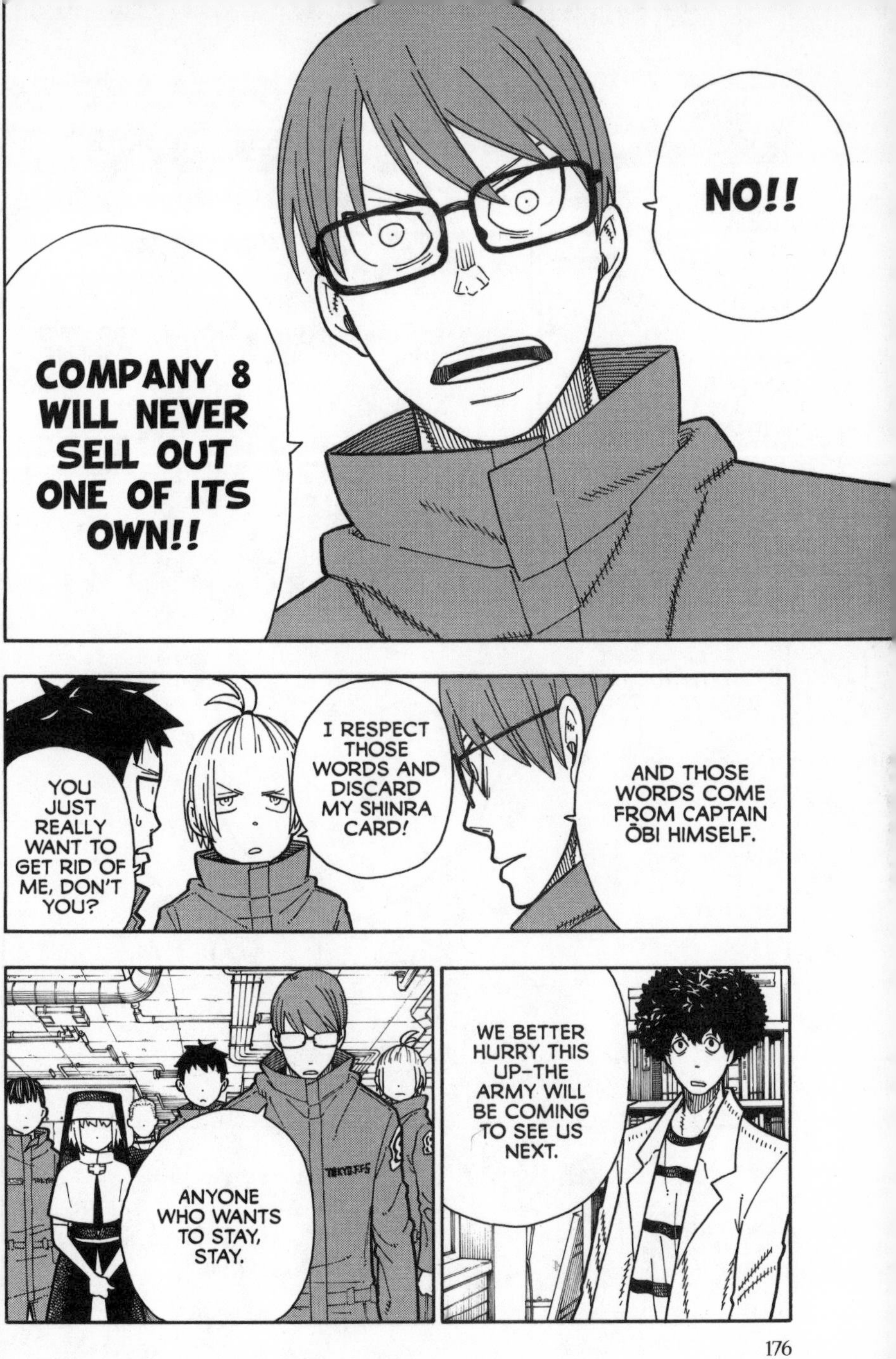
NO!!
COMPANY 8 WILL NEVER SELL OUT ONE OF ITS OWN!!
AND THOSE WORDS COME FROM CAPTAIN ŌBI HIMSELF.
I RESPECT THOSE WORDS AND DISCARD MY SHINRA CARD!
YOU JUST REALLY WANT TO GET RID OF ME, DON'T YOU?
WE BETTER HURRY THIS UP–THE ARMY WILL BE COMING TO SEE US NEXT.
ANYONE WHO WANTS TO STAY, STAY.

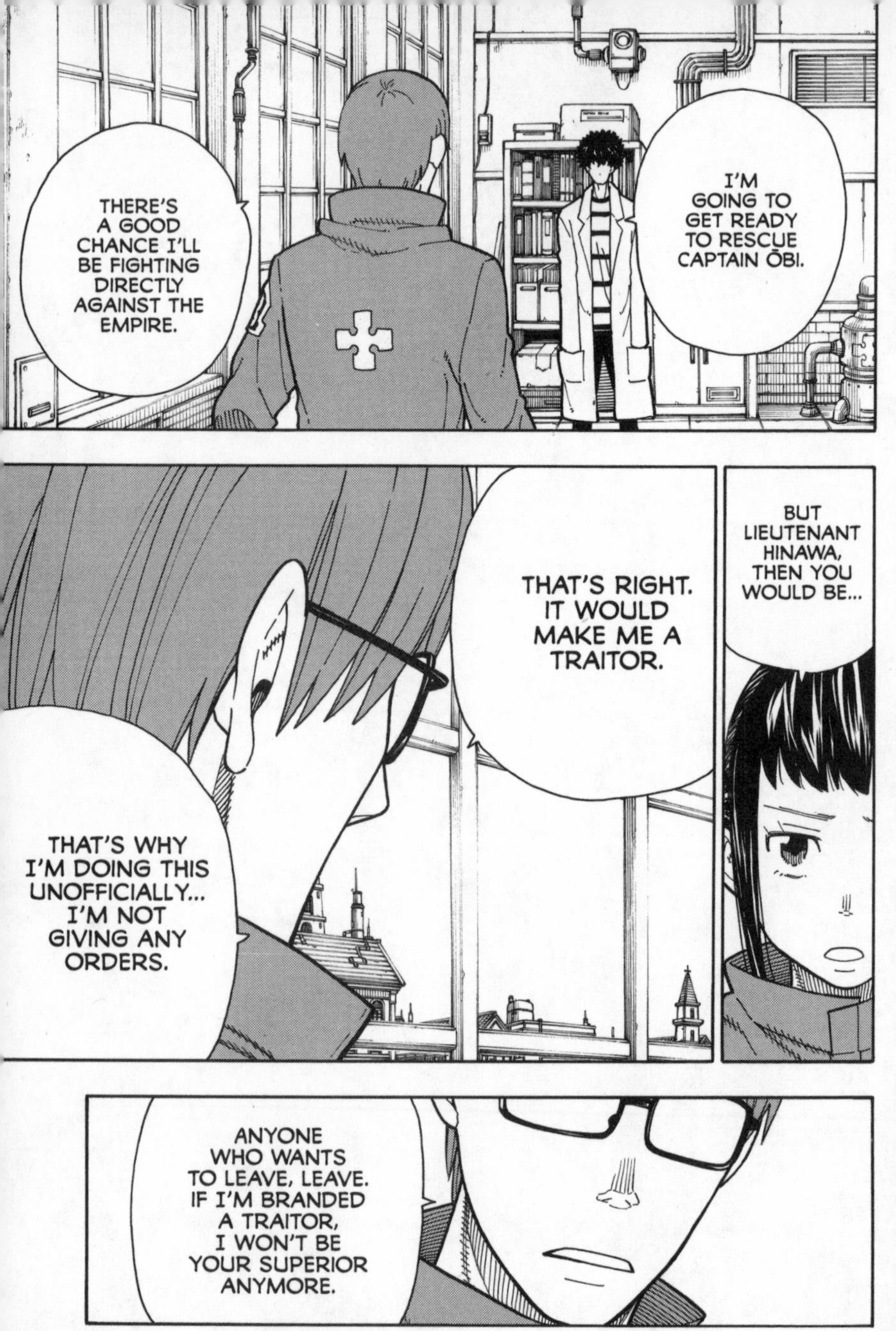
I'M GOING TO GET READY TO RESCUE CAPTAIN ŌBI.
THERE'S A GOOD CHANCE I'LL BE FIGHTING DIRECTLY AGAINST THE EMPIRE.
BUT LIEUTENANT HINAWA, THEN YOU WOULD BE...
THAT'S RIGHT. IT WOULD MAKE ME A TRAITOR.
THAT'S WHY I'M DOING THIS UNOFFICIALLY... I'M NOT GIVING ANY ORDERS.
ANYONE WHO WANTS TO LEAVE, LEAVE. IF I'M BRANDED A TRAITOR, I WON'T BE YOUR SUPERIOR ANYMORE.

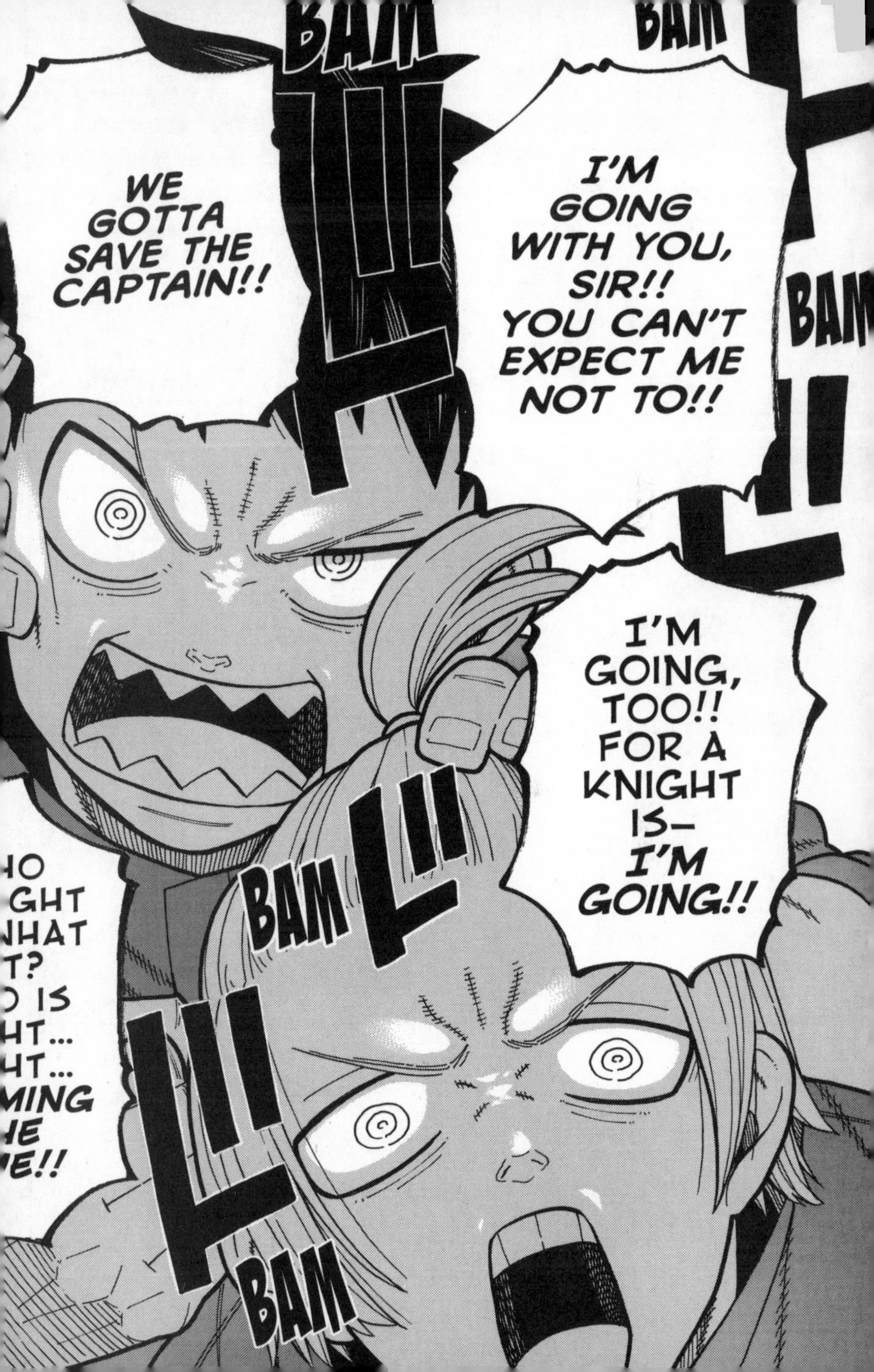
BAM
I'M GOING WITH YOU, SIR!! YOU CAN'T EXPECT ME NOT TO!!
BAM
WE GOTTA SAVE THE CAPTAIN!!
BAM
I'M GOING, TOO!! FOR A KNIGHT IS— I'M GOING!!
BAM
BAM

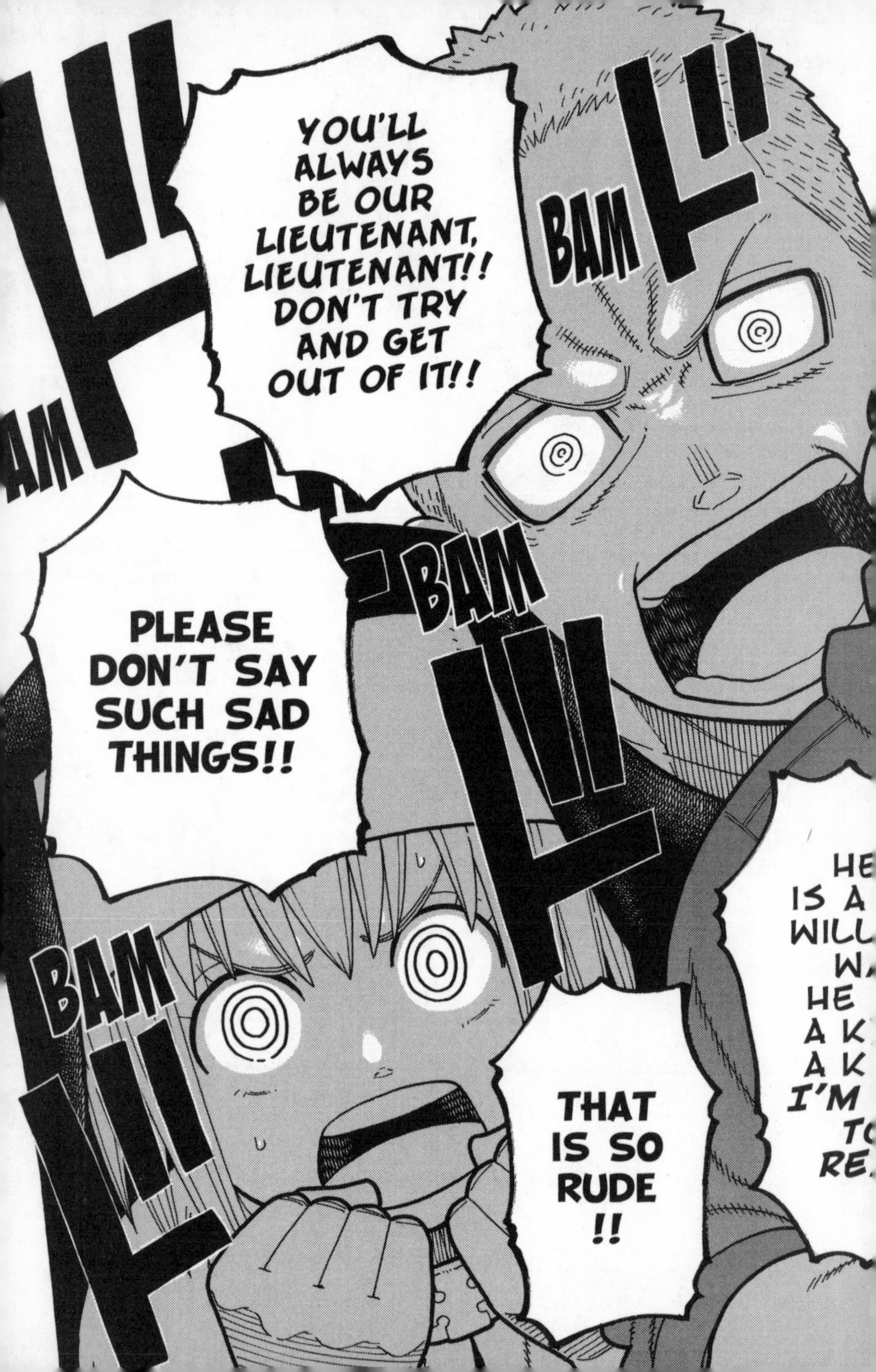
BAM!!
YOU'LL ALWAYS BE OUR LIEUTENANT, LIEUTENANT!! DON'T TRY AND GET OUT OF IT!!
AM!!
BAM!!
PLEASE DON'T SAY SUCH SAD THINGS!!
THAT IS SO RUDE!!
BAM!!

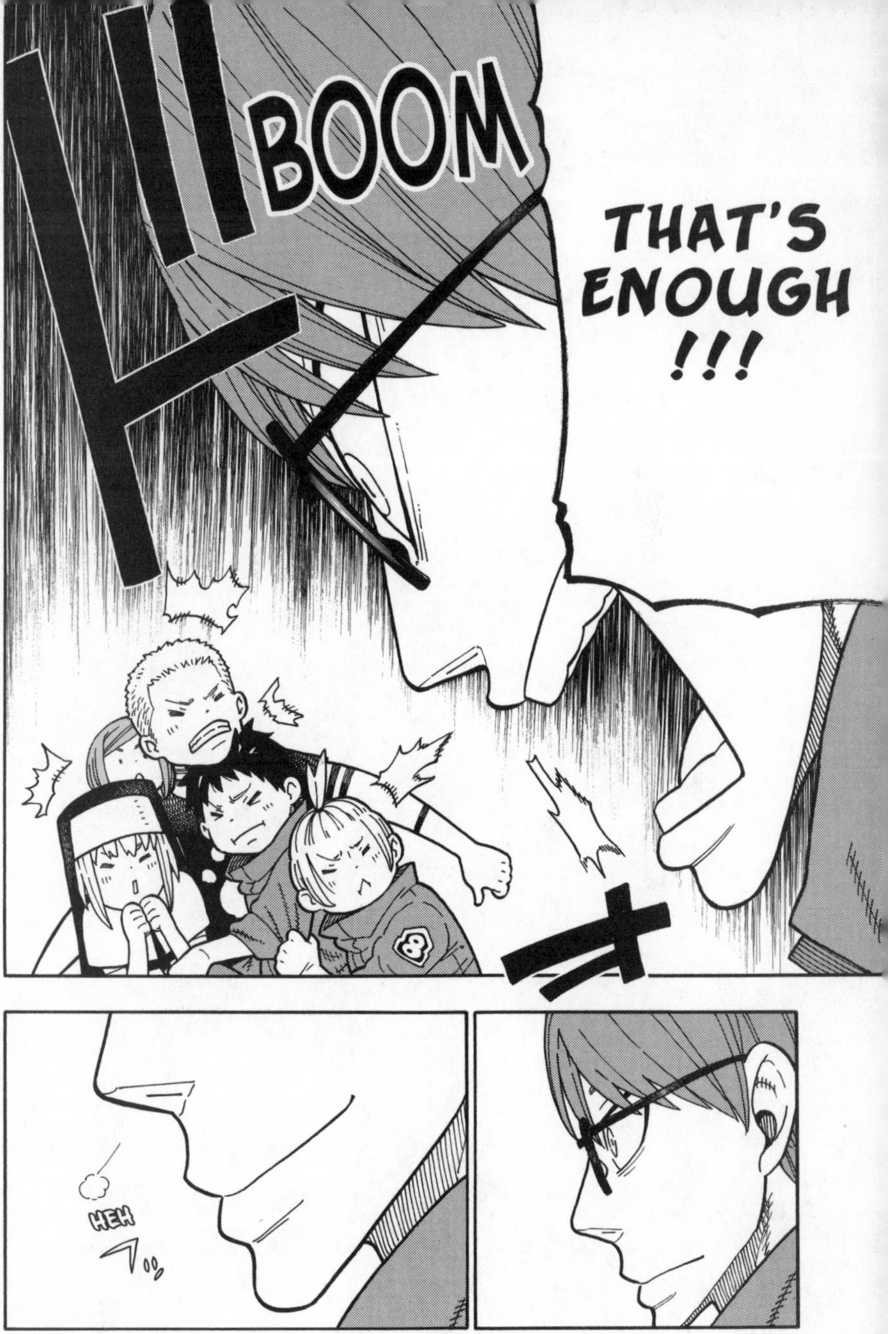
THAT'S ENOUGH !!!
BOOM
HEH

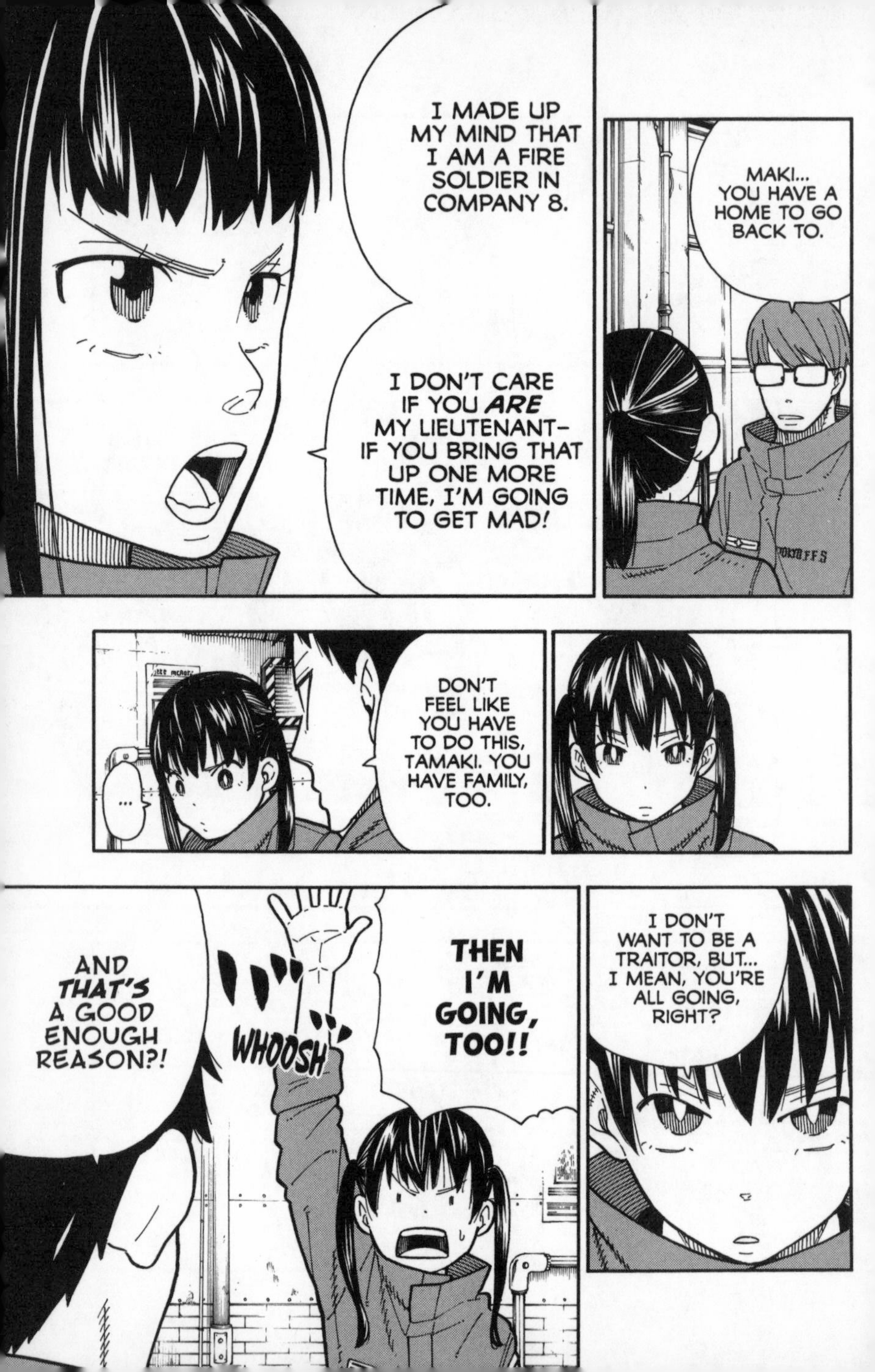
MAKI... YOU HAVE A HOME TO GO BACK TO.
I MADE UP MY MIND THAT I AM A FIRE SOLDIER IN COMPANY 8.
I DON'T CARE IF YOU *ARE* MY LIEUTENANT– IF YOU BRING THAT UP ONE MORE TIME, I'M GOING TO GET MAD!
DON'T FEEL LIKE YOU HAVE TO DO THIS, TAMAKI. YOU HAVE FAMILY, TOO.
...
I DON'T WANT TO BE A TRAITOR, BUT... I MEAN, YOU'RE ALL GOING, RIGHT?
THEN I'M GOING, TOO!!
WHOOSH
AND *THAT'S* A GOOD ENOUGH REASON?!

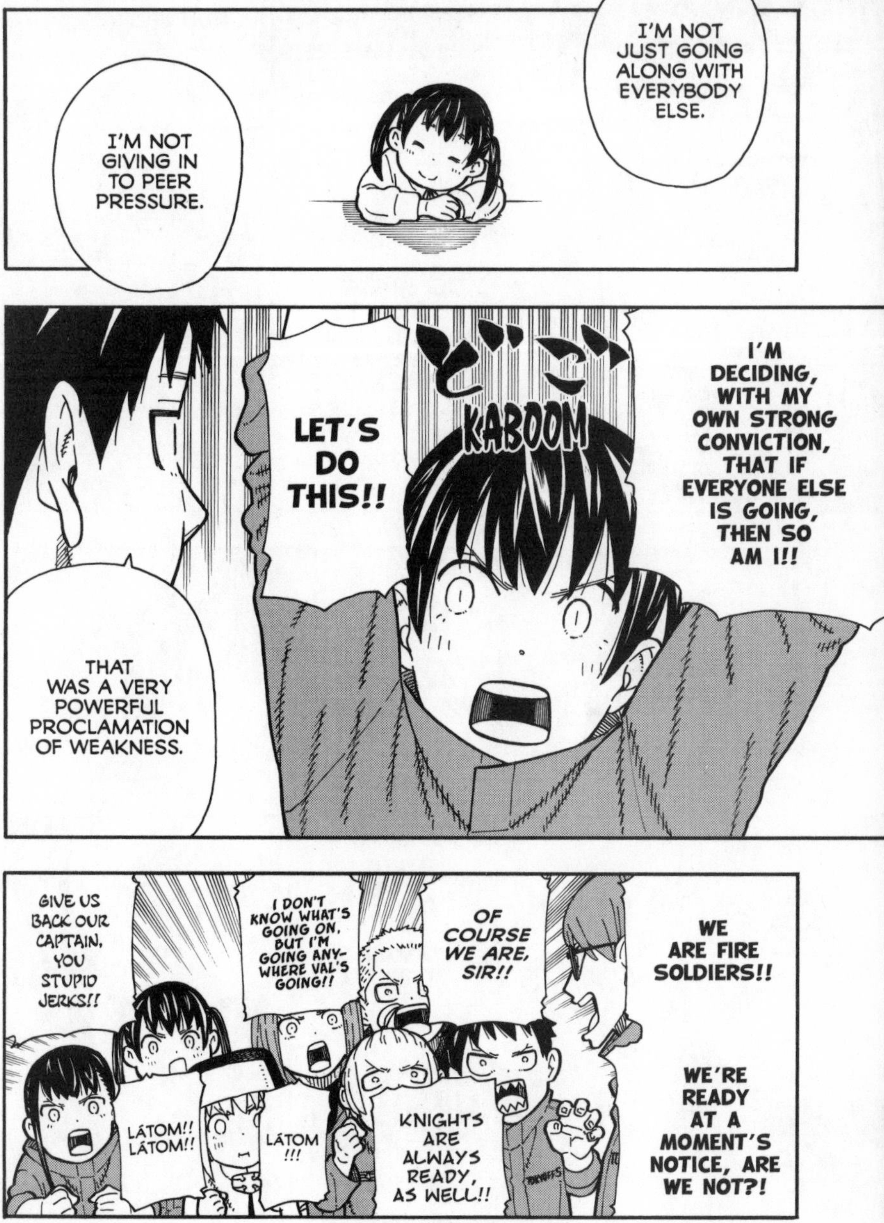
I'M NOT JUST GOING ALONG WITH EVERYBODY ELSE.
I'M NOT GIVING IN TO PEER PRESSURE.
I'M DECIDING, WITH MY OWN STRONG CONVICTION, THAT IF EVERYONE ELSE IS GOING, THEN SO AM I!!
KABOOM
LET'S DO THIS!!
THAT WAS A VERY POWERFUL PROCLAMATION OF WEAKNESS.
WE ARE FIRE SOLDIERS!!
WE'RE READY AT A MOMENT'S NOTICE, ARE WE NOT?!
OF COURSE WE ARE, SIR!!
KNIGHTS ARE ALWAYS READY, AS WELL!!
I DON'T KNOW WHAT'S GOING ON, BUT I'M GOING ANYWHERE VAL'S GOING!!
LÁTOM !!!
LÁTOM!! LÁTOM!!
GIVE US BACK OUR CAPTAIN, YOU STUPID JERKS!!

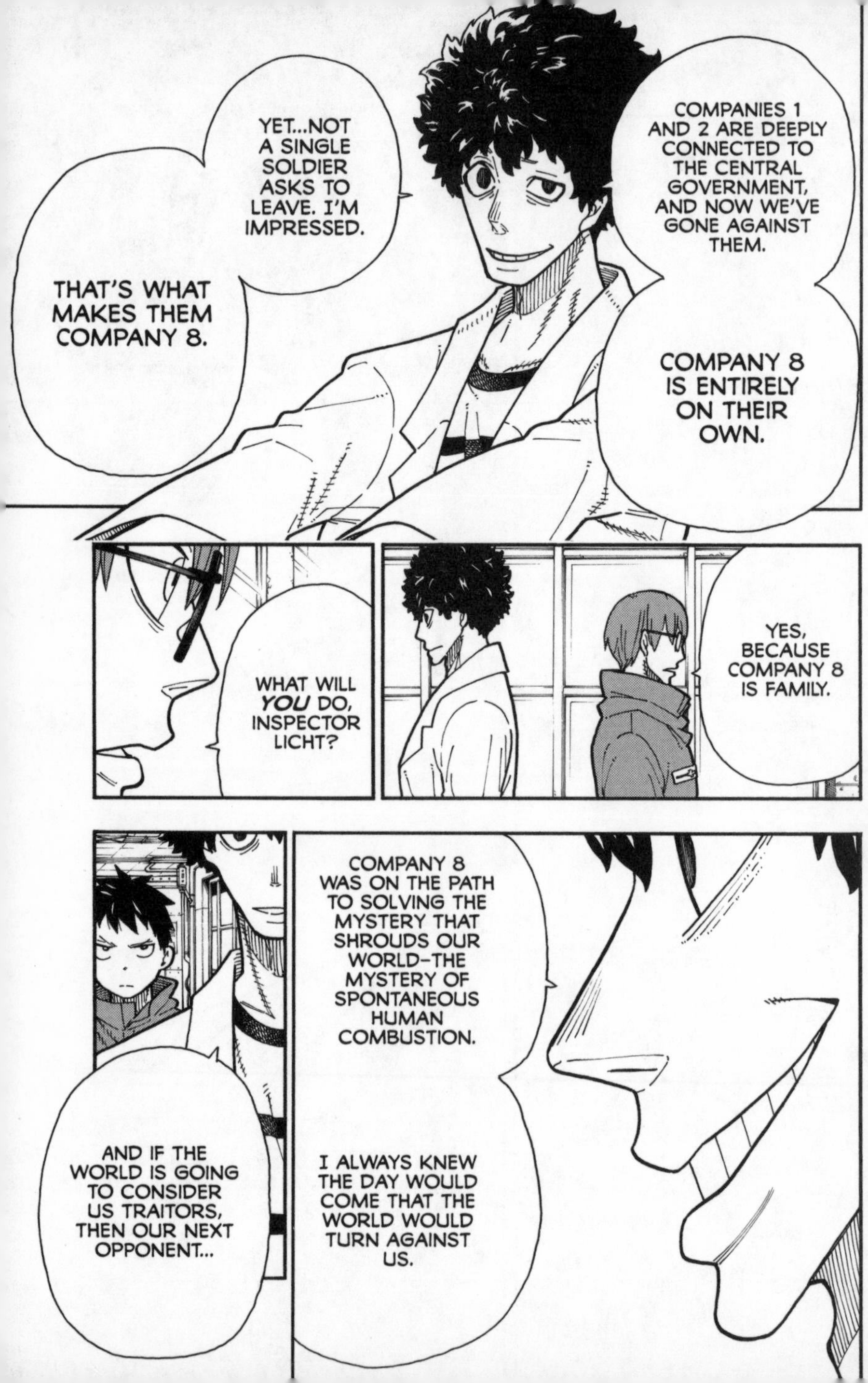
COMPANIES 1 AND 2 ARE DEEPLY CONNECTED TO THE CENTRAL GOVERNMENT, AND NOW WE'VE GONE AGAINST THEM.
COMPANY 8 IS ENTIRELY ON THEIR OWN.
YET...NOT A SINGLE SOLDIER ASKS TO LEAVE. I'M IMPRESSED.
THAT'S WHAT MAKES THEM COMPANY 8.
YES, BECAUSE COMPANY 8 IS FAMILY.
WHAT WILL *YOU* DO, INSPECTOR LICHT?
COMPANY 8 WAS ON THE PATH TO SOLVING THE MYSTERY THAT SHROUDS OUR WORLD–THE MYSTERY OF SPONTANEOUS HUMAN COMBUSTION.
I ALWAYS KNEW THE DAY WOULD COME THAT THE WORLD WOULD TURN AGAINST US.
AND IF THE WORLD IS GOING TO CONSIDER US TRAITORS, THEN OUR NEXT OPPONENT...

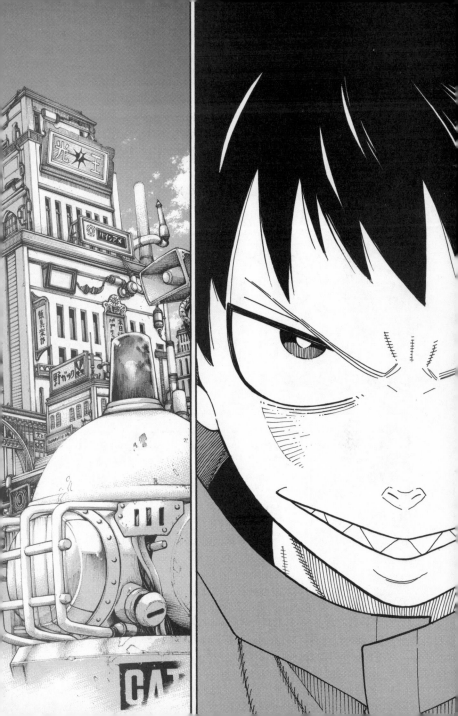

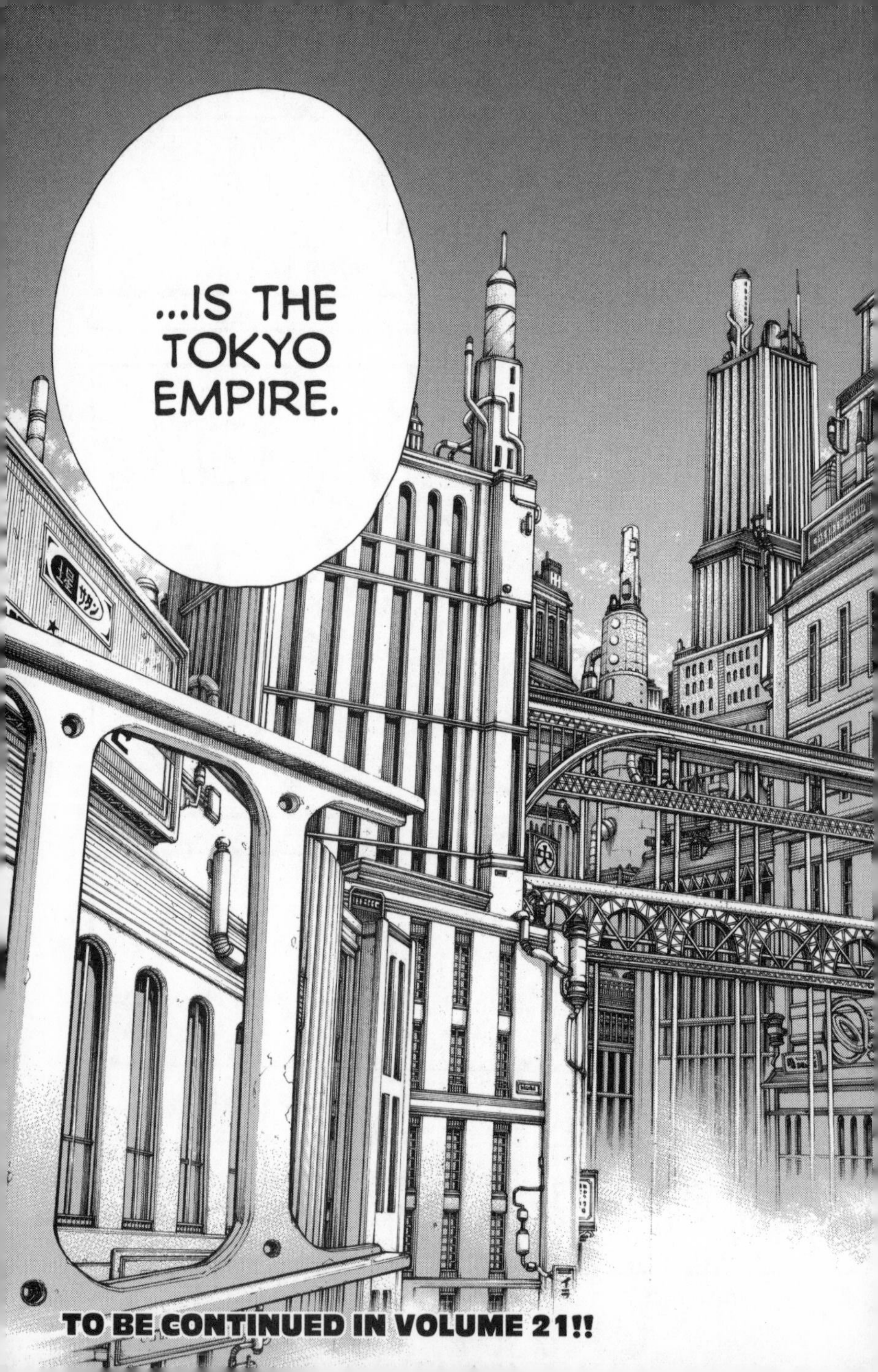
...IS THE TOKYO EMPIRE.
TO BE CONTINUED IN VOLUME 21!!

AFTERWORD MANGA: ATSUSHIYA

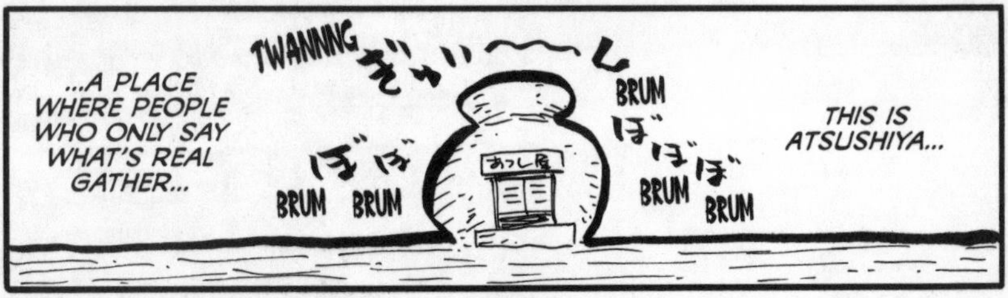
THIS IS ATSUSHIYA...
BRUM
ぼ
ぼぼ
BRUM
BRUM
TWANNNG
ぎゅい〜〜ん
あつし屋
ぼぼ
BRUM
BRUM
...A PLACE WHERE PEOPLE WHO ONLY SAY WHAT'S REAL GATHER...

Sign: Atsushiya

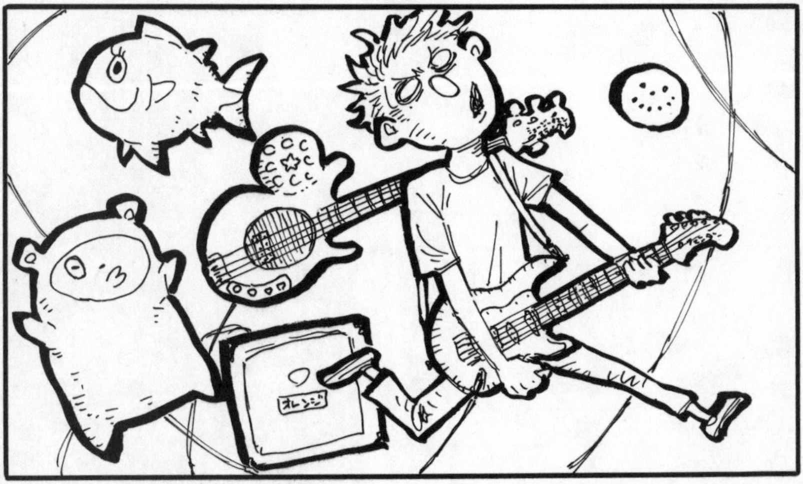
オレンジ

Label: Orange

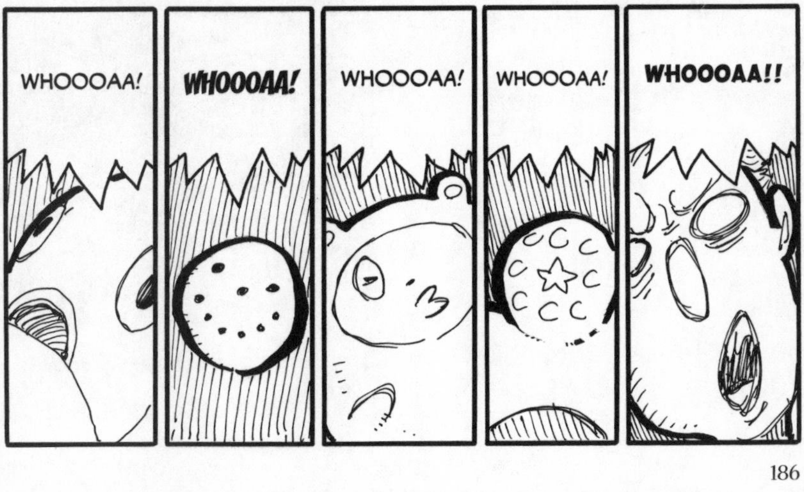
WHOOOAA!!
WHOOOAA!
WHOOOAA!
WHOOOAA!
WHOOOAA!

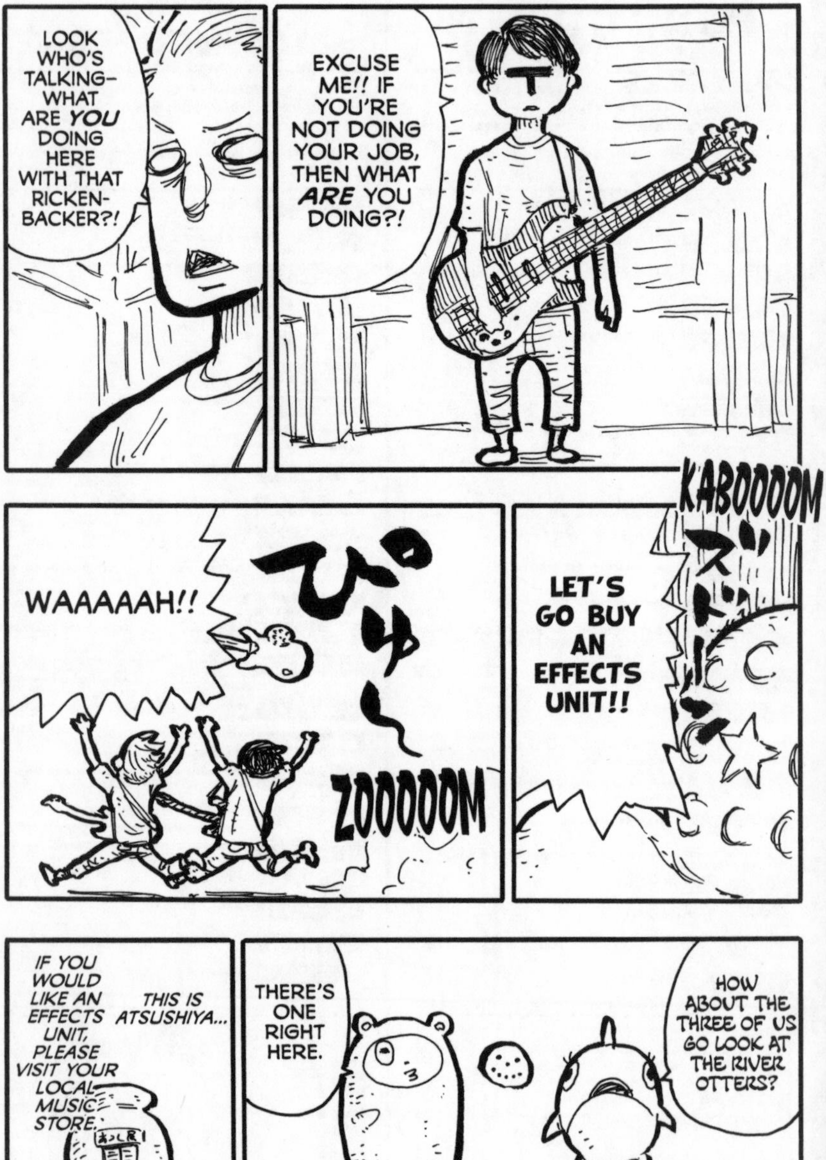
EXCUSE ME!! IF YOU'RE NOT DOING YOUR JOB, THEN WHAT *ARE* YOU DOING?!
LOOK WHO'S TALKING—WHAT ARE *YOU* DOING HERE WITH THAT RICKEN-BACKER?!
KABOOOOM
LET'S GO BUY AN EFFECTS UNIT!!
WAAAAAH!!
ZOOOOOM
HOW ABOUT THE THREE OF US GO LOOK AT THE RIVER OTTERS?
THERE'S ONE RIGHT HERE.
THIS IS ATSUSHIYA...
IF YOU WOULD LIKE AN EFFECTS UNIT, PLEASE VISIT YOUR LOCAL MUSIC STORE.
Sign: Atsushiya

PURT CO PAN

AFFILIATION: FWEET FWEET (SPECIAL FIRE FORCE COMPANY 4)
RANK: FWI-FWEET (LIEUTENANT)
ABILITY: FWEEEET-FWIT (THIRD GENERATION PYROKINETIC)

Sends heat energy to others, giving them various strength enhancements.

Height	FWI-FWEET FWIT (179cm [5'10.5"])
Weight	FWIT FWI-FWEET (73kg [161lbs.])
Age	FWEET FWIT (30)
Birthday	FWEET FWEET FWIT (February 20)
Sign	FWEE-FWEET FWIT (Pisces)
Bloodtype	FWEET (O)
Nickname	FWEET FWEET (The Piper of Company 4)
Self-Proclaimed	FWI-FWEET FWEET FWIT
Favorite Foods	FWEET FWEET FWEET (Hamburgers)
Least Favorite Food	FWIT (Food with holes in it like *chikuwa* fish sticks or Red Vines, because people give it to me all the time.)
Favorite Music	FWEET-FWIT (Classical: Clarinet)
Favorite Animal	Cute little FWEET FWEETers
Favorite Color	FWI-FWEET FWIT (Pink)
Favorite Type	FWEET FWEET FWI-FWIT FWI-FWEET-FWIT-FWIT FWI-FWEET FWEET FWEET-FWI-FWEET FWIT-FWIT FWEEEEEEEET
Who He Respects	FWIT-FWEET (Captain Hague)
Who He Hates	FNONE (None)
Who He's Afraid Of	FWEEEET… (People who threaten to lick other people's whistles.)
Hobbies	Bicycle riding, cooking, collecting healthcare products.
Daily Routine	I live a very routine life.
Dream	To stay in this line of work without getting hurt.
Shoe Size	26.5cm [8.5]
Eyesight	1.2 [20/16]
Favorite Subject	Health and Physical Education, Home Economics
Least Favorite Subject	FWEET (Math)

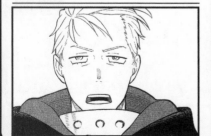

OGUN MONTGOMERY

AFFILIATION: SPECIAL FIRE FORCE COMPANY 4
RANK: SECOND CLASS FIRE SOLDIER
ABILITY: THIRD GENERATION PYROKINETIC

Controls tattoos that raise his physical abilities using thermal energy.

Height	175cm [5'9"]
Weight	69kg [152.1lbs.]
Age	17
Birthday	March 3
Sign	Pisces
Bloodtype	B
Nickname	King of the Park, The Black Star
Self-Proclaimed	Burger King
Favorite Foods	Hamburgers
Least Favorite Food	Anything that doesn't fill me up.
Favorite Music	Reggae, hip hop
Favorite Animal	I don't really know the animals in the Empire that well…
Favorite Color	Orange
Favorite Type	I really liked Ally-chan back in grade school. That was pure love.
Who He Respects	Captain Hague, Lieutenant Pan. And a really long time ago, I heard there was, like, a star in a gang? That's awesome.
Who He Hates	No one in particular. But Shinra and Arthur gave me a lot of headaches.
Who He's Afraid Of	Just between us, Captain Hague scared me in his later years.
Hobbies	Basketball and sports involving boards, like skateboarding. I want to try snowboarding!
Daily Routine	Playing sports in the park. It's hard, because nobody will play with me unless I give them easier rules.
Dream	I heard they used to have big global sporting events. I'd like to see one of those.
Shoe Size	26.5cm [8.5]
Eyesight	1.5 [20/12.5]
Favorite Subject	History, Math
Least Favorite Subject	Language Arts

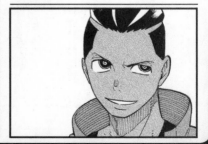

Translation Notes:

Wisdom King Acala, page 78

Known in Japan as *Fudō Myō-ō*, Acala is a Buddhist protective deity who is often portrayed surrounded by flames which consume evil. He is highly venerated in Japanese Buddhism, and is known for guiding the deceased.

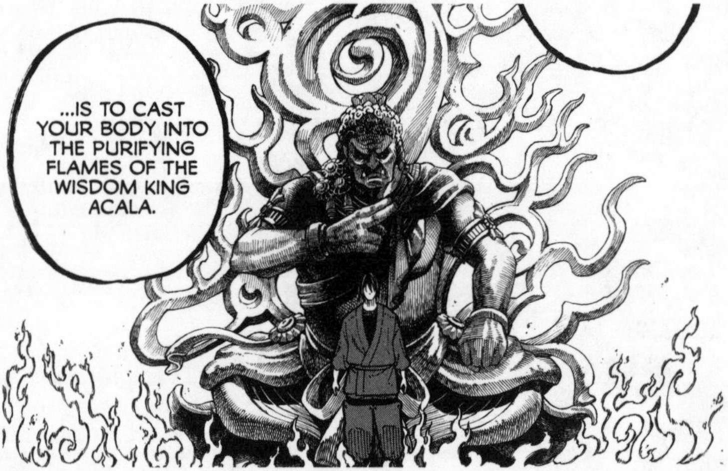
...IS TO CAST YOUR BODY INTO THE PURIFYING FLAMES OF THE WISDOM KING ACALA.

Stigma, page 101

In the Japanese text, they use both the Latin word "stigma" or "stigmata" in the plural, and the Japanese word *seikon*, meaning "holy scar." The Latin word "stigma" means "mark."

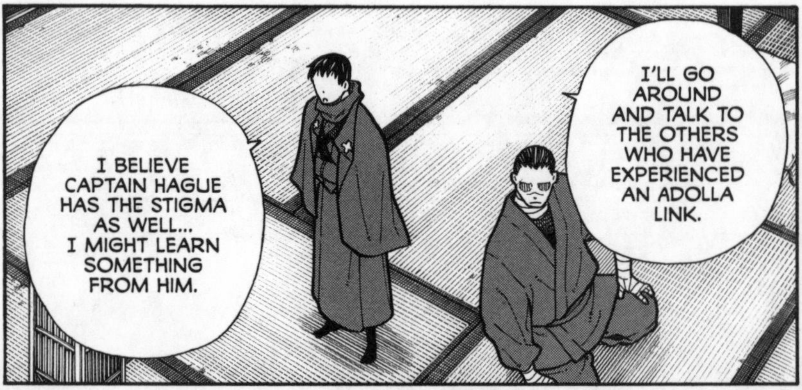
I'LL GO AROUND AND TALK TO THE OTHERS WHO HAVE EXPERIENCED AN ADOLLA LINK.
I BELIEVE CAPTAIN HAGUE HAS THE STIGMA AS WELL... I MIGHT LEARN SOMETHING FROM HIM.

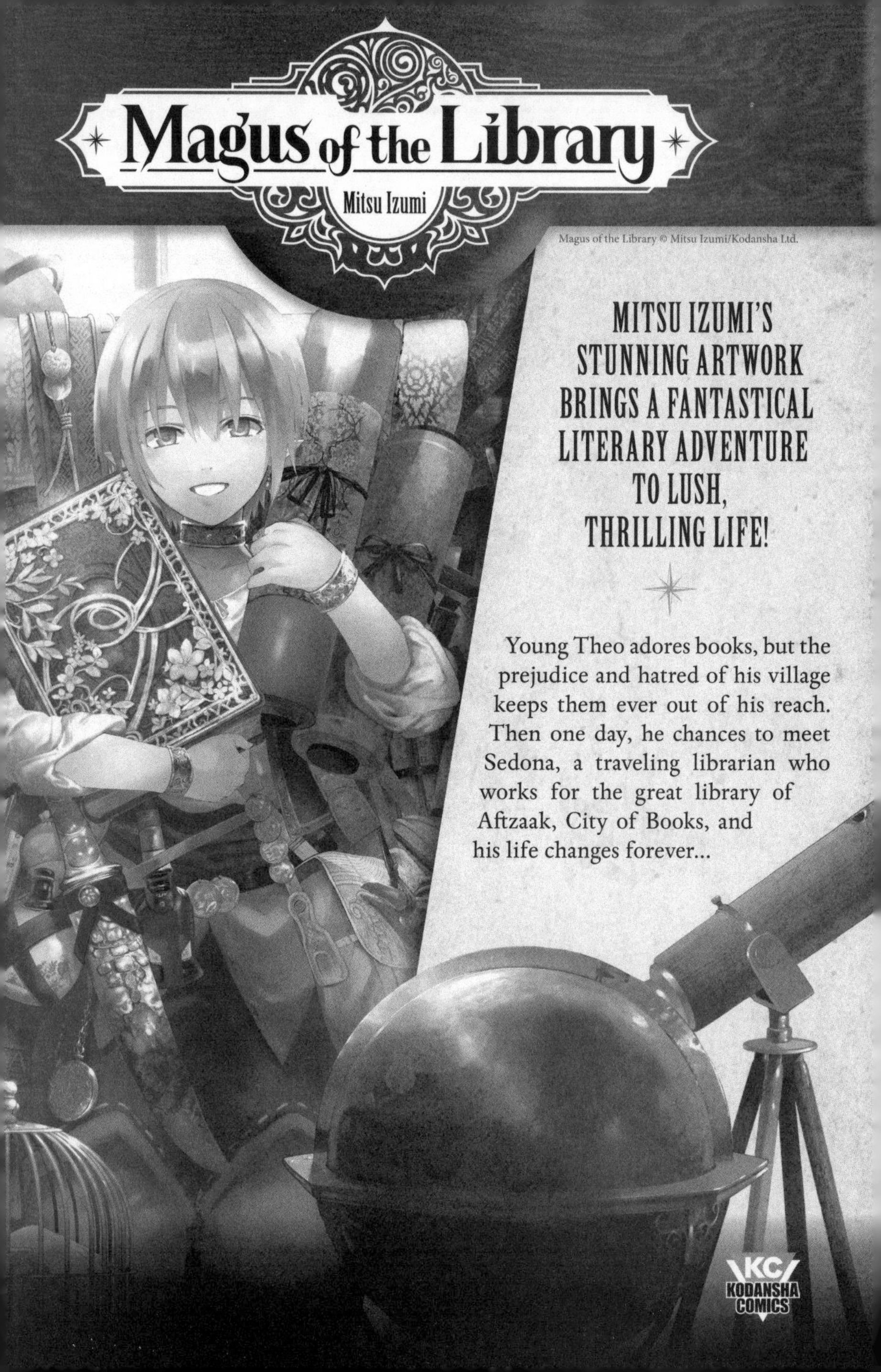
Magus of the Library
Mitsu Izumi
Magus of the Library © Mitsu Izumi/Kodansha Ltd.
MITSU IZUMI'S STUNNING ARTWORK BRINGS A FANTASTICAL LITERARY ADVENTURE TO LUSH, THRILLING LIFE!
Young Theo adores books, but the prejudice and hatred of his village keeps them ever out of his reach. Then one day, he chances to meet Sedona, a traveling librarian who works for the great library of Aftzaak, City of Books, and his life changes forever...
KC
KODANSHA COMICS

world
es one.

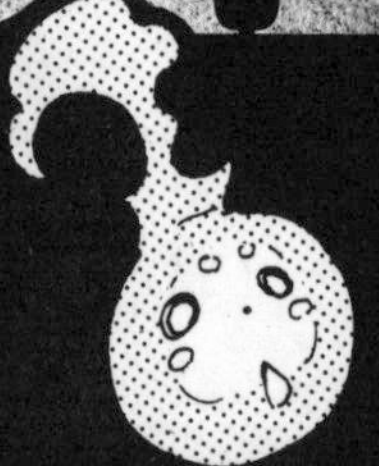

VOL. 20

ATSUSHI OHKUBO

FIRE FORCE

ATSUSHI
OHKUBO

20

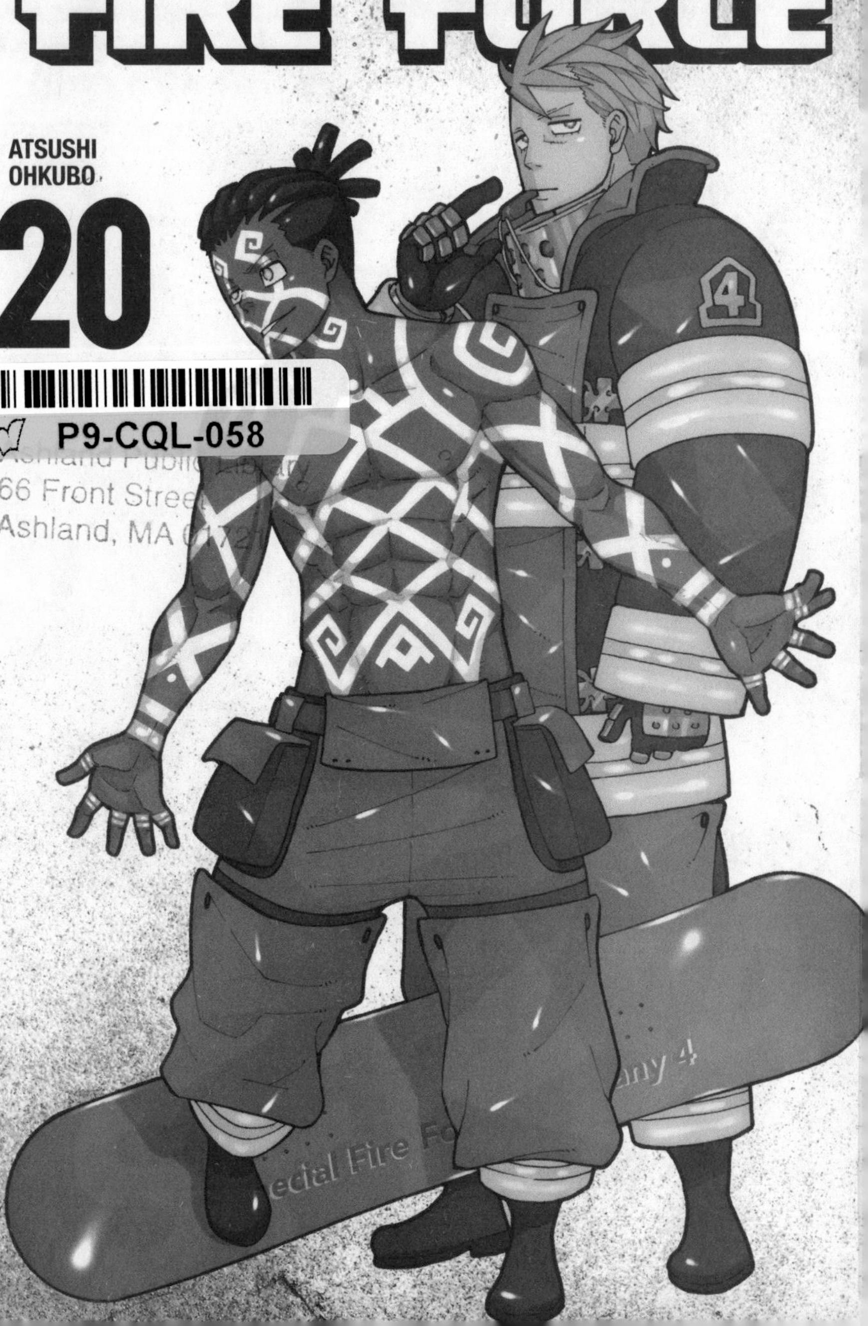